The Skeptical Visionary

BOOKS BY SEYMOUR SARASON

The Skeptical Visionary

A Seymour Sarason Education Reader

EDITED BY

Robert L. Fried

TEMPLE UNIVERSITY PRESS

PHILADELPHIA

Temple University Press, Philadelphia 19122
Copyright © 2003 by Temple University
All rights reserved
Published 2003
Printed in the United States of America

Library of Congress Cataloging-in-Publication Data

Sarason, Seymour Bernard, 1919–
    The skeptical visionary : a Seymour Sarason education reader /
  edited by Robert L. Fried.
      p.   cm.
    Includes bibliographical references.
    ISBN 1-56639-979-3 (alk. paper) — ISBN 1-56639-980-7 (pbk. : alk. paper)
      1. Education—Aims and objectives—United States.   2. Education—Social
  aspects—United States.   3. Educational change—United States.   I. Fried, Robert L.
  II. Title.

  LA217.2 .S28 2002
  370'.973—dc21

                                                                    2002018086

ISBN 13: 978-1-56639-980-7 (pbk.: alk. paper)

082611P

To Seymour Sarason, mentor and friend,

whose personal warmth and zest for ideas

are wholly without skepticism

Contents

Part III: Students and Parents

Part IV: The Political and Policy Agenda

Part V: Tables of Contents from Sarason's Books on Education

Editor's Note and
Acknowledgments

There is a certain anxiety, coupled with humility, involved in selecting from Seymour Sarason's published work on education for an anthology such as this. It is inevitable that much of great value and profound influence will be left out, including works which may not deal directly with education but which are critical to our understanding of Sarason's approach to organizing the contexts in which teachers try to teach and students to learn. Books such as *The Creation of Settings and the Future Societies* (1972), his works on art and psychology, on social psychology, and the books he co-authored with Elizabeth Lorenz on how we are to redefine "resources" come immediately to mind as victims of my selection process.

But choices must be made. I have made them, and I take full responsibility for the disappointment that some of Sarason's followers will feel when they discover that one or more of their favorite chapters has not been included. Left on my own, without the constraints imposed by the publisher of this volume and the publishers of his previous works, I, like the little old man in Wanda Gág's children's book *Millions of Cats*, would likely have "chosen them all."

Seymour Sarason has generously lent me his out-of-print books, his counsel, and, as you will see in the introductions to these selections, his contemporary reflections on a number of the issues that course through these pages. He has cheerfully agreed to the edits and occasional chapter combinations I was compelled to make to his original texts to comply with the aforementioned constraints. He has even pored over the completed volume with me to respond to the copy editor's meticulous inquiries. My appreciation for his support is deep and heartfelt.

Where material has been edited, I have inserted ellipses. In the few instances where my own explanations of excised material have been necessary, I have put them between brackets. Where I have combined material from more than one of his original chapters or renamed selections to reflect more accurately the focus of the material, I have so indicated. In many cases, Sarason refers in his text to other chapters from excerpted books;

I have left those cross-references in, to alert the reader about where to find more information on that topic. The tables of contents of twenty-seven of his books—those most central to his discussions of education—are in Part V of this volume. They will, I hope, serve the curious reader who seeks more of what Seymour Sarason has to say.

I want to acknowledge the assistance of several people who have helped this book come into being. Micah Kleit, my editor at Temple University Press, has enthusiastically championed this book from the moment I brought the idea to his attention. Lesley Iura, senior editor at Jossey-Bass Publishers (now part of John Wiley and Sons), has been most generous in granting me permission to freely include a wealth of Sarason's writings published by them. Carole Saltz and Amy Kline of Teacher's College Press have been very cooperative with respect to Sarason's more recent books published by TCP. And Agnes Fisher of Simon and Schuster helped secure permission for the final selection of this anthology. I also wish to acknowledge the superb and meticulous copy-editing of Bev Rokes and of Naren Gupte of P. M. Gordon Associates.

Closer to home, I want to recognize the very fine photographic work of my son, Zachary Fried, whose portrait of Seymour Sarason adorns the paperback cover of this book. And anyone who knows me is quite aware that without the loving support of my wife, Patricia Wilczynski, my efforts to bring this volume into being would have run aground months ago, a victim of my own chronic disorganization. Thank you all.

The Skeptical Visionary

EDITOR'S INTRODUCTION

Seymour Sarason:
Sculptor of Ideas

A Walking Contradiction

Seymour Bernard Sarason is a man on whom we might bestow a most unusual set of labels: "cheerful curmudgeon," "dour optimist," "cautious radical," "pragmatic idealist," "doubtful visionary." And these oxymorons are not the only lenses through which to observe this most contradictory scholar. Is he, essentially, a psychologist or an educator? An academic or a practitioner? A writer or an activist? Is he a champion of school reformers or a persistent gadfly of the school reform movement?

Is Sarason, at heart, a psychologist who has adopted public education as his field of practice, or is he an educational philosopher who uses his background in psychology to try to help us understand why our schools are failing? If an educator, what is his specialty—education for students with disabilities or general education? Why does he staunchly defend classroom teachers in one breath and then scold them roundly for their failure to read the professional literature? Who has he decided deserves the blame for the persistent failure of schools to become interesting places for children and teachers to learn—teacher preparatory institutions or teacher unions? Building principals or district policymakers? Local, state, or national government leaders? And whom does he call on to solve endemic educational problems—the president of the United States or an ad hoc group of parents and teachers who ought to get rid of the school board and the principal and take control of local schools?

And, if one should claim that Seymour Sarason is, at one and the same time, *all* of these people, that he holds forth on *every one* of these seemingly contradictory positions, how can he avoid being viewed by academic experts as someone who spreads himself much too thinly, to the detriment of good scholarship?

Why should we take this man seriously, when no governor, education secretary, or academic dean—in *any* of the disciplines he writes about—seems to have adopted his philosophy? Why bother to collect selections from this man's forty-odd published books, when it is so hard to get a handle on just what kind of scholar he really *is?*

Seymour Sarason would himself entertain these questions—with a heavy dose of skepticism. He begins each new book with a chapter entitled something like, "Who Really Needs a Book Like This, Anyway?" In private, and in public, he is his own severest critic, even though he declines to view himself in terms of the contradictions that have been noted. As he disclosed in a recent conversation, he sees himself rather as a man "continually adding to an individual mosaic of ideas." He described himself as someone who pursues apparently contradictory thoughts "until the fog of my confusion gives way, slowly, to clarity of thought," adding, after a pause, "I only wish that part about 'clarity of thought' were true."

He is a man who, for sixty years, has struggled to determine how well our institutions and social systems serve the people they were designed to help, be they people with mental retardation, children in our beleaguered public schools, graduate students in psychology, or teachers and professors at all levels. For sixty years, he has agonized about why our institutions and social systems so rarely succeed in achieving the visions of those who created them, despite the sincere and hardworking efforts of people of good will.

He is a man who, over a half century of thinking, writing, and teaching, has worked to bring together disciplines, often segregated within academic circles, that he believes deeply influence one another: art and psychology, history and education, politics and schools, communities and universities, performing arts and teaching. For all this time, he has relentlessly challenged our conventional thinking about how systems evolve, why much-desired and often well-funded changes fail to bear fruit, and why our schools seem so resistant to adopting even those reforms whose validity has long been proven.

This walking contradiction is Seymour Sarason, and far too few of those who are engaged in education, psychology, and human services—particularly teachers and students of education—know much about him, despite the more than three dozen books that he has published over the life of his career, before and since his retirement in 1989 as professor of clinical psychology at Yale University.

A Sculptor of Ideas

I have known Seymour Sarason as friend and mentor since 1995, and for me his greatness lies in yet another identity, as "a sculptor of ideas." Some scholars and reformers gain renown because they propose major new directions in their fields and then organize coalitions of people and institutions to carry their ideas forward. One thinks of Theodore Sizer's Coalition of Essential Schools, or Mortimer Adler's Paideia Project, or E. D. Hirsch's cultural literacy movement, or the Comer schools modeled on the research of James Comer. Others become known as exemplary practitioners whose writings extend from their own successful settings to attempt to broaden the impact of their discoveries. Deborah Meier comes to mind, as do Nancie Atwell and William Glasser, among many others.

There are also people who establish themselves primarily as social critics, such as John Holt, bell hooks, Alfie Kohn, and Jonathan Kozol, who are more renowned for their cogent criticism than for the clarity of their reform proposals. Still others are celebrated for the relevance of their research, conducted in new settings or presented in ways that challenge conventional assumptions. Jeannie Oakes's work on tracking, Lisa Delpit's work on African American and other minority languages and cultures, and Mike Rose's interviews of working-class students are wonderful examples.

Seymour Sarason's writing shares certain characteristics with all of these distinguished writers. But his most important contributions to education are the ideas, notions, and concepts he has articulated that, over the course of six decades, have helped shape the thinking of many of these scholars, reformers, and philosophers of education. His ideas have been influential far beyond the breadth of his readership among educational practitioners and teachers-to-be. A number of his books—such as *The Culture of the School and the Problem of Change* and *The Predictable Failure of Educational Reform* have sold very well, and most of his education titles are still in print. But partly because his thoughts have been spread over more than twenty-five books on educational themes, his words reach only a small percentage of the audience that he deserves. The present volume is an attempt to close this gap.

What are those ideas and concepts I claim are so vital? At risk of oversimplifying them, I will summarize a dozen of them here.

1. *Every school has a culture that manifestly defines how people within it operate.* A school is not just a building containing classrooms, teachers, and students, all of whom operate according to state and local district policies. It also has, and *is*, a "culture," and, as such, it affects people in ways that they acknowledge as well as ways that are hidden from their consciousness. As examples, consider how rare it is in most schools for teachers to get together, on their own initiative, to talk about promising new ideas for improving instruction, or how rarely students volunteer questions about the meaning of what they are learning, or how new teachers are often left on their own to "sink or swim." Only when we acknowledge this culture and ask ourselves how well, or how poorly, it reflects our values and goals for diverse learners of all ages can we take charge of our lives as teachers, parents, or students.

2. *The "regularities" of that culture—patterns, rules, and procedures that are mostly unseen and assumed—tend to undermine the basic purposes of educating our youth.* These regularities are what might be called "ways of doing business in school." They are rarely questioned, but to an alien observer (in Sarason's favorite image, "the Man from Mars"), they seem curious, irrational, and counterproductive of the announced mission of schools. Among such regularities are the absence of most parents from active participation with the teacher in guiding their child's learning, and the fact that the school building bustles with activity for six hours a day, five days a week, and then is largely abandoned for any academic purpose. These regularities are not immutable "laws of nature," nor are they the result of careful assessment of the efficacies of prac-

tice. They persist because they go unexamined and unchallenged ("But we've always done it that way!"). Only when we uncover such regularities can we decide whether they serve our purposes as educators.

3. *The overarching purpose of school ought to be that children should want to keep learning more about themselves, others, and the world, yet that purpose is mostly ignored.* Why should kids go to school? To learn the basics as they prepare for a career? So that we can pass our cultural heritage to another generation? So that we can inoculate them with bits of knowledge—dates, formulas, vocabulary lists—that we deem to be "basic"? Is that it? Is that enough? Or do we want them to become better learners, more confident, more capable, more curious? Is there any other goal that even comes close in importance to having students increase their desire to learn more about themselves, others, and the world? If not, why is this goal so rarely articulated and even more rarely assessed to see if, in fact, students leave our schools at least as interested in learning as when they entered?

4. *The educational "system" has an oppressive impact, and when that system continues unseen and unacknowledged, progress is stifled.* The search for culprits—bad teachers, bad students, bad parents, bad schools—who are supposedly responsible for failures in education is a popular, politically sanctioned activity. But the real culprit is the system itself, a system nobody designed, nobody champions, nobody in their right mind would duplicate, and almost nobody challenges. The system is so pervasive that it seems invisible to those who work within it. For example, at every level of schooling people tend to distrust and resent those (e.g., administrators) who wield more power than they, even as they are likely to show disdain or disrespect toward those (e.g., students) who have less power. Ignorance of "the system" perpetuates its worst attributes.

5. *The system, as it currently functions, is intractable, not easily reformed, and reform efforts that ignore systemic regularities and inherent obstacles will predictably fail.* The most significant feature of the educational system is its propensity to perpetuate itself, to just roll along in the face of considerable research illuminating its inefficiencies and failures. Reform efforts that do not acknowledge and address the undesirable features of the system itself are doomed to failure, because change gets stymied or sabotaged by the very dysfunctional aspects one is attempting to alter. For example, it is common in schools for changes to be handed down from on high—new rules, new tests, new priorities—and yet this way of initiating change almost always leads to resentment, apathy, subversion, and failure. Such failures only get compounded when a new reform effort repeats old mistakes.

6. *More specifically, reforms that do not change the power relationships between and among people in schools are fated to suffer paralyzing inertia, if not direct opposition.* Power is unjustly and inequitably distributed in schools and school systems, such that each group feels victimized by those with seemingly more power. We have to address these inequities and imbalances head-on, to ask ourselves why we behave as we do toward those above and below us in the hierarchy of power and how we can change those

relationships so that they reflect our democratic values and promote shared decision making.

7. *Sustained and productive contexts of learning cannot exist for students if they do not simultaneously exist for teachers.* Everyone within a school needs to work together to create an environment in which learners feel motivated and supported as they build on what they know and seek to learn more. But unless teachers also feel that they, too, are part of a high quality and respectful learning environment—that they are learning in a sustained and productive way—we cannot expect more than a few of such teachers to create that environment for their students.

8. *Applying labels to people, especially children, based on pseudo-scientific presumptions about their intelligence, their disabilities, or their academic potential is futile and unjust.* Since the thirties, with the introduction of IQ tests, and continuing with increasing fervor today, millions of children have had their academic careers misshaped by being tested and put into categories that often have had little to do with their real potential as learners. Even the humanizing promise of legislation for the handicapped, such as P. L. 94-142, The Education for All Handicapped Children Act, has been undermined by the tendency of schools and school districts to "code" and label students.

9. *The democratic principle, while celebrated in America, is undermined or ignored in our schools and school systems.* This nation was founded on the revolutionary principle that those who will be affected by a decision have a right to be included in helping to shape that decision—except, evidently, in schools, where the exclusion of parents, students, and teachers from responsible roles in decision making continues unabated. Sarason is that most annoying of patriots. An unabashed champion of American constitutional values, he insists that we live up to them.

10. *Parents are vital partners, teachers are qualified leaders, and both (acting together) are potential governors of schools.* It is easy to proclaim the value of parent participation or involvement. But such advocacy is meaningless when parents are sidelined by school traditions that trivialize roles allotted to parents. Parents, along with teachers, deserve a much greater role—even if that means eliminating school boards and empowering parents and teachers to run the schools.

11. *U.S. presidents (with the exception of Jefferson) have failed to understand the systemic features of our education system.* The pathetic tendency of our highest political leaders to view schools as merely collections of classrooms, each made up of one teacher and a bunch of kids, is inexcusable. This failure is compounded every time a new president sets forth another list of a dozen goals, a "model program," or a battery of high-stakes tests to be foisted on teachers and kids. If the same haphazard strategy had been applied to international affairs, the United States would have lost every war it has fought.

12. *American psychology has been reluctant to address, or has disdained to examine, critical issues in schools.* How can the very discipline that was pioneered, in this

country, by William James and John Dewey—both of whom were fascinated by the nature of learning—so neglect the plight of learners in schools and out? Psychology needs to own, once again, its responsibility to public institutions, including schools, and regain its historical role as a contributor to the improvement of human institutions.

"The Culture of the School"—The Impact of a Notion

The influence of Sarason's ideas has been much more widespread than is generally known even within the education community (let alone the book-reading public). Many if not most of the leading progressive theoreticians and scholars in education credit Sarason with helping to shape their thinking about schools and society. Such people as Theodore Sizer, Linda Darling-Hammond, Michael Fullan, John Goodlad, Deborah Meier, Ernesto Cortes, and the late Al Shanker acclaim Sarason's ideas for playing a major role in the formation of their philosophical stances.

The one place most of us begin is Sarason's notion of the culture of the school. The school culture is so evident, so pervasive, yet so invisible. We know a school as a building, a group of classrooms, a bunch of students, a staff of teachers and administrators, a curriculum of studies, a library, a playground. But how is it also a "culture"? And why is it so important that the main features of that culture be identified, examined, challenged, and changed? If we continue to fail to see the school as a culture, Sarason argues, we will be continually disappointed by the inability of people in school to make those changes that are called for by research, public will, economic necessity, intellectual honesty, and democratic principles. We will fail to see the forest for the trees.

What became increasingly apparent to Sarason, especially during the sixties, was that certain problems involving obstacles to school improvement were recurring with maddening frequency. Whatever the setting, whatever the context, changes that were designed to improve the operation of educational institutions were being sidelined, sweet talked to death, ignored, or sabotaged.

It was from this stagnation that Sarason's most influential work, *The Culture of the School and the Problem of Change,* emerged in 1971. This book brought to the world of education the most cogent challenge to the status quo since the writings of John Dewey a good half century earlier. And, indeed, Sarason is recognized as one of Dewey's heirs in progressive education, as well as for sharing Dewey's fascination with the nature of human learning.

Other books followed, on educational and psychological themes, plus essays on social criticism and the arts. By the time he retired from Yale, in 1989, as professor emeritus, Sarason had published twenty-two books. Time to sit back, relax, and enjoy some leisure after a long career of hard work.

Maybe for some; not for Sarason. Writing, formerly a central academic interest, has become his dominant passion. Books have flowed from the yellow legal pads covered with pencil marks decipherable only by a loyal secretary, Lisa Pagliaro. Between his retirement from Yale and the end of the twentieth century, Sarason published an additional fourteen books. When I proposed the idea of this anthology to him in 1999, following the publication of *Teaching as a Performing Art* in that year, Seymour Sarason believed (as did I) that he had said pretty much all he needed or wanted to say about education.

I should have known better. While I was preparing this book, he was writing four new ones, three of them on education and the fourth including essays on education. Several of these books should appear at about the same time this anthology does. Sarason swears he is finally finished with writing about education. I do not believe him.

"Take the Poison!"

Seymour Sarason, now in his mid-eighties, often ends our telephone conversations with a joke, usually on a Jewish theme. One of his favorites concerns a timid man, living in a hamlet in Eastern Europe, who goes to the village rabbi and, quaking with fear, tells the rabbi that he thinks his wife is planning to poison him. "Nonsense," says the rabbi. "Why would she do a thing like that?" "I'm scared to death," says the man. "You've got to help me." "Well," says the rabbi, "I will come to the house and talk with her, if you insist. And then you'll see how foolish your fears are."

The rabbi appears at the door of the one-room house and is welcomed in. Since the husband is still frightened and upset, the rabbi tells him to sit outside while he speaks with the wife. For the first half hour, the man hears murmured conversation from within. During the second half hour, he hears his wife's voice complaining steadily, with only occasional pauses. Then comes another half hour in which his wife screams and yells almost constantly. At this point, the rabbi emerges from the house, his eyes bloodshot, his prayer shawl in disarray. As he heads down the path to the village, he turns to the husband sitting there and, shaking his head, advises, "Take the poison!"

This joke offers an ironic glimpse of Seymour Sarason's own approach to life. An exuberantly cheerful and idealistic person, he often takes a dim view of the possibilities of significant improvement in those institutions to which he has devoted more than a half century of professional work and thought.

In one sense, Seymour Sarason has "taken the poison"—he has accepted the hand that life has dealt him, including polio at age fourteen (which cut short his boyhood dream of becoming a football player). In person, he plays down the impact of this disability as an obstacle, but there is little doubt that it has spurred his ambition to "do great things" intellectually.

Born into a working-class Jewish family, the son of a cutter of children's clothing (which, as he comments in his 1988 autobiography, was considered a "low status" job among his father's Jewish contemporaries), Sarason had to overcome the influence of poverty in his family of origin. College, graduate school, a Ph.D., and a university career were far above the expectations of a person of his background. He was able to get tuition aid to attend a commuter college only because his state government considered it a pathway to self-sufficiency for a victim of polio who might not otherwise find gainful employment.

Something happened to him as a young college student. First, he got politics—the politics of Marxism, a very attractive alternative for intellectuals growing up during the Great Depression. Then, he got psychology—an abiding interest in how the mind works and why people act the way they do. He abandoned the Marxism, as history showed him how similar Stalinism and fascism became in practice. He held onto the psychology. But the field of American psychology in the thirties and forties was fundamentally different from that of the post–World War II era. Freud was virtually ignored. Psychology, as a clinical approach to healing emotional disorders in people, was an uncertain and under-recognized discipline in higher education. Studying rats in cages and rats in mazes was "where it was at." Being accepted into the graduate program in psychology at Clark University was another unexpected achievement for Sarason.

Receiving his Ph.D. in psychology in 1942, Sarason found the job market all but closed. As he commented, "I was the only one of three graduating students at Clark University in 1941–42 who never received a reply from the colleges to which I had applied for a position. I attributed that to the fact that I did not conceal that I was Jewish." The only position available to him was as a resident psychological "tester" at the "state-of-the-art" Southbury Training School, in rural Connecticut, for people with severe mental retardation. So, that is where Sarason headed with his wife, Esther (also a psychology graduate of Clark University, and his lifelong partner until her death in an auto accident in 1993). The Southbury experience changed his life and deeply affected his growth in understanding about the nature of human institutions.

After three years at Southbury, Sarason was invited to apply to Yale University for a position in clinical psychology. He comments, "If anyone had told me when I came to Southbury in 1942 that I would be at Yale in 1945, my diagnosis and prognosis of their mental condition would have been gloomy indeed." But thanks in part to his growing list of academic publications, he won the position, the first acknowledged Jew in his department.

While teaching graduate students in psychology, Sarason reached out to embrace the challenge of public education—at the very time that Yale was getting rid of its graduate program in education! He focused his critical attention in such areas as student test anxiety, teacher preparation, education for the handicapped, parent empowerment, and urban schools—areas that were, and are, generally avoided by American psychologists.

And once his research into public education produced the "bitter pill" of the system's intractability to significant reform and change, Sarason accepted that poison, too, even though it meant his being unable to share the optimism of school reformers of the sixties, seventies, eighties, and nineties, who thought that their new approach might be "the answer" to the system's failure to educate all children.

Sarason's response to all of this poison, however, has been anything but resignation. He has continued to write, to illuminate the nature of the obstacles and dilemmas, to challenge himself with even tougher questions than he poses to others. He has dared school superintendents, college deans, business leaders, and U.S. presidents to open their eyes to systemic realities rather than hide behind slogans or pieties or simplistic solutions. In doing so, Seymour Sarason has thus far shared the fate of Priam's daughter Cassandra, who was endowed with power to predict the future but cursed by Apollo such that nobody would believe her predictions, however accurate.

It is often said of visionary people, of men and women who are passionately devoted to principles of equality, of democracy, of social justice, that, faced with formidable and overwhelming obstacles to their ideals by the forces of repression, they "would rather light one candle than curse the darkness." Seymour Sarason has, in his sixty years of teaching and writing, managed to light many a candle. But it is the uncompromising nature of his intellect, his refusal to soft-pedal the truth of systems and their cultures, that Sarason has maintained his right, also, to curse the darkness.

It is that quality, that skeptical vision, that makes Seymour Sarason indispensable to those of us who wish to bring light to our work with children and with the systems that attempt to educate them.

Robert L. Fried
Boston, 2002

Part I

The Teacher

CHAPTER 1

Powerlessness Unanticipated

In this first selection, Seymour Sarason reminds us that teachers-to-be need more than a positive attitude toward kids and the requisite course work to prepare themselves for a career in education. He contends that those who enter teaching must have "a better comprehension of what life as a teacher too frequently is" and notes that "the conditions for a productive, satisfying career require . . . a social-intellectual-professional atmosphere" in which teachers can develop as professionals with real knowledge of the problems and promises of that profession. He finds that "those who choose teaching as a career are inadequately sensitized to the problems they will confront and what *they* can and *should* do about them."

Question for Seymour Sarason

If you were teaching an "Introduction to Education" course for students contemplating teaching as a career, how would you begin the process of sensitizing them to the problems that lie ahead?

Sarason's Response

At the end of the first class I would ask them to write a five-page paper on their experience of their school years. The paper would address, for example, these questions: "How often were you stimulated or bored?" "How many teachers turned you on?" "What is the most important thing you learned about yourself as a person and a learner?" "How well do you think your teachers knew you?" I would devote two to three sessions to a discussion of these "memory" papers.

In my book *The Case for Change* I have a chapter on an elective, year-long course on the culture of the school. I discuss the experiences they would be provided with, for example, attending board of education meetings and school faculty meetings, following

From the preface, acknowledgments, and "Justifying This Book" in *You Are Thinking of Teaching? Opportunities, Problems, Realities* by Seymour Sarason. Copyright © 1993 by Seymour Sarason. This material is used by permission of Jossey-Bass, Inc., a subsidiary of John Wiley & Sons, Inc.

the superintendent around for at least two days (also the principal, social worker, etc.). No one has taken me up on that suggestion.

Today, I would make something like that course *required* of anyone who seeks to become a teacher. The beginning teacher is scandalously ignorant of the culture of the school. I regard that chapter as containing one of the most constructive suggestions I have ever made.

More about the preparation of teachers may be found in:

Teaching as a Performing Art (1999)
How Schools Might Be Governed and Why (1997)
School Change: The Personal Development of a Point of View (1995)
The Case for Change: Rethinking the Preparation of Educators (1992)
The Preparation of Teachers: An Unstudied Problem in Education (1962)

. . . I resisted writing this book for fear that what I would say would be perceived as having an effect contrary to my intention, which is to portray to those considering a career in teaching a picture containing exciting opportunities to understand themselves, students, and our society. The source of my resistance was that those opportunities would be believable only if those contemplating a career in teaching knew the nature of the challenges they would confront. I long ago learned that too many people chose such a career abysmally unsophisticated about what they would be up against staying intellectually and professionally alive. Despite such a lack, some teachers had the courage and motivation to continue growing, learning, and changing. Too many teachers did not, and in saying that I intend no criticism whatsoever. The conditions for a productive, satisfying career require more than personal characteristics; they also require a social-intellectual-professional atmosphere in which those characteristics stand a chance to be expressed. What I found impressive were those instances where that atmosphere existed minimally or not at all but where individual teachers successfully sought to change that atmosphere.

It took me too many years finally to "hear" what almost all teachers were telling me: "I wish I had been made more knowledgeable about and sensitive to the realities of teaching real kids in a real school. If I knew when I started a fraction of what I know now, I might or might not have chosen a career in teaching, but I would have reacted to the realities in a better way." One teacher articulated well something that for me had the clear, loud ring of truth: "It took me at least five years to overcome the tendency to regard myself as powerless to do anything to make my school an alive place. In my preparatory program, my instructors and supervisors—who were well-intentioned, sincere people—conveyed the impression that my major, even sole responsibility was to the students in my classroom. What was happening in the rest of the school was important *but none of my business* [her emphasis]. That, of course, was not true. When I had that insight, my whole outlook changed, and so did my role in the school. I helped change that school. I became a more happy teacher *and person* [her emphasis]. If I didn't feel all-powerful, I certainly didn't wallow in feelings of powerlessness. It wasn't easy, but it has paid off." That was said to me twenty-five years ago, long before the issue of the role of teachers in educational decision making gained currency. If it has gained currency, albeit far more on the level of rhetoric than in practice, the fact remains that today those who choose teaching as a career are inadequately sensitized to the problems they will confront and what *they* can and *should* do about them. That is a central theme in this book. It is a theme, a belief, that literally forced me to write this book. "Salvation" has its internal and external sources and conditions.

If I believe anything, it is that unless and until those who enter teaching have a better comprehension of what life as a teacher too frequently is, *and what it should and can be,* improving our schools is a doomed affair. Yes, other things have to happen, other changes have to be made. But unless teachers are better prepared to play a more active, even militant role in such changes, improvement will be minuscule. It is that belief that permits me to emphasize . . . that those who today choose teaching as a career are doing so at a time when, individually and as a group, they can make a difference. No career other than teaching allows one as much possibility of meeting and coping with a threefold challenge: better understanding of oneself, others (students, parents), *and the society in which we live.* This is not an easy challenge. It is not for the fainthearted or those who view *the* teacher in *a* classroom as a desirable (or possible) monastic existence. It is a challenge that when understood and realistically confronted guarantees excitement, frustration, and personal-intellectual-professional growth.

What I say in this book to those contemplating a career in teaching can be put this way: "You may perceive what I say as coming from a pessimist who says the bottle is half-empty. I hope you will see it as coming from someone who sees the bottle is half-full and believes that you can increase its contents." . . .

. . . If in the past I have been critical of what and how teachers teach their students, I am delighted to be able to say that teachers have taught me a great deal about teaching, teachers, and schools. I must single out two teachers, now my friends, who "instructed" me well. One is Ed Meyer, who at great personal cost, but not at the expense of dearly held values and intellectual integrity, has been a constructive and persistent critic of the preparation of teachers. The other is Robert Echter, who helped me understand how keenly teachers feel the lack of collegiality in their schools, a sense of community they passionately desire but were not helped to think about or to assume the obligation to achieve. . . .

. . . We are all familiar with the quip that the two things we can count on in our lives are death and taxes. There is a third thing: In our past, present, and future, something we thought was "right" was or will be wrong. That is as true for me as for the reader. I say that as a way of indicating that this book reflects an agonizing review of what I have learned from my experiences, mistakes, and successes. In one or another way I have been connected with schools for almost fifty years, either as a clinical psychologist, a researcher in schools, a consultant, or an active participant in teacher training programs. And those have been years during which the society generally and schools in particular have undergone dramatic change, although one should never confuse change with progress. It was hard, I would say impossible, for anyone living through those decades to continue to think in accustomed ways. If it was true in those decades, it is still true today.

The immediate stimulus for this book is my bedrock belief that nothing will desirably change in our schools until those who enter teaching have a more realistic grasp of what life in a school is, can, and should be. It took me years to realize that those who were choosing teaching as a career did so more on the basis of fantasy than on reality-based expectations. That is understandable. After all, a person choosing a career in teaching is, relatively speaking, young, inexperienced, idealistic, unformed, and uninformed. There is truth to that, but I have had to conclude that it is a very partial truth, which obscures what can be with what is. No one can know all that one should know about choosing a particular career, but that is no excuse for not trying to help that person become aware, to some degree at least, of the problems one will predictably encounter in that career. And when I say "help," I mean not only providing information but alerting the person to a most fateful question: Is there a match between the obligations, responsibilities, and problems inherent in that career and the individual's personal style, needs, and goals? That is a question many professionals failed to struggle with at the point of making a career decision, with the consequence that they have some regret about the choice they made. That is as true for teachers as it is for lawyers, physicians, engineers, and businesspeople.

We are living at a time when there are scads of proposals to improve our schools. . . . However widely and wildly these proposals differ, they rest on the assumption that those who enter teaching have a working grasp of what it means to live life in a school. On the basis of hundreds (perhaps thousands) of conversations and interactions with teachers, I can assure the reader that that assumption is wholly or in large measure invalid. This is not to say that most of these teachers regretted their choice of career, although some did, but rather that they wished that they had made the choice with more scrutiny, that someone had alerted them to what they later came to see as predictable problems a teacher will encounter. As one teacher said to me, "I do not regret having chosen teaching, but I do regret that I made the choice on grounds that guaranteed I would have a lot of personal and professional problems, not about my classroom but about my place in the school and school system." One teacher summed up what scores of teachers told me: "Before I became a teacher, I imagined that I would be part of a school family, that I would be part of an intimate, stimulating group of friends who shared experiences and had common goals. It hasn't worked out that way, but at least I know from teachers in other schools that I should not blame myself." Still another teacher, relatively new to teaching, articulated what I frequently heard from others: "When I decided to go into teaching, no one told me that my self-respect would force me to be assertive, even confronting about how decisions affecting me were made. Fortunately, I am no shrinking violet but, frankly, I didn't expect to have to be as forthright as I have become."

If what these teachers said does not paint the rosiest of pictures, the fact is that there are schools, by no means numerous, in which teachers feel worthy, respected, consulted, a sense of personal-intellectual collegiality, the sense that they belong. And some of these schools are what are termed "ghetto" schools, where the appearance of physical decay, inadequate resources, and a slumlike surrounding masks the reality of a devoted, closely knit, energy-demanding, creative group of educators who would not want to be elsewhere. What is noteworthy about these schools is they are what they are in large part because teachers exercised initiative and leadership about matters beyond their classrooms. So when I say that little of the goals of reform efforts will be realized unless and until teachers are better prepared to understand, deal with, and change the quality of personal and intellectual life in schools, I am saying that those who contemplate a career in teaching have to examine who and what they are and want to become. Not everyone seeking a career in medicine or law or psychology has the personal and temperamental characteristics such a career requires, both practically and ideally. It is no different for those seeking to enter the profession of teaching.

It is a truism to say that each of us is literally a unique person. It is also a truism to say that each profession has its unique aspects: for example, where and how that profession is practiced, the responsibilities and obligations of such a professional, the demands on life-style such a profession makes, and the kinds of personal and intellectual problems that will predictably be encountered over a professional lifetime. If you conclude that teaching is not for you, that is no basis for self-criticism. Teaching is not for everyone. If you conclude that teaching is for you, it should be on the basis that *you* know who and what you are, the ways in which you will be challenged, and that you are prepared to be other than a silent, passive participant in the socially fateful and crucial effort to improve our schools; that is, the particular school or schools in which you work. It is unfair and unrealistic to expect teachers to change the society. It is not unfair or unrealistic to expect teachers to change, in part if not wholly, the conditions in which they and their students experience personal and intellectual growth. Teachers have brought about such changes. If the number of instances is smaller than we like, let us not gloss over the fact that some groups of teachers successfully departed from tradition and the results have been both exciting and gratifying, despite all sorts of frustration and uphill climbs. These teachers were truly not shrinking violets. They were not content to live their professional lives in an encapsulated classroom in an encapsulated school.

I said that the immediate stimulus for this book is my belief that little or nothing will desirably change in our schools unless or until those who enter teaching have a more realistic grasp of what life in a school is, can, and should be. In discussing that belief, I have also answered the question about how I, who have never taught in a public school, can justify writing a book for those thinking about teaching as a career. The answer is simple: What I say in this book is what teachers have told me. I do not want to give the impression that I met with teachers, I asked questions, and out came answers. It was not as simple as that. What I learned from teachers—and in this respect, they were my teachers—I got after I had spent time in their classroom and school, after they perceived me as someone interested in how they thought and felt as teachers, after they came to believe me when I said that teaching is (that is, can be) a wondrous combination of intellectual challenge, interpersonal sensitivity, superhuman patience, creativity, a healthy degree of frustration tolerance, and more. And some of these teachers had the courage and candor to say that they fell short of the mark.

There is one pervasive theme in this book that was rarely verbalized by teachers and represents a conclusion to which I was forced. Simply put, it is that teachers vastly underestimate their power to change things. Teachers tend to see themselves at the bottom of the hierarchy of power in educational decision making. That is the way things are, although that is slowly changing. And yet what teachers were telling me *implied* that unless their sense of powerlessness changed, the effort to reform schools would be another instance of "the more things change, the more they remain the same." More than that, their basic stance was that alterations in their relationship to educational decision making would come from those higher in the hierarchy of power. That will not happen, in my opinion, except infrequently and (probably) begrudgingly. It will come primarily from teachers exercising initiative, leadership, and courage. That is why I regard who will choose teaching as a career to be so crucial in determining what will happen to our schools in the long- and short-term future. . . .

CHAPTER 2

You Know More Than You Think and More Than They Give You Credit For

Here, Sarason invites prospective teachers to reflect on their own experiences as students in K–12 classrooms and to use these experiences as a framework through which to envision their careers as teachers. "My goal in this chapter," he begins, "is to convince you that its title has validity."

Toward the end of the chapter he avers, "If you can do for your students what your best teacher did for you in the ways he or she did it, you will have justified your professional existence." Throughout this book, the tone is informal and warm, as though Sarason is trying to both encourage and caution teachers-to-be about the perils of their intended profession.

Question for Seymour Sarason

In recounting your memories of your own public school teachers, you say, "As I have looked back and replayed my school days on my internal video screen, there were very few teachers I can say I trusted." Because, admittedly, you received a pretty good education in public school, just how important is it for new teachers to create a trusting environment?

Sarason's Response

I did *not* receive a good education. I was forever scarred by math and algebra teachers who were utterly insensitive to—and seemingly uninterested in—why I was having trouble. My chemistry teacher made chemistry a memory game. The only subject I truly enjoyed was history. I had two teachers who made subject matter come alive in a way that had *personal significance*. These two teachers I think about frequently today, seventy years later. There was a third teacher I valued, whom I have discussed in a couple of books. She was, of all things, a Latin teacher who demonstrated and emphasized how so much of English derives from Latin—relationships that opened a new world to me. I came to find dictionaries fascinating.

> More about the preparation of teachers may be found in:
>
> *Teaching as a Performing Art* (1999)
> *How Schools Might Be Governed and Why* (1997)
> *School Change: The Personal Development of a Point of View* (1995)
> *The Case for Change: Rethinking the Preparation of Educators* (1992)
> *The Preparation of Teachers: An Unstudied Problem in Education* (1962)

My goal in this chapter is to convince you that its title has validity. That is important for at least two major reasons. In the previous chapters, I emphasized that because of your inexperience and lack of relevant knowledge, you must make every effort to seek and digest as much knowledge as possible about what a career in teaching will require of you. That advice still holds good. You do have "deficits" in knowledge, but, as I shall endeavor to persuade you, you have some crucially important "assets" in experience that you should mine. You are far from being an ignoramus! The other major reason is that not only should your experiential assets enter into your decision, but once you have decided on such a career, you must use those assets as a basis for judging how well what you will be asked to learn in a preparatory program helps you make sense of those experiential assets. What you must avoid is falling into the trap of passively accepting attitudes about and conceptions of a teacher's role that conflict with your experience. I am not suggesting that you be argumentative with your college teachers but rather that you be true to yourself—that is, you will not lightly dismiss or forget or give up conclusions you came to as a student who spent twelve years in elementary, middle, and high school. Those conclusions inevitably will contain errors of different sorts, but they will also contain some important truths.

You owe it to yourself to listen to and reflect upon what you will be taught, but not at the expense of giving up all you have *learned about learning* in those twelve years. Some college teachers have the understandable but still inexcusable tendency to view students as having empty heads that need to be filled. As a college teacher, it took me years to realize that I vastly underestimated what students knew. After all, I was teaching *psychology*, and on what basis was I assuming that my students had empty psyches, that they had not had experiences directly relevant to what naive I assumed would be for them completely new knowledge? If I say such a stance is understandable, it is in large part because my students presented themselves as if they had no experiential assets I could or should exploit. And that is the point: Students too readily assumed that they had no basis for using their experience to question in any way the "truths" I was giving them. When teacher and students collude in accepting that assumption, it is a recipe for nonproductive learning.

Teachers teach and students learn! Productive learning occurs when students and teachers teach each other. Teachers do know more than students, but unless that more takes into account what students know and have experienced, the students are robbed of the opportunity of examining, critiquing, and enlarging their personal and intellectual horizons. In the course of your professional education, you will frequently hear the maxim "You teach children, not subject matter." That maxim is intended to emphasize that you be sensitive to "what and where children are." Teaching should always deal with two subject matters: the world of the learner and the content and structure of the subject matter. That maxim is as valid for the individual in a teacher preparatory program as it is for a first-grade child. Too frequently, it is a maxim honored more in the breach than in the practice.

Let us start with the first major reason justifying this chapter's title, and let us do so by asking this question: When you review your twelve years as a student, which teachers come quickly to mind? Let me personally answer the question. Because I am undoubtedly a very senior citizen, I have to point out that the teachers I remember now are the same teachers I remembered when I was much younger. For example, when I was in graduate school—approximately six or seven years after being graduated from high school—a number of my student colleagues and I were discussing the nature of memory, in the course of which someone suggested that each of us write down the names of the teachers we had in our public school days. We were quite surprised at the relative shortness of our lists. (We could recall in our mind's eye several teachers whose names could not be dredged up.)

My list then was what it is today, and in this order: Miss Stephenson, Mr. Coleman, Miss Collins, Mr. Triest, Mr. Hunkins, Mrs. Schweig, Mr. McDonald. The last two names were not teachers. Mr. McDonald was the principal of my elementary (K–8) school, and Mrs. Schweig was the assistant principal. But they were unforgettable because I and others viewed them as fearsome, punishing, if not child-devouring. The fact is that I can recall not a single instance when I interacted in any way with either of them, and I can recall no instance when I saw them in any way punish or discipline a child. But to the children in that school, Mr. McDonald and Mrs. Schweig were to be avoided like the plague. If you were in the hall and you saw either of them, your heartbeat mightily escalated, especially if they appeared to be approaching you. Why are they, who were not my teachers, on my list? For one thing, I cannot think of my elementary school days without their images being conjured up. I *feared* them. For all I know, they may have been lovely, decent, sensitive, supportive people, but you couldn't prove that by my testimony or that of my classmates. They never did or said anything to give students the feeling that they could be trusted. There is a difference between fear and respect. We *feared* them. We saw them as seeing us as potential criminals. We loved and respected Tom Kelly, the police officer who directed traffic at the busy intersection where the school was located. He was a delightful, friendly, joking, lovable person. When he was killed by a car at that intersection, we cried. If that had happened to Mr. McDonald or Mrs. Schweig, we probably would have been sad, but we would not have cried.

Why do I start with Mr. McDonald and Mrs. Schweig? For one thing, I wish to emphasize that how a child views an adult in the school may be dramatically discrepant with how that adult intends or would like to be viewed. I have no doubt whatsoever that Mr. McDonald and Mrs. Schweig did not want to be feared. But I can recall nothing said by either of them or any of my teachers to change my basic stance of fear, my belief that if they approached me, I was in trouble. (It was not until I was an adult that I learned that that is precisely what many parents believe: If they are asked to come to see the principal, they are going to hear bad news. Parents are not accustomed to being summoned to school to be told good news.) The more general point I wish to make is that young children, *like everyone else*, form impressions of others less on the basis of what they say or do not say and more (much more) on what they experience in their give-and-take with others. And by *experience*, I mean circumscribed instances in which the needs, expectations, and goals of a child are positively or negatively affected by the words and actions of an adult. It is not that actions speak louder than words but that actions are incomparably more fateful than words. I may very well have been told that Mr. McDonald and Mrs. Schweig were not to be feared, but there was nothing in my personal experience to lead me to change my mind. Fear is the enemy of trust, and trust is the interpersonal vehicle by means of which different personal worlds can begin to overlap. I had absolutely no basis for trusting Mr. McDonald and Mrs. Schweig.

As I have looked back and replayed my school days on my internal video screen, there were very few teachers I can say I trusted. Let me hasten to add that I never feared a teacher the way I did Mr. McDonald and Mrs. Schweig. Why, then, were there so few whom I did trust? Why when I think of trust do I think only of Mr. Coleman and Miss Stephenson? One reason is that I believed they were interested not only in my academic performance but in *me;* that is, what I thought and felt. When I gave a wrong answer to a question, they did not say "That is wrong" and call on another student. They tried to determine why and how I arrived at the wrong answer. And they did that calmly, patiently, as if I had piqued their curiosity, which they had to satisfy. With other teachers, I would not volunteer an answer unless I was *absolutely,* 100 percent sure my answer was correct. With Mr. Coleman and Miss Stephenson, I was relaxed and not fearful of appearing stupid. In fact, I enjoyed those give-and-take interactions. Their classes were interesting, they asked us interesting, even puzzling questions, they challenged us to draw on our out-of-class experience. And in doing so, they did one other thing: They revealed why and how *they* thought as they did. We learned a lot about them as people. If I had to put in one sentence what has stayed with me from their classes, it would go like this: "There is more than one way to think about and solve a problem."

When I think of these two people (they were more than the label *teacher* conventionally conjures up), the word *fair* always comes to mind. That is a hard word to define briefly. For my present purposes, let me just say that it appeared as if who you were, and how "smart" you were, were never grounds for ignoring or devaluing you. Regardless of who and what you were—and the students were very heterogeneous on any variable you can name—you *counted.*

Let me now tell you about Miss Collins, whom I had in the ninth grade and who influenced my life. She did not have the "open," challenging style of Miss Stephenson or Mr. Coleman. I never felt I knew her or that she was particularly interested in me other than as a performing student. She was a prim, constricted, low-key, curriculum-oriented woman who in her quiet way ran a quiet class. If she rarely smiled or expressed any strong feeling, she was not intimidating. She taught Latin. In those days (shortly after the Civil War!), you took Latin if you were college-bound. You would be right if you assumed that students took Latin with the same enthusiasm they took a horrible tasting medicine. For the first month of class, it was all medicine. Then, slowly but steadily, Miss Collins began to demonstrate how some of the words we used every day derived from Latin. To me and a few other students, it came as a revelation that English mightily derived and developed from Latin. Yes, it was a Latin class, but to me it was also a class in the English language, *my* language. It was Miss Collins who stimulated us to look upon a dictionary as a kind of detective story. If Miss Collins was not an interpersonally interesting teacher, she was an intellectually mind-expanding teacher. She made "dead" Latin personally "alive."

Now to Mr. Hunkins and Mr. Triest (and many others whose names I cannot recall). The first word that comes to mind is *uninteresting.* Not only were they uninterested in me (or any other student), but they did not seem interested in *anything,* including the subject matter. It is as if they came to a class with a recipe (= lesson plan) that said "Do this first, that second, and that third, and if you follow instructions, you will end up with a palatable dish you will enjoy." There was nothing to enjoy! We were treated and felt like robots. More correctly, it is as if we had empty heads and hearts. The fact is that a lot was going on in my head and heart, but God forbid that I should put it into words. My job was to learn what I was told to learn even though in my "unformed" mind, I knew there was a difference between learning and understanding. And I learned one other thing: Even if I learned but did not understand, do not ask questions, do not reveal your stupidity, do not ask "why" questions, do not take up valuable teacher time. By conventional standards, I was a "good" learner. By my own standards, I was a very poor understander. The classroom was no place to seek or expect to gain understanding. It was a place to get good grades, to appear as if you understood, not a place to ask questions that nobody else seemed to have (which, of course, was not true), but a place in which you had better be able to answer the seemingly scores of questions the teacher asked. None of these teachers *invited* questions. On the contrary, they made you feel that if you asked questions, you were either stupid or a show-off. None of the teachers responded to questions the way Miss Collins did. I said she was prim, low-key, undemonstrative of feeling. But when you asked her a question about whether a particular word in English derived from Latin, her eyes took on an excited cast, an ever so small smile seemed to struggle for expression, and she helped you to answer your question. I can sum up by saying that in these other classrooms, productive learning was defined by the number of questions I could answer, how well I could regurgitate what I was supposed to learn. That definition does contain a kernel of truth, but only a kernel. Another way of summing up is to say that the bulk of my classrooms were uninteresting, boring, and without much point.

Why do Mr. Triest and Mr. Hunkins stand out in my memory? Why do I remember their names and not those of similar teachers for whom subject matter was infinitely more important than what was going on in our hearts and minds? The answer is that I did not respect them. There were many teachers who were riveted on subject matter, but in some inchoate way, I concluded that they cared about the subject matter, if not about us. Mr. Triest and Mr. Hunkins, I and others had to conclude, cared about nothing except getting through class without once getting up from their chairs. Their classes were ones in which nothing seemed to make sense. Mr. Hunkins taught introductory chemistry, Mr. Triest introductory German. We ended up having no respect for or interest in Mr. Triest, Mr. Hunkins, chemistry, or German. There are people today who assert that the level of learning in a classroom is largely affected by factors extrinsic to the classroom, for example, family socioeconomic status. They never had the likes of Mr. Triest and Mr. Hunkins!

I could go on and on, but I do not see the point. I have revealed enough to buttress the conclusion that by the time I finished high school, I had had experiences quite relevant to conceptions of what makes life in a classroom interesting and challenging or boring and even deadly. Needless to say, I did not know that I had learned a lot about the ingredients working for and against productive learning. I was *just* a high school graduate. It could never occur to me that I had experiential assets relevant to matters educational. Who was I to pass judgment on teachers, classrooms, and the nature of learning? Is there any doubt whatsoever that my teachers would view me as without assets on the basis of which I was justified to come to conclusions? If after high school I had entered a teacher preparatory program—and in those days, you could do just that—it would have been with the attitude that nothing in my school years was of value in learning to become a teacher. I would have looked at my college teachers from precisely the same stance from which I had looked at my public school teachers: I knew nothing, they knew it all; their job was to pour in, mine was to absorb; I had only deficits, they would provide me assets; they were entitled to opinions because they had experience, I was not so entitled because I lacked experience.

What do you come up with when you review your school years? Which teachers stand out and why? Who turned you on or off? In which classes did you find yourself *willingly* eager to learn more? How frequent were boredom, lack of interest, and pointlessness? On which teachers would you confer sainthood because in some way or other you now know that something about what they were as teachers and/or people rang a bell you still hear? Is what I related about my school years (which were well over sixty years ago!) markedly different from what you recall? That there will be differences among us can be taken for granted. But are those differences of such a degree as to cause you to disagree with these statements:

1. In too many of our classrooms, children rarely, sometimes never, have what I will for the sake of brevity call a mind-expanding experience.

2. In too many of our classrooms, the structure and ambience do not encourage children to give voice to their questions about subject matter, personal experience, and the world they live in. Put another way, children live in two worlds, and the twain shall never meet.

3. From the standpoint of the student, there is no separation between what is being taught and who is teaching it. To the student, the teacher is a person whose words and actions determine whether or not he or she will feel understood, fairly judged, valued, encouraged, as someone who counts, someone whose feelings and needs are not taken for granted, someone who wants to feel *interpersonally safe* to be expressive, spontaneous, even probing and "wrong."

4. Teachers, *all* of your teachers, contributed to your admittedly vague sense of the ingredients that make for productive learning. And that sense is always based on a comparison, a contrast between a Miss Stephenson and a Mr. Hunkins.

The point is not whether you find yourself agreeing with all, part, or none of these statements but rather that you have had valuable experience relevant to learning about learning (which is always social in nature). You do have assets. So, if you are contemplating a career in teaching, it should not be from the stance that you will be entering a completely new world for which you have no personal compass. That does not mean that these assets are a form of hands-on-the-Bible truths that will not require amending, enlarging, recasting. But it does mean that you know where you stand and what you stand for and that you will not easily give up your beliefs because someone says you are wrong. Your beliefs came from your experience, and you should change those beliefs on the basis of new experience and not because someone *says* you are mistaken. Your obligation to yourself and your teachers is to listen, to "hear" what they say, to reflect on it, not passively to assume that the voice of authority requires submission. Productive learning is a struggle, a willing struggle from which comes a sense of change and growth. It makes no difference whether you are a first-grader or someone entering a teacher preparation program. Productive learning has its joys, but they are a consequence of intellectual and personal struggle.

This chapter had a goal beyond trying to convince you that you have valuable assets. If I have, in part at least, been convincing, you will then better understand why being a teacher is among the most constructively impactful roles there are. *If you can do for your students what your best teacher did for you in the ways he or she did it, you will have justified your professional existence.* Your goal is not to become *a* teacher but to become one consistent with the personal style and intellectual creativity of those teachers whom you have cause to remember with gratitude.

It is easy to say "be true to yourself." Like all clichés, that saying contains a kernel of truth. The problem is to determine what you mean by "yourself." What I have endeavored to do in this chapter (and previous ones) is to suggest that in regard to becoming a teacher, "yourself" is, among other things, a condensation of attitudes, perceptions, and values forged in years of experience that led you, albeit vaguely, to define the conditions in which *you* came alive, in contrast to those in which *you* were going through the motions. *You* know when "yourself" was and is engaged. It is that engagement that you owe to your students. It is not a matter of imitation. It is a matter of personal-intellectual-professional *development,* and I italicize that word in order to make the obvious point that however clear the image of your best teachers is in your mind's eye, you are a unique individual who will have to find your own way to be true to that image. As a teacher, I undoubtedly looked quite different from Miss Stephenson, Mr. Coleman, and Miss Collins. I would like to believe that whatever my style, it reflected what these teachers stood for and did for me. If I was not the superb teacher they were, I have never forgotten what the best is. And if I have never forgotten that, I never have forgotten my worst teachers, who, in a strange way, were very impactful on my developing self.

CHAPTER 3

Why Teachers Must Also Be Psychologists

Sarason compares teachers to psychologists and argues that teachers must be both, as Dewey suggested, if only to help students connect learning with living. But to assume such a role demands that would-be teachers, while they prepare for the profession of teaching, be accorded the respect and care they deserve from their university professors.

Continuing on the theme of teacher preparation, Sarason exposes the disparity between how idealistically we like to envision ourselves teaching kids and how patronizingly we treat those whom we are training as prospective teachers. He includes two lists—"the thoughts that run through the mind of a beginning teacher on the first day of teaching," and "the questions that occupy the minds of students on the first day of school"—and concludes, "The phenomenology of the teacher and student is, in principle, virtually identical." Like teachers, students are anxious and curious. Yet, as Sarason says, "I have yet to meet a beginning teacher who had been prepared to be sensitive to and act on that identity."

Question for Seymour Sarason

What would you have college students do—individually or collectively—should they find themselves being treated in a disrespectful or patronizing way by their professors? How can a student in a teacher preparatory program act upon the idea that "the phenomenology of the teacher and student is, in principle, virtually identical"?

Sarason's Response

When students are viewed by teachers as underdeveloped countries who are too dumb and primitive to ask questions, or to disagree with those who have all the answers, or

Reprinted from "Teaching Teachers and Teaching Children: Ignorance Assumed and Assets Unmined," in *The Case for Change: Rethinking the Preparation of Educators* by Seymour Sarason. Copyright © 1992 by Seymour Sarason. This material is used by permission of Jossey-Bass, Inc., a subsidiary of John Wiley & Sons, Inc.

whose minds are empty and need to be filled, they should revolt. They should band together and, in writing, let the teacher know that "We the People" declare independence.
Being a professor is no excuse for ego trips.

That will not be easy for students to do, I know. But to suffer in silence is to reinforce
obtuseness and tyranny, which is what a lot of school kids experience every day. This
question is very difficult for me to handle because I get too upset when I see instances
of demeaning behavior, even though the perpetrators usually see themselves as well intentioned.

More about the preparation of teachers may be found in:

Teaching as a Performing Art (1999)
How Schools Might Be Governed and Why (1997)
School Change: The Personal Development of a Point of View (1995)
You Are Thinking of Teaching? Opportunities, Problems, Realities (1993)
The Preparation of Teachers: An Unstudied Problem in Education (1962)

Teaching teachers, like teaching children, is not a morally neutral affair. It is the discharging and instilling of obligations, the primary one of which is the sense of discovery and growth in what may be termed the learning process. It is not an aim only for
pupils. It is also one for the teacher for whom, no less than for pupils, that sense is the
sole antidote to mindless routinization of thought and action. What we owe children we
owe teachers. No one will say that teachers are only or primarily conduits for information and the articulation of abstract principles. We expect more of teachers and that
more is that they have identified in their own experience the nature and context of productive learning and have taken on the obligation to create similar conditions for pupils.
This ideal holds for the teacher of teachers and the teacher of children. Even though it
is an ideal impossible to attain, or if attained impossible to sustain, it is one by which
we should judge any teacher. The realities of classrooms and schools are obstacles to ap-
proximating the ideal, but that is no excuse for forgetting it. We know that "love thy
neighbor" is a statement of an ideal our world and our frailties seem intent to subvert
but we also know that it is a statement by which we should judge ourselves and others.
In the quiet of the night we know we should expect more of ourselves and others. Ideals
are double-edged swords: they tell us what we should be even though we know at best
we will be only partially successful in attaining them.

I have said that the primary aim of education is fostering the sense of discovery and
growth in the learning process of teachers and students. The learning process in the
world of real classrooms involves more than what we conventionally call subject matter. In the course of any one day things happen in a classroom for which that aim is as
relevant as it is for learning to read or write; this requires an understanding and a course
of action consistent with the primary aim. For example, a teacher discovers that a child
has lied or cheated. How would we want the teacher to understand and respond to that
knowledge? We would, I assume, not be satisfied if the teacher only punished the child:
Break the law, pay the penalty. That would bother us for the same reason that we feel

if a child got all or mostly wrong answers on an arithmetic test, the teacher should go well beyond merely indicating that the answers are wrong. We expect the teacher to seek to discover why the child performed so poorly. Of course the child has "a problem" but so does the teacher. Indeed, the teacher has two problems: to reexamine her way of teaching that child and to determine what other factors may be at work. *For any untoward event in a classroom the teacher, consistent with the primary aim, has to look both inward and outward, a stance that makes discovery and growth possible.* It is also a stance that makes discovery and growth possible for the child. In the case of the child who lied or cheated I am not one who believes that punishment is unnecessary or undesirable. But before punishment is pronounced is it not the obligation of the teacher to try to understand the lying and cheating and to help the child in ways that might prevent such occurrences in the future?

We hear much today about the teaching of values. What we do not hear is that in the course of one day a teacher inevitably faces and has to deal with value issues arising from or impacting on the learning process. Is it not likely that our dissatisfaction with educational outcomes, deriving as those outcomes do from teaching subject matter and not children, is what makes the "clarification of values" a matter of chance in the modal classroom? I cannot refrain from saying that we need a new curriculum for values like we need a hole in our heads. If you think that statement is unwarranted, then I suggest that you sit in any classroom for a day and note the number of times moral and ethical issues, implicit or explicit, arise and are ignored, glossed over, superficially discussed, or handled in counterproductive ways.

Years ago I had several colleagues sit every day for a month in elementary school classrooms and note each time something occurred that was relevant to and illuminated the "constitution" of that classroom, that is, the "values" without which what went on in the classroom was inexplicable, and who "wrote" that constitution which said, so to speak, what the rights, duties, and obligations of students *and* teacher were—what the "laws" were. The occurrences were many. In each classroom, however, the constitution was "written," proclaimed, and enforced by the one adult. If some of the laws you will note lack the specificity of the Ten Commandments, from the standpoint of the children the teacher was, like Moses, confronted by pagans who did not know right from wrong, who needed to be subdued. I am not an advocate for participatory democracy in which everyone's opinion should have equal weight, but if you are to be consistent with the primary aim, then how the constitution of a classroom is forged has a pervasive effect on learning subject matter and assimilating values. To set the teaching of values apart from the teaching of subject matter makes as much sense as separating the teaching of subject matter from the teaching of children. It makes less sense in that it betrays an ignorance or insensitivity to what life is like in the classroom.

The training of educational personnel inadequately prepares them for what life is like in real classrooms in real schools and leaves them unable to capitalize on opportunities to be consistent with the primary aim. The preparation of such personnel should begin not with theory or history or research findings or pedagogical technique but with concrete issues of classroom life: the practical, inevitable, action-requiring issues on the basis of which the would-be teacher can judge and utilize theory and research.

It apparently is easy for the teacher of teachers to forget that the would-be teacher is not without experience or assets. That individual has been a student for years and can identify those contexts in which he or she experienced discovery and growth, the difference between values espoused and values practiced, the teachers whom he or she trusted and the ones who were feared, and the difference between having one's feelings sought and understood and having them ignored or misunderstood. *Far from being without assets, the would-be teacher has loads of assets that the teacher or teachers should help the student recognize, mine, articulate, and apply.*

It is not only the teacher of teachers who sees the student as having no assets, however. That is the way most students see themselves: empty vessels possessing the understandable "deficit" of ignorance and inexperience, waiting to be filled with facts, knowledge, wisdom, and technical skills. Getting students to see themselves otherwise is, will, and should be no easy task, and that also holds for the teachers of teachers who have to change their attitudes about the assets of the would-be teacher. None of this can be accomplished quickly and none of this can be learned in a "once and for all way." It is something we have to learn again and again in relation to the myriad happenings in classroom life. It is not a stance or habit you can learn in a single course or in regard to a particular subject matter. It is a stance that, among other things, should be the object of inquiry and use throughout the preparatory process.

What I have said thus far in this chapter has been by way of prologue to discussion of more conventionally labeled topics. It is a prologue that contained three assertions:

- The primary aim of education is to nurture the sense of discovery and growth in students and teacher. If educational personnel are not committed to that ideal (or to a similar one couched in different language), if for whatever reason they forget or ignore that ideal, their role is robbed of moral justification.
- The arena of classrooms and schools contains mammoth obstacles to actions consistent with the primary aim. That, today, is a given, a glimpse of the obvious, that has numerous sources, one of which (and *only* one of which) is how educational personnel are inadequately prepared for what they will confront—conceptually, personally, interpersonally, morally—as independent practitioners. Unless and until the preparation of educational personnel deals directly with those confrontations and enables candidates to see that there are ways of thinking and acting consistent with the primary aim, those personnel will remain *one* of the sources of inadequacies in our schools.
- Those who seek to become educators have a major asset: They have spent years as "learners" in classrooms. The asset consists not in sheer experience, or the validity or invalidity of whatever conclusions they may have come to, but in the potential that asset has for intellectually and personally grasping the nature and practical consequences of the primary aim.

I anticipate several critical reactions to these assertions and others that will follow. Let me deal with them here so as not to have to repeat them later. The first is this: "What you state as the ideal, the primary aim, sounds like the musings of a university professor who believes that each child is capable of becoming an intellectual, a devotee of the life of the mind." My critic will be surprised to learn that he is partly right in that I believe Piaget and Freud were absolutely correct that from its earliest days each child is a question-asking, answer-seeking organism trying to make sense of self and the world, a budding "intellectual" already containing the seeds of complex thinking: asking questions, arriving at answers (more often than not invalid), experimenting in the sense of trying things out, and knowing in inchoate ways the sense of and the satisfactions from discovery and growth. When I state the primary aim I am saying that our task as educators is to recognize and nurture features already characteristic of the child.

Lest you think that I regard the preschool child in narrow intellectual or cognitive terms, I must refer you to my book *The Challenge of Art to Psychology* (1990a). That book deals with this question: The observational and research evidence is overwhelming that young children everywhere seek and engage in creative, artistic activity, so why *in our society* does that activity virtually disappear as a self-initiated activity when they begin formal schooling? No, my primary aim in no way implies or assumes that all children are capable of becoming committed intellectuals, let alone university professors. It does imply that our obligation is to foster the sense of discovery and growth about self and the world in whatever ways we can (subject matter being but one), knowing that the outcomes of our efforts are far from predictable. Regardless of what a child appears to be, the primary aim dictates that you begin by giving the child the benefit of any doubt you may have.

The second critical reaction is in principle similar to the first, except now it concerns my expectations of teachers: "You, like many others, have commented on the number of different roles society asks teachers to adopt, for example, parent, social worker, policeman, psychiatrist. You now seem to be adding the role of psychologist, and a very sensitive and astute one at that. Not any kind of psychologist but one who can identify and understand and appropriately react to a wide variety of behaviors, feelings, and events. Apart from what that role requires in terms of classroom time, why do you assume that most of those who seek careers in education are capable of becoming effective in that role?"

My answer is in several parts. The first is that teachers have always operated as psychologists. They, like the rest of us, have a "psychology" that informs their thinking and actions. What we are dissatisfied with is that their psychology is inadequate in regard to recognizing and preventing problems. Put in another way, their thinking and actions violate the maxim that you teach children, not subject matter, and that there are myriad non–subject matter opportunities to further discovery and growth. Once you take the maxim seriously you are, so to speak, hoist with your own petard: The psychology of the teacher takes center stage in regard to subject matter and other things. Better *not* to take it seriously than to mouth it and then ignore it, to reinforce the charade in which the utterance of truths remains on the level of cliché.

The second part of my answer is that if my critic does not view favorably the capabilities of those who seek a career in education, then my critic is raising two very important questions: How do we get to the point where preparatory programs can *select* appropriate candidates rather than having to take whoever comes through the doors? And what do we know on the basis of systematic experience or research about the criteria for selection we should employ? The second question is, unfortunately, easy to answer: We know precious little, and that may be an overstatement. Implied in my critic's reaction is the assumption that because those who seek a career in education have, on average, discernibly lower scores on intelligence and aptitude tests than those in the more prestigious professions, it is asking too much of them to expect them to become psychologically sophisticated.

Studies on this point are very few but they confirm the conclusion from my own experience that the correlation between intelligence test scores and the grasp and application of psychologic principles is not far from zero. Future research—assuming that an important problem like this gets the attention and study it deserves, an unlikely assumption—may demonstrate otherwise. So I have to say to my critic that in redesigning preparatory programs we have no alternative but to assume that teachers are capable of becoming better psychologists. To assume otherwise is to indulge the self-fulfilling prophecy, which is what too many teachers indulge with their students.

The third critical reaction goes like this: "If teachers become better psychologists and appropriately take advantage of the many opportunities in the classroom to nurture the sense of discovery and growth in students, would that not cut into the time teachers allot to learning subject matter? Given the brute fact that teachers are under increasing pressure to complete the curriculum in ways that get reflected in achievement test scores, how much time could or should a teacher devote to other aspects of a child's development?" My critic is getting at the heart of the matter which is how long we will continue to require teachers and students to adhere to and meet criteria in ways that are ultimately self-defeating of the productive development both of teachers and students. The issue is not subject matter. The issue is the assimilation of subject matter in ways that capitalize on, stimulate, and reinforce the sense of discovery and growth in regard to self and the world. Subject matter, any formal subject matter, is taught in a social context in which diverse factors have consequences for how that subject matter will be approached, judged, and learned. Subject matter is crucial, so crucial for life that we cannot be other than aghast that most students experience learning of subject matter as a form of harassment and child abuse. Implied in the primary aim is that students should *want* to learn subject matter, not to feel that it is an exercise that an uncomprehending adult world foists on them, an exercise quickly forgotten when the curriculum has been completed.

Of course what I am suggesting may well cut into the time allotted to formal subject matter. But should we not realize that increasing the time devoted (in the most narrow ways) to subject matter has been either fruitless, or has raised test scores to a minuscule degree, or has had the counterproductive effect of guaranteeing that in the development of children subject matter has no personal or intellectual significance for them? Subject matter is too important to be learned but not assimilated, to suffer the fate of enthusiastically motivated memory loss. Yes, I expect a lot from and for teachers and students. And if those expectations require changes in classrooms and schools, the preparation of educational personnel cannot remain what it is.

As I look back at the reform efforts in the post–World War II era, it is truly remarkable how cosmetic the changes have been in the preparation of educational personnel, amounting to little more than add-ons to conformity-reinforcing programs. So, for example, we have been told that teachers should be far more steeped in the subject matters they teach. How can you quarrel with that cliché? How can you be against virtue and motherhood? But how can you ignore the fact that the preparation of educational personnel ill equips them to make subject matter intellectually and personally meaningful to students? How do you get would-be educators to recognize and act on what they know *before* they enter a preparatory program: the differences between productive and mind-stultifying learning experiences? And how do we discharge our moral obligation to the would-be educators to make them knowledgeable about the obstacles they will confront when they become independent practitioners in schools where trying to act consistently in regard to what they know will be so difficult? Do we have a viable alternative that holds promise for preventing, to a degree at least, disillusionment, burnout, ritualization, and retreat into routine on the part of teachers and, therefore, intellectual passivity in students?

Changes in any traditional, complicated type of organization do not derive from one source. Changes always have internal and external sources that are not always compatible with each other. What I have said and will say suggests changes for which the general public is not prepared. For too long it has been given superficial, issue-avoiding "solutions" that turned out to be failures. Although I do not expect the educational community warmly to embrace my proposals, there are two things about which I am certain. The first is that that community does not need to be persuaded that the current situation is either desirable or to be tolerated. The second is that a surprising number of educators (among those who write) have been saying what I have said. If our rationales and proposals are not identical, the most informed critiques of the way things are have come from within the educational community. I do not believe that I have a corner on the truth. I justify this book on the basis of two facts and one belief. The first fact is that for the past thirty years I have been correct in predicting that reform efforts will fail. It could be that I was right for the wrong reasons, but I obviously prefer another explanation! The second fact is that the reform efforts have, for all practical purposes, ignored preparatory programs. My belief, like that of Goodlad, is that these programs need to be completely rethought and redesigned and that if over time those programs do change, they will serve better the purposes of primary prevention.

I have described a stance that should undergird the approach of teachers of teachers in every aspect of the preparatory program. Let me illustrate this further by two questions with which the would-be teacher should be presented. The first question is this: What will be the thoughts, feelings, and expectations of the would-be teacher on his or her first day of teaching, be it the first day of practice teaching or the first day as an independent practitioner? That question is a concrete instance of a more general question: What goes through the mind of anyone who has to demonstrate competence in a new role or task before some kind of a judging public? Long before the would-be teacher entered a preparatory program he or she has had many "audition" experiences, which is to say that the would-be teacher is not devoid of any experiential assets when asked to think about the first day of teaching. In any event, what would we want the would-be teacher to become aware of? What should that person know about an event that will inevitably be challenging? How can we prevent its more destabilizing consequences? Let me briefly list some of the thoughts that run through the mind of that teacher:

- Will I be adequate or competent?
- Will I be liked and respected?
- What will I do if a child challenges what I say or do? Will I be able to do what I know I should do if a child does something flagrantly wrong?
- Will the principal and other teachers show they understand how I feel, that I may screw up, that they want to be helpful?
- What if a child asks me a question I can't answer? Will I be able to say I don't know, I want to think about it?
- What if I do something wrong? Will I be able to say out loud I made a mistake, and that I, like my students, have to learn from my mistakes? Will I have enough control and self-confidence to be consistent with the principle that *I* am a model of how *they* should think and act?

The reader, educator or not, will have no difficulty comprehending the phenomenology of the beginning teacher. Others may employ a different phraseology or come up with a longer list, but every list will reflect one common theme: The beginning teacher is an anxiously curious individual, curious about self, others, and social context. That individual is no different from an actor on opening night, a lawyer trying his first case, or a surgeon performing her first operation.

Now for the second question we ask the would-be teacher to ponder: What are children curious about on the first day of school? Let me list a few of the questions that will occupy the student, putting them in adult language.

- What kind of a person does my teacher appear to be? Should I, will I, like her, trust her? Will she like me?
- Is he going to be fair and consistent? How will he react if I get wrong answers or I do something he thinks is not right?
- Will I be one of the smart ones or one who doesn't catch on quickly? If I don't understand what she asks the class to do, will she help me, talk to me, or make me look dumb in front of the class?
- Will I get up in the morning eager to go to school? Will school be interesting?

The phenomenology of the teacher and student is, in principle, virtually identical. I have yet to meet a beginning teacher who had been prepared to be sensitive to and act on that identity. It is understandable if the teacher is self-absorbed, but when that self-absorption, as is too frequently the case, renders her insensitive to what children are feeling and asking themselves, it can initiate a dynamic not conducive to a context of discovery and growth. I am *not* saying that what happens on the first day or days is fateful for all days thereafter, but my experience has forced me to conclude that those very early

days are, unfortunately, representative of the substance and level of many teachers' understanding of "where children are coming from." Teachers have two theories of learning: one for them (adults) and one for students. That, of course, is theoretical nonsense,
just as it would be nonsense to say that we need one theory for the oxygen atom and
another for the hydrogen atom.

Children are not adults, but that does not mean that their needs are totally different
or that faced with similar situations, their reactions will in no way be similar. I am reminded here of a teacher whose understanding and handling of students I had to regard
as inadequate and insensitive. One day the principal appeared, whispered something to
the teacher, and then left. The teacher then told the class to continue with their seat assignments because she wanted to talk with Kenneth Stone at her desk. I was seated in
the back of the room and could only see their interaction. What I saw was a woman
tenderly talking to a child in tears, one of her arms around his shoulders as if she was
going to embrace him, the hand of her other arm cupped gently under his chin so that
eye contact was unavoidable, tears were streaming down his face. She then kissed him
on the forehead, turned to the class and said she would be back in a few minutes, and
left with the boy. I, like the children in the class, watched the interaction with fascination. When the teacher returned, she immediately assumed her "role" of teacher: The
"lesson" continued.

Two things were remarkable about this incident. The principal had told the teacher
that the boy's mother had been in an auto accident, was in the hospital, and the boy's
father was coming to pick him up. The principal had asked the teacher to talk briefly
with the boy and then bring him to the office. What was more remarkable to me than
the "out of role" behavior of the teacher with the boy was her volunteered explanation
to me of what crossed her mind when the principal relayed the news: "I remembered
how I felt when I was in the sixth grade and my mother came to school to tell me that
my father had died. My heart went out to Kenneth." The second remarkable thing was
that her interaction with the boy, on which everybody's eyes had been riveted, was never
discussed in that class, except to inform them that someone in the boy's family was ill.

The point of this anecdote is that in the course of a day the behavior of this teacher
seemed to be based on the assumption that there was nothing in her experience as a student relevant to her understanding and managing of her students. Her experience was
unused and unusable. It took a fortuitous and unfortunate set of circumstances to allow her unreflectively, spontaneously, to use her experience to comfort the boy in the
most exemplary way.

The reader should ponder this question: In what ways could a teacher capitalize on
such an incident for *educational* purposes? I italicize the adjective *educational* in order
to disabuse the reader of the impression that I am advocating using the incident only or
mainly for therapeutic or cathartic purposes. One thing we know: The children (and I)
saw something that was atypically moving and about which they (and I) were curious
and full of questions. Who was ill in the family? What was the illness? Was that person
going to die? Was the person in the hospital? When would Kenneth come back to
school? How would he make up the lessons he would miss? How can we help him?

There was one other thing I can assure the reader was true: For the rest of that morning the minds of those children were not on subject matter. And I confess that for the rest of that morning I was puzzling over the discrepancy between the usual and unusual behavior of this teacher.

I once discussed this incident with a group of teachers. Here are a few summary highlights of that discussion:

- By the end of a two-hour seminar class, there was general agreement that the teacher should have known the students would be preoccupied with questions when they saw her with tearful Kenneth. Those questions should have been discussed, if only because ignoring them interfered with learning the formal curriculum. Most of these teachers, however, felt that to call such surfacing and discussion *educational* was defining the word much too broadly. Granted that the children would learn something, the teachers still considered the discussion of Kenneth's problem something of an interference or luxury.

- There are countless times during a school year when things happen in and out of the classroom that arouse interest and questions in children. If a teacher were to respond, to try to capitalize on even a small number of these happenings, that would measurably cut into the time required to teach the formal curriculum. Also, to respond to these happenings "in the way you are suggesting requires a degree of psychological sophistication we don't have. We would like to have it, but we don't."

- One of the teachers taught math. "I'll tell you what I would have liked to have done but would not because of the time it would take. I would have asked the class if they were interested in these questions: How many auto accidents are there in one year? Do auto accidents happen more on certain days than on others, more on certain times of the day and night? Who gets in more accidents, men or women? Young people or old people? Do American cars stand up better in accidents than foreign cars? Do seat belts prevent serious injuries?" She must have reeled off a dozen or so questions. And then she said, "I would discuss with them how and where we could get answers, prepare tables and graphs, and do other things that require number concepts. Sure, you can, in your words, capitalize on the Kenneth incident for educational purposes but what if what they learn is not on the achievement tests they take in the spring?" That, I replied, was a legitimate question but I also regarded my answer as legitimate: Learning arithmetic and math in ways and for purposes unrelated to the world of children's interests and activities has been an educational catastrophe.

One more example. President Kennedy was assassinated on a Friday. Schools in New Haven did not open until Wednesday, which was the day of the week I met with first-year teachers after school. When I walked into the conference room of the Yale Psycho-Educational Clinic, the twelve teachers were sharing a common experience: It had been next to impossible to get their pupils to attend to the lessons of the day. As one teacher put it, "This was not a day to teach children anything."

The point of this anecdote is not only that there was a great deal that the children could have and wanted to learn, but that these teachers were so focused on subject matter that they could not respond to what was on minds of all pupils, indeed everyone in the country. These teachers were not unaware of what the children had experienced, nor were they unimaginative souls possessing no spark of creativity. In fact, all but three were recent graduates of prestigious liberal arts programs, they had all taken a couple of educational courses in a local teacher preparatory program the previous summer and were now taking more courses leading to a teaching certificate. And, yet, after three months of teaching they felt under pressure to stick to a prescribed curriculum, come what may.

I trust the reader will agree that the aim of preparing educational personnel is *not* to instill in them a conformity to the way things are. That does not mean that the aim is to prepare revolutionaries who will storm the barricades. But it does mean that they will be knowledgeable about and sensitive to the obstacles to taking seriously what we know about children and productive learning. More than that, they will feel more secure, intellectually and personally, in justifying their departures from the way things are and their obligation to seek to influence educational policy, never forgetting that what is at stake are their fates and those of their pupils. That, to some people, may seem to be asking too much of these personnel.

I find it ironic that this criticism has tended to come from people who indict teachers for not expecting enough from their students. Yes, I expect educational personnel not only to grasp the nature of the ideal but to strive for it even though that striving is an uphill battle. Preparatory programs that ignore or gloss over these issues contribute to the manufacture of problems in both educators and their students.

The principles educators need to grasp, the realities the implementation of those principles will encounter, cannot be learned only by reading or listening to lectures or observing the implementation of those principles by others. These are important modalities, but unless they are embedded in or accompanied by personal, hands-on supervised experience *throughout the preparatory process*—and I literally mean from day one—the chances are that the principles and the ideal will remain abstractions, lacking that sense of concrete experience that alone provides the basis for understanding the relations between ideas and actions. To wed thought and action requires that we overcome the too-frequent divorce between thought and action. At the present time preparatory programs are inadequate in two respects: The gulf between thought and action, principles and action, is very wide; the gulf between how educators are prepared and the realities they will encounter is no less wide. It is one thing to comprehend and explain those gulfs in light of the history, traditions, and formal laws and regulations which have shaped them. It is quite another thing to excuse them. We are living at a time in regard to matters educational when to understand all is no warrant to forgive all. We are at a time for judgment.

It was to John Dewey a glimpse of the obvious that teachers are psychologists. He never advocated that educators should "learn psychology" and *then* become educators, the kind of separation against which he was the most thoughtful critic. And Dewey never expected or suggested that educators should become whatever is meant by a "sophisticated" psychologist. What Dewey did advocate was that educators grasp and appropriately implement psychological principles essential to their task as educators. Dewey stated explicitly that those who had the awesome responsibility to prepare educators should be psychologically sophisticated, a kind of what he called a "middleman" who understood children, classrooms, schools, and the moral and intellectual purposes of education. In setting up his lab school at the University of Chicago at the end of the nineteenth century, Dewey was, of course, the model middleman. He was not on an ego trip when he insisted that he would come to Chicago only if he could head up a department of psychology and pedagogy. His insistence was not based solely on the signal contributions he had already made to the new field of psychology and his desire to relate the potentials of that field to the educational arena. Nor did it stem only from his extraordinary awareness of the relation between social-economic inequities and their perpetuation by educational practices of the time. Those background factors were important but so was the fact that Dewey had been a school teacher. Dewey's concept of the role of the middleman did not come out of the blue.

Teaching teachers involves every psychological issue and principle involved in teaching children. The would-be educators, like the pupils they will later teach, are not unformed, empty vessels, devoid of knowledge, assets, interests, and experience in matters educational. To ignore what the would-be teacher knows and has experienced, what that teacher aspires to be and achieve, is to seal off a gold mine in the face of poverty.

On several occasions I have presented the contents of this chapter to groups of teachers of teachers. Because I assume that their major reactions will be those of many readers of this book, . . . I take them up here. The first reaction went like this: "It's hard to argue with the implications you draw from the maxim that you teach children, not subject matter. And we cannot quarrel with your suggestion that would-be teachers are not devoid of knowledge and experience about productive learning. But when you say that capitalizing on those assets and instilling in our students what the maxim means in practice should begin on day one and should be center stage throughout the program, *we* don't know what that means for *us* and the way our *programs* are structured. You say you are not opposed to courses but everything you say suggests a kind of one-on-one relationship that, you will have to admit, is quite impractical, even utopian. But let us assume that we decide to move in that direction. What kinds of facilities would we need, what kind of techniques could we employ, to make the relationship between principles and actions more meaningful and consistent?"

My answer is in several parts. The first is that form follows function; how you design a program depends on what you want to accomplish. If traditional courses and their sequencing are not accomplishing a stated purpose, then what will? It is true that I look with disfavor on a program that says you have to take this course and then that one, on the assumption that acquiring knowledge is a necessary and sufficient basis for applying that knowledge appropriately in a classroom. The knowledge acquired in course x or y may be valid in a scientific or consensual sense. For example, what is learned in a math, history, psychology, or methods course may be completely valid as sheer knowledge, but the students in these courses will be *practitioners* who are supposed to be able to make subject matter something of interest and curiosity in children, not things unrelated to their past, present, and future. Subject matter is not something to be delivered as we deliver mail but something that is willingly digested, intellectually and personally, and reinforces the sense of discovery and growth. The subject matter of any course takes on appropriate significance *for the practitioner* only if it provides a basis for creating the conditions that make the acquisition of that subject matter productive for students. Far too frequently, those who teach subject matter courses are partisans of subject matter, not of children in classrooms. Of course teachers should be steeped in subject matter, but they should no less be steeped in what makes that information digestible to children. It is this dual obligation that makes teaching as challenging as it is difficult. I am not opposed to courses. I am opposed to courses in which that dual obligation is ignored.

There is an irony here. University professors have been among the most vocal critics of teachers and our schools, especially in regard to teachers' superficial grounding in subject matter and, therefore, to the poor performance of their students. By whatever criteria you employ for "good" teaching, there is no evidence that the quality of college teaching is obviously better, on average, than that of school teachers. But it is my opinion—and it is no more than an opinion—that college students, again on average, gain more than school children from their courses. If that is true, it is not because (certainly not *only* because) college teaching is superior but in large part because college students have more opportunity to take courses that they think interest them, that is, they *want* to take those courses.

Often school children do not want to learn what is given them. That is not to say they do not want to learn a lot about a lot of things but rather that what they are asked (that is, forced) to learn has no special intellectual or personal significance. I could count on students wanting to take my courses. That kind of wanting, however, is rare in the modal school classroom with the modal teacher. The aim of a preparatory program is to nurture that kind of wanting, a wanting with which children started school but which went quickly underground.

The second part of my answer is that my hold on reality is not so shaky as to allow me to suggest a one-on-one relationship between instructor and student, although I am suggesting that such a relationship should be far more frequent than it is. There is no one way of acting on my suggestions. In this day of wondrous technologies there are myriad ways they can be used in preparatory programs. Let me give but one example . . . : how a teacher should relate to parents.

Decades ago I taught a seminar on educational issues for graduate students in clinical psychology. One segment concerned how to convey to a parent that his or her child was mentally retarded. I had a student from the drama school act the role of the parent telling him only that he would be in the role of a parent whose child had been failing in school and he had been called in to talk with the school psychologist. The student in my seminar was told: "You have observed the child, spoken to the teacher, tested the child, and the unambiguous conclusion is that the child has to be placed in a special class. Your job is to convey this information in a helpful way." Famous last words! The drama student made mincemeat of my would-be psychologist.

In the intervening decades I have taken advantage of every opportunity to try to convince educators and others to develop a series of films that could be used in preparatory

programs to illustrate the difficult problems one encounters in interacting with parents—and I do not mean only "how to do it" films in which errors of omission and commission are left out. I also suggested that every would-be educator have the opportunity
to be filmed in real or simulated conditions. (I also have tried to persuade people to consider films about how to think about and chair faculty meetings.) My powers of per-
suasion obviously leave much to be desired; to my knowledge, no one has taken the suggestion to heart or mind. The point here is that the technology exists whereby real and
realistically simulated educational issues, events, *and* settings can be used in the preparation of educators. It is not a technology that should be employed so as put the student
in the passive role of a viewer of films. As in the case of any subject matter, the task is
to help students integrate attitudes, knowledge, and action in regard to events that will
be central to their professional careers.

William James and John Dewey alerted us a century ago to the dangers of designing
laboratory experiments that were unrelated to the real-world phenomena those studies
were meant to illuminate. They were not opposed to rigorous research but rather to research which, by virtue of the conditions created, did not permit generalization to events
outside the laboratory. The preparation of educators is not a formal experiment but the
dangers James and Dewey articulated are, unfortunately, too characteristic of too many
preparatory programs. The thrust of my entire argument in this book is that those dangers have to be confronted and overcome to whatever degree possible.

The third part of my answer to the reactions of teachers of teachers is that, like Goodlad, I am advocating a total redesigning of preparatory programs. I am not advocating
add-ons or strengthening what now exists. Obviously, this redesigning will not, cannot,
occur quickly. To redesign assumes that there is a new rationale, a new set of governing
principles that have been thought through and accepted, that there is the courage to realize that one is setting sail on somewhat uncharted seas, and that the fear of failure
works against change and creativity. . . .

Our nation was quite taken with President Kennedy's "Ask not what your country can
do for you. Ask what you can do for your country." In regard to our dissatisfactions
with our schools, educators should articulate what they feel our country should do for
schools, children, and educators. Where they stand should not be kept private. *At the
same time, however, they should be no less clear about what they can and should do
for themselves.* If they ask of our country what they have asked in the past, it will reinforce a view of educators as self-serving, unimaginative, feckless conveyors of ideas and
programs that have failed in the past. But if educators begin to convince the general public that what they advocate is not cosmetic, that they are willing and able to take responsibility for helping themselves, they will have started a change in how the general
public will perceive educational issues. They can show their willingness to make radical changes in preparatory programs, to take primary prevention seriously, to act on
what we know (and know well) about children, productive learning and productive contexts, and to be prepared to alter the relationships between teacher and child, between
teachers and teachers, and between educators and communities. . . .

CHAPTER 4

Teaching as a Lonely Profession

This title originally appeared in 1966 as a chapter in the book *Psychology in Community Settings: Clinical, Educational, Vocational, Social Aspects* (John Wiley) that Sarason co-wrote with colleagues at the Yale Psycho-Educational Clinic. In the chapter, he reviews his earlier findings and concludes that, unlike other "performers," teachers do their most important work in isolation, cut off from the support of colleagues with whom they should be linked by virtue of the students they have in common and the school environment they share.

Sarason believes that the impact of such isolation and "the absence of anything resembling professional collegiality," over time, contributes to the much-noted resistance of teachers "to change their accustomed beliefs and practices." He again criticizes teacher preparatory programs for their failure to "expose their students to the opportunities, dilemmas, and frustrations of group living in a school."

Question for Seymour Sarason

How do you answer those who charge that teaching *attracts* people who seek the isolation and security of the solitary classroom; thus, to impose collegiality on teachers will appear to be just another example of administrative disrespect?

Sarason's Response

I have never heard this criticism! It is psychologically superficial and can be expressed only by someone who has never worked with—held discussions with—beginning teachers. What the culture of the school does (much too effectively) is to make collegiality a no-no, fraught with danger. I have to assume that such critics are also opposed to the use of group/cooperative learning in the classroom, despite the fact that cooperative learning has validity demonstrated through research.

I truly have difficulty believing that *anyone* in our field is so unbelievably stupid. Rob, if there are such people, please make sure I never meet them.

Reprinted with the permission of Teachers College Press from "The Classroom and the School Culture" in *Teaching as a Performing Art* by Seymour Sarason (New York: Teachers College Press, 1999).

More about teacher isolation, collegiality, and professionalism may found in.

Charter Schools: Another Flawed Educational Reform? (1998)
Revisiting "The Culture of the School and the Problem of Change" (1996)
School Change: The Personal Development of a Point of View (1995)
You Are Thinking of Teaching? Opportunities, Problems, Realities (1993)
The Case for Change: Rethinking the Preparation of Educators (1992)
Schooling in America: Scapegoat and Salvation (1983)

. . . "Teaching is a lonely profession"—that is the title of a chapter written by Dr. Murray Levine in a book several of us at the Yale Psycho-Educational Clinic wrote in 1966 (Sarason, Levine, Goldenberg, Cherlin, & Bennett, 1966). Of all the chapters in that book, that was the one about which we received the largest number of unsolicited approving letters from teachers. As one teacher put it, "Finally, someone recognizes that although we spend the day with students, as an adult we feel alone in the world, especially those of us who are expected to eat our lunch with the kids." That theme has two significances. The first is that unlike those in other performing arts which require (demand) finely tuned, interconnectedness among all those on the stage, the social-political organization of the school is one in which such face-to-face interconnectedness is absent or minimal. Each teacher is, so to speak, a law unto him- or herself. Not only does the teacher look askance at a principal who seeks to change his or her pedagogy and style but also at other teachers who articulate or imply something critical. In other performing arts it is a glimpse of the obvious to the student in training that one is part of a mutuality among the members of the group that exercises restraint over the tendency to do things in one's own way. In the case of teachers, preparatory programs have as one of their "of course" goals to prepare a sole performer, someone who will discharge responsibilities independently. It is as if these preparatory programs say, "Yes, you will be part of a social organization that has purposes, rules, regulations, but you will decide for yourself how best to interpret and implement them." It is, therefore, not surprising that the neophyte teacher approaches the opening of school with a good deal of anxiety about being able effectively to act and be independent; to hide anxieties and "mistakes" from other teachers. The neophyte both fears and treasures independence and isolation; over time, the safety of independence and isolation swamps the strength of the fears.

If anything is incontrovertible in the literature on educational reform, it is how difficult it is to get teachers to change their accustomed beliefs and practices. (That is true of others in the educational hierarchy, but let us stay with teachers.) Their resistance to change should occasion no surprise. None of us likes to change. All of us in the face of change find that we like our "symptoms," that the pain associated with change appears greater than the pain the symptoms engender. But in the case of educational reform the stimulus for change comes far less from teachers than from "higher-ups" or other external forces, and teachers regard that pressure as an unwarranted criticism of what they have been doing. In some reform efforts the aim is to increase the strength and the ways in which teachers as a group can assume new responsibilities, an aim as difficult to achieve as it is laudable. Indeed, some teachers look favorably on such a goal not only as an escape from an unwanted privacy but as a recognition of respect for what teachers can and should do. Sometimes that alteration goes relatively smoothly, but more often it engenders such differences in opinion, arouses heretofore unverbalized interpersonal rivalries, and puts such demands on available time as to cause some teachers to opt out or to drastically limit the achievement of the goals of the reform. Someone has said that the life of an educational reform effort is no more than 5 years, which is another way of saying that the death rattle was audible long before final death. Preparatory programs in no way expose their students to the opportunities, dilemmas, and frustrations of group living in a school, especially when the school is being pressured to change.

Those who are in the conventional performing arts have two types of motivations. The first is that they know they have a personal obligation to develop their craft. They know they are expected to do that. One can put it this way: They are motivated to learn more and to change; they do not want to feel or be perceived as one-dimensional. In part that motivation is built-in because the directors of artistic productions exert such pressure; they are not content merely to accept what the artist does, their self-interest demands that they help the artist develop and change. Both in opera and the theater, artists, even well-known ones, seek coaches who serve as supportive critics and teachers. And in all instances performing artists, especially those of neophyte status, carefully and eagerly observe and learn from more experienced performers with whom they are working.

The second motivation, related to the first, is that the performing artist seeks diversity in role and repertoire. No actor wants to be typecast. . . . No opera singer wants to sing only Verdi, or Wagner, or Puccini. No pianist wants to be known as competent only to play Mozart, or Beethoven, or Chopin. No dancer wants to perform only in the ballets of Balanchine, Graham, or Ashton. The performing artist seeks the challenge of diversity. We are used to hearing that when asked why he seeks to scale Mt. Everest, the mountain climber's answer is, "Because it is there." In each of the performing arts there are Mt. Everests where the danger is not injury or death but the possibility that the artist will not do justice to the role.

It is radically different with teachers. The classroom is the domain they rule, but the ruler is *alone*. They do not seek to invite others into the classroom to be observed, advised, or criticized. They do not ask to observe other teachers. There is little or no professional collegiality if by that you mean a serious discussion of the pedagogical issues and problems teachers confront. There are in some schools "in-service" staff development days when some external expert talks about his or her expertise. With rare exceptions teachers regard these one-shot sessions as uninteresting and unrelated to their daily practice. In many states teachers are required to take some graduate courses to maintain their certification and receive a modest salary increase. Teachers find these courses little more interesting than in-service days.

There is little or nothing in the organization and culture of schools that spurs a teacher to regard change and development as necessary, personally and intellectually rewarding, and *safe*. I emphasize safe because in the culture of the school the teacher who seeks help or coaching from others is one whose competence is called into question. The teacher is expected to handle all problems that arise in the classroom, and it is a sign of weakness if it becomes apparent that that is not the case. No teacher will deny that the beginning teacher is one plagued by anxiety, self-doubt, and fear of exposure. In all my experience over the decades I never knew of a school that made it easy and safe for the beginning teacher to admit some inadequacy and ask for help. This is not to say that experienced teachers are unsympathetic to the neophyte, but rather that they assume offers of help may add to the neophyte's sense of incompetency; besides, it is the rare neophyte who will ask for help. I should emphasize that the school day is not organized to make visitations possible, let alone easy.

What happens over time to teachers when year in and year out they teach the same thing to the same kinds of audiences? What are the sources, internal and external, to give them the sense of growth, to cause them willingly to enlarge or alter their role and repertoire, to prevent the feeling that they have settled into a safe, comfortable routine? The answer is: precious little. The absence of anything resembling professional collegiality, the lack of motivation to read the professional literature (Sarason, 1993c), the adversarial strains and tensions in the school culture between teachers and the administrative hierarchy, the sense of aloneness in a densely populated setting—these are some of the factors conducive to the routinization of thought and practice. These problems are especially relevant to teachers in urban schools where educators are under constant pressure to improve student performance, pressure which has not been successful. In these schools routinization of thought and practice is a process that over time interacts with the equally insidious process of teacher burnout in which teachers conclude that the time, energy, and commitment they give to their students are grossly disproportionate to student outcomes. . . . Beginning in the 1960s professional burnout became a "hot" topic generally and among teachers in particular. That was the decade in which every major societal institution was subject to critical scrutiny and pressure to change, and schools were not exempt. By the end of that decade, and continuing thereafter, a significant number of teachers and administrators left the field or looked forward to early retirement. The explanation is by no means a simple one, but part of that explanation was an unwillingness or inability to adapt to changing times, attitudes, and roles, an adaptation made difficult or impossible by a school culture which never contained or supported the conditions which make professional growth and change safe and desirable. On the contrary, it was a culture which reinforced routinization of thought and practice, as well as narrowness of role.

In all my writing about schools and their personnel I have emphasized what I consider to be a glimpse of the obvious: If the conditions for productive learning do not exist for teachers, they cannot create and *sustain* those conditions for students. So, if you ask college and university faculty to justify the existence of these institutions, the common thread in their answers is that they exist in order to create the conditions in which faculty learn, explore, change, and "grow." When you ask educators to justify the existence of schools, the answer is that they exist for students, period. No two explanations can be more different from each other. What would be surprising is if teachers generally (there are always exceptions) experienced over time the sense of learning, exploring, changing. In the conventional performing arts, performers seek novelty and challenge. *They are expected to seek them.* It occasions no surprise when a leading actor in the theater signs a contract not for the entire run of the play, but for a specified number of months; he or she wants and needs new challenges, not satisfied to remain within the confines of challenges met and overcome. There are new worlds to conquer! I have met very, very few teachers who view their futures in that way. Whether they are justified or not, after 5 years in the classroom teachers (again generally speaking) feel they have met the challenge and envision a future as a carbon copy of the present, unaware of the dangers of routinization of thought and practice.

In 1996 I attended in Germany an international conference on teacher burnout. Although my perspective on schools and teaching should not have allowed me to assume that teacher burnout was more serious and frequent in the United States than in countries with very different cultures and systems of education, I was not prepared to learn that it was no less serious and frequent elsewhere. Indeed, in some countries which unlike in the United States have highly centralized, bureaucratically layered and controlled school systems, teacher burnout was reported as no less a problem than in our country. And in all countries dissatisfaction by the public with their schools was loud and getting clearer. Although it was recognized that directing criticism to teachers was an instance of blaming the victim, there was relatively little discussion about what changes would be required to transform schools and preparatory programs so as to make teachers more motivated to enlarge their understanding of themselves and their audiences. . . .

CHAPTER 5

Power Relationships
in the Classroom

For teachers, especially (and for everyone else in a school), the idea of power relation-ships represents a kind of third rail—too dangerous to touch. Sarason begins this dis-cussion by paying homage to the political scientist Machiavelli, who in his time looked realistically at power politics in ways that, even today, make people uncomfortable. But discomfort is no excuse, Sarason says, for remaining ignorant about the phenomenon of who wields what kind of power in school systems.

The price we pay for our willed ignorance of power politics is that change is stifled. For a beginning teacher, "power relationships" invariably mean one thing only: maintaining control of the class. Even in those classrooms where students and teacher appear to work together in a relaxed, respectful manner, the fear of loss of control is usually present (or the teacher feels "lucky to have a good class this year"). So Sarason asks, "How does power get defined in the classroom?" and what opportunities are lost when children are excluded from the process of understanding power relationships? He finds that teachers get little help, here, from most parents, who are as confused about this issue within the family context as are teachers in school.

Question for Seymour Sarason

How does a new teacher who seeks to provide a warm and empowering classroom avoid being stigmatized (or worse) by colleagues who believe that such an approach represents "coddling" children and that it puts at risk necessary teacher authority and control?

Sarason's Response

I respond to this question with the same disdain as I did to the previous one, albeit for different reasons. The word *coddling* is used as a pejorative, implying that the teacher who coddles does so to all of her students, mindlessly, as if all students need it. Or is "coddling" a euphemism for indulgence and permissiveness? The question is when, why, and whom a teacher coddles. Before you indict the teacher you have to know why she coddles this child and not that one. Of course if she employs coddling mindlessly, inappropriately, and indiscriminately, she may be causing harm.

Let us assume that she cannot justify her coddling. In the real world of the culture of the school, who can be helpful to her? And by helpful I mean that there need to be other teachers or a principal who has a relationship of trust with her and who is not out to be critical or demeaning or, worse yet, intent on "laying down the law."

To be helpful to the teacher (or for a teacher to help a student), you have to be sensitive, empathic, patient: All of these are the ingredients of a supportive collegiality in which no one claims perfection. As I have said countless times, you start where the learner or teacher is and your strategy is to build on that knowledge—unless you believe that everybody is the same and needs the same reaction.

Such help rarely exists in any schools. I truly feel sorry for beginning "idealistic" teachers. Idealism is and can be an asset. But if there is no one and no context that recognizes such an asset, the teacher retreats to an unwanted, professionally impoverished privacy, just as many students do.

Incidentally, Rob, I resent questions that require me to appear to be a sour, dyspeptic, disillusioned octogenarian!

More about issues of power relationships in classrooms and schools may be found in:

How Schools Might Be Governed and Why (1997)
Barometers of Change: Individual, Educational, and Social Transformation (1996)
Revisiting "The Culture of the School and the Problem of Change" (1996)
Parental Involvement and the Political Principle (1995)
The Case for Change: Rethinking the Preparation of Educators (1992)
The Predictable Failure of Educational Reform (1990)
Schooling in America: Scapegoat and Salvation (1983)

Political science claims Machiavelli as one of its founders. That may come as a surprise to most people, for whom the adjective *Machiavellian* is a pejorative signifying immorality, deceit, and manipulativeness. The fact is that no scholar of Machiavelli regards him in such terms. What Machiavelli was concerned with was an examination of power as opportunity and dilemma for leaders seeking the attainment of public welfare goals. In the case of Machiavelli, that meant the unification of Italy—that is, welding the Italian people into a sovereign nation free from domination by foreign countries who essentially had carved up Italy into many fiefdoms. The exercise of power for the sake of power was anathema to him. The task of an Italian leader was to gain and use power for the Italian people, not as a means of personal aggrandizement. It was one thing to gain or have power—that was relatively easy, although its costs were many; it was quite another thing to use power in ways that would allow the people willingly to grant power. Machiavelli's advice to such a leader was based on the way things were at that long ago time. And he pleaded with such a leader not to confuse the way things were with what he would like them to be. In the world of action one deals with things as they are, however seamy, complex, and problematic the context in which power has to be used. What the world could not countenance in Machiavelli was his description and analysis of the way things were and what that meant for action. Just as the world disparaged Freud because of his description of infantile sexuality—it could not believe, let alone accept, his theories—it earlier had denied validity to Machiavelli's description of the realities of power, that is, of political relationships.

If I begin this chapter with homage to Machiavelli (whom few outside of political science read), it is to make two points. The first is that the field of education has never been of much interest to political scientists, despite the fact that it is egregiously clear that schools and school systems are political organizations in which power is an organizing feature. With but a few exceptions, when political scientists have looked at schools, their descriptions and analyses have been centered on matters of policy and not on the uses and allocation of power.[1] The second point, explained in part by the first, is that the failure to examine school systems in terms of the myriad of ways in which power suffuses them has rendered efforts at reform ineffective. In no part of the school system is this failure more complete than in regard to the individual classroom.

We do not think of the classroom as a political organization. Our usual imagery of the classroom contains an adult who is "in charge" and pupils who conform to the teacher's rules, regulations, and standards. If students think and act in conformity to the teacher's wishes, they will learn what they are supposed to learn. We are not used to saying that a teacher has "power" and that students are and should be powerless. That sounds too fascistic. We are more used to saying that a teacher has authority which students should respect, precisely as those students should respect parental authority. But, as any teacher (or parent) will attest, the conventional imagery borders on fantasy. From the standpoint of the teacher, especially at the beginning of the school year and especially in the case of the beginning teacher, the name of the game is power: quickly and effectively to establish who is boss of the turf, to make it clear that the authority of the teacher is powered by the power to punish. It is no secret that the performance of the beginning teacher is viewed by his or her colleagues with bated breath. Will that teacher be able to maintain control? Will he or she be able to handle the different challenges to the teacher's authority? Will we have to come to the rescue? Is that teacher an effective disciplinarian?

Several years ago I had the opportunity to interview nine people who had begun teaching several months earlier. The focus of the interviews was on how they evaluated their training for what they experienced when they were alone in the classroom. Although the focus went far beyond matters of control or discipline, I restrict myself here only to these matters. There was unanimity on three points. First, they had been told by their mentors that establishing the authority and power of the teacher was absolutely essential. Although there was variation in what they were advised to do to achieve that goal, there was none in regard to the primacy of that goal. Second, the first few weeks of teaching were among the most stressful experiences they had ever had, far more stressful than they had expected, because they found themselves frequently on the brink of saying and doing things they knew were "psychologically wrong." Third, they feared that their inadequacies would come to the attention of the principal and other teachers—that is, those who were perceived as having power or influence to devalue them. Three of the nine teachers were still having "control problems"; the rest felt they were wrestling adequately with those problems, albeit they were omnipresent problems. All of these teachers were in New York City schools, but none of them was in what could be considered an inner-city school.

What I have related thus far is not intended to convey the impression that children are generally an unruly lot intent on making life unbearable for teachers (although some teachers might think so). Nor do I want to convey the belief that there is a way to prepare teachers for the social realities of the classroom that would prevent issues of control and power from arising. Being on one's "professional own" for the first time is inevitably stressful; in the case of teachers such stress is guaranteed, precisely because the establishment of their authority and power is so central to how they and others judge their professional competence. The phenomenology of the beginning teacher was emphasized because it illustrates to a compelling degree what all teachers experience to a lesser degree. Power is a ubiquitous feature of classroom living. Anyone familiar with schools or the educational literature will agree that what I have described is an old story.

It is not difficult to find classrooms where issues of power and authority seem absent —that is, where the teacher and students are relaxed, the students are willingly engaged in their assigned task, and the overall ambience is friendly. If you ask these teachers to explain why this is so, they give two answers. The first is that for reasons of chance selection, no student was set to challenge the teacher's authority and power. That is to say, the students recognized and accepted the power and authority of the teacher. That power and authority were and are always silently in the picture. The second answer, usually given quickly after the first, can be put this way: "What you see now, tomorrow, this year in my classroom you may not see next year in my classroom. The students next year may be another cup of tea, a bitter brew, and I may strike you as a much less friendly, permissive, happy teacher. The dream class does not come around at all frequently. When I come to the first day of class I pray that I will not have to be a disciplinarian."

In these matters I have long felt kinship with the public school teacher. I taught at Yale for forty-four years, and within a few years after I started teaching, I came to recognize how remarkably different successive cohorts of first-year graduate students could be in terms of motivation, intellectual curiosity, and, yes, challenges (hostile or otherwise) to my authority. There were years when in class I could sit back after some opening remarks and act as moderator of heated discussions. There were years when getting a discussion going was almost impossible. There were years when a student or two made it clear, by oral or body language, that they did not highly regard the substance and style of my teaching. One thing that was always in the picture for both the students and me was that I had to grade them, and the grade I gave them could be fateful for their professional futures as well as their status in the department. I had power and I and they knew it; that brute fact governed both of us. It was no less a problem for me than it was for them, although it is safe to assume that they did not see this as a problem for me. If we are not accustomed to think of the public school classroom in political terms—in terms of the nature and consequences of power where power is asymmetrically allocated —we are similarly unaccustomed to think of the university classroom in those terms. Unaccustomed, that is, until the dynamics of that power explode into full view, as happened in the sizzling sixties in the university, secondary schools, and every other major societal institution. If educators in our schools and universities were taken by surprise at this challenge to their authority and power, it was because they had never had reason to view or question how institutions in which they were embedded—and to which they had been socialized—were implicitly and silently based on power and relationships waiting to surface.

Just as teachers are extraordinarily alert to issues of power—sensitive to behavior that may or will require exercise of power, as well as to individual differences among students—so are the students. If substitute teachers have control problems, it says as much about the knowledgeability of students about power as it does about the substitutes' unfamiliarity with the traditions of their classrooms and the casts of characters. Issues of power are always a function of the perceptions and actions of student *and* teacher. Here is an extreme example. In the course of working in classrooms in an inner-city school, I saw a nine-year-old boy literally climb the wall. The school was almost a hundred years old and the steam pipes were exposed, enabling the youngster to climb to the ceiling. His teacher was utterly inadequate to handle him and others in that classroom. I said to the boy: "Next year you will be in Mrs. Esposito's classroom. Is that the way you will act there?" With practically no reaction time, he replied: "I would never do it in *her* classroom. She would kick the shit out of me."

How does power get defined in the classroom? What understanding of power do we want children to obtain? Should students have some kind of role in defining power, thus giving them some sense of ownership not only in regard to definition but also to implementation? Is the unilateral definition and exercise of power desirable for the development of children? Does it tend to breed the opposite of what it intends to achieve?

It was these kinds of questions that stimulated me to do the following. In several elementary school classrooms I arranged for observers to be there from the first day of school to the end of the month. I was after what I described as the forging of the classroom's "constitution." What were the rules and regulations that governed the classroom and how were they arrived at? The task of the observers was to record and describe any instance relevant to the articulation of rules and regulations: when and how these instances arose and who was involved. Who wrote the constitution of the classroom? The answer—to which there was no exception—was that the teachers wrote the constitution. They articulated the rules and regulations (frequently post hoc) but provided no rationale. There was absolutely no discussion about the rationale. It was as if the teachers, Moses-like, came down from Mt. Sinai with the constitution. (The response of the

Israelites, remember, was far from warm.) It never occurred to these teachers, who by conventional standards were very good, that students should be provided with a rationale, which deserved extended discussion, and that students should have the opportunity to voice their opinions. How should we live together and why? These were suburban classrooms to which almost all students came with respect for teachers—that is, they knew that they were expected to conform to the teacher's rules and regulations, or else. In these matters it was as if teachers had no respect for the needs and opinions of students. Students were and should be powerless in these matters. Their time would come when they "grew up." In all but one or two of these classrooms, there were clear examples of rule formulation or rule implementation to which some of the students did not take kindly. They never received clarifying discussion.

It is ironic that today we hear much about how unfair it is that teachers are powerless to influence policies (read: constitution) that mightily affect them. As I write these words, the metropolitan mass media are giving a lot of play to the new chancellor-designate of the New York City school system who, as head of the Dade County school system in Florida, has empowered teachers (and others) in formulating policies for their schools. In a television interview, Dr. Fernandez stated that "the evidence is not yet in" about whether what he has done in Dade County will have the intended desirable consequences. He was unambiguous, however, in stating that for teachers to be held accountable for educational outcomes required that they have more power than tradition has accorded them. To state it oxymoronically, Fernandez is a skeptical utopian. The media are giving a good deal of play to the criticism directed to Fernandez by the head of the administrators union, who regards teachers the way teachers regard students. And therein is the irony: Teachers regard students the way their superiors regard them—that is, as incapable of dealing responsibly with issues of power, even on the level of discussion. The head of the administrators union does not say that teachers have to grow up to handle power, because if he did, he would have to face the question: How do you grow up in or to a role in which you are denied experience or access? When do you start? It is no different in the case of the student in the classroom. When should students begin to experience the nature and dilemmas of power in group living?

I have focused on the classroom not to make the obvious point that power is one of its distinctive features but to suggest that the sense of powerlessness frequently breeds reduced interest and motivation, at best a kind of passionless conformity and at worst a rejection of learning. When one has no stake in the way things are, when one's needs or opinions are provided no forum, when one sees oneself as the object of unilateral actions, it takes no particular wisdom to suggest that one would rather be elsewhere. We are used to hearing today that too many students lack interest, motivation, and intellectual curiosity. An explanation is by no means simple, but surely one of its ingredients is the fact that schools are uninteresting places for many students (and teachers). I discussed this at some length in my book *Schooling in America: Scapegoat and Salvation* (1983). Here I wish only to emphasize that if classrooms are uninteresting places, it is in part (and only in part) because students feel, and are made to feel, powerless to influence the traditional regularities of the classroom. One of the regularities is that determining what is right and wrong, just and fair, is solely in the province of the teacher and completely off limits to students. Teachers are legislators, executives, and judiciary. Underlying this behavioral regularity is the assumption that students are incapable of exercising power responsibly in any way or on any level. Furthermore, it is dangerous to accord them power.

Here is an example. I was sitting in a first-grade classroom in an elementary school. The new school year had begun a week earlier. One child was sitting in her seat, head down, crying silently. Occasionally, the child would slowly approach the teacher and nestle against her. The teacher would then take the child back to her seat, saying sympathetically: "When school is over, your mother will come for you. Stay in your seat and try to do what the other students are doing." Later the teacher told me that each day the child cried when the mother brought her to school. What the child wanted, the teacher said, was to be held, cuddled, and soothed. My conversation with the teacher went something like this:

SBS. The girl asked to be held?

T. Yes. She would raise her hands for me to pick her up.

SBS. Did you?

T. No.

SBS. Why not?

T (with a surprised look). If I picked her up and cuddled her, then that is what other children would want me to do for them.

SBS. In other words, the other children would want to get in on the act?

T. You are so right!

SBS (after a long pause). What if you were to discuss this with your class? What if you were to explain to them that Gail misses her mother terribly and that is why she is so unhappy and wants to be picked up and held by you. What should a teacher do in such a case? Should she accede to the child's needs and wishes? I am willing to bet that their answer would be a definite yes. And what if you were to say that what you would do for Gail you are prepared to do for others who would feel about leaving their mothers as Gail does?

The anecdote illustrates two related points. The first is that discussing the dilemma with the class was foreign to this teacher's conception of her role, which is that she does not take up such issues with students, and that she alone decides what is the right course of action. Second, she feels that these young children are incapable of understanding, let alone articulating, the issues involved. Indeed, it would be dangerous to discuss the matter because what they might say is unpredictable. Leave well enough alone.

It would be a gross misunderstanding of what I am suggesting if it conjured up imagery of a classroom in which the teacher is a market researcher seeking to determine what children want her or him to do. It would be no less wrong if the reader concluded that I am suggesting that teachers give up the power to make final decisions. What I am advocating is that the teacher should accord students the right *and* responsibility to participate in forums where the constitution of the classroom is forged. The classroom should be a place where those in it come to feel that they will be governed by rules and values they have had an opportunity to discuss. The overarching goal is not to come up with rules but to begin to comprehend the complexities of power in a complicated group setting. Put another way, the goal is to instill in students an understanding of a commitment to the classroom constitution, a sense of ownership, and an awareness that their opinions will be respected, even when not accepted.

For purposes of this discussion, I divide the world of parents into two groups, one far smaller than the other. The small group comprises those parents set to be sensitive to and respectful of the opinions of their children, not in order to go along with them but rather to determine with what they are dealing. These are parents who seek to avoid adversariness and the need to exercise naked power. They are prepared to compromise but not to surrender. They know when and how to "flex," to take risks, and also to put their foot down. Inside this cake of virtue are, among other things, anxiety, puzzlement, indecision, and ambivalence. What appears on the surface is one thing; what goes on inside is far more volatile and even confused. But whatever goes on inside does not prevent these parents from listening to, respecting, and mulling over what their children are saying and requesting, or demanding. Just as the children know that their parents have power—of this the children have no doubt—the parents have no doubt that their children have power to affect them. What the parents seek is a modus vivendi with which both "great powers" can live.

The much larger group consists of parents who are, if not polar opposites, on different points of the continuum. The polar opposites are those parents for whom unilaterally exercised power creates what one part of them seeks to avoid. The great powers are in struggle.

Teachers are kin to parents, which is why so many of them experience their students in terms of a power struggle. In recent years the term *parenting* has gained a good deal of currency. Courses in parenting are becoming part of the secondary school and college curriculum. And, especially since World War II, the number of books published on parenting seems to be increasing exponentially; at some future date there may be more such books than there are parents. This social phenomenon says a good deal about how problematic parenting has become. It is astonishing, however, that parenting in the classroom—not as a technical but as a fundamental set of issues fateful for learning and growth—has received virtually no recognition or discussion in any of the many commission reports on educational reform. When these reports say anything, it is to affirm "law and order" in the classroom, an affirmation of the traditional view that the power to govern resides solely in the teacher. As I said to a commission member: "No one is opposed to law and order. What should be at issue is how laws arise and how order is experienced and, fatefully, how those processes contribute to productive learning and desirable social living. None of your recommendations speaks to that issue, as if the basis for life in the classroom is in no way an object of scrutiny and reform." He looked at me as if I were one of those bleeding-heart sentimentalists whose misguided ideas deserve no response. I later learned that he described me as being in the John Dewey tradition. He was, of course, absolutely correct. I would bet, and give very attractive odds, that he never read anything by John Dewey. Sloganeering as a defense against the acquisition of knowledge is all too frequent.[2]

There is another reason I have focused on the classroom in this chapter. After reading the reports on educational reform, I had to conclude that they were written by people who either had only the foggiest notion of what goes on in classrooms or had once been or taught in the classroom but had amnesia for what they had experienced. For example, in no report—and it is no less true in the general education literature—is anything said about question-asking behavior in the classroom. Why question-asking behavior? The answer in brief is that humans are very distinctive question-asking organisms, and question asking is not only a reflection of curiosity but also one of the royal roads to productive knowledge and action. It is surprising how little attention has been given to this characteristic in educational research and the preparation of educational personnel. If the research is scanty, it is extraordinarily compelling and unanimous in findings. In the modal classroom (for example, a social studies period of forty minutes) the average number of questions asked by students is two, and those two questions could have been asked by one student. Teachers' rate of question asking varies from about 40 to 150. No one, including developmentalists and teachers, to whom the findings of this research have been presented has ever said that these are desirable results. It is beyond my purposes to explain this regularity in any detail. But it does suggest, central to my present purposes, that students do not feel secure in exercising the right or power to ask questions. Indeed, too frequently, students fear asking questions—testimony again to the role of power in classroom living. And when fear is not a factor—and I do not want to overplay its frequency—it is because students accept or conform to their perception of the rules of the game implicitly or explicitly set by the teacher. And yet, in the scores of recommendations for educational reform, no question is ever raised about question asking. The explicit ultimate goal of all of these recommendations is to improve educational outcomes. The assumption undergirding these recommendations seems to be that those outcomes can be achieved without any significant alteration in the behavioral-constitutional-social regularities of the modal classroom. It is an assumption as obfuscating as it is invalid. One can change curricula, standards, and a lot of other things by legislation or fiat, but if the regularities of the classroom remain unexamined and unchanged, the failure of the reforms is guaranteed.

What responsibility in the classroom are students given for their learning? As I have indicated, the student's responsibility is an individual one: to do, by himself or herself, the tasks assigned by the teacher. Indeed, it is implicit, and frequently explicit, that students work by themselves. What assumptions undergird this regularity? One assumption is that students are generally incapable of working in a cooperative, productive way with other students. A second assumption is that even if that incapability is unjustified, the products that emerge from small-group activity do not permit evaluation of individual contributions—that is, individual contributions become "ungradable." A third assumption is that the dynamics of power in such groups can be anti-educational for many students.

The exercise of power in the classroom is a feature not only of teacher-student relationships; it is no less a feature of student-student relationships, which, it is assumed,
can get out of hand in small task-oriented groups. These assumptions, singly or in combination, justify the present regularity, which seems so right, natural, and proper. How
classroom learning is structured is a derivative of the power of the teacher. That means
that the teacher has the power to alter, even radically, how learning is structured. He or
she can decide, in regard to any subject matter or task, to structure things differently —
for example, to form small groups each of which is given responsibility to do the task
as it sees fit. The nature of the task is clear; how the small group meets the task is its responsibility. The members of the groups are given the power to organize themselves as
they see fit. They are given a degree of power, of control. That does not mean that the
teacher sits by passively unavailable for help and advice, but that each small group has
been given responsibility for and control over its outcomes.

I do not bring up these considerations only to emphasize again the sources and exercise of power in the classroom. Another reason is to note that in recent decades there
has been a growing research literature comparing two kinds of classrooms: those in
which the teacher conventionally teaches the whole class, and those in which teachers
have been trained in the organization and supervision of classrooms where students
have been organized into small groups (cooperative learning). One major conclusion
that can be drawn from this research literature is that where cooperative learning is implemented, classrooms do not become disorganized, disorganizing, and chaotic places.
Law and order are not replaced by anarchy or mob behavior. This is not to say that peace
and quiet reign supreme, but the expectation that students will mischievously misuse
and subvert their groups is not realized. A second conclusion is that the level of student
interest and motivation is far higher than in the usual "whole class" method of teaching. A third conclusion is that using the criterion of academic achievement, the cooperative, small-group approach is as effective as the conventional one and, more often than
not, is superior. A final conclusion is that, depending on the particular focus of the research study and the outcome measures used, the small-group method changes racial
and ethnic attitude in a desirable direction. Despite these findings, there is no evidence
that they are influencing either the preparation of teachers or classroom practice.[3]

The small-group method is no panacea. We do not, at this time, know its limitations.
It is not being paraded, nor should it be, as the answer to the improvement of educational outcomes. But in two crucial respects this literature is refreshing indeed. I refer,
first, to its focus on life in the classroom, the place where all of the intended goals of
educational reform are to be influential. And it is a literature that explicitly holds that
how life and learning in the classroom are structured makes a difference, and that the
existing structure is ineffective — more accurately, it is part of the problem and not the
solution. Secondly, the proponents of the small-group method leave no doubt that implementing the method requires the unlearning of conventional attitudes, practices, and
assumptions and the learning of new ones, a difficult task for anyone. It cannot be
achieved by fiat or simply high motivation. It requires literally a re-education, which
these researchers do not gloss over. In several studies the efforts of the researchers just
to prepare teachers for implementation approached the heroic. In fact, in reading this

literature one has to keep in mind that participating teachers were almost always volunteers. Even so, life was not easy for them.

Changing the regularities in the classroom is a very complex, demanding, and personally upsetting affair even when motivation is high.[4] (People who willingly enter psychotherapy to change regularities in their thinking and actions know what I mean. If love is not enough, neither is motivation.) When I read this literature, which inevitably varies in quality, I am always reminded of what happened in the sixties and seventies when educational policymakers legislated the wholesale introduction of the new math, the new biology, the new physics, the new social studies, and a lot of other new things. They were scandalously insensitive to what was involved in changing classroom regularities. Teachers had to teach a new curricula, usually after a workshop of several days, as unrealistic a time perspective as has ever been employed. It was as if teaching the new curricula was a technical or engineering task that could be learned in short order by any biologically intact teacher. Like today's educational reformers, their grasp of life in the classroom was, to put it charitably, unknowledgeable.

Let us return for a moment to children's question asking: When do you not answer a child's question but rather help the child use his or her resources to get an answer? Obviously, if you think the child is capable of finding an answer, you should encourage him or her to do so. Because a child asks a question is no reason automatically to provide an answer. How you respond should depend in part on your assessment of how much responsibility a child can assume for pursuing an answer. Generally speaking, in and out of the classroom, we underestimate the capability of children to pursue answers on their own. We respond as if they are irresponsible in this regard, and we usually end up proving the self-fulfilling prophecy. One of the major sources of resistance to the use of cooperative learning is the assumption that students are incapable of taking some responsibility for their learning. . . .

Notes

1. One of the exceptions is Willis Hawley. His article on the commentary page of *Education Week* for November 1, 1989—in the form of an imaginary conversation with the president of the country taking office in 1993—is a concise summary of many thoughts discussed in this book. I knew Hawley a couple of decades ago when he was immersed in the development and study of an alternative public school in New Haven. He learned the game and he knows the score. I also recommend an earlier article by Hawey (1988).

2. It is appropriate here to say that many of the issues I discuss in this book are explicitly or implicitly contained in John Dewey's writings on education. Also, anyone who reads Alfred North Whitehead's *The Aims of Education*, a collection of essays published in 1929, will quickly see why he was so influential in my thinking. . . . One of my favorite sentences in Whitehead is: "In training a child to activity of thought, above all things we must beware of what I call 'inert ideas'— that is to say, ideas that are merely received into the mind without being utilized, or tested, or thrown into fresh combinations." Also: "Except at rare intervals of intellectual ferment, education in the past has been radically infested with inert ideas. that is the reason uneducated, clever

women, who have seen much of the world, are in middle life so much the most cultured part of the community." That, of course, was said long before the women's liberation movement really gained momentum, and one has to ask whether today women have the same burden of inert ideas as men!

3. The reader who wishes to become familiar with this research literature should reach the following, each of which contains a more extensive reading list: Johnson and Johnson (1987); Johnson, Johnson, and Maruyama (1983); Sharan (1980); Sharan and others (1984); Slavin (1983).

4. To introduce teachers *and* a school to cooperative learning is no easy task. Introduction is easy but implementation is not, because it encounters a host of predictable problems deriving from the nature of the school culture. The most succinct and sophisticated account I have read of the process is a chapter by Sharan and Sharan in a forthcoming book, *Current Perspectives on School Culture*, edited by Nancy Wyner.

CHAPTER 6

Constitutional Issues
in the Classroom

In this chapter from his groundbreaking book *The Culture of the School and the Problem of Change* (first published in 1971 by Allyn & Bacon and reissued in 1982), Sarason examines how the rules are created that govern how a classroom will operate. He sent observers to several suburban classrooms to see how such "constitutional issues" were dealt with. From their observations, he concludes that most teachers invariably do to their students the very thing they themselves most resented from their university professors and now resent from their principals and other supervisors, namely, they disregard their students as participants in decision making within a democratic environment.

Sarason extends his inquiry to the area of learning itself, especially the role of teachers as learners and of students as participants in the investigation of learning. He finds that, for teachers, concerns about maintaining classroom control outweigh all other pedagogical considerations. Sarason further theorizes that "the social aspects of classroom organization" may be better understood by pupils than by their teachers, and he concludes that the possibilities of positive change in classrooms are very much limited by certain "covert principles and theories" that usually go unrecognized.

Question for Seymour Sarason

Would you advise a relatively inexperienced teacher to deal openly with "power relationships"—to talk about them, to explain her values, to invite students to participate in framing a class constitution? Or should she wait until she has established a "firm but friendly" climate in the classroom and then ease into such conversations?

Sarason's Response

I really cannot do justice to this question unless I write another book. I am surprised that no one has seen fit to describe how a teacher might or should handle, in the first two or

Reprinted with the permission of Teachers College Press from "The Teacher: Constitutional Issues in the Classroom" in *Revisiting "The Culture of the School and the Problem of Change"* by Seymour Sarason (New York: Teachers College Press, 1996).

three days, these "constitutional matters." Let me just say that by "handle" I mean many things, among which are:

1. What the teacher owes the students.
2. What the students owe the teacher and other students.
3. What students owe themselves.
4. Why students must feel safe in order to ask questions, voice disagreements, express opinions—*all related to number 1, above.*
5. When teachers ought to learn from students.
6. Why, when push comes to shove, the teacher is the final arbiter of how life and learning in the classroom should be conducted. In this regard teachers can make mistakes just like students; they are not perfect.
7. Why whatever "final" authority teachers have is what the community and parents have given them.

None of these points should be conveyed to new teachers by speeches or sermonizing. I have used the concept of "owing" because living and learning have a moral basis, without which our personal rudders are neither productive nor satisfying.

Also, neither students nor teachers should be bound by rules that cannot be amended; the dynamics and process of learning are how we change and grow. Life is with people, and nowhere is that more true than in the classroom. I have not done justice to the question.

More about the obstacles to educational change at the classroom level may be found in:

Educational Reform: A Self-Scrutinizing Memoir (2002)
Teaching as a Performing Art (1999)
Revisiting "The Culture of the School and the Problem of Change" (1996)
Parental Involvement and the Political Principle (1995)
You Are Thinking of Teaching? Opportunities, Problems, Realities (1993)
The Case for Change: Rethinking the Preparation of Educators (1992)
The Predictable Failure of Educational Reform (1990)
Schooling in America: Scapegoat and Salvation (1983)

Constitutional Issues

. . . Almost all teachers meet a new group of pupils on the first day of school. The beginning phase of the school year certainly extends beyond the first day, but by the third or fourth week a routine is established, and teacher and pupils have, so to speak, sized up each other; the rules of the game by which everyone will be governed are fairly well known. How does this come about? How do teachers present and explain these rules of group living? Are these rules discussed? Are they for children only? What role do pupils play, if any, in the formation of rules? These questions and others comprise what

I like to call the constitutional questions because in each classroom there is a constitution, verbalized or unverbalized, consistent or inconsistent, capable or incapable of amendment, that governs behavior. Constitutions tell us a good deal about history, tradition, and conceptions of human behavior.

We did an informal observational study of six classrooms, two each in grades 3, 4, and 5 in a suburban school system. In each of these six classrooms we had an observer who sat in the classroom for the first month of school beginning on the first day. The task of the observer was to record any statement by teacher and child that was relevant to "constitutional issues." The results were quite clear:

1. The constitution was invariably determined by the teacher. No teacher ever discussed why a constitution was necessary.
2. The teacher never solicited the opinions and feelings of any pupil about a constitutional question.
3. In three of the classrooms the rules of the game were verbalized by the end of the first week of school. In two others the rules were clear by the end of the month. In one it was never clear what the constitution was.
4. Except for the one chaotic classroom, neither children nor teachers evidenced any discomfort with the content of constitutions—it was as if everyone agreed that this is the way things are and should be.
5. In all instances constitutional issues involved what *children* could or could not, should or should not, do. The issue of what a *teacher* could or could not, should or should not, do, never arose.

On a number of occasions I have presented these findings to groups of teachers with the question: How do we explain them? In every group the question produced silence. In one group a teacher responded in a way that I think verbalized what most teachers were thinking: *What* is there to explain? I would then follow my initial question with another question: What do we have to assume to be true about children and teachers in order to justify these findings? These discussions were by no means easy or pleasant, and understandably so, if only because the teachers had never been called upon to make explicit the conceptions and values upon which these practices were based. But what were some of the assumptions that teachers could, after prolonged discussion, recognize and state?

1. Teacher knows best.
2. Children cannot participate constructively in the development of a classroom constitution.
3. Children want and expect the teacher to determine the rules of the game.
4. Children are not interested in constitutional issues.
5. Children should be governed by what a teacher thinks is right or wrong, but a teacher should not be governed by what children think is right or wrong.
6. The ethics of adults are obviously different from and superior to the ethics of children.

7. Children should not be given responsibility for something they cannot handle or for which they are not accountable.
8. If constitutional issues were handled differently, chaos might result.

If one does not make these assumptions, which is to say that one thinks differently about what children are and can do, one is very likely to think differently about what the role of the teacher might be. In this connection it is instructive to note that as I pursued the issues with the groups of teachers, and the assumptions could be clearly verbalized, *many of the teachers found themselves disagreeing with assumptions they themselves recognized as underlying their classroom behavior.* Equally as instructive was the awareness on the part of a few that if one changed assumptions one would have to change the character of one's role, and this was strange and upsetting, as indeed it should be because they realized that life in the classroom for them and the children would become different.

The problem we are discussing goes beyond the classroom, and its generality hit me with full force during one of these discussions with teachers. That it hit me with such force in this particular group was in part due to the fact that several of the teachers were quite adamant in maintaining that young children had to have their lives structured for them by adults because they were too immature to participate in and take responsibility for important decisions governing classroom life. *What I became aware of during the discussion was that these teachers thought about children in precisely the same way that teachers say that school administrators think about teachers; that is, administrators do not discuss matters with teachers, they do not act as if the opinions of teachers were important, they treat teachers like a bunch of children, and so on.* And should not these analogies be extended to include the way in which school personnel regard community representatives in relation to participation in educational policy?

In earlier chapters I emphasized the significance of power, and people's view towards it, in understanding relationships within the school culture and between those within and without the school setting. The failure of efforts to introduce and sustain educational change have foundered largely because they have not come to grips with the power aspects of existing relationships, and by coming to grips I obviously do not mean change by fiat or appeal to people's good will or to token gestures that everyone recognizes as a degrading charade. . . . One of the major findings of Berman and McLaughlin was that successful educational change required the serious and active participation of the classroom teacher. Similarly, Cowen (Cowen et al., 1975), whose program in the Rochester schools is the most long-lived successful intervention that will be found in the research literature, emphasizes the centrality of the classroom teacher in planning and implementation. Unlike most proponents for change, Cowen altered the teacher's accustomed feelings of powerlessness, a change that had remarkable effects on the teacher's motivation, creativity, and industry. The point that must not be overlooked, however, is that teachers tend to regard children in a way that arouses hostility and lowers motivation in teachers when others regard them in that same way. The use and militancy of teacher organizations have a complex history, but one of the most important factors was the unwillingness of teachers to be governed by a tradition in which they had no part in decisions and plans that affected them. During the turbulent sixties and early seventies, a period during which teacher militancy dramatically increased in strength and consequence, there was a similar militancy on the part of pupils (largely in middle and high schools) centering around dissatisfaction with the powerlessness of students in regard to life in schools. Students no longer were content to be the traditional students—passive receptacles of learning. They clamored to be regarded as capable of participating in and taking some responsibility for their formal education. Just as teacher militancy was perceived as a threat to the decision-making power of administrators and boards of education, and just as the militancy of community groups was perceived as a threat to the power of educators, so was the militancy of students perceived by school personnel. The creation of alternative schools has to be seen in the context of the different power struggles that were going on.

One should not overlook the fact that what was going on in the public schools was also going on in college and universities: Students were challenging their accustomed role of powerlessness in the classroom. A constitutional change seemed to be occurring. The amending of constitutions has been and always will be accompanied by strong conflict for two reasons: There are differences in conception of what people (teachers, students) are, and it is recognized that what is at issue is what life in a school is and could be. The conflicts wax and wane depending on what is happening in the larger society. The issue of power has long been the basis for competing educational theories, but it requires sea-swell forces in the society to illuminate dramatically the practical significances of these competing theories for institutional change.

To change the quality of life in a classroom, especially when that change involves changes in power relationships, involves no less than a basic change in the culture of the school. It is not a change that can happen quickly. It is certainly not a change that can take place only from within what we traditionally call a school system. It is a change, in whatever degree, that will occur through alterations in the transactions between school and society.

It is not the purpose of this book, except in a very secondary way, to say how things should be. The primary purpose is to describe some of the important regularities in the culture of the school and to relate them to the conceptions and theories that "justify" these regularities. In order to do this I have tried, wherever possible, to contrast these existing relationships with the ever present but neglected universe of alternatives of conceptions from which derives a universe of alternative actions. This tactic not only serves to make one aware how the weight of habit and tradition can obscure the difference between what is and could be, but it also helps force those who want to introduce changes to be more precise about what it is they want to change. The "constitutional problem" is a case in point. I have known many teachers, principals, and school administrators who pride themselves on their adherence to democratic principles and feel strongly that the needs and rights of children have to be taken into account. In addition, these same people can point to colleagues whom they label as authoritarian or restrictive, with the implication that these characteristics are antieducational in spirit and effect. Without denying in the slightest that these differences exist, I have also to say that, constitutionally speaking, the differences are not all that great; in terms of how and on what basis the classroom constitution is determined, the "democratic" and "authoritarian" teachers are not as far apart as one might think.[1]

In both cases I have been impressed by three things: Constitutions are for children and not teachers, complete power is retained by the teacher, and children passively accept the constitution developed for them. Those who wish to change life in the classroom are dealing with constitutional issues and not, as is too frequently the case, with high-sounding slogans whose conceptual underpinnings remain unexamined, with the usual result that there is a discrepancy between what is said and what is done.[2]

As a reminder, in this chapter we are attempting to understand the relationship between what teachers do (or do not do) and how they think about children and themselves, to understand the "theories" of teachers—not their feelings or values, but their conceptions of what people are. And teachers, like the rest of us, have such conceptions, which, again like for the rest of us, are usually implicit rather than explicit. In this connection we now turn to another issue that was the major reason we did our little observational study.

The Student's and Teacher's Conception of Learning

Prior to the observational study, I had, in connection with numerous studies on anxiety in elementary school children (Sarason et al., 1960), sat in scores of classrooms. It took quite some time for me to become aware that something was missing, and that was discussion in class of why and how people learned. It is obvious enough that however one defines such words as *learning, schooling,* and *education,* they refer to things or processes that take place in a school. They can and do take place outside of a school, but they are involved in what goes on in a classroom. What do children in a classroom think about the business of learning? Do children have their own theories (as indeed they do) about how and why one learns? Are there discrepancies between the theories children think about and the theories they are asked or required to adopt? Would children like to talk about these matters? Are they able to talk about them? How do teachers explain and discuss their theories of learning and thinking with their students? In short, to what extent were the whys and hows of learning and thinking an explicit focus and subject of discussion in the classroom? My observations left no doubt that how children thought about the processes of learning and thinking rarely came up for scrutiny in the classroom, but I was not as certain that the teacher's theories were as rarely presented and discussed. Therefore, we placed observers in classrooms to study this, and we chose the first month of school on the assumption that it would be during this interval that a teacher was most likely to make his or her own thinking explicit to the students. The most general instruction given to the observers was to note anything that a teacher said bearing on the whys and hows of learning and thinking. More specifically, they were asked to record anything relevant to the following questions:

1. When a child did not know or could not do something, did the teacher's response in any way attempt to find out how the child had been thinking or how the child might think—in contrast, for example, to telling and showing *a* correct procedure?
2. How frequently did a teacher say "I don't know" and go on to discuss how he or she would think about going and *knowing*?
3. How frequently and in what ways [did] a teacher take up and discuss the role of question asking in intellectual inquiry or problem solving?

There were other questions, but I expect from these that one will understand that we were interested in the degree to which such topics as thinking and problem solving were discussed in the classroom. The results were quite clear: Such discussions did not take place. Although unverbalized, the ground rules were not difficult to discern. First, the task of the student was to get the right answer and this was more important than how one arrived at the answer. By "more important" I mean simply that the right answer was what teacher and student obviously treasured. Second, for any one problem or question there was *a* correct way of thinking about and answering it. Third, *thinking was really not a complicated affair.*

There is nothing new or surprising in this. For example, Wertheimer (1945) well described, in the case of a geometry class, how the students were taught by their teacher to solve the parallelogram problem. When Wertheimer then tried to get the students to consider alternative ways of solving the problem, they were hardly able to grasp the idea that there was more than one way one could think about the problem. When he demonstrated alternative proofs, the students said he was wrong because he did not do it "the right way."[3]

What happens when I take up these observations with teachers? One of the most frequent reactions is . . . : "That is the way things should be." In a real sense these teachers were responding in a manner identical to that of Wertheimer's students, who could not accept the idea that there were other ways of thinking. But most instructive of all were those occasions when I could raise these issues with teachers *after* a discussion in which they had critically examined their experiences as students in their college courses. *What I confronted them with was the startling identity between their complaints as students in college and what their own students might complain about if they could but talk.* Some teachers could immediately see the possible connection. Other teachers could not accept the idea that how they felt could bear resemblance to how their students felt; that is, children did not think about thinking or learning the way teachers did. Leaving aside these reactions, there were two reservations that teachers verbalized. First, there was little or nothing in their training that would enable them to handle the issues in the classrooms. Second, even if they wanted to or could handle them, the demands of curriculum coverage leave little time for such matters.

Life in the classroom can be viewed and understood from different vantage points, but in my opinion, one of the most important ones is that which looks at the implicit theories teachers have about thinking and learning.[4] What I have tried to suggest in this section is that many teachers have two theories: *one that applies to them and one that applies to children.* Put in another way, many teachers are quite aware from their own experiences of the differences in characteristics between dull and exciting conditions of intellectual activity. But their inability to see or assume some kind of identity between their pupils and themselves leads them unwittingly to create those conditions that they would personally find boring. Classroom learning is primarily determined by teachers' perceived differences between children and adults, a fact that makes recognition of communalities almost impossible. . . .

The Teacher as a Thinking Model

Thus far in this chapter I have been, in one or another way, raising a descriptive type of question: What and how much do children know about what a teacher thinks? It is inevitable that children will know something about how a teacher thinks—how much depends on the teacher. I have never heard anyone argue that a teacher is not a model for children of how one should think and act. It is not a matter of *should* a teacher be a model, but rather that he or she *is* a model. But the fact that the teacher is a model of a particular kind and degree very definitely involves a variety of "shoulds," such as what children should learn, what a teacher should do, and so on. The point I wish to emphasize is that it appears that children know relatively little about how a teacher thinks about the classroom; that is, what the teacher takes into account, the alternatives the teacher thinks about, the things that puzzle the teacher about children and about learning, what the teacher does when unsure of what should be done, how the teacher feels when he or she does something wrong—there is quite a bit that goes on in a teacher's head that is never made public to children.

Am I advocating that teachers act like patients on an analyst's couch and give forth with all that is inside them? Obviously not, in addition to which I am not advocating *anything*. I am merely pointing out that the degree to which teachers make their thinking public inevitably reflects the kind of "thinking model" to which they adhere. Put in another way, it reflects a conception of what is helpful to children. How does one decide what is helpful? For example, if it were true that how a teacher thinks about the classroom is something about which children are curious, is it helpful *not* to satisfy this curiosity? Is there any reason to believe that it is helpful to children to know how a teacher thinks?

Unfortunately, we do not have a truly firm foundation for answering the question. However, there is a good deal of anecdotal evidence strongly indicating that the more a teacher can make his or her own thinking public and subject for discussion—in the same way one expects of children—the more interesting and stimulating the classroom becomes for students, and I assume that is a helpful state of affairs. Phillip Booth (1969) put it beautifully in a review of a book by the teacher and poet Mark Van Doren: "His unique genius as a teacher was to speculate publicly; in opening the play of his mind to students, he gave each student a self-assigned role in resolving these questions his teaching dramatized." I would quite surprised if Professor Van Doren's "unique genius" was not in some measure a reflection of a clear conception of what would be helpful to his students. . . .

... If my experience with school children—in fact, with all levels of students, from elementary through graduate school—is any guide, that large part of a teacher's "thinking about thinking," which is never made public, is precisely what the children are interested in and excited by on those rare occasions when it becomes public. . . .

Let me now turn to two related questions I have asked teachers regarding student behavior and misbehavior: Is there something about children that makes them *completely* unable to participate in discussion and formulation of crime and punishment in the classroom? Please note that I italicized "completely" because I have never seen a classroom (although I am sure they exist) in which children participated in such discussion and formulation—and we are back, of course, to the constitutional issue. The second question: Assuming that they are incapable, is it also true that they do not think about or are not concerned about crime and punishment in the classroom? To say they are completely unable is at least unjustified and at worst sheer ignorance of what children do outside of school in their spontaneous play groups. One does not need the support of formal research to assert that children in their relationships to each other have some concept of fairness—one needs only good eyes and ears.

The fact of the matter is that the great bulk of teachers assert (1) that children are not completely unable, and (2) that children do think about crime and punishment in the classroom. *Whatever thinking allows teachers to make these positive assertions is not reflected in what they do or, more specifically, in the justification of the prepotent response.*

. . . When a teacher thinks about misbehavior, one thinks primarily in terms of individual children. When the teacher thinks about action, one also tends to think about action in relation to individual children. Although the teacher is quite aware that there is a group of children, this plays far less of a role in thinking and action than one might think. . . .

. . . I have by now asked hundreds of teachers the following two questions: "How many times in the last month have you, aside from the report card, made it your business to communicate to parents that their child was not doing well, or he was misbehaving, or one or another kind of problem?" I never kept an accurate count, but I would guess that 25 percent of the teachers indicated that they had gone out of their way to contact parents about a child's problem. The second question was: "How many times in the last month have you, aside from the report card, made it your business to communicate to parents that their child was doing well, or very well, or very much better than previously?" At most, 1 percent of the teachers indicated that they had initiated such a contact.

The Goals of Change in the Classroom

One does not have to document the statement that there are many people, both from within and without schools, who feel that the quality of life and learning in the classroom needs to be changed. The goals of change vary in their scope and phraseology; for example, the classroom should be more child-centered, it should be more democratically organized and run, it should be more relevant to the world that children do and will live in, teachers should be more creative, and so on. A basic assumption in these statements of virtue is that the teacher will be the agent of change; the teacher will possess that way of thinking, as well as appropriately derived procedures and tactics, that will bring about the desired kind of classroom life. It is rare, indeed, to find in these discussions serious consideration of the consequences of this basic assumption for the change process. That is to say, there is a remarkable blindness to the fact that one is confronted with the extremely difficult problem of how one changes how people think. This is all the more strange when one recognizes that underlying the different criticisms of classroom life is the more basic criticism that one does not agree with how the modal teacher thinks.

The more I have read about and personally observed efforts to introduce change in the classroom, the more clear several things have become. First, those who attempt to introduce a change rarely, if ever, begin the process by being clear as to where the teachers *are;* that is, how and why they think as they do. In short, they are guilty of the very criticism they make of teachers: *not being sensitive to what and how and why children think as they do.* As a result, teachers react in much the same way that many children do, and that is with the feeling they are both wrong and stupid (Holt, 1964). Second, those who attempt to introduce a change seem unaware that they are asking teachers to unlearn and learn. Third, if there is any one principle common to efforts at change, it is that one effects change by *telling* people what is the "right" way to act and think. *Here, too, those who want change do exactly that for which they criticize teachers.*

The main purpose of this chapter has been to obtain glimpses of how the modal teacher thinks and how this determines, in large part, life in the classroom. Put in another way: The overt regularities that can be discerned in the classroom reflect covert principles and theories. If we wish to change the overt regularities, we have as our first task to become clear about the covert principles and theories: those assumptions and conceptions that are so overlearned that one no longer questions or thinks about them. They are "second nature," so to speak. If these assumptions and conceptions remain unverbalized and unquestioned, which is to say that thinking does not change, the likelihood that any of the overt regularities one wants to change will in fact change is drastically reduced. It would all be so simple if one could legislate changes in thinking.

It is likely that some readers will use the contents of this chapter as grist for their internal mill of prejudice and snobbery. It is not difficult, if one is so disposed, to feel superior to teachers—and many university critics (and others) are so disposed. This would not be worthy of comment were it not for two facts: Many university critics spearhead the change process, and, as anyone familiar with the history of anthropology knows, the feeling of superiority ("bringing culture to the primitives") is lethal for the process of understanding and change.

My former colleague, Dr. Murray Levine, developed a concept on the basis of his intensive work with teachers in inner-city schools.

The Child Comes by His Problem Honestly

From the point of view of the teacher who is concerned about teaching a large group of children any child who presents special difficulties is a nuisance. As long as education is defined in terms of the preparation and presentation of material to children, the teacher's first inclination, when faced with a difficult child, is to experience the child as trouble. Finding her own efforts frustrated or finding that she must divide her attention in more ways than she feels capable of doing, the teacher frequently feels angered and resentful of a child who demands something different by virtue of his behavior. She may also feel anxious because her image of herself as a competent professional person is threatened. Although we are taught that human behavior stems from sufficient causes, in the classroom situation the teacher is not always able or prepared to seek causes. Understandably, from her viewpoint, the child is at fault for acting as he does, and it is her feeling that both she and the child would be better off if the child were away from her. Sometimes the consultant can serve an important function by helping the teacher to see that the problem has a background. When the teacher sees that a child does come by his problems honestly, so to speak, her tolerance for the problem and her willingness to make the effort to work with the child are sometimes increased. (Sarason et al., 1966)

Dr. Levine gives case examples of how the thinking and actions of teachers changed in relation to certain children once they understood that indeed they come by their problems honestly, which is another way of saying that teachers understood the children in *their* terms and life experience. If we believe teachers likewise have problems, and they do, we will not get very far in helping them if we do not understand that they too come by their problems quite honestly.

Notes

1. This conclusion is similar to that made by Jules Henry (1963), based on his observations of life in the suburban classroom. Henry is one of the very few anthropologists who has directly studied the classroom. His description and discussion of life in the classroom are illuminating and provocative. Given the emphasis in anthropology on foreign and so-called primitive cultures, it is not surprising that this important discipline has not focused on the classroom in our society (e.g., Spindler (ed.), 1963).

2. The constitutional issues, as well as others to be raised in this chapter, could be regarded as relevant to, or subsumed under, a theory of instruction. This would be a matter of indifference to me were it not that theories of instruction do not deal with constitutional issues but rather focus on the cognitive characteristics of the individual child, and on how these characteristics develop and could be taken account of in curriculum building. As often as not the theory talks about *a* child, and not a child in a group of children. Any theory of instruction that does not confront the reality that the teacher does not instruct *a* child but a group of children is not worth very much, to teachers at least. Even where the teacher intends to instruct a particular child, it takes place psychologically (for the child, teacher, and the other children) in the context of being part of a larger group and set of relationships. I quite agree with Jones' critique (1968) of Bruner's (1966) theory of instruction; that is, his overemphasis on cognitive skills and curricular skills and underemphasis on the affective. Jones comes close to including the constitutional question in his the-

ory of instruction, but it is far from as explicit as I think will be found to be necessary. This may be because Jones, in reacting to Bruner's overemphasis on the cognitive side, gets riveted on the expression of the affective side, and what tends to get sidetracked are the constitutional arrangements between teacher and class that maximize such expression. Depending as Jones does on Freud's and Erikson's conceptions about individual development, he cannot develop what is needed: a truly social psychological theory of instruction. These objections aside, I consider Jones' book a distinct contribution.

3. One of the several justifications for the development of the new math was to counteract the kinds of things Wertheimer and others have described. That is to say, one wanted children to grasp the idea that there were different ways one could use and think about the world of numbers. Nonetheless, the new math is taught in much the same ways as the old math. It could not be otherwise if for no other reason than those who pushed for the change seemed unaware that the theories of learning and thinking that guide teachers, in addition to the constitutional issues discussed earlier, do not permit the processes of thinking to be an object of inquiry in the classroom.

4. Fuchs' (1969) *Teachers Talk* is relevant here. Most of Dr. Fuchs' book consists of excerpts from journals kept by fourteen new teachers during the first semester in the classroom in city schools. These excerpts constitute compelling confirmation of many points I have made in this and previous chapters. My favorite excerpt (because of the importance I place on constitutional issues) is from a teacher's report of the first day of school: "Then I established class routines: how we would put away our clothing; how we would get our clothing; raising your hand when you have something to say, not calling out; not talking when I'm talking; not talking when I haven't given permission to talk; not talking when you are doing something. I told them that we would have free time for talking. Then we discussed fire drills, what we would do and how we would line up, and our behavior in the hall and in the yard. I also covered supplies, the things that I requested that they bring in, and any problems. I complimented them on how they were dressed and how I would like them to come to school from now on, dressed neatly and clean; we discussed routines at home, the time we go to bed at night, how we take our bath, what happens when you get up in the morning. We discussed why breakfast is called breakfast and why we eat breakfast. Before we knew it the whole morning had gone and it had been a very good morning." The book is a storehouse of accounts of life in the classroom and school.

CHAPTER 7

The "Nonreading" Professional

In this final chapter of *You Are Thinking of Teaching?* Sarason does two things he rarely does. One is to be explicitly critical of teachers, and the other is to, in his words, "consciously and deliberately . . . sermonize." What goads him are the circumstances that combine to produce a nation of teachers of children and young adults who are, as educators, mostly nonreaders in their field. He laments teachers' failure "to *want* to know what others are thinking and writing because they feel they *need* to know in order to have the sense that they are intellectually-professionally alive and enlarging their horizons."

The irony of teachers bemoaning "the fact that most students look upon books as uninteresting, unimportant and irrelevant to their lives" is not lost on him. He compares educators to other professionals and finds both a disturbing similarity among medical practitioners and a horror at the very idea that one's doctor or lawyer might "read next to nothing in his or her field." He asks, *"Would you not consider finding someone else to whom to bring your problems?"*

What Sarason asks of future teachers is not just that they read educational research and practice, but that they do so with a critical eye. And he cautions that such reading "is hard work, a struggle, precisely because that kind of reading requires you to walk that fine line between uncritical acceptance and premature dismissal of new ideas." He ends up praising the struggle itself as an enhancement of one's intellectual and professional life.

Question for Seymour Sarason

With literally dozens of "worthwhile" educational books and hundreds of cogent articles published each year, how does a teacher avoid becoming inundated and confused by a flood of often-contradictory advice? How, as a professional, do you begin to be a serious reader?

From "The 'Nonreading' Professional," in *You Are Thinking of Teaching?* by Seymour Sarason. Copyright © 1993 by Seymour Sarason. This material is used by permission of Jossey-Bass, Inc., a subsidiary of John Wiley & Sons, Inc.

Sarason's Response

When you go shopping for clothes, or a car, or a new house, or a gift for somebody, you "case the joint" because you want, so to speak, to get us much bang as you can for your buck. A professional is one who needs or wants to know what is relevant to his or her obligations and purposes, someone who asks, "What have other people written that will help me do a better job for my students and my own sense and need to grow?" You may find little you consider relevant, but at the very least you will know what is being attempted, and discussed, by others.

In this regard, I am amazed and discouraged with how little most school personnel know, for example, about vouchers and charter schools. They have opinions and prejudices even though most of them have read nothing about them. That is why when the Heinemann Publishing Company asked me to write a small book about vouchers and charter schools, I agreed to do so. It will be published in early winter 2002. It is titled *Questions You Should Ask About Charter Schools and Vouchers.*

More about Sarason's views of the teaching profession may be found in:

Educational Reform: A Self-Scrutinizing Memoir (2002)
Teaching as a Performing Art (1999)
Political Leadership and Educational Failure (1998)
Revisiting "The Culture of the School and the Problem of Change" (1996)
The Case for Change: Rethinking the Preparation of Educators (1992)
The Preparation of Teachers: An Unstudied Problem in Education (1962)

In a book like this it is hard to avoid sermonizing. In this final chapter I consciously and deliberately will sermonize.

In the case of teachers, one hopes that they never give up trying to "save lives," regardless of how long they have been teaching. In my case, a very obvious senior citizen, I still seek to save the lives of those entering the educational profession! Let us leave aside the thorny question of which criteria we should employ to judge whether we have "saved" the life of a professional. But there is one criterion about which I feel so strongly, and about which there is general agreement, that it deserves a sermon! Unfortunately, despite such agreement in the abstract, it is a criterion honored more in the breach than in the practice—one of the preconditions for giving a sermon. Sermons tell us what we already know we should think and do; the purpose of the sermon is to remind us that we have fallen short of the mark and we should try to do better.

A prefatory note of caution. What I say in this chapter is not peculiar to those in education. There is no evidence to suggest that educational practitioners are dramatically different from other practitioners in their failure to read the literature in their fields; that is, to *want* to know what others are thinking and writing because they feel they *need* to know in order to have the sense that they are intellectually-professionally alive and enlarging their horizons. It is really irrelevant to my purposes whether educators are more or less "nonreaders" than those in other professions. In my experience, too many practitioners in education have little interest in reading what others are thinking and writing in regard to issues in the field.

How many times have you heard educators and others bemoan the fact that most students look upon books as uninteresting, unimportant, and irrelevant to their lives? How many times have you heard that one of the adverse consequences of TV is that reading books (or even the newspaper) has been further eroded as a source of intellectual pleasure? Are we not dismayed (too weak a word) when we are told about studies demonstrating that young people's knowledge of the world they live in is scandalously poor? And are we not taken aback (again too weak a phrase) when we learn that they are *uninterested* in that world? It is irrelevant whether the results of these studies are no different or worse than what studies from the most distant past may have indicated. As one researcher said to me, "Anyone who takes comfort in the argument that this is the way it has always been has learned nothing from history." It was the same researcher who went on to say, "How many people know that the founding fathers who gave us our wondrous Constitution were, as a group, the most voracious readers of the history of the issues with which they were confronted, more voracious than any comparable group in human history?" Let me interrupt this sermon with a story.

Back in the sixties, I invited a friend to talk to my colleagues and graduate students. Edward Cohart was a physician and an internationally respected epidemiologist. The point of his talk was in the form of a question: Why is it that in the United States the treatment of choice for breast cancer in women is radical mastectomy, while in England surgeons opt for lumpectomy, a much less invasive and pervasive procedure? The difference between the two countries, he said, was so striking as to suggest that one of them had to be "wrong"; that is, the psychological and bodily consequences of the two approaches for women were too obvious to permit one to justify either as the dominant procedure. He then went on to compare the results in both countries in terms of longevity, morbidity, and other indices of outcomes. The most cautious conclusion the comparisons permitted was that there were *no* differences in outcomes. A less cautious but still justified conclusion was that the outcomes favored lumpectomy. Both conclusions obviously should have caused the medical community in the United States to ponder the frequency with which it resorted to radical mastectomy. But it did not! Not in the mid sixties, when Cohart gave his talk. It took two or more decades before American surgeons began to reduce the frequency of radical mastectomy as the surgery of choice.

How do we explain this? One partial answer is that it is an instance of the way people resist changing highly overlearned ways of thinking and acting, even when the "objective" evidence suggests that a change in viewpoint is in order. American surgeons were trained to believe that radical mastectomy was the procedure of choice. They learned that from their teachers, and they learned it well. (Obviously, that is the risk you run whether you are in medical school or in a teacher preparatory program!)

But there is another part of the answer, and it has to do with reading. Of course, there were some American surgeons who had read the British studies, but it was apparently the case that most surgeons had not read them. Among practicing surgeons (as among practitioners in other professions), the number who read, really read, the literature in their field is not large. I understand the argument that the demands made on professionals (for example, physicians and teachers) are so great, so persistent, so energy draining as to make serious reading in their fields at best a luxury and at worst an unpleasant bore. But to understand all is not to forgive all! It is my opinion that if more physicians had read the British studies, it might have spurred more of them to rethink their practices. In recent years, there has been a steady increase in the United States in lumpectomies. If more surgeons had earlier read and digested the impact of those studies, that increase might have started long before it did. The important point here is that practitioners in diverse professions read very little in their fields. I cannot cite studies to prove that assertion. All I can say is that whenever I have talked with leading people in this or that profession, one of their complaints is that the "everyday" practitioner does not read, does not keep up with new research findings, new ideas. As one such leader said, "They are in a rut, withering on the vine, and don't know it. What bothers me more than not reading in the field—that I can understand up to a point—is that too many of them are *uninterested* in reading."

This problem has been so general and worrisome as to cause professional organizations *and* state legislatures to *require* educational and medical practitioners to take more courses or attend workshops. I italicize *require* because it confirms what has long been obvious: Too many practitioners do not read what they should be reading. I have nothing against continuing education, but I have to confess that I am not impressed with what some people (adults and children) learn when learning is mandated, when it is not internally dictated and sought. I have attended and given workshops, and I have heard and given scores more lectures in continuing education programs. Audiences, I have concluded, comprise two groups: those who are there because they want to be there, and those who are there because they are required or expected to be there. I may be accused of undue pessimism when I say that the number in the latter group exceeds the number in the former.

My wife is an avid attendee at workshops, and I tag along, dutifully and reluctantly. Rarely have I regretted attending. Workshops can be stimulating. They have an important role to play, especially if they not only spur you to reflection about how you think and act but also stimulate you to read more extensively about the issues. Being a passive but interested listener to someone giving you his or her version of truth is one thing; actively seeking to read, analyze, and digest what different people have written about a particular idea or practice is quite another thing. Truth has many versions.

Let us take an example from the educational arena. Almost twenty years ago, the federal government commissioned an extensive study to evaluate the outcomes of federal efforts to improve education. It is a landmark study (in several volumes!). There are two ways you can respond to the study. One is with discouragement because the outcomes were far from favorable. The other is with encouragement because one of the few clear findings was that favorable outcomes were associated with schools where teachers and administrators (and frequently parents) cooperatively planned and implemented actions for change; that is, the proposals for change were themselves outcomes of intellectual-professional discussions reflective of a collegiality making for commitment on the part of all participants.

That was a very important finding, the significance of which cannot be overestimated, flying, as it does, in the face of the "traditional" way proposals for change originate and are implemented in our schools. That is not only my opinion but that of others who read the study. If there were people who read the study, how do I explain the sad fact that among the many scores of teachers I asked, *none* had read the study and only a handful had even "heard" about it? Before you scapegoat teachers, you should know that *none* of them had ever been exposed to that study in their preparatory programs. Having said that, however, I have to point out that the study received a good deal of play in professional journals, weeklies, newspapers, and newsletters. Even if the teachers with whom I spoke had not been told about the study in their preparatory programs, it is not unfair to say that there were numerous opportunities for them to become aware of that study. But only if they felt the obligation to read what was going on in the field. Not to feel such an obligation is, I must in all candor say, inexcusable.

A professional person is, among other things, someone whose responsibilities include knowing what others in the field think, do, and have found and reported. *If you knew that your physician, or lawyer, or tax accountant read next to nothing in his or her field, would you not consider finding someone else to whom to bring your problems?* In recent years, there has been a dramatic escalation in the number of malpractice suits against physicians. That escalation has several valid and invalid sources, but let us not forget that one basis for a malpractice suit is that the person did not know something he or she *should* have known; that is, if the person had read what he or she should have been reading in the *normal* course of professional living, that person should have acted otherwise. A professional person is not one who stopped reading after finishing formal training. Reading is more than desirable, it is crucial. If I were czar of education, I would seek to stimulate and support the professionals in each school to devote at least one hour each week to a meeting in which is discussed a published study, report, or book that everyone had read beforehand. Professionals should always be "going to school."

You should read articles and books the way you listen to your instructors: carefully, respectfully, but critically. Because someone says something or has written something does not mean that you should accept it. In listening or reading, you have two tasks or, better yet, obligations. The first is to seek to understand the rationale; that is, to understand it in terms of the writer's experience and his or her use of formal studies and the experiences of others that are the basis for the rationale. Put another way, you should seek to comprehend "where the person is coming from." It may surprise you when I say that this kind of reading is not easy, especially when what we are reading is unfamiliar or clearly discrepant with our way of thinking and practicing. When we read something that challenges our accustomed ways, our internal resistances to change come to the fore and can interfere with even a semidispassionate comprehension of the writer's argument. I speak here from personal experience. Reading for the purpose of truly comprehending another person's way of thinking and acting is the opposite of a routine practice. It is hard. We do not take kindly to new ideas. By not reading, of course, you eliminate that difficulty, but at the expense of your intellectual-personal-professional development.

The flip side of the problem is no less dangerous: uncritically accepting what you read (or you hear in lectures) as gospel. Thus, the second task is to read with a critical eye. Because a "voice of authority" has said or written something does not mean that you should accept it. Such voices have what we call a "demand characteristic"; that is, "If Professor or writer X says Y, the message is that I should believe it and do it." I am reminded here of a medical colleague who was one of the greats in radiology. One of the first things he would do with a new cohort of interns was to present them with x-rays of several people, ask them to study them, and then to give their opinions about what the x-rays revealed. The interns would unfailingly come up with lists of pathologies. After all, if Professor Henry Kaplan, *the* Professor Kaplan, asked them to study the x-rays, something was amiss in those patients. The interns were, to say the least, chagrined to learn that the x-rays were those of normal people. It was their first lesson about how easy it is, how dangerous it is, to see what you think a voice of authority says you should see. It is a lesson no less valid for reading than for seeing.

I am not advocating reading for pleasure. Reading for the express purpose of enlarging your intellectual-personal horizons is hard work, a struggle, precisely because that kind of reading requires you to walk that fine line between uncritical acceptance and premature dismissal of new ideas. The pleasure from such reading comes when you can say that you have engaged in a struggle, you have tried to be fair to yourself and the writer, and you can justify the resolution of the struggle on grounds other than habit, sheer feeling, or prejudice.

We are living in times when education and educators—in our public schools, colleges, and universities—are subject to all kinds of criticism and pressure to change. The issues are many, complicated, fateful, and they will not go away. The day is past when anyone entering *any* human service profession can remain ignorant of those issues, the different positions taken, and their implications for action. How these issues get played out will depend on many factors, predictable and unpredictable. But certainly one of those factors will be the outlook, knowledge, creativity, and courage of those who will enter these professions. In the case of our public schools, a major factor will be those who become teachers. You can react to that prediction as a problem or an opportunity. Obviously, I regard it as an opportunity for those who seek to understand themselves, their students, and the society in which we live. No longer can a teacher's horizons be circumscribed by a classroom, or a school, or a school system.

It has *never* been the case that schools were impervious to societal forces and dynamics. But up until the post–World War II era, our schools acted as if they were truly oases walled off from their surrounding. That is no longer possible. World War II, like all other major wars in human history, ushered in societal changes that changed everybody and everything. Indeed, the crisis in education today inheres in the fact that educators have to deal with those larger social forces, like it or not. Some have not liked it. For them, it is a problem, not an opportunity requiring change, adaptation, innovation, and understanding. For those who see it as an opportunity, the challenge is both formidable and exciting. It is not the kind of challenge appropriate for those who see the classroom as a retreat from the larger society. And it is not the kind of challenge for those content to let others—in and outside of schools—decide how teachers should think and act. I am not suggesting that teachers go it alone, that there are not other voices that should be heard in decision making.

What I am asserting is that teachers have to become sophisticated about several things: the allocation and uses of power, the processes of decision making, the role and uses of community groups and resources, the nature and consequences of the legislative process, the history of the educational crisis with which we are confronted, and the sources of the diverse conflicting rationales about the goals of education. In the course of your professional preparation, you will be exposed to some of these things, although not as much as you should be (in my opinion). In any event, however adequate or inadequate that preparation may be, you should feel obliged to assume the responsibility to become and remain knowledgeable about what is happening in your field. There is no one way to accomplish that. Reading is one of the best ways. *Your* professional "salvation" will not come from outside of yourself. A professional is someone who has something *to profess.* Your obligation to yourself and your profession is to know what is going on; that is, what others are experiencing, studying, and writing. Teaching need not be, must not be, a lonely profession. Reading is one of the better prescriptions for diluting the sense of intellectual-professional isolation as well as the sense that you stopped developing. No profession more than education provides as exciting an opportunity to understand the society in which we live: how it has changed, will change, should change. Will there be problems, frustrations, ups and downs, second thoughts, even despair? Of course. Is personal, intellectual, professional "growing up" easy? Of course not. End of sermon!

Part II

The School

CHAPTER 8

The School Culture and Processes of Change

This selection, from Sarason's Brechbill Lecture at the University of Maryland on January 10, 1966, contains his first statement of issues that emerge in *The Culture of the School and the Problem of Change* (Allyn & Bacon, 1971). It includes his analysis of the disaster of "The New Math," along with sections on the critical importance of school-based relationships and the complex issue of school culture. This selection will help readers trace the development of some of Sarason's major conceptual contributions to education and psychology.

Question for Seymour Sarason

It has been more than thirty years since this essay was published, followed as it was, two years later, by *The Culture of the School and the Problem of Change.* In 1996, you published *Revisiting "The Culture of the School and the Problem of Change."* As you revisit the question of culture and change yet again, in the twenty-first century, does it seem that educators are, in general, paying more attention to issues relating to a school's culture? Or do we manifestly refuse to "get it"?

Sarason's Response

I have to postpone answering this question, because it should be raised only after people have a more comprehensive idea why educational reform efforts are so paltry in their effects. That requires reading. Good intentions are not enough. But one thing I can say to any teacher who wants to influence his or her colleagues with respect to "culture" is this: "You may find, at best, only a superficial collegiality in the school; there is likely to be no forum where ideas and possibilities can and are expected to be raised and discussed. So, you might as well save yourself from trouble by keeping quiet."

Reprinted from "The School Culture and Processes of Change" in *The Psycho-Educational Clinic: Papers and Research Studies* by Seymour Sarason (Boston: Massachusetts Department of Mental Health, 1969).

I am not being flip. Your question is deceptive. Reformers with far more status, money, and administrative support than an individual teacher have learned through painful experience how much they had oversimplified the obstacles that must be faced when trying to change schools. I have discussed this in various of my books, especially the charter school book and my most recent one—*Educational Reform: A Self-Scrutinizing Memoir.*

More about the concept of a school and its culture may be found in:

Educational Reform: A Self-Scrutinizing Memoir (2002)
Teaching as a Performing Art (1999)
Revisiting "The Culture of the School and the Problem of Change" (1996)
School Change: The Personal Development of a Point of View (1995)
The Predictable Failure of Educational Reform (1990)
Schooling in America: Scapegoat and Salvation (1983)

A Basic Assumption

. . . In approaching the problem of change, I am making an assumption that the school *is* a subculture in our society since it has traditions, goals, dynamics, organization, and materials which set it apart from other settings in our society. Let us put it in another way: Those who are part of the school setting see themselves as different, in numerous ways, from those who work in or are a part of other settings, e.g., a factory, a mental hygiene clinic, or a political club. What is involved is not merely the feeling of being different, but the awareness that one possesses special knowledge, values, and obligations which have a history not only in the life of the individual but in the larger context of history. There is a sense of individual and group identity derived from a past that gives structure and meaning to the present and future. Those in the school culture "know" what they are in the same way that a newspaper reporter knows what he is, or an Australian bushman knows what he is, or a physician knows what he is.

The school culture is, of course, a highly differentiated one. There are elementary, junior, and senior high schools; there are superintendents, teachers, principals, and supervisors; there are urban, suburban, and rural schools; and there are boards of education. In addition, the school culture has many points of contact with the larger society—parent groups, schools of education, business, law enforcement, and mental health clinics. Despite the differentiation within the school culture and the fluidity of its boundaries with the larger society, I assume that those within it possess values, self-perceptions, goals, technical skills, training, and expectations which have a distinctive organization or patterning. It needs to be emphasized that the distinctiveness resides in not just one of these characteristics but in their overall relation to each other.

Is it warranted to make this basic assumption? It could be argued that schools and school personnel vary so fantastically on so many different levels that attempts to arrive at communalities or distinctive patterns of behavior and attitudes are rendered meaningless or fruitless. From this standpoint each school, or even each classroom, is a unique entity which can only be understood in its own terms and which has little or nothing in common with what goes on in other schools or classrooms. There is truth to this in the same way that there is truth to the statement that no two people are alike. But the fact of uniqueness in no way invalidates the perception of similarities. The significance of uniqueness or similarities depends on what one wants to do. The fact that no two teachers are alike would in no way impede one from predicting similarity in response to an increase in pay or a reduction in class size.

The fact of the matter is that the assumption of a school culture has hardly been examined or studied. This is not to say that there is not a good deal to be learned about schools from the many studies which have been done on scores of educational issues, problems, and practices. For example, one can devote one's life just to reading what has been written about reading—one lifetime probably being in the nature of a gross underestimate. What bearing does the literature on reading have on our understanding of the culture of the school? Asking that is clearly to beg the question of what I mean by culture. It is realistic self-appraisal rather than modesty that compels me to say that far wiser and more knowledgeable people than myself have asked this question and have left it unanswered or have given answers which left them and others far from happy. I will not attempt a definition but rather will give examples of the kinds of things to which the concept of the school culture refers.

Example I

There is a physical education program in every school I know or have heard about. In almost all instances there is a particular place in the school where this program is conducted. Those who conduct these programs are expected to have special training. What happens when, as I have done on numerous occasions, I say to groups of teachers that I simply do not comprehend why there should be physical education programs in the schools? As you might imagine, the most frequent response is staring disbelief followed by a request to reformulate the statement. Without going into the details of the discussion—which is usually quite heated—I shall indicate the significance I attribute to the initial response and the ensuing discussion. First, there is the implicit recognition by both the teachers and myself that we operate in different worlds, i.e., I perceive them and they see me as having different backgrounds and experiences. Second, it is inconceivable to the teachers that a school could or should be without a physical education program. They have a conception of a school which, if subject to change or challenged, they strongly defend. Far from being indifferent to the conception they defend it to a degree which illuminates the extent to which their sense of identity is related to this conception. Third, they justify the physical education program in terms of what they think children are and need; their justification is both psychological and philosophical.

The concept of the school culture refers to those aspects of the setting that are viewed by school personnel as "givens" or essential features, which they would strenuously defend against elimination or marked change, and which to them reflect psychological concepts and value judgments. It is important to note that the frequency or regularity of an activity does not inform one as to its significance in the school culture. For example, I have been in many elementary school classrooms at the beginning of the school day, and in each instance the day began with the salute to the flag. On several occasions I have said to groups of teachers that I did not understand why children had to salute the flag each day. The responses to this statement are much more varied than to my statement about physical education. Some teachers respond by saying that the daily salute to the flag is an empty ritual which they would like to dispense with or reduce in frequency. Others say that it reinforces feelings of patriotism and contributes to the school's goal of making good citizens. Some teachers go on to point out that the salute to the flag is mandatory by law or administrative regulations. Rarely has the response been one of bewilderment or disbelief.[1] Aside from suggesting that frequency of an activity is not in itself a revealing characteristic, this example suggests that not all activities, however frequent, are considered by school personnel as equally important or relevant to their conception of the school or of themselves as professional people in the school.

There is one other thing that can be said about these two examples and again it is not something that is discernible from observing and recording ongoing activities in the school. I refer here to those activities which school personnel feel they must perform or engage in regardless of personal views, in contrast to those activities for which no such feeling is experienced because it is so syntonic with their view of things. It is interesting to note that although some teachers say explicitly that they are required to have their children salute the flag daily, no teacher says that about physical education programs even though in most, if not all, instances these programs are also required by law or administrative regulation. In other words, the culture of the school cannot be derived by examining laws and regulations just as it cannot be derived from knowledge of types of activities or their frequency.

. . . One of the ways to get at aspects of the school culture is to focus initially on activities that characterize the setting. The next, and more important and difficult, step is to determine how each activity is justified, and its centrality to the individual's conception of a school and sense of identity with it. It is not enough to determine the different bases for justification. One must determine, in addition, the degree to which the presence or absence of, or a change in, the activity is capable of affecting the individual's equilibrium.

I would expect two major consequences of the approach I have described. The first would be a clearer picture of what school personnel consider to be essential activities in the setting without which they would not apply the label *school* to it. The second consequence would be a much more explicit statement and understanding of the thinking and reasoning of the school personnel. Finally, and this is crucial, what we would learn about school personnel would differ in important respects from similar studies by non-school personnel, since school personnel characteristically view and think about school activities in a distinctive (although not necessarily unique) way.

Some may regard what I have said as a glimpse of the obvious. I do not think so, of course, but if it is obvious it will not be the first time that the obvious has not been taken seriously.

Relationships

There is much more to the concept of the school culture than can be discerned by focusing on activities. Of crucial importance are the different kinds of people who work in a school and the significance of "kinds of people" to the nature of relationships. To a person outside the school setting a principal is not a very differentiated kind of person. To someone in the school setting the principal is a very complicated kind of person because he is perceived and judged on factors that only become explicit when one becomes part of the setting. His years in the position, the help of an educational kind that he gives to teachers in classrooms, the help that he gives to teachers in regard to the management of children, the degree to which he "fights for" his staff in matters of salaries and working conditions, the quality of the evaluations he makes of his faculty, the degree to which he establishes personal as contrasted to professional relationships—all these are some of the factors which should prevent one from assuming that the relationship between the principal and his staff is a simple one or that the principal's role is not a very differentiated one. You undoubtedly noted that I omitted a very important characteristic— the sex of the principal. Is there anyone who would deny that the sex of a principal makes a difference in the culture of a school? Is it fortuitous that the significance of this factor is rarely raised or discussed in educational literature and research? Is this an oversight or is it a symptom of the fact that too little attention has been paid to understanding the school as a social system?

I would like to make clear that I have not been talking about the personality or other factors (race, religion, or political affiliation) about the principal which may be of great importance by virtue of their interaction with the factors I have mentioned. My focus has been on those aspects which are inherent in the job of principal and which make for the variety of relationships he has with others in the school.

Let me now ask another of those apparently, and perhaps truly, silly questions. Is it necessary for each school to have a principal? I have put this question to friends who are not connected with schools. There are three types of responses to this question. The first is one of mild surprise that the question should be asked. The second response is that the individual simply has no basis for considering alternatives, although in principle he would not be opposed to alternatives. The third and least frequent response is one in which alternatives are stated and the pros and cons evaluated. If I have sensed anything common to these responses it is that the question is an open and interesting one. Now, how do teachers respond to the question? As you might expect, their response is far stronger than it is to my question about physical education programs. Once emotions are relatively out of the way, a variety of answers are given although they tend to have one thing in common: There are "practical" matters of an everyday sort (that do or could occur) which could bring the operations of a school to a halt if the principal were not present. Who would keep the attendance data? Order supplies? Handle behavior problems and sick children? Supervise fire drills? Talk to parents when they phoned or visited? One could go on listing housekeeping matters which are considered to require the presence of a principal. What is most interesting to me is that teachers rarely, if ever, respond in terms of the factors I presented earlier—the principal's educational or leadership role, his evaluation functions, his role as representative of the teachers to other administrative bodies, and the importance of personal as contrasted to professional relationships with him. In other words, teachers tend not to respond in terms of the variety of relationships they actually have with the principal. And yet I have the distinct feeling, although perhaps without external evidence, that the teachers have a strong need to have *one* authority figure in the school who is "above" everybody else.

How does this shed light on the culture of the school? Again I would want to emphasize how inconceivable it is to teachers to think of a school without a principal. I confess that I stress this because it is conceivable to me that a school does not require a principal to attain its educational objectives. What I think, however, is far less important than what teachers think, rightly or wrongly, if one is interested in bringing about changes—*and this is what most innovators fail to realize.* Of equal significance is the possibility that the relationships which teachers have with the principal—relationships which stem from the duties and obligations of the principal—are far less important to the teacher than one might suppose. That is, the importance which teachers attach to the role of the principal does not reflect relationships they have with him in his role as an educational leader.

. . . In fact, rather than look to the principal as an educational leader and expert, teachers tend to shy away from meaningful discussions of these matters with the principal. I should quickly add that it is our distinct impression that principals feel most uncomfortable in their role as educational leader, that they prefer to have teachers solve their own problems, and that they infrequently visit classrooms to ascertain what is going on and its relationship to educational-psychological goals.

The principal-teacher relationship is but one means by which one can begin to understand the realities of the school culture as opposed to what may be deduced from job descriptions or untested statements of practices. Far more complicated than this relationship are those which exist among teachers. Age, years of teaching, marital status, perceived competence, sex, the grade being taught, psychological and educational orientation—these are some of the lines along which teachers vary and which affect their relationships with each other. I think there is a tendency for those outside a particular social organization to view those within it as a cohesive and interacting group, particularly if they share a common label, e.g., teachers. This naive but understandable view prepares the way for the surprise one feels when one learns that relationships within the system are otherwise. I am sure that it is akin to bringing coals to Newcastle when I say that in any one school the relationships among teachers are quite complex. I cannot go into detail about these complex relationships since they have hardly been the object of study. I will only state, but not expand upon, the assumption that when important human relationships occurring within a particular social system have not been the object of study, it is symptomatic of the need either to deny reality or to hide it from outsiders. When one considers the vast amount of educational research done in this and previous decades, is it not surprising that the relationships among teachers have received little attention? I cannot believe, and our experience clearly contradicts, that these relationships are not among the most revealing features of the school culture.

There is one aspect of teacher relationships which happens to fascinate me and which also relates to what was said above about principal-teacher relationships. I think I can make the point most clearly if I tell you something about the Psycho-Educational Clinic, more specifically, about our Fridays.

> ▶ All members of the Clinic are expected to be there all day on Friday. We are the type of Clinic in which staff members and interns spend a good deal of time in the schools and in other community settings. Consequently, Friday is set aside for group discussions, and for staff members and interns to have smaller meetings as the need may be. From 9:00 to 11:00 A.M., a member of the staff usually presents something about his work to the entire group. His presentation may be concerned with any problem to which he wants the group to react, i.e., it may concern a teacher, a child, a school, or a research problem which poses some kind of issue. At the end of this meeting there is a short break after which a second two-hour meeting is held. During this meeting, a staff member or intern presents his work with a child at the Clinic. Whereas the focus of the first meeting is a problem encountered away from the Clinic, the second is more narrowly focused on a child as seen in the Clinic. Between 1:00 and 3:30 P.M. there are no group meetings but there are informal discussions, planned and unplanned. Between 3:30 and 5:00 P.M., there is another group meeting, but this time devoted to some ongoing group work being conducted by a staff member in one of the community settings in which we work. ◀

Obviously we are very verbal characters. If I had the time to go into detail I could no doubt convince you that these meetings tend to have a "no-holds-barred" quality and that whatever other consequences they may have, they serve to make clear how each of us thinks and approaches common problems. We influence each other and recognize that we become changed by virtue of these meetings. We do not seek controversy but we do not avoid it. Personal feelings enter into or are reflected in discussions that can be quite stormy. We do not seek to be a happy family at the expense of candid discussion.

The major reason for the above description of our Fridays is to give you some idea of the importance we attach to the presentation and discussion of what we think and do. Aside from crowding everything into one day, we are probably no different from other clinical settings devoted to understanding and helping other people.

What does this have to do with teacher relationships? It serves as a contrast to the relative lack of meaningful, open, and sustained discussion among school personnel about their work, goals, professional problems, and explicit or implicit theoretical orientation. Let us not forget that everyone in the teaching and helping professions has an explicit or implicit, variably organized theory about human behavior which, in part at least, governs his or her professional actions. "Sharing" among teachers tends to be as productive of learning and communication as the "share and tell" periods are for elementary school children.

This state of affairs raises three questions: Why should this be so? Do school personnel wish it to be otherwise? What are the direct and indirect effects of this lack of communication on teachers and children in classrooms? I am not prepared to attempt to answer the first question. As for the second question, our experience at the Clinic . . . indicates that school personnel are ambivalent about the aloneness of teachers. In regard to the third question our experience is quite clear, particularly in relation to the neophyte teacher; the beginning teacher (especially in our large urban settings) tends to anticipate failure, is plagued by all kinds of doubts, is fearful of a negative evaluation, is thankful for her relative isolation due to fleeting and infrequent visitation by administrative superiors, and yet is acutely aware that she needs and wants help, guidance, and support uncomplicated by the implied threat of a negative evaluation. We have seen numerous beginning teachers and their pupils suffer the consequences of a state of affairs in which help through candid and meaningful relationship with professional colleagues is distinctive by its absence. That such relationships are indeed rare says something about the social system we call a school.

The Complexity of the Problem

There is much more to the school culture than can be described by a discussion of activities and professional relationships. . . . There are "peripheral personnel" (nurse, secretary, custodian) in the school whose activities and relationships with the children and teachers are not as simple or as uninfluential as their titles might suggest. There are, of course, the material or instrumental aspects of the school culture—those aspects through which information is communicated, skills are learned, traditions are explained, and attitudes are inculcated. Through the written word and other sensory media one can see most clearly that which the society considers its most prized traditions and significant historical events and movements, its expectations of its citizens, and its conceptions of human nature and development. It took, among other things, a Russian Sputnik and a civil rights movement to force many to the realization that the curriculum in our schools was based on philosophical and psychological assumptions which needed scrutiny and change.

Many other complex factors comprise the school culture. . . . On the surface it looks like a self-evident type of social system, aspects of which can be delineated by organizational charts, job descriptions, budgets, goals, and materials. This naive view could be tolerated if it did not serve as a basis for introducing change into the school, i.e., the way you effect change is to spend more money, erect more functional buildings, hire more people, add new services, and change what is between the covers of our textbooks. Lest I be accused of cynicism at best and of nihilism at worst let me state clearly that I have no doubt that changes introduced in these ways will have some positive effects. But, as I said at the outset and shall elaborate upon below, the degree of desired change will be much less than expected because of the failure to take into account some of the characteristics of the school culture I have discussed or alluded to.

Processes of Change

I will illustrate my point by a "case history" which although taken from the past has relevance for the present. I learned a lot from this instance and still have feelings of guilt because my role, however well intentioned, produced some unhappiness in others and failure was the end product.

A number of years ago I was asked by a Superintendent of Schools to visit him and his Board of Education in order to discuss his proposal to organize a department of research in the school system. After a two-day visit I learned the following things. First, the Superintendent felt very strongly that it was an obligation of a school system to evaluate the effectiveness of its program. Second, he had many doubts about certain ongoing programs but had no firm basis for making decisions about their continuation. Third, he felt that a school system should support not only applied educational studies but basic research in the learning process. Fourth, the Board of Education (which seemed on all counts to be unusually interested and informed) basically supported the idea of a department of research but was uncertain as to how to justify the necessary expenditures —this being a time when our school systems were already overwhelmed by the great number of children born during the years following World War II. Fifth, the Superintendent was a bright, decisive, energetic individual who was in the process of finishing his research for a doctorate, perhaps an irrelevant but nevertheless interesting fact. I returned to New Haven with the feeling that it had been a good visit. After all, I had heard people say what I wanted to hear, and they had listened respectfully to what I had had to say. To add material pleasure to personal joy they had also paid me for my time. The decisive reinforcement to my self-esteem was a letter from the Superintendent stating that approval for his ideas had been obtained and asking me to recommend someone for the top position. I quickly got in touch with a former student of mine, explained to him the excellent potentialities in the situation, and urged him to apply for the position; he did so and was chosen for the job.

Permit me to review the beginning of the story from the vantage point of subsequent years of experience in schools since what I have thus far related to you set the stage for later failure, my ignorance being an effective barrier to seeing the obvious. I shall list and discuss very briefly four related factors in the situation.

1. The decision to innovate was made not only from on high but by one individual.
2. There was no indication then, and this was subsequently confirmed, that the decision was other than cursorily discussed with other directors or supervisory personnel in the system. It need hardly be said that nobody below the supervisory level had even an inkling that a department of research was to come into being.
3. There apparently was no consideration or anticipation of the possibility that a department of research would be viewed as a *threat* to school personnel. That is, a department of research presumably *evaluates* ongoing programs and there is always the possibility that these programs would be found ineffective. The important point is that most school personnel take a dim view of research and researchers.

4. The fact that the person who was given the position was not in the narrow sense of
the word an educator but rather a clinical psychologist was not viewed as a potential source of difficulty for the psychologist or the more traditional kinds of school
personnel. The fact that there would be a "stranger" in the system, both in terms of
role and training background, was not thought of.

What does the above indicate about the culture of the school? It is, in my experience,
characteristic that decisions frequently are made at the top of the administrative hierarchy without regard for two likely consequences: the reactions of individuals and
groups to the *manner or means* by which decisions are made, announced, and implemented, and equally as important, their reactions to the *contents* of the decision in light
of prevailing attitudes, relationships, and ongoing activities. Decisions are made as if
there is no means-ends problem and as if one were not dealing with a social system in
which the introduction of change is no small matter. I think it important to emphasize
that decisions are made by people who are part of the system but who act in ways which
suggest that they do not know the system in some of its more socio-psychological characteristics.

What happened to my poor student? A less selfish question would be to ask what
happened to all the actors in a drama which had not been written but was nevertheless
being enacted. My former student came to the situation unaware that he was entering
a social system which he did not understand and for which his training did not prepare
him. Ignorance is one thing but when it is accompanied by a strong motivation to
change and influence people and settings—and there is no doubt in my mind that too
many research psychologists have an insufferably superior attitude to people in general
and educators in particular—we have the necessary but not sufficient basis for interpersonal disaster. The near sufficient basis is provided when the individual is viewed by
those within the system as unwelcome, potentially harmful, unnecessary, and an alien
within their midst.

What happened, very briefly, was that the psychologist (who in this instance was a
relatively humble and unaggressive individual) got caught up in a never-ending series of
political maneuvers having diverse aims, e.g., to circumscribe his activities and prerog-
atives, to influence his choice of research problems, to saddle him with the most time-
consuming and meaningless types of data collection, to have him stay out of the schools
and classrooms, to "prove" that certain existing programs were ineffective, and, finally,
to really rock the boat. By the time he resigned his position, many within the system felt
their worst fears had been confirmed while he felt that his status had deteriorated from
that of a stranger to that of an outcast.

One could say that the situation I have described is not peculiar to a school and that
one could find countless similar stories in other types of settings, for example, business,
industry, and so on. . . . Wherein then does the situation reveal the distinctive culture of
the school? The distinctiveness is contained in the fact that the participants, each in his
own way, were stating and defending attitudes, beliefs, theories—call them what you
will—about the purposes of education, the nature of teaching, the role of teachers, how

children learn, and how the school setting should be organized. It would be missing the point to view the situation as resulting only from personality clashes and resistance stemming from the operational fatigue characteristic of bureaucratic structures. Equally as important as these features are the points of view about people and learning which have histories and traditions that give meaning to activities and to the sense of professional identity. It is these points of view which are distinctive to the school setting. The attempt to innovate or change which does not take these points of view into account is inviting failure, assuming that such an invitation has not already been extended through autocratic decision-making and a confusion between laudable intent and self-defeating actions.

Another story concerns the "new math" which was being introduced into this school system at the same time my former student was starting in his position.[2] The new math had been introduced to the teachers in the previous summer through specially arranged workshops. From the standpoint of the administrative personnel, the introduction of the new math was considered the hallmark of their progressiveness, especially since at that time there were not many school systems which had made the transition from the old to the new. The psychologist was in his element; *he* wanted to learn the new math, observe it being taught in classrooms, and ultimately to devise studies comparing it to the old math. To his puzzlement there was little positive response to his interest and enthusiasm. It would be more correct to say that in diverse ways he was encouraged to focus on other problems. It was not until months later that he found out the following.

1. The teachers were never consulted about the change to the new math.
2. Although it was stated verbally that attendance at the summer workshop was not mandatory, it was the teachers' view that they had no alternative but to attend.
3. For some, perhaps many, teachers the learning of the new math was far from easy and was accompanied by much concern about their ability to teach it to their pupils when school opened.
4. The manuals which the teachers were to use were not considered by them to possess the virtue of clarity.
5. After the workshop and at the beginning of the school year most of the teachers were tense, anxious, hostile, dependent, and semimutinous about the new math. Weekly meetings with supervisors were instituted in an attempt to handle the problems the teachers were having, but with little apparent success.
6. There was apparently a marked discrepancy between what teachers said in public and what they said private about the new math.

And my poor former student, coming from another world, could not understand why his desire to learn and evaluate the new math received a cool reception!

And what light does this anecdote shed on the culture of the school? In my experience, it is representative of numerous instances and allows for the following generalizations.

1. Innovations or changes practically never reflect the initiative of teachers but rather come from the highest level of administration. As a group within a single school, or as the largest subgroup within a system, teachers are remarkably unrelated to the initiation of change. I can think of no other professional group which in its own setting takes as passive a role in the initiation of change. Teachers react to change, they do not initiate it.

2. Those who initiate change generally adopt means which maximize the strength of reactions which in turn only dilutes or subverts the intent of the innovation. Although this is not peculiar to the school setting, I think it occurs with a frequency which makes it a distinctive characteristic of the school culture.

3. In practice, schools and school systems are authoritarian social systems in which the "proletariat" (the teachers) overtly conform to what is expected of them but covertly resent their lack of power. This is particularly true of the urban school culture. One frequently hears teachers state that the public no longer has the degree of respect for teachers that it once had. What teachers tend not to say publicly is that they do not feel that they are accorded respect by those in administrative or supervisory positions in the schools.

4. Pervasive in the school culture is a suspiciousness of, hostility toward, and derogation of formal attempts to evaluate the effectiveness of educational, activities and programs. It is true, but nevertheless a misleading oversimplification, that these attitudes and reactions are unfortunate as well as obstacles to change. What is so frequently overlooked by critics is that reality frequently confirms the teachers' view that research and evaluation studies are initiated without seeking their opinions or suggestions, that these studies are inadequate or irrelevant, and that in one way or another these studies will serve as a basis for explicit or implicit criticism of teachers. From the standpoint of teachers they are the most frequent and convenient objects of criticism (from within as well as without the system) in regard to policies and programs which are not of their making.

Some might say that what I have been describing is not peculiar to the school setting and could in principle be found, for example, in business and industry. It is certainly not my position that schools are unique settings in that they are governed or explainable by principles which hold for no other social setting. The school setting is one in which, by virtue of traditions and the larger society, there are distinctive relationships among people, role attitudes, values, materials, and goals; and these distinctive relationships have a content, strength, and dynamic quality which crucially determine the fate of attempts to change any aspect of the culture or setting. Although these statements may be in the nature of the obvious, it is my contention that the failure to recognize the obvious or take it into account is primarily responsible for past and present resistance to change and for the tendency of change to fall far short of its intended mark.

Let me illustrate a few of my points by reacting to some statements by a proponent of the new math (School Mathematics Study Group, Stanford University, 1961). In concluding a presentation on student achievement in SMSG courses the following is said:

Suppose a school administrator asks, "Can I use SMSG or similar courses in my school? My teachers are inexperienced, or their background is poor. Few have attended summer institutes." On the basis of our present evidence we must answer, "We know of no reason why you cannot, providing your teachers have the proper attitude. If they are willing to try new courses, and if they try to judge the materials critically, there is no reason to expect trouble. If you can arrange for a mathematical consultant or an in-service program during the first year, so much the better!"

I interpret this statement to imply that the success or failure of the program will be a function of the *teachers' attitudes and the teachers only*. No caution is given to the school administrator about *his* responsibilities and attitudes, *his* way of presenting and carrying out proposals for change. There is no recognition that there is a means-ends problem which, when overlooked, can produce trouble, independent of teacher attitude and capability. In recent years I have had numerous opportunities to observe the teaching of new math and to have prolonged discussions with teachers about their experiences with and attitudes toward it. My experiences unequivocally support two conclusions: (1) Many teachers are in trouble with the new math; (2) the sources of trouble are many but among the most important are the consequences of how it was introduced to the teachers, the difficulty the teachers have in voicing questions, problems, and doubts which they fear will be construed as a lack of intelligence and competence, and the tendency on the part of administrators and supervisors to relate to teachers in a way that is not conducive to two-way conversations. When will we take seriously the blatant fact that a teacher is part of a complicated social system and that her effectiveness as a teacher must, *in part* at least, reflect her place in and her relationships with that system? The disadvantage of this way of thinking is that it removes the teacher as the convenient scapegoat for the ills of our schools.

One final point. My observations on the teaching of new math have convinced me that children learn the new math in much the same way they learned the old math, i.e., by drill and rote memory which is also the way many teachers had to learn it in a workshop. Most children can learn the new math. However, if you are one of those people who does not equate learning with thinking, and performance with competence, it must become clear to you that we must also be on guard against the dangers of equating change with progress.

Notes

1. It has significance in understanding the school culture that the private views of teachers to certain school activities are by no means similar to those they may voice in public. Whenever I have raised the flag-salute question with teachers, it has been after we have established a working relationship and a situation of mutual trust has developed.

2. The introduction of new math into a school system is described in more detail in Chapter 4.

CHAPTER 9

Underestimating Complexity

In this chapter Sarason examines the significant obstacles teachers face in seeking to extend the impact of successful ideas or practices beyond their own classrooms. When teachers make significant progress, they feel a natural inclination to want to spread the effects to their colleagues. But their efforts are nearly always thwarted by a the lack of adequate leadership training compounded by the unwritten codes that restrict teacher conversation mostly to the sharing of "war stories" rather than encourage the sharing of more positive results of teaching within a professional climate of collegiality.

Sarason reiterates, here, an example drawn from a proposal he first published in the journal *Teachers College Record* (May 1976)—to have teachers meet with the parents of their students, in one-on-one sessions, before the school year begins—and he analyzes the obstacles to implementing such an obviously useful idea.

Question for Seymour Sarason

Supposing an individual teacher does, in fact, wish to "try to have an impact on an entire school" instead of focusing solely on his or her classroom. What *personal qualities* seem most propitious of successful efforts—and what attributes tend to get individual teachers in trouble with their peers?

Sarason's Response

As I said with the previous question, the usual exceptions aside, a teacher's peers are likely to just not "get it." But one thing has changed, and that is the increased number of educators who in the quiet of the night conclude that schools—as they now are—are unrescuable. And the recently passed federal legislation (2001) will only make the situation worse in that it will increase the disparity between urban and suburban schools, a disparity that is already appalling. The more things change the more they remain the same. Again, there are exceptions, but when you examine them closely, they tend to confirm the general rule.

This does not mean that individuals who seek genuinely to improve the climate and the culture of the schools they work in should abandon the effort. Far from it. It just means that they should have no illusions that this work will be easy or rewarding. What does it take to "change" one's colleagues? I could list some qualities any self-propelled change agent might wish to possess, without giving any assurance that these qualities are all that is required. The list would begin with a willingness to take risks; to be self-reflective and self-critical; to reach out to parents and to students as full partners in teaching and learning; to treat colleagues not as "nay-sayers" or "blockers" but rather as people whose will to act has been severely damaged by the regularities of "the system." Need I continue? A sense of humor is also a useful thing to have.

On a most serious level, the name of the game is "constituency-building." That means that you build in step-by-step fashion a group who, together with you, will decide each of the next actions in the process of making a difference in the culture. The single individual wanting to change a school is not enough.

More about the obstacles to educational change in the classroom and school may be found in:

Educational Reform: A Self-Scrutinizing Memoir (2002)
Teaching as a Performing Art (1999)
Revisiting "The Culture of the School and the Problem of Change" (1996)
Parental Involvement and the Political Principle (1995)
You Are Thinking of Teaching? Opportunities, Problems, Realities (1993)
The Predictable Failure of Educational Reform (1990)
Schooling in America: Scapegoat and Salvation (1983)

When people advocate improvement of the quality of education, we cannot judge their advocacy unless we know who they are, that is, in what relation they stand to schools and the decision-making process. If the advocate for such a laudable goal is a classroom teacher, we assume that he or she is in a position to change something in a single classroom. We take for granted that whatever resources the teacher has are relevant to the goal of improving the educational experience and performance of students in that classroom. Let us imagine a teacher who has become convinced that instead of teaching by the "whole class" method, he or she will divide the pupils into small working groups in which students will take on more responsibility for their own learning: They will no longer be passive recipients of teacher input and direction, they will learn to use each other to handle assignments, they will have a more personal stake in what they do. Whether the teacher is right or wrong in being convinced is not at issue. The point is that we assume the teacher can institute such a change; we applaud a teacher who is dissatisfied with the way things have been and sets out to "reform" his or her classroom. One classroom, one teacher, one effort at improvement.[1]

But when teachers advocate educational reform, however, they almost never are referring to what they can or should do in their own classrooms. They refer to people and factors outside the classroom, which they see as being in need of change that would presumably have a positive impact on what happens in classrooms. Indeed, it almost has the status of a law to say that those who advocate an educational reform seek not to reform themselves but to change someone or something else. So, let us imagine that the teacher who gave up the "whole class" method of teaching concludes at the end of the school year that the change has had dramatically positive results, by whatever criteria one could employ. And now that teacher, stimulated by success, seeks to convince other teachers and the principal to change their attitudes and practices. Whereas before we could take for granted that in the single classroom the teacher had the resources, the responsibility, and the authority to institute a change, we cannot take for granted that in seeking to effect a change in all classrooms in that school the teacher has similar powers and responsibility. In fact, we would be justified in assuming that the teacher has taken on a task for which he or she is not prepared by formal training or even knowledge. Is that teacher perceived by others as a leader, an opinion maker? Does the teacher have the interpersonal skills to undertake such a task? Is the teacher willing to devote out-of-school time to discussing the issues and problems the change would require? Are there forums in that school at which the changes can be raised, discussed, and judged? Does the school or school system have resources and supportive services that can be utilized?

It is infrequent, bordering on rare, for an individual teacher to try to have an impact on an entire school. For one thing, there is nothing in the preparation of teachers that is relevant to such a task. And, as I have said countless times in the past, the culture of schools is inimical to collegiality in regard to intellectual-education-reform matters. But even leaving these facts aside, teachers can relate "war stories" about what can happen to those who try to change something outside of their classrooms, or about what happens to teachers who are the objects of someone else's proposal for reform.

There have been times, however, when a teacher has not been intimidated by others' failures and has spearheaded actions that changed a school in important ways. And in recent years, formal, system-initiated changes have taken place that give teachers responsibility to make changes. (Just as some teachers have organized their classrooms to give more responsibility to students, there are schools where teachers are being given new responsibilities.) Two problems have arisen. These were predictable, except no one dealt with the predictable. The first is that the new responsibilities required attitudes, knowledge, and understanding for which teachers had not been prepared. Learning to act in ways consistent with new roles collided with the need for and difficulty of *unlearning* old ways. At best, learning new ways is difficult; at worst, the old ways win out rather quickly. The second problem is that teachers vastly underestimated what one confronts in *sustaining* a change. In brief, what many teachers have learned is that reforming an existing organization and its problems is best left to those with unfulfilled reservoirs of masochism. There are exceptions, of course, and in later pages I shall return to why they have succeeded and are so rare.

Let me now give an example of a proposal that contrasts to existing practice, a proposal that illuminates the difference between repair and prevention. It is a proposal I first floated in 1975 (Sarason, 1976) and have managed to refloat every time I have talked with groups of educators, and those times have been many. Two points are noteworthy. First, never has any person disagreed with the proposal. Second, no one has seen fit to take it seriously in practice. In part, failure to implement the proposal may be explained by the fact that I stand in no formal relationship with a school and school system. There are other reasons, which will become clear after I present the proposal. Here is how I put it in 1976:

> I must confess that when I hear people say "we want to meet the needs of all children so that each child has the opportunity to realize his potentials" I do not know whether to laugh or cry—to laugh because behind that statement is the invalid assumption that to accomplish these goals all we need do is to hire more and more of the kinds of personnel who now inhabit our schools. This assumption, even if it were true, is scandalously unrealistic. And I want to cry because that well-intentioned statement fails to recognize that the problem primarily reflects our accustomed ways of thinking of what a teacher is, how a classroom should look, and how a school should be organized.
>
> Let me give an example with which most adults are familiar. When do most parents come to their child's school? One of these times is when they have been asked to come to discuss a problem in connection with their child. That is to say, they come *after* the school is fairly sure there is a problem, and usually that is well after the school found itself asking *if* there was a problem. The other time is several weeks after the school year has begun, when there is "open house" or "parent's night" usually in conjunction with the first PTA meeting. Parents are encouraged to come and visit their child's classroom, meet the teacher, hear about the curriculum, and to talk with the teacher about their child, if they so desire. These evenings are, by common consent, among the most uncomfortable, unsatisfying social rituals invented by humans—albeit one of the less hostile examples of man's inhumanity to man. At the end of the evening everyone breathes a sigh of relief that this charade is over, that a function designed to be informative and to redound to the interests of children has been lived through without casualties (except for the purposes for which the meeting was intended).
>
> Is there another way of thinking about how to get parents and teachers meeting around the individual needs of children? Can this be done so that the interests and knowledge of both stand a chance of being articulated in a way which could be used to meet the needs of individual children—at least to recognize these needs to a greater extent than they now are? Suppose that before the first day of class appointments are made with the parents of each child. (To make it possible for both parents to come, teachers would be available in the evenings and even over a weekend—you deliberately and willingly adapt to the circumstances of parents and not vice versa.) And suppose that the teacher said to the parents: "I was eager to get together with you before class begins because I wanted to learn as much as possible about your child so that I can be of as much help to him (her) as possible. Obviously, you know your child extremely well and even after I have gotten to know him I will not know him in the same way you do. You know his likes and dislikes, his strong points and weak points, what turns him on and what turns him off, what works with him and what doesn't. You know a great deal I ought to know if I am to treat and teach your child in ways suited to him—some ways are more suitable for some children than they are for others. So you can see that if I am to help your child you have to help me with what you know."

Note that you cannot talk to parents in this way unless you truly believe that what they can tell you will be helpful to you in your relationship with their child. If you view parents as hopelessly prejudiced and blind about their child, as people who do not or cannot recognize positive and negative features in their child, as people who would rather withhold than reveal information about their child—if you tend to view parents in these ways you usually structure your relationship with them so that you end up proving you were right in the first place. If, however, you are not intent on proving your superiority to parents, your all-knowingness, and you have no trouble accepting as a fact that parents can be helpful to you, that they can reveal "bad" things about their child, that indeed many parents want to do just that without the fear that it will be held against their child, you will learn a great deal which will help you react differentially to their child. In short, I am not suggesting role-playing but rather some values and a way of thinking about how you learn about individual children and how you begin a relationship with parents that is not likely to become an adversarial one, or one in which people talk to and not with each other. Whatever its other benefits would be, the relationship I am suggesting is far more humane than the dishonesties of Parent's Night or the usual after-school parent-teacher conference characterized by as much openness and candidness as a high-stakes poker game. Can there be any doubt that my suggestion holds out greater hope than present practice that a teacher will learn something which could be useful in meeting individual needs? To follow my proposal requires no additional money or personnel, just another way of thinking. But where will teachers be aided to think in these ways? As we (Sarason, Davidson, and Blatt, 1962) pointed out years ago: even though talking to parents is considered a crucial function of teachers—a function they are *required* to perform—they receive absolutely no instruction for the function in their training. Similarly, even though principals and other administrators spend a fair amount of their time organizing and running meetings, they too receive no exposure in their training to the issues (technical, theoretical, and moral) contained in such a function. Unless one believes that performing such functions is a matter of genes or divine guidance the issues have to be directly confronted in training. (Sarason, 1976, p. 578)

The obstacles to implementing such an approach are several. First, it requires a sincere belief that parents have knowledge important to your purposes. That, it must be emphasized, does not mean that what they tell you is hands-on-the-Bible truth. Let us remember that that is no less true for what *we* know and say. No less than parents, our knowledge and explanations are inevitably incomplete and in certain respects wrong. But the purpose of putting the cards on the table is to alter, enlarge, and combine differing perceptions and understandings. More than that, the purpose is to gain commitment from the participants to take on new, shared responsibilities. Educating children is not and should not be the sole responsibility of educators.

A second obstacle, of course, is time, the ubiquitous variable. In my 1976 remarks I said that the approach requires another way of thinking, not more money and new personnel. It is unlikely that all teachers would be willing to give that time freely. If that is true, it says less about greediness than it does about the adversarial relationship between teachers and administrators. There is one conclusion I have come to from my experience and that of others: When teachers, indeed all educators, come to see that a course of action is in their self-interest—that it will be personally, intellectually, and educationally productive—time as an obstacle is surmounted. One of the reasons most reforms fail is that they deal with the "form" of a problem and not its substance or context. You can proclaim the virtues of parental involvement, you can even legislate such involvement, but if you are ignorant of or insensitive to how the parties define their self-interests, you are engaging in self-defeating actions. You are making problems, not preventing them. The word *self-interest* tends to be viewed as reflective of selfishness or callousness. I trust it is clear that when I use that word I am referring to how people define themselves in regard to roles, goals, and obligations. It is glib to say to a group of educators, parents, and others that "we all share the commitment to a quality education for our children." Everyone nods in agreement but no one is prepared to acknowledge that different groups do not define their roles and obligations to that commitment in the same ways. To ignore those differences or to assume that goodwill alone will solve them is the grossest of misunderstandings of the nature, power, and inevitability of perceived self-interests. . . .

Note

1. The clearest, most succinct and balanced presentation of the theoretical basis of cooperative learning is that by Shlomo Sharan (forthcoming). As he points out, cooperative learning is a generic name that refers to several methods for the organization and conduct of classroom instruction, each method constructed on the basis of different theoretical orientations. His focus is on one type of "Group Investigation." What is so refreshing about this paper is that Sharan emphasizes, as he has in other writings, that for a teacher to *unlearn* the traditional "whole class" method of teaching and to *learn* and *appropriately* apply small group methodology is a personally and intellectually demanding and even upsetting process. That process is well known to the psychotherapist who having worked only with individual clients decides to try his or her hand at group psychotherapy. It is a different ball game, not one in which good intentions are sufficient. I have personally observed classrooms organized on a small group methodology but which in practice were suppressed with all of the features of the whole class method. . . .

CHAPTER 10

Programmatic and Behavioral Regularities

All schools have norms and procedures. But, as Sarason discusses here, we should not be deluded that these ways of "doing business" stem from a conscious and inclusive process of deciding what is best for the school environment. Into this discussion, Sarason introduces the notion of "programmatic regularities" and "behavioral regularities," forces that represent the weight of custom and are divorced from a rational assessment of educators' goals and purposes.

Because these mostly unexamined assumptions, about the way schools are and ought to be, often have "no intrinsic relationship to learning and education," they hobble change efforts from their inception. One such unexamined assumption concerns question asking. Sarason discusses the disturbing regularity that students —the beneficiaries of our instruction—ask very few questions pertaining to the material being taught (aside from those relating to assignments or upcoming exams).

This selection introduces Sarason's metaphor of the "Man from Mars" who peers down at our schools and cannot understand the logic of what he sees.

Question for Seymour Sarason

How does a teacher begin the process of encouraging colleagues (and perhaps also parents) to identify and examine existing "regularities" without coming across as a dangerous radical, an iconoclast, or a nitpicker?

Sarason's Response

I don't know. Actually, it is not that I don't know but that initiating a change process is not for the naive or faint of heart. Good intentions are not enough. One must also have

Reprinted with the permission of Teachers College Press from "Programmatic and Behavioral Regularities" in *Revisiting "The Culture of the School and the Problem of Change"* by Seymour Sarason (New York: Teachers College Press, 1996).

a relatively well-formulated conception of the obstacles ahead, as well as a time perspective that realistically assesses the strength of those obstacles.

As just one example, the goal of school literacy programs is to enable students to read. Fine. But—and with me there is always a "but"—if learning to read does not instill a *wanting* to read, to read *for pleasure* and for the stimulation of fantasy and imagination, the results offer no cause for satisfaction. The regularities of literacy instruction emphasize vocabulary lists and formulaic book reports. Unfortunately, teacher preparatory programs do little or nothing to engender *wanting to read*, and neither does the school culture.

More about school "regularities" as obstacles to educational change may be found in:

Educational Reform: A Self-Scrutinizing Memoir (2002)
Charter Schools: Another Flawed Educational Reform? (1998)
Teaching as a Performing Art (1999)
Revisiting "The Culture of the School and the Problem of Change" (1996)
Parental Involvement and the Political Principle (1995)
The Case for Change: Rethinking the Preparation of Educators (1992)
The Predictable Failure of Educational Reform (1990)
Schooling in America: Scapegoat and Salvation (1983)

The attempt to introduce a change into the school setting makes at least two assumptions: The change is desirable according to some set of values, and the intended outcomes are clear. . . .

The Existing Regularities

Let us approach the general problem of outcomes by indulging in a fantasy. Imagine a being from outer space who finds himself and his invisible space platform directly above an elementary school. Being superior to earthly beings he is able to see everything that goes on in the school. But he does operate under certain restrictions: He does not comprehend the meaning of written or spoken language, and it can never occur to him that things go on inside of what we call heads. He can see and hear everything and, being an *avant garde* outer-spacer, he, of course, possesses a kind of computer that records and categorizes events on any number of dimensions, allowing him to discern what we shall call the existing regularities. (Let me anticipate the discussion of the latter part of this chapter by advancing the hypothesis that *any attempt to introduce change into the school setting requires, among other things, changing the existing regularities in some way. The intended outcomes involve changing an existing regularity, eliminating one or more of them, or producing new ones.*)

Let us start with one of the more obvious regularities. Our outer-spacer will discern (but not understand) that for five consecutive days the school is densely populated while for two consecutive days it is devoid of humans. That puzzles him. Why this 5-2 pattern? Why not a 4-3 or some other kind of pattern like 2-1-2-1-1?

What if the outer-spacer could talk to us and demanded an explanation for this existing regularity? Many of us earthlings would quickly become aware that we have a tendency to assume that the way things are is the way things should be. But our outer-spacer persists. Is this the way it has always been? Is this the way it is in other countries? Is it demonstrably the best pattern for achieving the purposes of schooling? Does the existing regularity reflect noneducational considerations like religion, work patterns, and leisure time? Is it possible that the existing regularity has no intrinsic relationship to learning and education?[1]

The significance of an existing regularity is that it forces, or should force, one to ask two questions: *What is the rationale for the regularity?* and *What is the universe of alternatives that could be considered?* Put in another way: Can the existing regularity be understood without considering its relationship to the alternatives of which it is but one possibility? I would suggest that if we could peruse this issue in the case of the 5-2 pattern we would become increasingly aware not only of the universe of alternatives but also of the degree to which the existing pattern reflects considerations that have little or nothing to do with the intended objectives of schooling.

Let us take another "population" regularity. After a period of time our outer-spacer notes that at regular intervals (what earthlings call once a month) a group of people come together at a particular time in the evening. No small people are there, only big people. With few exceptions, the big people tend not to have been seen in the school during the day. The exceptions are those who are in rooms during the day with small people.

At this meeting most of the people sit in orderly rows, very quietly, and rarely say anything. When someone in these rows says something it is most frequently preceded by the raising of his or her right hand. There are a few people who do most of the talking and they sit in front at a table.

Several things puzzle the outer-spacer. For example, his computer tells him that there is no relationship between this meeting and any existing regularity during the day; that is, any existing regularity during the day is in no way affected by the occurrence of these meetings. This puzzles the outer-spacer because there are obvious similarities between the evening meeting and what goes on in the daytime. For example, both times most people sit quietly in orderly rows—in the evening big people sit quietly, while during the day it is the little people who sit quietly. At both times it is the big people "in front" who do most of the talking—in the evening there is one big person who talks the most, while during the day it is the only big person in the room who does most of the talking. What complicates matters for the outer-spacer is that he has seen that in both instances as soon as the people leave their rooms they speak much more, and they have a much greater variety of facial expression.

How do we respond to our celestial friend when he learns English and demands explanations for these regularities and similarities? What do we say to him about why there is no apparent relationship between what goes on at a PTA meeting and anything else that goes on at the school? What do we say when he demands that we tell him the alternative ways that were considered for organizing a PTA meeting or classroom, and the basis used for making a choice?[2]

Earlier in this chapter I said that "any attempt to introduce change into the school setting requires, among other things, changing the existing regularities in some way." At this point I would further suggest that this statement should be preceded by the statement that *the attempt to introduce a change into the school setting usually (if not always) stems from the perception of a regularity that one does not like.* We, like the outer-spacer, are set to see regularities, but unlike the inhabitant of the space platform we are not set either to observe the tremendous range of existing regularities or to inquire naively about the rationale for any one of them and the nature of the universe of alternatives of which the existing regularity is but one possibility.

Let us now leave both fantasy and heavenly friend and take up several existing regularities that not only illustrate the fruitfulness of this approach for understanding the school culture but also help clarify the problem of how to state intended outcomes in ways that are testable. . . .

The Arithmetic-Mathematics Programmatic Regularity

We turn to the arithmetic-mathematics regularity in order to see how easy it is to assume that the way things are is the way they should be, and to help grasp how difficult it is to examine what I have called the universe of alternatives. In an earlier chapter I alluded to the following programmatic regularity: beginning in the first grade and on every school day thereafter until graduation from high school the child receives instruction and drill in the use and understanding of numbers. Like eating and sleeping regularly, one may assume that this degree of regularity reflects considerations vital to the development of children.

The naive person might ask several questions: Would academic and intellectual development be adversely affected if the exposure was for four days a week instead of five? Or three instead of five? What would happen if the exposure began in the second or third grade? What if the exposure was in alternate years? Obviously, one can generate many more questions, each of which suggests an alternative to the existing programmatic regularity. From this universe of alternatives how does one justify the existing regularity?

Before taking up this question we must first deal with the emotional reactions I have gotten when on numerous occasions I have asked different groups (e.g., educators, psychologists, and parents) questions that challenge what exists and implicitly suggest that there may be other ways of thinking and acting. I focus on the emotional reactions because they reveal the distinctive characteristics of the culture more than other ways of understanding the setting, particularly if one is or has been a member of that setting. Because we have spent so much of our own lives in schools, and watched our own children in school, we may never be aware of the process whereby we uncritically confuse what is with what might be. In fact, in diverse ways, one of the most significant effects of school on children is to get them to accept existing regularities as the best and only possible state of affairs, although frequently this is neither verbally stated nor consciously decided.

The first response to my statement of alternatives is essentially one of humor; that is, the listener assumes that I intended something akin to a funny joke.[3] Having established myself as a comic, however, I usually persist and insist that I am quite serious. To keep the discussion going I then say the following:

> ▶ Let me tell you the results of an informal poll I have been conducting among friends and colleagues, and I will take this opportunity to get your answers to this question: When you think back over the past few months, how many times have you used numbers other than to do *simple* addition, subtraction, multiplication, and division? The results of the poll are clear: Highly educated, productive people very rarely use numbers other than in the most simple ways, leaving aside, of course, those individuals whose work requires more advanced number concepts (e.g., mathematicians). On what basis is it illegitimate to suggest that these results have no significance for the fact that a large part of what children learn in twelve years of arithmetic and mathematics is content other than the simple computations? Incidentally, I have also polled many far less educated individuals and, needless to say, the results contain no exception to the use only of simple computations. ◀

And now the fur begins to fly. Among the more charitable accusations is the one that I am anti-intellectual. Among the least charitable reactions (for me) is simply an unwillingness to pursue the matter further. (On one occasion some individuals left the meeting in obvious disgust.) One can always count on some individuals asserting that mathematics "trains or disciplines the mind" and the more of it the better, much like Latin used to be justified as essential to the curriculum.[4]

The fact is that whenever I have presented these thoughts I have been extremely careful to state them so that the words and sentences I employ do not contain any preference for any alternative, *simply because I have no adequate basis for choosing among the universe of alternatives*—and neither do the audiences. The intent of the thoughts is twofold: to indicate that there is always a universe of alternatives from which to choose, and to show that when any programmatic regularity is no longer viewed in terms of that universe of alternatives, rational thought and evaluation of intended outcomes are no longer in the picture, overwhelmed as they are by the power of faith, tradition, and habit.

A final example. What are the rites of passage for becoming a teacher? In most instances, following graduation from high school the person selects a college that has a teacher trainee program. The first two years of college are devoted to courses in the arts and sciences, and it is usually in the third year that education courses are taken preparatory to practice teaching and more advanced seminars. What if one required that anyone graduating high school and intent on becoming a teacher would have to spend one year learning the culture of the school? That is to say, it would be a year during which the person would have duties in different places (elementary, middle, and high schools; pupil personnel department; board of education meetings, etc.) that would *begin* to expand and deepen his or her understanding of educational rites. This would be a carefully organized and supervised year geared to observation of and experience with problems and issues that are distinctive to the educational scene. Some college credit would be given. How do I justify this recommendation when I present it to groups of teachers, administrators, and college faculty? For one thing, I point out, the usual teacher training program gives the student very narrow experience in schools . . . , an informational and conceptual narrowness that in no way can be considered adaptive. For another thing, at the present time the student taking education courses has no experiential basis for determining whether the picture of schools reflects the realities of schools. Put in another way, too many college faculty no longer have a firsthand, sustained experience with schools and, therefore, they ill prepare the student for what he or she will encounter. But the most clear, empirical justification for coming up with alternatives to present practices is, as Lortie (1975) has indicated, the feeling among teachers that their professional preparation was markedly inadequate. The reaction to my proposal has never been favorable. "Do you mean," I am asked, "that you would give responsibilities to people who never had an education course?" I answer, "Why not?" "Do you mean that someone right out of high school would be allowed to spend the year as you described?" "Yes."

I did not offer my proposal because I was convinced that it would be more effective than either the existing practice or any other alternative I or someone else could come up with. The fact is that I believe my proposal has some merit, but I believe even more strongly that the present practice has not been maintained *because* of its demonstrable superiority to alternatives. In listening to the defenders of the present practice, one comes away with the feeling that any departure along the lines of my proposal would be predictably harmful. They are unaware that for decades in the last and the present century those who became teachers had somewhat less than a four-year high school education following which they became teachers very quickly. And although we like to believe that anything we do today is obviously superior to the way we did those things in earlier times, we should try to be sensitive to the possibility that we are victims of "generational chauvinism."

These defenders of today's regularities are also unaware that at the height of the population explosion in the fifties and sixties, when there was a formidable teacher shortage, people were allowed to start teaching with no formal professional background whatsoever. Nobody has ever demonstrated that these people on average were more or less ineffective than teachers who had the formal preparation. The perceived universe of alternatives expands somewhat when there is an institutional crisis as there was during the population explosion. That expansion is dramatically greater when it is a societal crisis, e.g., during war. In wartime there is quick and willing alteration in standards, practices, and training, and here too there is no compelling evidence of harmful consequences.

The point of my proposal is that present practices are not choices rationally selected from a universe of alternatives. That we justify them as if they were so selected says far more about our capacity to delude ourselves and to resist the consequences of change than it does about the effectiveness of the present practice. This is not peculiar to people in the school culture. If I use the phrase "culture of the school," it is, of course, to suggest that there are features of that setting that differ from those of other settings. But in response to proposals for change, people in schools and other distinctive types of settings are similarly allergic to the implications of the concept of the universe of alternatives.

Thus far in this chapter we have discussed examples of regularities to which all within the school must adapt, since there is little or no element of individual choice. They are predetermined characteristics of the setting. Let us now turn to what might be termed *behavioral regularities,* which have to do with the frequency of overt behaviors. Laughing, crying, fighting, talking, concentrating, working, writing, question-asking, question-answering, test behavior and performance, stealing, cheating, unattending—these are *some* of the overt behaviors that occur with varying frequency among children in school. That they occur is important to, and expected by, school personnel. But what is equally important is that they are expected to change over time. *Behavioral regularities and their changes represent some of the most important intended outcomes of programmatic regularities. Deliberate changes in programmatic regularities are intended to change the occurrence and frequency of behavioral regularities.*

Some behavioral regularities are concerned with individual pupils while others reflect pupil-pupil interactions, such as boys with girls, older pupils with younger pupils, and black with white. As important as any of these are the behavioral regularities characterizing teacher-pupil interactions. We shall take up now a teacher-pupil behavioral regularity fateful for the intended outcome of any change in programmatic regularities.

Question-Asking:
A Behavioral Regularity

As in our discussion of programmatic regularities I shall not start with questions about assumptions, values, intended outcomes, or alternative patterns, but rather with the discernible regularity. It is, I think, only when one is confronted with a clear regularity that one stands a chance of clarifying the relationship between theory and practice, intention and outcome. Let us, therefore, start by asking two questions: At what rate do teachers ask questions in the classroom? At what rate do children ask questions of teachers?

From a theoretical and practical standpoint—by which I mean theories of child development, intellectual growth, educational and learning theory, techniques of teaching, presentation and discussion of subject matter—the importance of question-asking has always been emphasized. It is surprising, therefore, that there have been very few studies focusing on this type of behavior. Susskind (1969, 1979) did a comprehensive review of the literature. He expresses surprise that a type of behavior considered by everyone to be of great importance has hardly been investigated. However, he points out that although the few studies vary greatly in investigative sophistication, they present a remarkably similar state of affairs. But before we summarize the findings, the readers may wish to try to answer Susskind's (1969) question:

> Before exploring the research literature we suggest that the reader attempt to estimate the rates of two classroom behaviors. Imagine yourself in a fifth grade, social studies classroom in a predominantly white, middle-class school. During a half-hour lesson, in which the teacher and the class talk to each other (there is no silent work), how many questions are asked (a) by the teacher, (b) by the students? How do the two rates correlate? (p. 38)

The first two questions are deceptively simple because, as Susskind has made clear, there are different types of questions, and there are problems as to how questions (and which questions) are to be counted. For example, if the teacher asks the same question of five children should it be counted once or five times? Susskind developed a comprehensive, workable set of categories, and the interested reader is referred to his work. We will now summarize the answers to the above questions in light of existing studies, including the ones by Susskind, whose findings are very similar to those from older studies.

1. Across the different studies the range of rate of teacher questions per half hour is from 45–150.
2. When asked, educators as well as other groups vastly underestimate the rate of teacher questions, the estimated range being 12–20 per half hour.
3. From 67 to 95 percent of all teacher questions require "straight recall" from the student.
4. Children ask *fewer* than two questions per half hour. That is to say, during this time period two questions by children will have been asked.
5. The greater the tendency for a teacher to ask straight recall questions, the fewer the questions initiated by children. This does not mean that children do not have time to ask questions. They do have time.
6. The more a teacher asks "personally relevant" questions, the higher the rate of questioning on the part of children.
7. The rate of questions by children does not seem to vary with IQ level or with social-class background.

These statements derive from existing studies, but, as Susskind points out, scores of people have come to similar conclusions from informal observations.

We have here a clear behavioral regularity. How should we think about this? Is this behavioral regularity an intended outcome? Put in another way, this is the way things are; is this the way things should be? I know of no psychological theory or theorist, particularly those who are or have been most influential on the educational scene, who would view this behavioral regularity as a desirable outcome, that is, as one kind of barometer indicating that an organized set of conceptions are being consistently implemented. In addition, I have never read of or spoken to curriculum specialists and reformers who would not view this behavioral regularity as evidence that their efforts were being neither understood nor implemented. Finally, the fact that teachers and other groups vastly underestimate the rate of teacher-questioning (in Susskind's study teachers were quite surprised when confronted with the rates obtained in *their* classrooms) suggests that this behavioral regularity is not an intended outcome according to some part of the thinking of teachers.[5]

We have, then, an outcome that practically nobody intends, a situation that would not be particularly upsetting were it not that practically everybody considers question-asking on the part of teachers and children one of the most crucial means of maintaining interest, supporting curiosity, acquiring knowledge, and facilitating change and growth. . . .

But we cannot understand the question-asking regularity without briefly trying to understand what aspects of the school culture contribute to a state of affairs that few, if anyone, feel is the way things should be.

1. *Teachers tend to teach the way in which they themselves were taught.* I am not only referring to the public schooling of teachers but to their college experiences as well — and I am not restricting myself to schools of education. In general, the question-asking regularity we have described does not, in my experience, differ markedly from what goes on in college classrooms. The culture of the school should be expected to reflect aspects of other types of educational cultures from which the teachers have come. As suggested in an earlier chapter, university critics of the public schools frequently are unable to see that their criticisms may well be true of their own educational culture. It would indeed be strange if teachers did not teach the way they had been taught.

2. *In their professional training (courses, practice teaching) teachers are minimally exposed to theories about question-asking and the technical problems of question-asking and question-producing behavior—the relationship between theory and practice.* To those who may be surprised at this, I would suggest consulting the most frequently used books in educational psychology, learning, or child development courses. Such readers may conclude either that it is not an important question or that the obvious is being overlooked.

3. *Whatever educational help or consultation is available to the teacher (principal, supervisors, workshops, etc.) does not concern itself directly with the question-asking regularity.* Particularly in the earliest months and years of teaching, the primary concern of everyone is "law and order," and the possibility that discipline may be related to, or can be affected by, the question-asking regularity is rarely recognized. The anxiety of the beginning teacher about maintaining discipline too frequently interferes with sensitivity to, and desire to accommodate to, the questions and interests of his or her pupils.

4. *The predetermined curriculum that suggests that teachers cover a certain amount of material within certain time intervals with the expectation that their pupils as a group will perform at certain levels at certain times is responded to by teachers in a way as to make for the fantastic discrepancy between the rate of teacher and student questions.* This factor touches on a very complicated state of affairs. From the standpoint of the teacher, the curriculum is not a suggestion but a requirement, for if it is not met the prin-

cipal and supervisors will consider the teaching inadequate. In addition, the teacher whom the pupils will have in the next year will consider them inadequately prepared. Therefore, the best and safest thing to do is to insure that the curriculum is covered, a view that reinforces the tendency to ask many "straight recall" questions.

From the administrator's standpoint the curriculum is only a guide, and the trouble arises because teachers are not "creative"; that is, the problem is not the curriculum but the teacher. As many administrative personnel have said, "We *tell* them to be creative but they still stick slavishly to the curriculum as if it were a bible." To which teachers reply, "What they want to know at the end of the year, and what I will be judged by, are the achievement test scores of my children."

Although both sides *correctly* perceive each other's behavioral regularity, the administrator feels unable to change the state of affairs—that is, he or she is of no help to the teacher—and the teacher continues to feel unfree to depart from the curriculum. In short, we are back to a familiar situation in which no one sees the universe of alternatives to current practices.

There are, of course, alternatives. For example, as Susskind's studies show, there is variation among teachers in the question-asking regularity; some teachers can utilize a curriculum without being a question-asking machine and without requiring pupils to respond primarily to "straight recall" questions. In addition, and a source of encouragement, Susskind obtained data suggesting that when a group of teachers were confronted with the question-asking regularities in their classroom, and this was discussed in terms of theory and intended outcomes, the teachers as a group were able to change the regularity. *But here one runs smack into the obstacle of another characteristic of the school culture: There are no vehicles of discussion, communication, or observation that allow for this kind of variation to be raised and productively used for purposes of help and change.* Faculty meetings, as teachers are acutely aware, are not noted for either their intellectual content or their sensitivity to issues that may be controversial or interpersonally conflictful.[6] (As our man from outer space could well have discerned, the classroom, the PTA meeting, and the faculty meeting are amazingly similar in the question-asking regularity.) . . .

For our purposes here, what is most important is not the particular behavioral regularity or the factors that may account for it, but the obvious fact that within the school culture these regularities, which are in the nature of intended outcomes, are not recognized, and it is not traditional to have means for their recognition. What is not recognized or verbalized cannot be dealt with, and if it is important and not recognized, efforts to introduce substantive change, particularly in the classroom, result in the illusion of change. . . .

The purposes of this chapter were to state and illustrate the following:

1. There are regularities of various kinds.
2. Existing programmatic and behavioral regularities should be described independent of one's own values or opinions.
3. Regularities exist because they are supposed to have intended outcomes.

4. There are at least two characteristics to intended outcomes: (1) aspects of them are discernible in overt behavior or interactions, and (2) they are justified by statements of value (i.e., what is good and what is bad).

5. There are frequent discrepancies between regularities and intended outcomes. Usually, no regularity is built into the school culture to facilitate the recognition of such discrepancies.

6. The significance of any regularity, particularly of the programmatic type, cannot be adequately comprehended apart from the universe of "regularity alternatives" of which the existing regularity is but one item. The failure to consider or recognize a universe of alternatives is one obstacle to change occurring from within the culture, and makes it likely that recognition of this universe of alternatives will await events and forces outside the culture.

7. Any attempt to introduce an important change in the school culture requires changing existing regularities to produce new intended outcomes. In practice, the regularities tend not to be changed and the intended outcomes, therefore, cannot occur; that is, the more things change, the more they remain the same.

8. It is probably true that the most important attempts to introduce change into the school culture *require* changing existing teacher-child regularities. When one examines the natural history of the change process it is precisely these regularities that remain untouched. Conspicuous by its absence in the school culture, or so low in priority as to be virtually absent, is evaluation of the regularities of the kind we have been discussing. We hear much talk today about "accountability," which reduces to achievement test performance of pupils. If the pupils perform at grade level, the teacher is "good"; if the pupils perform below grade level, the teacher is "bad." I in no way downplay the importance of achievement when I say that when it becomes overwhelmingly central to discussions of accountability, it is at the expense of recognizing the significance (fiscal and psychological) of behavioral and programmatic regularities in the school culture. For example, I would maintain that to look at achievement test scores independent of the question-asking regularity is short-sighted in the extreme. (There *is* a difference between quantity and quality control.) Similarly, ... to permit the institutionalization of expensive, time-consuming procedures that are supposed to serve important functions and then to have no way of evaluating their intended outcomes is, to say the least, wasteful game playing. The issue is not what priority should be given to evaluation or research, but the seriousness with which one views any behavioral or programmatic feature of the school culture. Current discussions about accountability show an amazing insensitivity to the existence of behavioral and programmatic regularities. . . .

Notes

1. It is an interesting digression to suggest that one of the major sources of the conflict between generations is that the younger generation has the annoying ability not only to discern existing regularities but also to force the older generation to the awareness that there are alternative reg-

ularities. This, of course, the older generation finds difficult to accept because of the tendency to confuse the way things are with the way things should or could be. I remember as a child being puzzled and annoyed that no one could satisfactorily explain to me why one could not eat fried chicken for breakfast. It was obvious what the existing breakfast regularities were, but I could not understand why the alternative of chicken aroused such strong feeling.

2. Most people are aware that a good part of the controversy surrounding large urban school systems arises precisely because some community groups are pushing for an alternative way of implementing "community control," a way that would presumably change, if not eliminate, some of the PTA and classroom regularities described above. I say "presumably" because I have neither seen, heard, nor read anything to indicate that aside from changing the curriculum (as in the case of new or old math) there is any intent to change the most significant existing regularities in the classroom, for example, the passivity of the learner or the teacher as talker and question-asker. My reservation may become more clear later in this chapter when we take up in detail some of the existing regularities in the classroom. The point I wish to emphasize here is that those who are in favor of "community control" state their intended outcomes for the classroom, when they state them at all, in terms so vague and virtuous that they would defy subsequent attempt at evaluation—quite in contrast to the specificity of intended outcomes as to the role of parents in decision-making.

3. This reminds me of the suggestion that a former colleague, quite eminent, made in the course of a discussion about how a university could get rid of tenured professors who were "dead wood" (i.e., whatever contribution they made was a long time ago and there was no reason to believe that they served any function other than to stand in the way of younger teachers). His suggestion was that all beginning instructors be given tenure and as they get promoted (from assistant, to associate, to full professor) they have increasingly less tenure so that when they become full professors they have no tenure at all. The suggestion, of course, was treated as a joke and no one (including myself) considered for a moment that there *were* alternatives to the existing structure (the way things are is the only way things should be).

4. It is important for an understanding of the school culture, although it certainly is not peculiar to it, that one not assume that the *public* positions taken by groups within that culture are those held *privately* by all or most individuals comprising those groups. Many within the school culture question many aspects of programmatic regularities and are willing to consider the universe of alternatives. However, several factors keep this seeking and questioning a private affair. First, there is the untested assumption that few others think in this way. As we have said elsewhere (Sarason et al., 1966) "teaching is a lonely profession" despite the fact that the school is densely populated. Second, existing vehicles for discussion and planning within the school (faculty meetings, teacher-principal contacts, teacher-supervisor contacts, etc.) are based on the principle of avoidance of controversy. Third, at all levels (teacher, principal, administrator) there is the feeling of individual impotence. Fourth, there is acceptance of another untested assumption: that the public will oppose any meaningful or drastic change in existing regularities. In short, these and other factors seem to allow almost everyone in the culture to act in terms of perceived group norms at the expense of the expression of "deviant" individual thoughts, a situation conducive neither to change nor to job satisfaction. It was only after I had worked intensively for months in schools, and had developed a relationship of mutual trust with school personnel, that I came to see that there was a difference between public statements and private positions.

5. Children are the one group who realistically estimate or know the behavioral regularity. My informal poll of scores of children leaves no doubt in my mind that they view the classroom as a place where teachers ask questions and children provide answers.

6. The absence in schools of the tradition of the case conference, a vehicle whereby teachers present to and learn from each other, is discussed in a later chapter, where we take up Public Law 94-142, popularly known as the "mainstreaming" law. That law requires the spirit and procedures of the case conference. It remains to be seen whether the case conference in the school takes hold as a learning device for staff and a helping device for pupils and parents. To my knowledge, in all the research that is going on in relation to 94-142, there is not a single study on the "placement team" meetings.

CHAPTER 11

Confronting Intractability

In this essay, which opens the book *The Predictable Failure of Educational Reform,* Sarason lays out the fundamental obstacles to reform within the education system—the unreasoned similarity of schools to one another with regard to "classroom organization, climate, and rationale for learning" as well as the complex organization of our schools and the existing power relationships within them. He explodes popular slogans such as "Our goal is to enable every child to reach his or her potential" and castigates the "empty rhetoric" of presidential proclamations on education. After listing five common goals of school reform, Sarason explores the notion of systemic intractability to help explain why progress in reforming our schools has been so slow.

Question for Seymour Sarason

Are school systems as intractable as they appeared to you ten years ago, or have there been at least some positive indications that these systems are questioning some of their basic practices and "regularities"?

Sarason's Response

I cannot allow the exceptions to change my prediction that things will get worse rather than better. I am fully aware that people will regard me as a depressed cynic, or worse. All I can say in defense is that what I predicted in 1965, when I first began seriously to study the impact of a school's culture on prospects for school change, has been confirmed and continues to be confirmed.

Please note that my 1965 prediction was similar if not identical with the prediction John Dewey made in his presidential address to the American Psychological Association in 1899, when he cautioned that unless the field of education was embraced by the social sciences, the inadequacies and the inequities of schools would not be remedied.

More about the obstacles to educational change at the system and national level may be found in:

Educational Reform: A Self-Scrutinizing Memoir (2002)
Charter Schools: Another Flawed Educational Reform? (1998)
How Schools Might Be Governed and Why (1997)
Revisiting "The Culture of the School and the Problem of Change" (1996)
School Change: The Personal Development of a Point of View (1995)
Letters to a Serious Education President (1993)
The Case for Change: Rethinking the Preparation of Educators (1992)
The Challenge of Art to Psychology (1990)
Schooling in America: Scapegoat and Salvation (1983)

The title of this book [*The Predictable Failure of Educational Reform*] requires a brief initial explanation, if only to disabuse the reader of the idea that I am suggesting that we give up on reforming our schools, forget them, cut our losses, and pray that they do not get worse than they are. There are those who feel that way—although they do not say that publicly—but I regard such conclusions as at best irresponsible and at worst nihilistic. What has happened and will happen in our schools is fateful for our society. I also believe it is fateful for the world, given our country's role in it and its pervasive influences, positive and negative, on that world. What happens here is a difference that makes a difference in this world. There is more to it than that, however, and that is the fundamental question: How can we liberate the human mind to use its capacities in ways that are productively expressive of those capacities at the same time that they strengthen a sense of community? That may sound to some like high-blown rhetoric, or do-good utopianism, or unrealistic idealism. Why climb Mount Everest? Because it is there, answers the mountain climber. Analogously, in regard to the growth of the mind, we should set our goals high, very high, because we know that most people are capable of more than they do or are. Unlike Mount Everest, which *can* be scaled, we can safely assume that our idealistic goals for education will not be met for everyone. But that is no warrant for starting out with modest goals that further the chances that the self-fulfilling prophecy will again be unfortunately confirmed.

The fact is that what I have just said is in no way contradicted by the rhetoric of educational reform. Have you heard anyone say that it is *not* the goal of education to enable every child "to realize his or her potential" or deny that "a wasted mind is an individual and social tragedy" or assert that we do not "owe" children the best of what we know or can do? Why call this rhetoric empty? If this is but empty rhetoric, how do we explain all of the past efforts to improve our schools? Were these efforts token gestures intended to ensure that the more things change the more they should *not* change? Was (is) there a grand conspiracy to seal over unpleasant messes, an unwillingness to give life to the rhetoric? Of course not (with the usual exceptions). I attribute to the proponents of these efforts a sincerity I would want my efforts to be accorded. They were and are no less idealistic than I am. I regard their rhetoric as empty for one reason: They have been and still are unable to explain, really to confront, two things—the deterioration in the accomplishments of our schools and the *intractability* of our schools with respect to reform efforts. It is the failure to confront goals with the realities over time that shows pronouncements of Mount Everest goals to be rituals devoid of meaning and unrelated to the realities.

In the fall of 1989 an unusual event occurred, one that had taken place only twice before in the history of this country. President Bush convened a meeting of all state governors to discuss educational reform, really to begin a process of interaction between federal and state governments. In his campaign for the presidency, Mr. Bush had said that he wanted to be the "education president." Some people criticized the meeting—held on the campus of the University of Virginia, which was designed and beloved by the truly first "education president," Thomas Jefferson—on the grounds that it was motivated as much by political-publicity considerations as by a sense of urgency and crisis. I assume that there is a kernel of truth to the criticism. President Bush is a politician, a word I do not use pejoratively. But I also assume that he knows, and that his educational staff has told him, that the deteriorating quality of our schools has become an albatross to our society, now and for the future. The criticism is, however, clearly unwarranted for the governors, many of whom, long before the meeting, were spearheading reform efforts. Just as teachers and other personnel are near or on the firing line where the action is, the governors are nearer the action than the president.

The empty rhetoric was predictably in evidence at the meeting. Many proposals surfaced—for example, the need for a national policy, national standards of educational achievement, and higher standards for certifying educational personnel. As best as I can determine from reading accounts of the meeting and seeing parts of it on television, there were two agreed-upon implicit assumptions: The patient is sick, getting worse, but still capable of recovery; money is not the only or primary mode of treatment—that is, additional funding may or will be required but funding is not the answer. Apparently, no one saw fit to ask why, in light of the fact that in the post–World War II era we have poured scores of billions of dollars into our schools, do we have little or nothing to show for it? Granted that we could or should have spent more, should we not have expected more positive results so that this kind of meeting would not have been so necessary? Why have our efforts—and they were many and expensive—met with intractability? Why should we expect that what we will now recommend will be any more effective than our past efforts? Because of its failure to ask and confront these questions, the well-intentioned rhetoric is empty. Hope may spring eternal even though it may be powered by a repetition compulsion. Compulsive behavior is not noted for its rationality or its relationship to reality.

Let me explain what I mean by intractability by first listing the usual aims of educational reform. The aims are not discrete but overlapping. Although I have put them the way I think them, they do not do violence to what is contained in the usual rhetoric.

1. To lessen the wide gulf between the educational accomplishments of children of different social-class and racial backgrounds.

2. To get students to experience schooling as a process to which they are willingly attracted, not a compulsory one they see as confining and boring.
3. To enable students to acquire knowledge and skills that are not the consequences of rote learning or of memory of abstractions devoid of personal experience but rather acquired in a way that interrelates and gives personal purpose to present and future.
4. To engender interest in and curiosity about human accomplishments, past and present. To get students to want to know how the present contains the past—that is, to want to know this as a way of enlarging a personal, social, and "citizen" identity.
5. To acquaint students with the domain of career options and how schooling relates to these options in a fast-changing world of work.

. . . Generally speaking, these goals have not been met despite all the efforts at educational reform. I say "generally speaking" because you can always find instances in which these goals have been approximated. But whatever lessons have been drawn from these isolated instances, they have not been successfully applied and institutionalized elsewhere. When I say that schools have been intractable to reform, I mean that for the large majority of students, including most from nonpoverty backgrounds, the declared aims of schooling are empty rhetoric that bears little relationship to their social experience.

Further, I mean that the failure of educational reform derives from a most superficial conception of how complicated settings are organized: their structure, their dynamics, their power relationships, and their underlying values and axioms. Schools today are not what they were twenty or thirty years ago. They have changed but in the spirit of the popular song containing the line "I am true to you *in my fashion*," which means that the changes are cosmetic and not fundamental. Schools will remain intractable to desired reform as long as we avoid confronting (among other things) their existing power relationships. . . . Avoiding those relationships is precisely what educational reformers have done, thus ensuring that the more things change, the more they will remain the same. This does not mean that if you change power relationships, desired outcomes will be achieved. It is not that simple. Changing existing power relationships is a necessary condition for reaching goals, but it is not sufficient.

I shall argue that schools are distinctive but by no means unique as complicated organizations. Insofar as changing them is concerned, they are no different in their response to change than other complicated settings. As I shall attempt to show, there are some compelling and instructive nonschool examples of system change that illustrate how changing power relationships is a precondition for achieving desired outcomes. If the examples are few in number, it is because altering power relationships requires a degree of insight, vision, and courage that is in short supply among leaders of complicated organizations.

Within the past few years the issue of power relationships in school systems has been raised, and there are cases in which it has been taken seriously in practice. Although the issue has generated a good deal of discussion, that should not obscure the fact that the instances in which it has been taken seriously are truly minuscule in number. There is no ground swell, no welcome mat. Two things are troubling about these instances: They are being promoted as if there is no question about outcomes, and there seems to be no awareness that to alter the power status of teachers and parents, however necessary and desirable (and problematic), without altering power relationships *in the classroom,* is to limit drastically the chances of improving educational outcomes. Nevertheless, the fact that the question of altering power relationships has been raised, however narrowly, has to be viewed as a positive step, although the number of school systems that have gone the route of implementation is pitifully small.

. . . I must warn the reader that the scope of my analysis is narrow, as I wished to emphasize only those issues too frequently ignored. Thus, I touch only lightly on the relationship between schools and university programs for the training and education of school personnel, and then only in regard to existing power relationships. I have discussed those relationships in previous books (1973; 1983; 1983; 1986; 1988, with Davidson and Blatt), and did not wish to rehash them here. Suffice it to say, these programs—their intellectual substance, the nature, length, and scope of field experience, their criteria for selection and credentialing—in all respects contain the same issues that make for controversy about how to educate children in the classrooms of our schools.

The proposal that we move, formally or informally, to national standards for student achievement, teacher competency, and school performance has a long history but has received more serious discussion in recent years. How, the argument runs, can one expect that the quality of education will improve when we have thousands of autonomous school districts differing widely and wildly on many dimensions? (This is akin to Charles de Gaulle's comment about governing France: "How can you govern a country that makes five hundred different cheeses?") Is it not time to forge national criteria of excellence to which all school districts would or should aspire? Although it is understandable why such proposals get made—reflecting as they do a response to the intractability of the bulk of autonomous school districts to demonstrate improvement—they are examples of two things: missing the point and ignoring the obvious.

The obvious they ignore is the point that John Goodlad (1984) makes in his heroic study of public schools: Despite the many and obvious ways in which schools differ, they are amazingly similar in terms of classroom organization, atmosphere, and rationale for learning. The point they miss is that the classroom, and the school and school system generally, are not comprehensible unless you flush out the power relationships that inform and control the behavior of everyone in these settings. Ignore those relationships, leave unexamined their rationale, and the existing "system" will defeat efforts at reform. This will happen not because there is a grand conspiracy or because of mulish stubbornness in resisting change or because educators are uniquely unimaginative or uncreative (which they are not) but rather because recognizing and trying to change power relationships, especially in complicated, traditional institutions, is among the most complex tasks human beings can undertake. The first step, recognition of the problem, is the most difficult, especially in regard to schools, because we all have been socialized most effectively to accept the power relationships characteristic of our schools as right, natural, and proper, outcomes to the contrary notwithstanding.

That is why in this book I discuss the parallels between the perceived inadequacies of our schools and the growing dissatisfaction with private-sector organizations—that is, their decline in quality of product and competition. In both arenas the acceptance of existing power relationships has been disastrous. In drawing these parallels, I hope to disabuse the reader of the belief that the core problems in education are unique. They are different, not unique. In saying that, I cannot refrain from noting one respect in which our schools and society are unique, a point that is as obvious as it is grievously ignored or simply not taken seriously. We are all familiar with studies that demonstrate that, in terms of student achievement, the United States is significantly poorer than many other countries, such as Japan and Korea. These disconcerting findings, we are told, are proof positive that our schools are inadequate and in need of overhaul. Because these other countries have powerful, centralized, national standards and programs, such findings are used by some in this country to support proposals that we go down that road (just as there are some who argue similarly for a stronger federal role to stem the international decline of our private sector). It is both inexplicable and discouraging that discussion of these findings has virtually ignored the fact that the United States is unique in this world in the racial-ethnic-cultural composition of its population, a heterogeneity that in the past and present has no precedent. Indeed, in light of this fantastic heterogeneity one might seek to explain not why schools are as bad as they are but rather why they are as good as they are. It may be true that no country in human history has ever had anything resembling our immigration experience. I do not, however, offer these conclusions as an excuse, let alone a justification, for our educational ills, or as an argument for inaction. They are conclusions that indicate again how difficult it is to take the obvious seriously.

If . . . I adopt what some may perceive as a narrow perspective from which to view educational reform, I have to plead guilty. My defense is that in restricting myself to issues of power relationships, I am addressing issues that, if left unexplored and undiscussed, will limit drastically the desirable outcomes sought by any effort on any educational problem. For those who find themselves agreeing with my argument, I need to stress that changing power relationships is no guarantee that those alterations will lead to improvement in educational outcomes. One seeks those alterations because one has a special vision about what people are and can be. To confuse change with progress is to confuse means with ends. Keeping those ends in mind, informing as they should the means in the most pervasive ways, is a responsibility that too often fades into the background in the turmoil of change. The means become ends in themselves and, therefore, the more things change the more they remain the same, or worse. It is the rare revolution that has been true to its initial vision.

CHAPTER 12

Conceptualizing the Educational System

Continuing his attack on the forces of "intractability," Sarason explores the "lethal obstacles to achieving even modest, narrow goals" that may be explained by the "characteristics, traditions and organizational dynamics of school systems." He chides us for our superficial notions of who "the villains" are and identifies pitfalls that those within or without school systems face in conceptualizing systemic reform, such as in finding ways to understand and ameliorate the overarching issue of inequitable "power relationships."

Question for Seymour Sarason

It seems that, after ignoring "systemic" educational issues for decades (generations?), governments at the state and federal level are at last putting forth what they herald as truly systemic reforms. I refer to such initiatives as mandated nationwide standardized student testing, linking federal dollars to demonstrated school improvements, and other efforts to hold schools "accountable" for their students' success. There are also proposals for school vouchers for parents and increasing support for charter school alternatives.

While few of these measures seem to have pleased progressive educators—followers of Dewey among them—don't they at least represent, to you, a change of thinking regarding education qua "system"? Your big complaint when you wrote *The Predictable Failure of Educational Reform* in 1990 was that most of the large-scale studies on education "accept the system as it is." Like it or not, you can no longer blame our leaders for that same obstinacy, can you?

Sarason's Response

One can think of all kinds of changes that could be called "systemic" and yet would be repudiated by thoughtful people in an out of government. One could propose doing

Reprinted from "Conceptualizing the Educational System" in *The Predictable Failure of Educational Reform* by Seymour Sarason. Copyright © 1990 by Seymour Sarason. This material is used by permission of Jossey-Bass, Inc., a subsidiary of John Wiley & Sons, Inc.

away with compulsory education, or instituting a mandated, lock-step national curriculum, or federal funding for sectarian schools. There is no magic in calling a bad idea "systemic." What President Bush (the younger) and his conservative allies in Congress and in
the state Houses have proposed are reforms that cloak themselves in slogans—"leave no
student behind," "empower poor parents with options." But these reforms amount to
little more than punitive, short-sighted endeavors that are "systemic" mainly in their desire to weaken public education and to place the penalties for educational failure on the
backs of those least equipped to bear them—poor and minority students who may lose
whatever chance they have to receive a high school diploma because of high-stakes tests.
As I have written in this chapter—and in many other books—any reform effort, systemic
or otherwise, that does not change the inequities of power relationships in our schools
will fail to bring forth changes of significance. *What seems clear thus far, in the movement to impose national standardized testing and draconian measures of so-called "accountability," is that power relationships are, if anything, more unbalanced and unequal
than before.*

More about the obstacles to educational change at the system and national level may
be found in:

Educational Reform: A Self-Scrutinizing Memoir (2002)
Charter Schools: Another Flawed Educational Reform? (1998)
How Schools Might Be Governed and Why (1997)
Revisiting "The Culture of the School and the Problem of Change" (1996)
School Change: The Personal Development of a Point of View (1995)
Letters to a Serious Education President (1993)
The Case for Change: Rethinking the Preparation of Educators (1992)
The Challenge of Art to Psychology (1990)
Schooling in America: Scapegoat and Salvation (1983)

. . . For almost half a century I have witnessed and have been a participant in efforts generally to improve our educational systems. For much of that time, and in very diverse
forums, I advocated for this or that kind of change, always assuming that what I recommended would, if appropriately implemented, have the desired effects. And what I
recommended went far beyond helping individual teachers or changing a single school.
I had demonstrated to my satisfaction, and to that of others, that such important but
narrow goals were achievable if certain conditions existed. But precisely because such
conditions were infrequent—and even when they were met, sustaining the desired
changes was by no means assured—I came to see what should have been obvious: The
characteristics, traditions, and organizational dynamics of school systems were more or
less lethal obstacles to achieving even modest, narrow goals.

How does one deal with the abstraction we call a system embedded in and reflective
of a society that created and nurtured that system? Can such a system be altered from
within? Does it require changes and pressures from without, or does it require some
kind of transactional readiness from both sources? And how do we determine whether

we are tinkering with and even bolstering the system rather than changing it? And what do we mean by educational system? Do we mean how people are selected to enter the system? How, once selected, they are prepared to be in the system? In what relation do they stand to decision-making forums that affect them? And can one conceptualize the system apart from its relations to the political system and its decision-making processes, formal and informal? Are parents and others part of the system? And can one think of the system without students: their developmental characteristics, their assigned roles, their perception of the system and their roles in it?

It is noteworthy, indeed symptomatic, that the proponents of educational reform do not talk about changing the educational system. They will couch their reforms in terms of improving schools or the quality of education. And if there is any doubt that they have other than the most superficial conception of the educational system, that doubt disappears when one examines their remedies, which add up to "we will do what we have been doing, or what we ought to be doing, only we will now do it better." In the past decade there have been scores of reports—by presidential and gubernatorial commissions, by foundation task forces—about how to improve educational outcomes. I have read most of them (for insomniacs they are far more effective than barbiturates) and none of them addresses interrelated questions: In what ways do our recommendations differ from those made by comparable groups twenty or even fifty years ago? How do we account for what seems to be the universal conclusion that there has been a marked deterioration in the climate and accomplishments of our schools? Why should the solutions we offer make a difference? If these questions were not raised in the reports, it is not because they were not discussed among those who wrote them.

In talking to these commission members, as I have, one is struck by two facts. First, they think they know who the villains are: inadequate teachers, irresponsible parents, irrelevant or inadequate curricula, unmotivated students from whom too little is expected or demanded, an improvement-defeating bureaucracy, a lowering of standards for promotion and graduation, and a lack of competitiveness that would serve as a goad for schools to take steps to improve themselves. I use the word *villain* advisedly because the assignment of blame allows them to pinpoint their recommendations for change. In a truly basic way they indict the motivations of this or that group or practice, as if current conditions were willed. It is no wonder that implied in their recommendations is a "shape up or ship out" attitude. Someone once said that it is hard to be completely wrong, and that is the case with these commission reports. There are kernels of truth in their criticisms but these have been identified before and have led to actions that were obviously ineffective. Why should similar diagnoses and actions today be more effective?

The second striking fact one learns from talking with those who wrote and sanctioned these reports is that they accept the system as it is. Whatever changes they seek to make do not require altering the nature of the relationships among those who make up the system. I am reminded here of a discussion I had a couple of decades ago with an executive of a foundation that was pouring a great deal of money into New Haven generally and the school system in particular. After one of his visits, he told me that he was unimpressed with the pace, direction, and effectiveness of the efforts at reform in the

New Haven schools. I asked him, "If you could do what you wanted in the New Haven schools, where would you start?" He answered, "I would send all of the school principals to Mexico City to a two-year convention." Change the personnel and improvement will follow! He did not want to change the role of the principal in regard to other roles or participants in the system; he wanted to select principals who could "think," who would adapt to new circumstances. It did not occur to him that the principals he derogated, almost all of whom he had never met, might once have been thinking people imbued with a sense of missionary zeal that had been extinguished by a variety of features of the system. Why over time should new principals not experience the same fate? Here, too, one could say that this foundation executive was not completely wrong in that some of the principals he found wanting or incompetent deserved criticism, and even removal. But he was egregiously wrong in suggesting that the inadequacies were due only to their personality makeup, and in no way reflected the effects over time of the system on those within it. I am not excusing ineffectiveness, incompetence, or mediocrity. But when one concludes that almost all people in a particular role are inadequate, should one not ask what there is about the system that makes or sustains such failures in performance? And if that question is not asked, how can one assume that the new cadre of principals will not experience the same fate?

One can see, touch, and interact with people and things, but not with the abstraction we call a system. System is a concept we create to enable us to indicate that in order to understand a part we have to study it in relation to other parts. It would be more correct to say that when we use the concept *system* it refers to the existence of parts, that those parts stand in diverse relationships to each other, and that between and among those parts are boundaries (another abstraction) of varying strength and permeability. Between system and surround are also boundaries, and trying to change any part of the system requires knowledge and understanding of how parts are interrelated. At the very least, taking the concept of system seriously is a control against overly simple cause-and-effect explanations and interventions that are based on tunnel vision.

When you read the myriad of recommendations these commission reports contain, it becomes clear that they are not informed by any conception of a system. That is a charitable assessment. It deserves emphasis that none of these reports confronts the question of why these recommendations for changing this or that part of the system, which have been made in the past, have been ineffective. More upsetting is the question of why so many people think the situation has not remained the same but has deteriorated. Why, in the quiet of the night, do so many people think that the situation is hopeless?

The reader may find it helpful to engage in the following exercise. Imagine a situation where you are empowered to initiate one change, and only one, in a school system. There is but one restriction: The change cannot cost discernibly more money than is now available. What would that change be and why would you choose that one from the universe of alternatives? If you start with some conception of the nature of a school system, you will not quickly arrive at an answer because there is, one can safely assume, a surfeit of changes you deem necessary. But, as you can make only one change, on what basis should your decision rest? Obviously, you will seek that change which, if appropriately implemented (quite an assumption!), will have over time desirable percolating effects on other problems in other parts of the system. The important point is that you do not choose a change because it addresses an important problem—of which there are many—but because what you seek to change is so embedded in a system of interacting parts that if it is changed, then changes elsewhere are likely to occur.

The kind of thinking this exercise requires clearly did not inform the scores of commission reports written in the past decades. The reasons are many, not the least of which is that we are not used to or comfortable with thinking in terms of systems. It is a difficult and humbling way of thinking because you quickly come to see the complexity you are trying to understand and how little you know about how its parts transact with each other. And if you discuss your understandings with others struggling with the same task, it becomes clear that this thing we call a school system engenders reactions no less diverse than those to an ink blot. And if that diversity is small, or even nonexistent, the chances are extremely high that there will be disagreement about what would be the most productive changes with which to start.

There is, however, a problem prior to thinking in terms of a system. How does one come to know a system—to have those experiences with it that will act as a control against overly simplified conceptualizing, the drawing of unrevealing diagrams and charts, and parochialism of outlook and roles? Almost all of the people who have served on these commissions have no first-hand experience in school systems, apart from having been students when they were young albeit in a somewhat different world than that of today. Although one should not write off such prior experience as useless, conclusions drawn from it are hardly a basis for recommending actions. . . .

I am not arguing that if you have not had experience in schools in the past two decades, you should remain silent. To make that point clear, let me relate a conversation with a business executive who was part of a local task force to improve the school system. He had taken over a company that was on the verge of bankruptcy and over a period of five years had transformed it into a very profitable enterprise. I had been invited to a task force meeting, during which it became clear that he was committed to public education; he was dismayed, to say the least, at the inadequacies of the local schools; he was convinced that the schools required more firm leadership, a more explicit statement of goals, and more systematic processes of accountability. It is correct to say that the management aspects of running our schools was his central recommendation—that is, he recommended that principles of effective management in the private sector should be applied to the schools.

I sought him out after the meeting and had a long talk with him. Part of the conversation went like this (reconstructed):

SBS. Let us imagine that a new superintendent has just been chosen and he or she comes to you for advice. What are some of the things you would say to this person?

CEO. That is a hard question and I could not be specific in answering. I think I know in a general way what I would advise but I don't know that that would be helpful. After all, I am not an educator.

SBS. What would some of these generalizations be?

CEO. Well, the first thing I would advise is that he or she articulate specific goals that are concrete, comprehensible, and would receive general agreement. For example, one such goal would be a reduction in absenteeism of students and staff. Who are these absentees? How quickly are those with the most frequent absences identified and who follows them up and how quickly are they helped to be where they are supposed to be? You don't collect such data at the end of a school year or every few months, long after a pattern has been established. You develop procedures that tell you or your staff quickly what is going on in these respects and require you to take remedial action.

SBS. That makes sense. What about another generalization that should lead to action?

CEO. What I am going to say now is touchy and truly is the test of leadership: You have to institute ways of evaluating the competency of your administrative staff to do what they are supposed to do. And that is also true for the teachers they supervise. In fact, I would tell the superintendent if at the end of the first year, you have not gotten rid of any employee, teacher or staff, or if the number is very small, something is wrong. Given what we know about this school system, and I have heard no one say that it is other than inadequate, it seems obvious that more than a handful of people should not be in the system. I would tell him or her that I am not advocating a witch hunt but an adherence to standards that must be met. If the superintendent waffles in these matters, that person is not doing his or her job.

SBS. What about one more piece of advice?

CEO. I suppose I should say what is obvious but rarely taken seriously by school systems, this one at least. There is a budget and you have to stay within it, a fact that should be made clear to everyone. It would be nice, of course, if the budget could be larger but that is not in the cards, given the nature of the economy of this city. There is a bottom line and that is fiscal responsibility.

SBS. May I shift the direction of our conversation? I know that several years ago you took over your company, which was near bankruptcy. Today it is thriving and growing. Why did you buy this company? More specifically, what experience did you have with the manufacture of the products they made?

CEO. I knew very little in a technical sense about their manufacturing process. I . . . knew their products, which had enjoyed quite a good reputation before they began the downhill slide. When I studied the situation—their financial sheets, conversations with some of their executives and managers—I decided that I could turn things around.

SBS. When you took over, what was your game plan? What were the *predictable* problems you would have to confront?

CEO. I am not sure I know what you mean. Obviously, I and the staff I brought with me would have to find out where the problems were. And by problems I mean people, departments, and processes. Some of the problems we knew, others we would have to discover.

SBS. Let me ask it in another way. What thought, if any, did you give to how people in the organization would view you?

CEO. I see what you mean. I expected two reactions: One was relief that new life would be breathed into the organization, and the other was fear that heads would roll, divisions would be eliminated, and all kinds of changes would be required.

SBS. Did that worry you?

CEO. It sure as hell did because those fears were not only real but if I didn't address them the situation could deteriorate quickly and really get out of hand.

SBS. So what did you do?

CEO. I spent one day drafting a two-page letter that went to everyone, but everyone. In it I told them that I knew how they felt and that they had reason to be concerned. But I also said that no quick action was planned. I outlined a plan by which people at different levels would meet among themselves and come up with recommendations about how the company could be improved. No one would sign their name to the report which would come to me. And what I emphasized was that I was serious about getting their recommendations.

SBS. What reason did you have to think that they would believe you?

CEO. I knew they wanted to believe me but that that belief was surrounded by doubt and fear. Look, I came up the hard and long way. I have worked at every level of a manufacturing company. I have seen companies from the bottom, the middle, and the top. And I am not patting myself on the back when I say I know how rank-and-file people see things. In fact, for a week after we came on the scene, I and my staff visited and discussed my letter with each division and arranged for them to meet several times for one hour. The message we conveyed was that we wanted to be judged by what we would do and not what we had said. We were not giving them "released time" as a sop as they went to the guillotine.

SBS. That strikes me as unusual thinking and action.

CEO. Maybe it is. But I have learned, and it pays off, I can assure you, that in these situations my self-preservation requires good morale in others. You not only have to listen, but you have to *hear* what people are saying and feeling, and you have to feel respect for them even though they are not telling you what you want to hear. That letter was only the first step in demonstrating *in action* that I would try never to act unilaterally.

SBS. It sounds as if you spend as much time listening as talking.

CEO. I spend more time listening.

SBS. Can you tell me briefly what you expected from these initial reports?

CEO. (Laughing.) Two things. The first is that I would learn a lot about what people at different levels in different divisions perceived to be important problems. The second, and the reason I laughed, is that I expected that people at a particular level would in some way see those below them as a source of problems. Not always, of course, because I expected that in a few instances those above them would be blamed. But in general I expected, and was right, that blame is downward assigned. Except, of course, for those at the bottom of the pyramid who can only assign blame upward. That is what I call standardized operating procedure for assigning blame and coming up smelling roses.

SBS. Are you saying that you cannot understand one part of the organization apart from the others? That problems are never self-contained? That it is truly a system of interlocking, interacting parts?

CEO. Isn't that obvious? You had better believe it.

SBS. One more question along these lines. Once you decided what the problems were and what needed to be done, what did you expect would happen?

CEO. I am not sure I know what you mean. One thing I knew for certain was that the big problems were ahead of me.

SBS. Now I am not sure what you mean.

CEO. To say it the way I thought it: I knew that when the changes were announced, it would be an example of the shit hitting the fan. Things were going to change and who, in these situations, likes change? In fact, I wrote another letter that went to everyone explaining the changes and saying in bold print that I knew that change was never easy and I sought their understanding, patience, and cooperation.

SBS. You expected resistance, in some quarters at least?

CEO. Of course. If I didn't know that, if the staff I brought with me didn't know it, we could be dead ducks. *I* owned the company but my fate was ultimately in their hands, which means everyone else in the company. Let me be clear on that point: I was never in doubt, and I made sure no one else was in doubt, about who would make final decisions. But I made it clear that no decisions would be made unilaterally—that is, without people feeling that they had had a hearing or that I or my staff had listened and discussed matters with them.

SBS. From what people have told me, things went well.

CEO. They went well but not easily, then or now. (Teasingly.) But I haven't told you my ace in the hole.

SBS. What was that?

CEO. I instituted a profit-sharing plan. If I win, they win.

SBS. It is getting late and I have to get back to New Haven. So let me put to you one more question that has bothered me in our conversation. It is less a question than it is a kind of paradox and I hope you will not take it as criticism. When I asked you earlier about the advice you would give to a new superintendent of schools, you articulated what I consider to be some superficial generalizations which in no way indicated that you had any usable knowledge about how hierarchically organized, complex human systems work and how they are experienced by those within them. But when you talked about how you went about changing a deteriorating complex organization—how you thought, the values you hold, your sensitivity to how people experience and can be adversely affected by a system, the obstacles to *and* the opportunities for change—a picture emerged that in no way informed what you said to a new superintendent taking over your schools.

CEO. You mean I know much more about school systems than I give myself credit for?

SBS. That you had better believe.

CEO. (Laughing.) Are you saying that I should or could be a superintendent of schools?

SBS. Yes and no. The answer is definitely no if your question implies that heads of large private businesses think and act the way you do. I have met and talked with many chief executive officers and very few have your style of thinking and acting. . . . They would advise a new superintendent the way you initially did. Indeed, in terms of style of thinking and acting, and the values that undergird them, superintendents and their "management staff" are more like than unlike private business executives. The answer is yes in *your* case if only because you strike me as someone with that rare capacity to transfer knowledge appropriately from one realm of experience to another, even if those realms seem to be wildly dissimilar. They are different in very important and crucial ways but far from totally different.

CEO. You don't sound optimistic about improving our schools. If what you say about superintendents is true—and intuitively I think you are right about them and my counterparts in the private sector—we are really in trouble.

SBS. I am the opposite of optimistic. But I do not want to scapegoat superintendents. They came up in the system and they are products of it. Like your counterparts, they are, with few exceptions, bright, well-intentioned, hard-working people. But they are products of a system and they are imprisoned in it. There are some exceptions.

CEO. I must confess that ever since I agreed to serve on this and that task force or committee having to do with the school system—and reluctantly had to decline nomination to the school board—I would occasionally entertain the thought that I could make a good superintendent.

SBS. I think you would, not because you are a successful businessman but because of several other factors: You have an articulated but sophisticated understanding of complex organizations; you are sensitive to what happens to and among people in a hierarchy; you are respectful of their attitudes and needs; and you seem to believe that anyone who will be affected by change should stand in some relationship to the formulation and implementation of that change.

CEO. Thanks for the compliments. I never would have described myself that way. Whenever I am asked to account for my success—and I find that a very embarrassing question I do not like to be asked—I say two things: I learn from my mistakes and I have no difficulty owning up to them quickly and publicly.

I have no doubt that if this unusual man had been on a presidential or governor's commission to make recommendations for improving schools, he would heartily have approved and signed a report that in no way reflected his experience in a complex human system. In his own bailiwick, he had a comprehensive conception of a system. Sitting on a task force, he saw only unconnected parts. Having little or no hands-on experience in schools is a very serious limitation on those with the responsibility to make recommendations for improving them. Ignorance is no virtue. It is, in this case, a mammoth obstacle because it reinforces the misconception that schools are not complex systems having many of the features of other types of complex systems. It is one thing to say that school systems are different, it is quite another to say they are unique. Having read scads of commission reports, I can only conclude that they rest on the invalid assumption that school systems are unique systems.

The reader should not conclude that I believe that educational reform should be left to educators—that is, that they possess a sophisticated conception of schools as systems. Teachers, principals, supervisors, curriculum specialists, superintendents, members of boards of education—with rare exceptions, those who belong to these groups think and perceive in terms of parts and not a complicated system: *their* parts, *their* tasks, *their* problems, *their* power or lack of it. If there is any doubt about this, one should pose, as I have, a specific problem or issue to each of these groups for their recommendations. The responses are so varied, often so conflicting, that one might conclude that a school system seems for its members to have the features of an ink blot. Of course, each group knows that there is a "system" but each sees it from a particular perspective which, by its narrowness, precludes understanding of any other perspective.

One might expect, for example, that those in administrative positions, each of whom had occupied lower-level positions (as teachers), would in their recommendations indicate a sensitivity to and comprehension of those below them—that is, one would expect a discernible degree of overlap in their perspectives. That is rarely the case. Predictably, they see themselves as adversaries. They literally do not understand each other, and by understand I mean being able to comprehend, to try to comprehend, how and why people in different roles see matters so differently, how and why the system engenders and sustains such radical differences in perspective, and why explanations of these differences in terms of "personality" contain but a small kernel of truth.

I have been in the habit, whenever I have met with educators in a system and it appeared opportune, of asking them why adversarial attitudes and stands are predictable features of a school system: a mini United Nations in which the pursuit of narrow self-interest is all-pervasive. I take pains to point out that I do not hold the utopian view that it is possible to have a complex social system in which intergroup conflict is truly minimal, let alone absent. But why, I ask, is the level of adversariness in school systems, especially urban ones, not only such a conspicuous feature but seemingly so self-defeating of everyone's goals? When taken together, the replies add up to a litany of blame assigned to those above or below the particular group's role level, mostly below. . . .

I have presented two conclusions which together explain in part why educational reform either is not attempted or is carried out in an institutional context of which the reformers have little or no knowledge. The first conclusion is that those outside the system with responsibility for articulating a program for reform have nothing resembling a holistic conception of the system they seek to influence. In principle, I have argued, that ignorance need not be lethal, although it almost always has been. The second conclusion is that being part of the system—part, so to speak, of the school culture—in no way guarantees that one understands the system in any comprehensive way.

This has been an old problem for the anthropologist planning a study of foreign culture. The anthropologist knows that as a stranger, an outsider, one can make some egregious errors of omission and commission even if one has read whatever is available about that culture. (Unlike outsiders on educational task forces, the anthropologist zealously tries to learn as much as possible about the subject.) There are advantages and disadvantages to being an outsider, but the anthropologist knows that, once on the scene, the live culture will differ in striking ways from what one has learned by reading the relevant literature. The anthropologist also knows or expects that different individuals in that culture will not describe the culture in identical ways. Indeed, for some of his or her purposes, no one in the culture can provide relevant information because what is sought rests on axioms that no one in the culture has put into words. In any event, the most fateful decision the anthropologist has to make once on the scene is to determine who would be reliable informants about what the culture is, how it works, and what are its interacting parts and system characteristics.

In short, the anthropologist does not want to make the mistakes that so many foreigners make when they come to study the United States, or that the United States made in its foreign aid programs after World War II. Mistakes in understanding are one thing; when they become the basis for action, it is quite another thing. In education the mistakes in conception and action have been many, and almost all of them derive from an inability to comprehend the nature of school systems. This inability prevents dealing with the question of how one decides where the change process should begin, because that is the starting point from which changes elsewhere will occur.

But one cannot ask that question if one's stance is: There is problem A we have to do something about, there is problem B, there is problem C, and so on. When each problem is posed and attacked separately, when each of a number of important problems is considered equally important in terms of its system implications, the chances of failure are very high. This is not to suggest that all important problems be attacked at the same time. It is necessary but not sufficient to try to understand how these problems are interrelated and reflect the nature of the system. What is crucial is to decide which of these problems should be a starting point, because if one deals successfully, even in part, with that problem, changes elsewhere in the system are likely to occur over time. The importance of a problem is but one criterion for choosing a starting point.

There is, I have come to conclude, a ubiquitous feature of complex human systems that should inform thinking and action in regard to educational reform. It is a feature that, if not taken seriously, invites failure. This is the fact that any social system can be described in terms of power relationships. Power is distributed unequally among the members of the system, and there is always a rationale for this unequal distribution of power. Put in another way, that differential allocation of power is justified by tradition and necessity; it is a way of ensuring that the overarching goals of the system will be effectively achieved. There is not only a division of labor but also a differential assignment of power in regard to planning, policy formulation, decision making, and implementation.

All of this is obvious and taken for granted until it becomes clear, as in the case of school systems, that the system is not achieving its stated goals. In the case of our schools, one would have hoped that there would be recognition of the probability that the failings of the system derive in part from the nature of existing power relationships—that this pattern of relationships is no longer adequate or appropriate. (The most inspiring and instructive example is how the constitutional convention of 1787 struggled with the issues of power in the face of the inadequacies of the power relationship contained in the earlier Articles of Confederation.) With two exceptions, the existing pattern of the distribution of power never informed the goals of and methods for change. There was nothing wrong with that pattern; the problem was defined as getting better people to use their assigned powers more effectively! The idea that the distribution of power needed to be changed was never addressed.

In the plethora of commission and task force reports of the last decade, the possibility that power relationships should be altered is never raised, even if one reads between the lines. And, yet, if anything is clear from the efforts to reform our schools in the post–World War II era, the relative or total failure of these efforts can in large measure be attributed to a gross insensitivity to how power was employed in the planning and implementation of change. Any effort to deal with or prevent a significant problem in a school system that is not based on a reallocation of power—a discernible change in power relationships—is doomed. This is not to say that in and of itself a particular reallocation of power will have positive consequences, but such a change is a recognition that a feature of the system has been confronted. And if the situation is favorable in regard to implementing and sustaining such a change, that change in power relationships can have percolating effects in the system qua system.

Now for the two exceptions. One is the rise in strength and influence of teacher unions, a development that at its core sought to change existing power relationships. The other exception is Public Law 94-142, the Education for All Handicapped Children legislation of 1975, a key feature of which was to change power relationships between parents and educational decision makers. In neither case did school systems react warmly—to indulge understatement—to this threat to existing power relationships. They were, so to speak, forced to accommodate to the threat. That should not occasion surprise. People rarely embrace a restriction or alteration in the scope of their accustomed powers. If reformers have steered clear of dealing with alternatives in patterns of power relationships, it is testimony to both a reluctance to change the system and an unwillingness to confront the conflicts such changes inevitably engender. The result has been that reformers rivet on problems they can deal with and gloss over problems they often regard as more important but too controversial.

In one report sponsored by a prestigious foundation, it is recommended that teachers should have a role in decision making, on the grounds that if teachers are to be truly professional they should have more power over matters affecting their everyday practices. That recommendation received a good deal of play in the public media, and was warmly supported on the editorial pages of our national newspapers. Unlike some other recommendations in that report, which were very clear, concrete, and specific in terms of action and funding, the one about increasing the power of teachers was couched in the most general terms. What should that recommendation mean for action? What educational decision-making processes should teachers be part of? Why will such a recommendation be difficult to initiate and sustain? Why is it likely, perhaps certain, that the recommendation will go nowhere? If one is an optimist, as I am, one is grateful for small favors and therefore heartened that this power issue has been raised, albeit generally and innocuously. If one is a pessimist, as I am, one is disappointed but not surprised that the report writers refrained from pursuing in any detail why the recommendation must and will encounter an obstacle course. . . . When the recommendation about changing the role of teachers in decision making was initially made, the then secretary of education, and the national organization representing school administrators, proclaimed publicly and unambiguously that they considered the recommendation stupid and an invitation to chaos. Again, their response should occasion no surprise. . . . Any educational reform that does not explicitly and courageously own up to issues surrounding changing patterns of power relationships is likely to fail. That prediction is based on the feckless consequence of educational reform in the past half-century.

CHAPTER 13

Predictable Features and Problems in the Creation of Charter Schools and Other New Organizational Settings

In this selection, drawn from two chapters of *Charter Schools: Another Flawed Educational Reform?*, Sarason includes charter schools within his critical observations about "new settings," a topic he explored in depth in *The Creation of Settings and the Future Societies* (1972). Here he focuses on the first year of a charter school's development—its sense of uniqueness, the constraints it labors under, how leadership is defined and enacted, how resources are viewed, and so forth. He comments on the "messiness" of new settings in relation to stated and cherished visions, and highlights the tremendous impact of time, leadership, and social forces in "the external surround," especially in the first year of an organization's existence.

Question for Seymour Sarason

You have been, in recent years, directly involved with charter school formation and development. Amid your high hopes that charter schools represent a holistic change strategy, you have worried that failure to rigorously document their successes and shortcomings will rob us of the ability to learn from them. Are you still as worried, or do you see that the significant success of at least some charter schools will keep the movement itself from the dismal fate of other reform efforts?

Sarason's Response

Charter schools will slowly become part of a history of failed reforms because, as you indicated, they were not set up to be seriously evaluated. We will never have the kinds of data that will stand up in a court of evidence. It is as simple and as sad and as depress-

Reprinted with the permission of Teachers College Press from "Charter Schools" and "Predictable Features and Problems" in *Charter Schools: Another Flawed Educational Reform?* by Seymour Sarason (New York: Teachers College Press, 1998).

ing as that. In my little book, *Questions You Should Ask About Charter Schools and Vouchers* [2002], I go into somewhat more detail about the sources of my deep pessimism and disappointment than I did in *Charter Schools: Another Flawed Educational Reform?* There recently was a most comprehensive review by the Rand Corporation of the published literature on vouchers and charter schools substantiating my prediction. The basis of my prediction—which goes beyond vouchers and charter schools—applies to all reform efforts, past or present. I deal with this in many pages of my most recent book, *Educational Reform: A Self-Scrutinizing Memoir.* In that book I scrutinize my own mistakes, errors of omission, commission, and misplaced emphasis, and I suggest how data relevant to a reform can be obtained.

I doubt that anyone will take me seriously; there are far too many people who view evaluation as a simple process to be scheduled for some time in the future rather than before and during implementation of the reform. I learned a lot about myself and the field from writing that book.

I mean, why be difficult when with a little bit of effort you can be impossible? I know that there are more than a few people who ask themselves that about me! I understand their irritation. What they do not comprehend is that the more you think, know, and act, the more you have to think, know, and act, because in the realm of human affairs there are no final solutions.

More about the creation of charter schools and other new educational settings may be found in:

Educational Reform: A Self-Scrutinizing Memoir (2002)
Questions You Should Ask About Charter Schools and Vouchers (2002)
Crossing Boundaries: Collaboration, Coordination, and the Redefinition of Resources [with Elizabeth Lorentz] (1998)
Political Leadership and Educational Failure (1998)
Barometers of Change: Individual, Educational, and Social Transformation (1996)
The Predictable Failure of Educational Reform (1990)
The Making of an American Psychologist: An Autobiography (1988)
The Challenge of the Resource Exchange Network (1979)
The Creation of a Community Setting [with F. K. Grossman and G. Zitney] (1972)
The Creation of Settings and the Future Societies (1972)
The Psycho-Educational Clinic: Papers and Research Studies (1969)
Psychology in Community Settings: Clinical, Educational, Vocational, Social Aspects [with Murray Levine, I. Ira Goldenberg, Dennis Cherlin, and Edward Bennett] (1966)

The charter school movement is the most radical challenge ever to the existing system. Although it has never been stated, let alone recognized, by national and state political leadership, you do not have to be a logician to conclude that charter schools are based on the opinion that the present system is unrescuable (Sarason, 1998). That is to say, the present system is by itself incapable of reforming itself, of innovating in ways that support or do not defeat the spirit of an innovation. What the legislation says to would-be innovators is, "If you have a way of improving the quality and outcomes of schooling and you cannot implement that way within the system, here is an opportunity to get out of the clutches of the system." A majority of the state legislatures have permitted a small number of charter schools to come into existence. In the 1996 presidential campaign the president said he would ask Congress to support the creation of 3,000 more charter schools.

Charter schools are as clear examples of the creation of new settings as one will find. At the present time most charter schools are in their early phase of existence. It is fair to say that we know little of how they are doing and why. In regard to the "before the beginning phase" nothing is known, as if all that preceded rolling out the welcome mat for entering students in no way did or would play a role in the life and outcomes of the school.

The fact is that no legislation, national or state, included funds to observe and record in an independent, dispassionate way the "story" of the school, including the before-the-beginning phase. That did not surprise me, and for two reasons. The first is that the creation of a new school—or any new setting—is associated with imagery of organizational-engineering-administrative issues, not with conceptual, interpersonal, philosophical, interinstitutional issues. And, I repeat, it is imagery that assumes that all that went before the setting became operational is best deposited in a museum of dead history, until, of course, later developments may stimulate you to visit that museum. The second reason is that political leaders, again national or state, almost never (I would say never) support an educational initiative with the funds and means on the basis of which it can be determined how experience with model A of the initiative should be used to develop model B. They proclaim the virtues of model A as if it will not require changes, as if in the real world of human affairs a new, complicated social-educational institution will not require revision and improvement. . . .

I have talked at length with four individuals who are in the process of creating a charter school, i.e., they are in the before-the-beginning phase, their proposal has been approved. Without exception they described a litany of obstacles "erected" by the school system from which the charter school personnel and parents came, or from the state department of education, or from local officials, or all of these. As one of them put it, "It is as if we were creating a leper colony." Precisely because a charter school is an implicit criticism of and challenge to the existing school system, opposition to it is not surprising. In each instance the opposition took subtle, or bureaucratic, even direct form, and in each instance the direct and indirect opposition came as a surprise to the creators. Indeed, in two instances the leaders were sorry they had engaged in the venture. One of these leaders—a person who had national visibility—made it her business to seek out others who were creating charter schools. She said, "Many of these people are afraid publicly to vent their spleen about the hurdles put in their way. They are afraid of offending because it may have adverse consequences down the road."

My sample of interviewees may be atypical but that is the point: Charter schools are not being created in a way that will permit us to determine how experience in the before-the-beginning phase affected the planning, morale, and cohesiveness of those responsible for these schools. I assume that charter schools will vary in what they experience and how they cope with that phase; they will not all be horror stories as my sample of interviewees might suggest. Relating what I have was primarily to emphasize that the before-the-beginning phase is a crucial one in the creation of a setting, a phase that cannot be ignored by anyone who wishes to understand the life course of that setting. . . .

No one seeks to create a new setting that will be a replica of an existing one. In some way or ways the new setting will be superior to, better than, more distinctive than comparable settings. The new setting is intended to demonstrate that its end "product" will be an improvement over comparable settings. In a purely psychological-phenomenological sense the new setting will be more than distinctive, it will be unique, it will not be a clone of comparably labeled settings. Its uniqueness may be a new idea, mode of organization, quality of end product (material or human), and the qualitative benefits members of the new setting will experience. It is the sense of uniqueness that is so powerfully motivating and captivating to the creators-leaders. It is that same sense of envisioned uniqueness that causes creators-leaders to be almost exclusively future oriented. Initially at least, they are far more clear about what the new setting will look like and accomplish than they are about what they will have to do, the resources they will need, and the time it will require to achieve their purposes. They know this in an abstract way, but they are so captivated by their vision of the future and the power of their sense of uniqueness that they hope and believe that with the "right" kind of people and resources attaining operational status will not present difficult problems. It is an exaggeration to say that the creators-leaders see the road ahead as paved with engineering issues, but it is not an exaggeration to say that they see that road as a straightforward one requiring the garnering and organizing of human and material resources.

External Constraints on Creators-Leaders

Far more often than not the new setting emerges from and is embedded in a larger existing organization which has decided a new setting is necessary or desirable. That decision may come about because someone has convinced the organization that such a new setting would enhance it and that he or she should create and direct it; or the decision is made because the person appropriate to lead it is available. Although the new setting is embedded in the larger organization, the new setting is seen as independent for all practical purposes. The point here is two-fold. First, there is verbal agreement about why the new setting is being created and what it will accomplish. Second, there is verbal agreement about what resources will be available to it. At this stage there is no thought to the maxims that "the hand that feeds you is the hand that can starve you" or "those who empower you are those who can disempower you." All is sweetness and light, there is no reason to expect serious problems. No one asks what will or might happen if there is change in leadership of the larger organization or there will have to be a decrease in support for the new setting; or as is frequent, the new setting requires more support than was expected.

There is another factor rooted in organizational realities: One can never assume that
the decision to create the new setting was happily greeted by all people of varying power
in the larger organization. Some will see the new setting from a zero-sum stance. What
the new setting gets, the older parts lose. Some will see the new setting as "privileged,"
as enjoying a freedom they do not have. Some will see it as an implied criticism of their
part in the larger organization. The leader of the new setting may know all of this—he
or she has experienced life in a complicated organization or system—but that knowledge is overwhelmed by the enthusiasm and optimism with which that person greets the
opportunity to create the new setting. He or she is preoccupied with the future, with
what needs to be done, with what will be, not with present or past organizational history, traditions, and what I call organizational craziness: the omnipresent struggles
around power, status, and resources.

I am not asserting that any or all of the above will play an important, negative role
in the creation and development of the new setting. I do assert that what I have described
are *potentially* powerful external constraints on the new settings, especially because the
leader of the new setting ignores them or does not devise means to keep the potential
constraints from becoming actual ones. It is beyond my purposes to suggest how these
potential constraints can be contained. But it is central to my purpose here to say that
almost all leaders of new settings I have known have said that they belatedly learned that
preoccupation with the internal development of the new setting blinded them to the importance of potential sources of constraint. As one of these leaders said to me, "I didn't
realize that I should have been not only secretary of internal affairs but foreign affairs
as well."

I have discussed potential sources of constraint coming from the larger organization
in which the new setting is embedded. In the large and sprawling arena of the human
services the external constraints on a new setting which is not embedded in a larger organization are far more actual than potential; more correctly, the potential becomes actual very quickly. For example, in the mid-sixties one of the War on Poverty programs
resulted in the creation of new community agencies in urban areas, the purpose of which
was to develop new and better programs for poor, underserved populations. I was involved in Community Progress Incorporated (CPI) programs in New Haven. Two things
were clear from the start. First, CPI would serve the inner city in ways that the traditional social agencies had not and could not serve. Indeed, the leader of CPI said to me
that he wanted to stay as far away as possible from any meaningful relationship with
those agencies which he regarded as dinosaurs. Second, those social agencies saw CPI
as a competitor for resources and as having an antiprofessional stance. Each had disdain for the other. Each wished the other would go away. Almost from day one it was
CPI versus a variety of social agencies.

The fact is that CPI could have benefited from some of the agencies' expertise, but its
stance was such and it was so preoccupied with its internal development that it never
sought to deal with those agencies. But it was also a fact that those agencies felt left out,
criticized, rejected. CPI had a hostile surround which it could ill afford. I cannot say that
if CPI had paid more sensitive attention to those agencies, to "foreign affairs," some of

its problems (which were many) would have been less severe. But I can say its stance made for constraints on what it wished to accomplish. Many of the War on Poverty programs had a short, checkered career, and at their root was the lack of any conception about the minefield the creation of settings has to traverse in today's communities. Legislation, money, enthusiasm, and the most laudable goals in no way guarantee that new settings will develop and survive. I urge the reader to consult Moynihan's *Maximum Feasible Misunderstanding* (1969).

Another instructive example are the hundreds of Youth Bureaus spawned by federal and state legislation. Youth Bureaus were never intended to provide direct service to young people but rather to interconnect existing independent community social agencies, each of which had programs for young people. Blumenkrantz (1992) has well described how existing agencies resented and resisted any such role for the Youth Bureaus, which they regarded as interlopers as well as reflective of an implied criticism that their programs could have greater impact by more connections among agencies. . . .

From the standpoint of the creation of settings the issue is not clarified by a "good guy vs. bad guy" dichotomy. The issue that those who create new settings cannot ignore, as they almost always do, is that by coming into existence the new setting will not be viewed neutrally or positively by all individuals and agencies in the community surround. Matters are not helped any if the leader of the new setting publicly proclaims that it has a more innovative, better, more important mission than existing agencies. Such proclamations may very well be true, but they carry a price: They flush out those individuals and agencies who, for one or another reason, will resent such a message and will seek ways to constrain the new setting. That price is not recognized because the leader of the new setting is so drawn to the future and the internal development of the setting that he or she pays little or no attention to "foreign affairs."

Time Perspective, Time as Enemy

I have known leaders of new settings who knew that there were external individuals and agencies who were potential critics of and constraints on the new setting but had never given thought to how the potential might be prevented from becoming actual or, at least, diluting the force of the actual when it might surface. In these instances, the single most important factor that caused the leader to pay little attention to such thinking and actions was time. That is to say, he or she comes quickly to perceive that the process of creating a new setting involves so many minor and major steps and problems that there is little or no time to deal with other than matters of internal development. That is especially the case when a date has been set (or required) for the new setting to open its doors. For most leaders this is the first time they have had the responsibility to create a new setting; they "grew up" in developed settings, the characteristics of which made the creation of a new one so alluring. In the abstract they knew that time is a limited, precious resource, but it is only when they begin confronting the realities of creating a new setting, that the abstraction takes on personal meaning; time does not pass, it seems to fly. The external surround recedes. Its potential for creating later problems gets little attention. The psychological here and now rivets on "getting things going," on "tooling up," and the external surround recedes more and more in to the background.

Let me paraphrase what creators of settings have said to me: "I get the import of your questions. You are implying that I and my colleagues should have dealt with a variety of individuals and agencies whom we knew might, for one or another reason, take a dim view of what we were creating and why. You are suggesting that we should have made a serious effort to get them on our side, to listen to their views, and to do this sincerely and respectfully. Today, now that we have become operational, I agree with you. We would not have some of the bedeviling problems we now have. But if we were having this discussion in the months before we opened, I would have said that you didn't understand how much time it would have taken to do what you seem to be suggesting we should have done, and that you were assuming the payoff would be worth it. Looking back, however, I would do things differently. We might, and I emphasize *might,* have made life easier for ourselves."

I quite agree with the use of the word *might;* there are no guarantees that dealing with potential sources of external criticism and constraint will be successful. But I have known of too many instances where not dealing with those sources early on aborted the creation of the setting, and there are even more instances where those sources, either in the before-the-beginning phase or in the early operational phase, influenced the new setting in ways that undercut or altered what was distinctive about the new setting. Time is a precious commodity, the use of which has to rest on a dispassionate judgment of who in the external surround may come to be an obstacle to the mission of the new setting. And, as some leaders will attest, some of those external sources come later to confirm the maxim that "with friends like that we have no need of enemies."

I am sure that the reader has already concluded that I regard the creation of a setting as both a kind of once-in-a-lifetime challenge and opportunity as well as an extraordinarily trying one. To engage in the venture with the expectation that a good idea, motivation, and enthusiasm will be sufficient, that our social-institutional world will be hospitable or easily bendable to the needs of the venture, that the success of the venture will depend solely or even primarily on its internal characteristics, is illusory; such expectations contribute to disillusionment, and what is predictably trying becomes even more so. There is no way the creation of a setting can avoid being a trying one. I do believe that when we begin to appreciate (indeed acknowledge) what creating a setting entails, the rate of failure will decrease. Let us go on to other features which in their own ways are as crucial as they can be trying.

The Core Group

Choosing a core group who will play major roles in the creation of the new setting is the first task of the leader. When the new setting is but a *possibility* in the leader's mind, that person has discussed the possibility with colleagues who the leader thinks will be supportive (at least) and perhaps would want to be part of the possible new venture. As we know, the word gets around and the number of people who approach the leader may be considerable because they view the possible new setting as more interesting and fulfilling than the one in which they are now working. Once it is made public that in fact the new setting will be created, the number of interested individuals further increases. Up until that time the leader may have tentatively decided whom he or she would want to have in the core group: those who will have major positions of responsibility. Once it is publicly known that the new setting will be created, the leader gets "down to business" with those he wants to attract. He talks individually with each of them.

Although usually unnecessary, the leader unreflectively adopts a "selling" stance which almost always (I would say always) conveys several messages: The new setting will be one happy family, the person will have the opportunity to implement the unique mission of the setting, personal and intellectual rewards and recognition will be considerable. This, of course, is what the person wants to hear. It is very understandable that these discussions are suffused with goodwill and high hopes. But it is almost always the case that these initial discussions lack substantive detail. That is to say, there is little or no discussion about governance and structure and style, resources and their allocation, development of constituencies, criteria by which to judge progress, and the role the core members will play in choosing the additional staff which will be needed. The implicit assumption is that once the core group has been chosen matters of substance and organization will get clarified. The other implicit assumption is that the core group and the leader are in such agreement about the significance of the goals of the setting that any disagreements that may come up will be satisfactorily resolved.

Not always, but very often, the members of the core group know each other at varying levels of intimacy. If they know each other, it may be they have never worked together. And to assume that they like and respect each other is to indulge in wish fulfillment. How they regard each other depends in part on how much of a voice each member had in selecting their counterparts. If the leader independently and serially selected the members, it becomes difficult for any of them to voice reservations about the choices; the disjunction between what one thinks and what one can say can have untoward consequences. Nor does the *order* in which the members were chosen go unnoticed. Like it or not, we all live in a world where we are made sensitive to symbols of importance and status. Choosing a core group may be a narrowly conceived personnel task, but it has or can have personal and interpersonal consequences which surface later, depending on the style and sensitivity of the leader. . . .

Once the core group has been selected, there follows a series of meetings about how to develop the setting consistent with its innovative purposes. What should be the first, second, and third steps? Where the housing of the new setting has already been decided, who will have what space for the functions for which he or she will be responsible? When housing has to be located, what locations are available and by what criteria should they be assessed? In light of available fiscal resources, what would be an acceptable compromise? When and by what procedures and criteria will such additional staff be chosen? Who will participate in selection? What can we do to avoid actions that are inconsistent with our purpose? The questions are many (if not endless) if only because creating a setting is a process in which one goes from an idea to an envisioned complicated reality in which a ruling principle is that solving one problem gives birth to new ones.

It is at these meetings when it becomes apparent that the members of the core group *and* the leader may not be in agreement about many things. Some of the core group may find that their conception of the new setting is not the same as that originally conveyed by the leader. Some may conclude that the leader is more attentive to and influenced by one or two members of the group. And it is inevitable that each core member begins to make judgments about the adequacy, judgment, trustworthiness of the other members. The extent and consequences of these judgments are largely determined by the leader's sensitivity, style, and interpersonal skills. What I am describing is complicated, subtle, tricky business, which does not mean that the consequences are always serious or lethal. But I have to say that of all the troubled settings I have known, observed, or read about, it was dynamics, composition, and conduct of those early planning meetings where the seeds of trouble were sown, and they did not sprout until some time later. Creating a setting is an intellectual and interpersonal affair, and we should not be surprised that it brings to the fore the best and the worst of people. Humans are social animals, which is to say that in their commerce with each other the manifestation of their assets and deficits will vary considerably, especially if the process and context is one they have never before confronted.

Leaders

There are parents who should not be parents, physicians who should not be physicians, teachers who should not be teachers, and psychologists (or psychiatrists) who should not be treating patients. And the same is true for leaders of organizations, especially if the organization is one yet to be created and which by design is intended to be distinctive and better than other organizations, an intention the leader has never had to actualize. Management theorists and researchers say that there are leaders who are effective only if the economy is robust and change, restructuring, and sacrifice are not necessary; there are other leaders whose style is tailor-made for periods of economic recession. So, I will amend what I said above by saying that a leader of a new setting that has failed of its purposes or went out of existence *may* be more successful in leading a chronologically mature organization. The important point is that there be a match between the leader and the requirements of a new setting. Most leaders of the new setting are self-selected because the conception was theirs, they have given time and energy to gain support for the venture, and they appear to have the appropriate administrative skills. Those who "officially" appoint the essentially self-selected leader have as little experience with or knowledge of the process and problems of creating a new setting as the person they appoint.

Let us begin with a deceptively simple question. Why does the person seek to create a new setting? The person will say that he or she wants to demonstrate that his or her innovative ideas and vision will not only prove to be superior to the outcomes of more traditional settings but will cause these other settings to change. It will be a demonstration that the particular field will be unable to ignore. I make no judgment how realistic those ideas and visions are. That is not the issue here. The issue is the degree of strength of the different motivations powering the seeking of leadership. It is understandable if conceiving of the necessity and importance of a new setting gives you a sense of ownership, of understanding, of competence in regard to overseeing the effort. It is also understandable if you wish to be recognized and applauded for the success of the venture; you may consider it unseemly to express that wish to others but the wish is always there. The wish for anonymity is of zero strength in those who seek leadership.

And it is also understandable if the sense of ownership motivates you to protect your ideas and role against criticism and change regardless of whether they are well intentioned or not. And precisely because it is highly likely that you have never created a setting before, you will strive to keep your doubts, insecurities, and anxieties to yourself, masking them by a display of confidence and the possession of a clear direction. And no one who seeks leadership believes that he or she lacks the skills to "handle people": to motivate them, to gain their loyalty, to get the best out of them, to forge a happy family in which everyone gives and gets. It is also a belief that one can handle situations in which members of the family in some ways interfere with "smooth" functioning of the setting.

Thousands of books have been written about leaders and leadership. Little in that literature is about leaders of new settings, and what there is is retrospective in nature, the retrospection coming years after the setting was created or went of existence. There is little about the complicated phenomenology of leaders of new settings, what in my 1972 book I have called the "socialization of the leader." From what I have read, personally experienced, and learned from the experience of others who have started new settings, there are several factors or attributes on each of which leaders vary and *in combination* vary even more from a positive to a negative extreme.

1. Power or authority is an omnipresent motive, although self-imposed controls over its manifestation can mask its strength. There are leaders in whom the power motive is so strong and unacknowledged as to justify characterizing their actions as an "ego trip." There are other leaders whose personal doubts, insecurities, or morality are so evident as to cause others to view him or her as lacking leadership qualities. I say *morality* because some of these people experience the display of power as the equivalent of an unwarranted expression of hostility, as a departure from the strictures of morality.

2. There is always a disjunction between what a leader thinks and feels about others in the setting and what the leader will say publicly. Some leaders strive to maintain a sense of treasured privacy and are almost totally unaware of how this is seen and in-

terpreted and reacted to by others. On the other extreme some leaders make a fetish of "openness" and are puzzled by the consternation and problems it engenders in others.

3. Leaders vary considerably (I would say wildly) in how sensitive they are to criticism, how they control the display of their sensitivity, and their tendency to interpret criticism as a general attack on their competence and ideas. Some leaders are incapable of admitting a weakness or mistake. Some are so insecure that they seek to mollify a critic by too readily accepting the criticism (and often the advice).

4. Because of the strength of the "happy family" fantasy, some leaders cannot accept the reality that there will always be problems, functions, and disagreements and slowly take actions which distance themselves from what is going on in the setting. On the other extreme are leaders who accept the reality but do not want to live with it: The leaders leave the setting. There are, albeit a few, leaders who accept the reality, deal with it forthrightly, and do not unduly blame themselves for problems that recur again and again. As one leader said, "I agree with President Truman. If it is too hot in the kitchen, get the hell out. I'm staying in this kitchen and taking the heat."

5. Creating a setting is a process which makes it very easy to forget that there is an external surround containing individuals and agencies who are potential sources of constraint. There are leaders who initially know that but soon forget it as they become more and more riveted on the myriads of problems with which the new setting confronts them. And then there are those leaders who begin to distance themselves from the setting by frequent forays into that surround as much to deal with "foreign affairs" as to avoid experiencing the surfeit of problems, many of which are instances of problem creation through problem solution.

None of these factors is discrete. They become interrelated in varying ways and strengths at different times. They are called into play when the leader selects and organizes the core group; when additional staff come on board; when a long series of meetings is held where the whys, wherefores, methods, governing rules put flesh on the bones of the abstractions contained in its distinctive mission; when the pressures and stresses increase as opening day looms; when after opening day it becomes apparent that not every contingency was planned for and that some aspects of the planning had been inadequate; when the realities of being operational put limits on collegiality and rational thinking; when the functions of each part of the organization become less aware of other parts and the overall mission is no longer the sole source of purpose and mission.

Throughout this developmental process the actions and behavior of everyone, including the leader, play both a cause and effect role. The socialization of the leader does not take place in a social vacuum, and that is no less true for everyone else. The actions and behavior of the leader are more pervasive and percolating than those of anyone else, but that should not obscure the fact that the actions and behavior of the leader are in part determined by what others say or do. A stimulus-response psychology to describe and understand what happens and why is utterly inadequate. If creating a setting is a horrendously—I use that word advisedly—complicated affair, so is the task of describing and comprehending what is going on and why. Indeed, the reason so many new settings fail of their purposes is that leaders underestimate the complexity they will encounter. Precisely because they never created a new setting, they have no conceptual road map by which to proceed. That is why leaders cling so dearly to the belief that goodwill and strong motivation will somehow or other allow them to overcome any and all obstacles.

We are used to hearing that the leader sets the "tone" of the setting. There is truth to that, but it is incomplete and even misleading. It is true in the sense that leaders do seek to set the tone, but if the leader expects that the tone will be interpreted and reacted to in the same way by everyone else, it can cause problems, minor or major. To confuse intent with accomplishment is a folly to which many leaders are victims. If eternal vigilance is the price we pay for liberty, eternal sensitivity is the price the leader pays to avoid the consequences of failing to take seriously that the tone he or she hears and projects is not the one *everyone else* has. That is a price that leaders on an ego trip are not able or willing to pay; deviations from the tone are regarded as inherently threatening, not a basis for self-questioning but rather a basis of criticism directed to others.

When we say the leader sets the tone, we ordinarily intend to convey in a shorthand way an overall affective feature of a setting: friendly, sullen, relaxed, tense, buoyant, subdued, etc. It is a way of characterizing the quality of relationships in the setting. However, precisely because a new setting is justified in terms of new ideas and concepts—it will be an improvement over comparable settings—tone is never independent of how clearly those ideas are articulated, examined, reexamined. Regardless of whether the setting is new or old, it will be comprised of people whose personalities—temperament—are not, to indulge understatement, made for each other. In a new setting there is the additional burden of two factors. The first is that few, if anyone, in the setting (including the leader) have ever been part of creating a new setting. Second, the new ideas and concepts are just that: new, not yet implemented in a surround over which the creators have relatively little control, an unpredictable world. Those two factors are sources of anxiety and pressure. How those sources are recognized and dealt with interact with other sources of interpersonal differences.

I trust the reader will now understand why I said that creating a setting is not for everyone who grasps the opportunity to do so. . . . At this point I turn to a feature that is bedeviling and whose impact and importance are either underestimated or miscalculated or both. Here, too, the lack of previous experience in creating distinctive new settings plays its usual, disruptive role.

Resources

I begin with my late cousin whose job was to estimate the cost of large buildings or housing developments. And by cost was meant the value of everything that would be needed to meet design-architectural specifications, ranging from labor to types of doorknobs, to stair railings. He had to estimate costs for literally hundreds of items. The reason, of course, was so that the builder-developer would know the total cost in order to set a selling (or rental) price that would permit him to make a profit. Large developers have learned the hard way that off-the-cuff estimates of costs can lead to unacceptable loss and bankruptcy. And they also have learned that the accuracy of estimates is imperiled if the estimates are determined by those emotionally involved in the venture. Accuracy requires not only knowledge but a kind of obsessive attention to detail. My cousin was a well-paid estimator with an excellent track record. Builders-developers trusted his estimates. He would be given the task, he would carry it out (it could take months), and he would be unconcerned about whether the builder-developer "liked" the estimates. Frequently, they did not like the estimates, and they would sit with him to determine where changes in design and specifications might lower the overall cost. I truly began to appreciate the demands of his assignments when, around the time New York's World Trade Center opened, a long article appeared in the *New York Times* on what had been involved and how long it took to estimate the cost of those skyscrapers; no one person did it or could have done it.

Creating a new setting requires estimation (not educated guesses) about the resources that will be needed. Let us assume that putting up a building will not be necessary or is simply out of the question because of limited resources. Even so, how to use or redivide or renovate existing space takes time and money, and if changes in plumbing, lighting, and electrical wiring will be needed the costs are not paltry. Depending on the nature and purposes of the new setting the number of physical changes that you feel desirable or necessary can be considerable so that what you judged to be an adequate budget proves to be otherwise. These and other miscalculations about the physical space become significant to the extent that they impact on funds budgeted for human resources: number of staff, salaries, and benefits; computer and duplicating services; books and subscriptions to professional-technical journals; travel to meetings; and more. In the minds of the creators the imagery of the new setting may not have deserved the label luxurious, but neither did it suggest one that would be uncongenial to the *purposes* of the different people in the setting. I italicize *purposes* because people may be willing to adjust to the physical aspects of the space if it is aesthetically unattractive but when it interferes with the purposes of one's functions, it is another story, especially if it appears that these interferences will not disappear in the future.

Whether any of the above factors or possibilities will become sources of personal or interpersonal grievance depends on what I call governance: By whom and in what types of forums are decisions made? Resources, human or fiscal, are limited and must be allocated by criteria that at best only minimally jeopardize the setting's purposes. The style and formal ways by which resources are allocated are from very early on a source of the greatest interest to everyone in the setting; no one is neutral about those ways, everyone judges those ways in terms of the importance they attach to their individual responsibilities. If they have no role in decision making and/or they regard the decisions as wrong and misguided or, worse yet, a reneging on promises made, the seeds of discontent are planted, and how quickly they grow (if they do) depends on the dynamics or factors I have discussed in previous sections. That is why I said what I did about the utter inadequacy of a stimulus-response explanation of what happens in a new setting. It is as if everything is related, both as cause and effect, to everything else, and to attribute cause x to effect y may satisfy the need for simple explanations but at the expense of sensitivity to or recognition of a complicated web of relationships in which any one factor does not, cannot, have encapsulated consequences. Those consequences may be observable or not, and their significance may not be understood until their connections to other goings on are triggered by a seemingly unrelated event, decision, or conflict.

Creating a new setting is a complicated affair which can become quite messy long before the setting becomes operational. Messiness is not an inherently negative feature except when those who are creating the setting bring with them the fantasy that love and strong motivation, plus laudably distinctive purposes, and a belief in a benevolent goddess of luck will be sufficient to overcome whatever problems they will encounter. And if in addition they have a most rosy picture of a happy family comprised of people not possessed of ambivalence, personal agendas, undue frailties, or a low level of frustration tolerance, the betting odds for failure are high. If anything is predictable in creating a new setting, it is that there will be unpredictable problems ahead, not only because it is new but that it is new with new distinctive purposes never before experienced by its creators and those they bring on board. . . .

Part III

Students and Parents

CHAPTER 14

Themes from Childhood and Adolescence

In this selection from a book that deals mostly with his life as a psychologist, Sarason remembers his high school years, including his ambivalent feelings toward his growing "noncompetitive" ambition to do great things and "the crucial importance of being regarded as intelligent." Looking back, his memories are filled with criticism of schools and their culture: "My job was to *do* algebra and geometry, not to understand them."

The selection gives the reader an insight into Seymour Sarason as a teenager, before he contracted polio, when his "interest in and understanding of our society were virtually nonexistent" and when he was a typical "self-absorbed adolescent for whom yesterday did not exist, today was all-important, and sports the be-all and end-all of masculine existence."

Sarason reports that, in writing his autobiography, he for the first time felt forced to confront questions about the meaning of one's life, taken as a whole, and of his place in society. He views himself as much a product of the classic "American dream" of success through hard work as a product of his cultural roots and "intra-psychic dynamics in the context of a Jewish family."

Question for Seymour Sarason

Is there something about being brought up in a Jewish or Asian family that particularly predisposes a greater percentage of children to do well in school cultures—and, if so, does that continue to place children from other backgrounds at a disadvantage? How should a conscientious school system address this?

Sarason's Response

This question disturbs me because it clouds the most important point, which is: The "disadvantaged" are not disadvantaged because of the presence of Jews and Asians. Blacks,

Reprinted from "Themes from Childhood and Adolescence" in *The Making of an American Psychologist: An Autobiography* by Seymour Sarason. Copyright © 1988 by Seymour Sarason. This material is used by permission of Jossey-Bass, Inc., a subsidiary of John Wiley & Sons, Inc.

for example, were disadvantaged long before other minorities were on the scene. African Americans did not come to these shores because they wanted to (as did other groups). I took this up in 1973 in an article entitled "Jewishness, Blackishness and the Nature–Nurture Controversy" published in the *American Psychologist.*

The point I make is that what has been honed in the Jewish psyche over the millennia is the exact opposite of what has been honed in blacks over centuries of slavery and racism. For African-Americans, as a group, to achieve full academic parity with other minorities may well take another century. The outstanding success of black students in certain exemplary urban schools is clouded, thus far, by the failure of the system to replicate such successes. Academic parity will occur only if educators—reflecting on what today passes for "urban education"—get clear in their minds the distinctions between contexts of *productive* vs. *unproductive* learning.

Not so incidentally, over the past forty to fifty years, Israel has absorbed about a million Jewish refugees from African-Muslim countries (where they were tenth-class citizens, if that), with the result that Israel has had and still has very "disadvantaged" Jews who intellectually and educationally have difficulty competing. They are doing better as time goes on, but that is not surprising when one remembers that they were "welcomed" in Israel to a degree that African-Americans were not welcomed on our shores.

I have given you a brief, oversimplified explanation. Your readers should not confuse it with the whole story, warts and all.

More about Psychology and Education may be found in:

American Psychology and Schools (2001)
Teaching as a Performing Art (1999)
Crossing Boundaries: Collaboration, Coordination, and the Redefinition of Resources
    [with Elizabeth Lorentz] (1998)
Barometers of Change: Individual, Educational, and Social Transformation (1996)
Psychoanalysis, General Custer and the Verdicts of History (1994)
Caring and Compassion in Clinical Practice (1986)
Schooling in America: Scapegoat and Salvation (1983)
Psychology and Social Action (1982)
Psychology Misdirected (1981)
Work, Aging, and Social Change (1977)
The Psychological Sense of Community (1974)
The Preparation of Teachers: An Unstudied Problem in Education (1962)
Anxiety in Elementary School Children: A Report of Research (1960)

You do not expect children and adolescents to take distance from their social scene, let alone from the society at large, and to identify on some level of generality the factors impinging on them or the sources of those factors. If we do not hold such expectations, it should not be assumed that teenagers, at least, are incapable at some level of such abstractions. We like to believe that young people, tied to concrete and immediate experience, and absorbed with an emerging self, have no interest in or capability for generalization about their social worlds; that is, whatever generalizations they make are so superficial as to cause one to question the use of the term *generalization*. That conclusion receives a jolt during times of social upheaval, when we hear youth discuss and pass judgment on features of the society they view as inimical to their roles as individuals and citizens. The clearest examples come from periods of re-evaluation in Third World countries when young people, eschewing an old ideology for a new one, identify features of the society that they seek to change. We label the ideology political, tending to forget that such an ideology at its core calls for basic changes in the nature of social relationships and in the content and use of means of communication. The ideology defines what is good and bad for the individual and the collectivity. Whether or not we accept the ideology does not permit us to gloss over the fact that its young adherents, and they can be young, possess interrelated generalizations about society as it is and should be. But we do not have to use Third World examples. As I pointed out earlier, during the Great Depression there were many youths of high school age who adopted a political ideology that allowed them to say that this or that feature of the society was a baleful influence that needed to be altered. And then, of course, there was the decade of the sixties. That was a decade during which I spent a great deal of time in the public schools, and it was a constant source of amazement to me how many children—white and black, male and female, rich and poor—identified and criticized features of their local and larger society. I do not want to exaggerate the level of sophistication of their critiques but rather to emphasize their articulate sensitivity to features of their society they saw as adverse to their futures. If their critiques had a deeply personal significance, they nevertheless directed attention to the nature of American society.

Up until I went to college, my interest in and understanding of our society were virtually nonexistent. I confirmed the stereotype of the self-absorbed adolescent for whom yesterday did not exist, today was all-important, and sports the be-all and end-all of masculine existence. Why was I whatever I was? How would I explain myself to myself? To others? These questions could not occur to me. They are questions that preoccupied me in later years but in a very unsystematic way. Writing this autobiography literally forced me to confront these questions. Like everybody else, I think I know the major characteristics of my "personality": the internal "stuff" of my mind and its relationship to overt behavior and action. Let us leave aside the inescapable fact that we are capable of mammoth self-deception and that there are inevitable discrepancies between how we see ourselves and how others see us. What we cannot leave aside is a consequence of the obligation of autobiography not merely to describe a complex life, but to explain it from the changing vantage points of different times in that life. Autobiography is a constructing and reconstructing process, a kind of jigsaw puzzle in response to which you seek organizing principles to give order to what you see, chastened by false perceptions and moves and humbled by your ability to ignore the obvious. And if you do not complete the puzzle, or it takes a long time to do so, the prepotent tendency is to blame yourself and to ignore the fact that the maker of the puzzle did not intend to make life easy for you. We are far more aware of our internal workings than of the nature of externals. A case in point is my ambitiousness. How to explain it?

I have always seen myself as ambitious but not competitive. That is to say, if anybody had asked me when I was a youngster whether I was ambitious—whether I wanted to achieve "great things" in life—I would have said yes, however unrealistic the realization of those ambitions might have then seemed. To *want* to achieve seemed natural, right, and proper. You could explain the strength of my ambitiousness by family tradition, structure, and dynamics. Such an explanation would certainly be in order, but only if it included the interaction between the Jewish immigrant experience and American culture; more correctly, the interaction of the tradition of learning and intellectual achievement with a culture that prized and glorified individual striving and achievement. If you did not have to be Jewish to like lox, cream cheese, and bagels, you did not have to be Jewish in America to take to ambitiousness.

The more I have plumbed my experience in the public schools, the more aware I have become of how in myriad ways we were taught to want to be ambitious, to achieve, to climb the ladder of success. There was a world to conquer, and our success would depend on individual motivation. If the social reality often made a mockery of the ideological message, the fact is that the message did not lack validity, and, it goes without saying, we were given example after example of what was valid in the message. Edison, Lindbergh, Ford, Lincoln, Franklin, Booker Washington, Babe Ruth, Paul Robeson, paralyzed Franklin Roosevelt—the names were legion, and each had by virtue of unrelenting striving and ambitiousness overcome the obstacle of mean beginnings, racial prejudice, or other handicap. Those were names we heard in school or read about on the sports page. That Babe Ruth grew up in an orphanage, that Paul Robeson and Jim Thorpe overcame racial prejudice to become pre-eminent athletes, was heady stuff for me. And if what I heard in school about ambitiousness needed reinforcement, I heard at home from parents about Al Jolson, Eddie Cantor, George Jessel, Douglas Fairbanks (Jewish and from Brooklyn, I think), and scores of others who had reached the pinnacles of success in the movies, theater, or radio. America was the success story of the world, and if you wanted to participate in that success, you could, but only if you were truly ambitious. My ambitiousness is inexplicable unless the variable of America is part of the explanation. Focusing on my intrapsychic dynamics in the context of a Jewish family is very incomplete and misleading, and for a long time that kind of explanation is how I explained myself to myself and to others, on and off the analytical couch.

Nothing better illustrates the point I am making than a radio program of the thirties to which the bulk of adolescents listened every weekday in the early evening. It was "Jack Armstrong, the All-American Boy." (Wheaties explained only a small part of Jack!) He encapsulated the virtues of perseverance, obstacle surmounting, and achievement-ambitiousness. And so did the Hardy Boys and Tom Swift and Horatio Alger. America made them, and they made America. They gave in their ways as one-sided a picture as that which rivets on family tradition and intrapsychic dynamics. American psychology has yet to integrate meaningfully those two pictures.

If I saw myself as ambitious, and was encouraged to be so, why was I (and do I continue to be) reluctant unequivocally to accept it in myself and to admit it to others? For one thing, as I indicated in the previous chapter, social-economic factors and the realities of physical handicap gave little basis for hoping that my fantasies could be realized. But, I have learned, there was another set of factors, which I then hardly understood, another example of emphasizing the internal over the external, the personal over the cultural. If there was anything I knew in my public school years, it was the crucial importance of being smart or intelligent—more correctly, the crucial importance of being regarded as intelligent. And being intelligent meant that you were not in the crowd, but above it.

One way of describing the culture of schools is that it defines and rewards intelligence, which, I repeat, meant that if you were not in a class by yourself, you were in a very small, select group of individuals. In practice, intelligence was more than doing well, it was doing better than the others on all tests in all subjects. No pupil was ever in doubt about who was regarded as intelligent, or bright, or smart. To be intelligent meant that you were successful, and if you were successful, it meant that you were intelligent. That is quintessentially American and therefore such a pervasive feature of our schools. What has stuck in my memory are those few classmates who could draw well—far better than anyone else—but who were not regarded as intelligent. Their classmates were awed by their drawings and paintings, as were their teachers, but that did not mean they were "intelligent."

And it was no different outside of schools. If someone was rich, it meant they were intelligent. If most of my aunts and uncles were far more affluent than we were, it meant that my father, a lowly cutter of children's clothing, was less intelligent than they were. To me, to possess the garments of success—a car, a telephone, your own house, or an apartment in a "nice" neighborhood—or to be sent by your parents to a summer camp, or to eat in a restaurant meant that you were smarter than someone like my father. None of this will be comprehensible to the adult reader who cannot comprehend how well children are made sensitive in countless ways, formal and informal, to messages from the culture, a process of absorption as powerful as it is subtle. I am saying nothing that in principle is not contained in the societal diagnosis by the women's liberation movement and by blacks and other minorities.

I did not regard myself as intelligent. I knew I was not "dumb," but that did not mean I was intelligent. I could list a couple of scores of names of classmates whom I believed teachers regarded as intelligent. I am not on that list. As I go over that list today, I am struck, truly struck, by how many on that list were perceived by me as coming from "well-off" families. I saw them as more self-assured and more assertive than I. I did not see myself as impressing anybody, least of all me. How I envied those classmates who seemed so quick to get the right answer, who seemed to have such a good opinion of themselves, who in terms of all-round performance were Jack Armstrongs or the female equivalent, and who lived in the best neighborhoods. It is true but facile to explain my opinion of myself in terms of family, identification with father, and that abstraction "social class" that obscures as much as it illuminates. If your explanation leaves out the diverse and pervasive ways by which children are judged in terms of intelligence, and how those judgments become part of the self-picture, with enormous consequences for motivation, aspiration, and the forging of a future perspective, you are leaving out a significant factor shaping the lives of American children.

Now for some objective facts that will complicate what I have said and cast it in a new light. I finished the eighth grade at the age of twelve, two years earlier than is usual. That came about in two ways. First, three times I found I had been skipped a grade. Second, one summer I went to school and got high enough grades to be advanced a year when school reopened. Clearly, I was regarded as intelligent as I defined it earlier. I must have been doing something right! And yet, I judged myself in a way discrepant with those facts. Here again, one can resort to an explanation involving the dynamics of my "personality," and that explanation would be valid but incomplete. It would be incomplete to the extent that it ignores some stultifying, mind-destroying features of the American classroom and school. Obviously, I met whatever academic standards that were set: I could answer questions teachers asked, I did my homework, and I did well on tests.

But it was equally obvious to me that, despite knowing the right answers, I did not *understand* why they were right answers. That was especially true in arithmetic. I could perform the operations (multiplication, division, fractions)—more correctly, I memorized the operations—but I did not understand why they worked and how they related to anything on this earth with which I was familiar. But I was a nice, dutiful, conforming pupil who learned what he was supposed to learn, even though it made no personal sense. From my vantage point, my *really* intelligent classmates understood what it was all about and why. I was a fraud. This came to a head in high school when I took algebra and geometry, which literally had no meaning for me. My job was to *do* algebra and geometry, not to understand them. That I had a strong need to understand (I know now) was very much a reflection of something deeply personal. But that is no warrant for ignoring how the American classroom is unwittingly geared to the production of "right answers" at the expense of understanding. Schoolteachers teach the way they were taught. They are victims no less than their pupils. They are not villains.

The discrepancy between how I judged myself and how others judged me was fateful for my career in psychology. By the time I entered graduate school, I was already convinced in the most personal and concrete ways that the concept of intelligence—its definition, measurement, and function in American society, and schools in particular—was at best nonsense and at worst symptomatic of abysmal ignorance about the transactions between organism and social contexts. To understand that concept, one had to understand it in light of American history and society, within which the worship of the technological and methodological is such a prominent feature. And it goes without saying that once I entered psychology, I was predisposed to be drawn to what goes on in schools. Becoming a psychologist meant not only that I wanted to understand myself better but that I wanted to change American psychology. Grandiosity aside, I entered psychology with an agenda.

Relevant here is my initial reaction (somewhere, sometime in college) to the assertion that women as a group were not as intelligent as men. It was an assertion buttressed by "studies," scores of studies. I was flabbergasted. That assertion made as much sense to me as geometry and algebra, except that, unlike the case with geometry and algebra, I had a wealth of personal experience that rendered that assertion dead wrong. It had never occurred to me that anyone could judge girls less intelligent than boys. And when in graduate school I pored over studies (and memorized their hypotheses, methods, and findings) demonstrating female inferiority, I responded precisely the way I did to algebra and geometry: It made no sense. So, when the women's liberation movement picked up steam in the post–World War II era, zeroing in on, among other things, the issue of intelligence, I needed neither instruction nor convincing. And if a century from now our world still exists, I have no doubt that the assertion of intellectual differences will be seen as another instance of how era and culture can imprison us.

There was another discrepancy, and that had to do with maleness. I saw myself as cowardly, a sissy, fearing any display of hostility by myself or other boys that might lead to a fight. I can remember only one time that I fought another boy, but that only confirmed my opinion of myself, because Harry Geiger, I knew, was more of a coward than I was. I lived with or near three cousins who were brothers, one whom I envied and two whom I worshiped. I envied Artie, a year older than I, because I saw him as bigger, stronger, and fearing nothing and nobody. I worshiped his older brothers, Oscar and Leo, because each had been on the first squad of Barringer High's football team. Leo went on to play for Cornell, and Oscar played for Brown, where he was on their famous Iron Man team. It is impossible for me to exaggerate how puny and inadequate I felt in relation to them. I never felt the way I thought a boy should feel. Matters were not helped any by the fact that I knew that everyone in our extended family said that Leo and Oscar were very intelligent, as indeed they were. Artie was not described in that way. He was the terror of the family, and to me he was lucky because he was a "real" boy. So I was a double fraud: I was not intelligent, and I was a coward. And I never saw myself as being an athlete. I lacked the physical agility and strength a real boy needs to play baseball, football, and basketball.

But writing this autobiography made me realize I was a good athlete if you go by conventional standards. We lived very close to a school that had a large playground, and during the summers there was a playground director who organized teams for intra- and interplayground tournaments. During any one summer, there must have been upwards of a couple of hundred boys and girls organized into teams. Something was always going on, even at night, because the playground had floodlights. The fact is that I was always on the first team. In baseball I was *the* pitcher, and I was a good switch hitter. And I was no slouch in the other sports. But the clincher in this picture is what happened when a spanking new high school was built in the neighborhood. I was in the first class to enter the school. How can you have a high school and not have a football team? Not in America! So when Weequahic High School opened in September, one of the first announcements was a call for candidates for the football team. I not only wanted to be on the team but I wanted to play center like Oscar and Leo. How I imagined myself in that football uniform! I need not detail the struggle with my mother to get permission to go out for the team. I won. Bear in mind that I was two or more years younger than any other candidate. I was shorter than anyone else. I weighed around 140 pounds, which was really puny because I wanted to play center, a position calculated to satisfy one's masochistic needs, which obviously were strong in me. It is a position from which one can give punishment, but that was not an aspect I relished; indeed, it bothered me. I felt like a child among giants. I still find it somewhat incomprehensible that I became the backup center to someone who looked to me to be ten feet tall, with weight appropriate to height. In practice scrimmages, I played against him. Why I did it is a little more clear to me than how I did it. I see myself as running here and there, looking *up* to try to see where the action is, where the play is going, avoiding direct contact, but ending up at the bottom of the pile. And what a pile it was! I feared injury, but I feared any display of unmasculinity far more.

Practice began early in September. Because it was a new team in a new school, no game was scheduled with a rival high school until mid-fall. Within a period of weeks, I had lost about twenty pounds, a loss not noted or picked up by the coaching staff. It was then that I came down with polio. I had won the battle with my mother. I had lost a larger war within myself. The fact is that after I contracted polio, there was a part of me—a part I would allow myself to recognize fleetingly and with guilt—that was relieved that I was removed from an arena in which I had to prove that I was a real male. And that was when fantasies about literary-theatrical achievement started to take over. The playing fields would be different; the ultimate goals remained the same.

The psychoanalytically inclined person would have a field day explaining the discrepancy between the way I saw myself as a young male and actual performance. But why a field day? More likely, a person would ask: So what else is new? An overprotective, Jewish mother, the oedipal triangle, the castration complex, a strong counterphobic tendency, the internal battle between activity and passivity, the self-protective nature of the process of sublimation—these and more can be employed to make me a textbook case of the content and processes of the young, developing male child. I do not question the validity of that clinical assessment. But it is not the whole story. What it leaves out is the strength of the myriad ways in which the young American male is literally bombarded with messages defining the nature of masculinity. Newspapers, radio, movies, peer groups, pulp magazines (especially westerns)—these were the major conveyors of the message of what a male should be: outward going, assertive (if not fearless), tolerant of pain, courageous, attractive to girls, unanxious, and capable of standing up for his rights even if that meant fighting. It was all right if a girl was a tomboy; it was shameful if a boy was a sissy. It was all right, indeed it was laudable, if you were courteous and respectful, but something was wrong if you were a Mama's boy. You should want to compete, to test and demonstrate your physical prowesses, not to shrink from or avoid competition. It was a message to and about the *individual* male child: his responsibility to *himself* and to the American ideal of the masculine child. All else was backdrop.

Parents and the family context are conveyors of societal messages, but only in part. By virtue of their socialization into American society, they have absorbed aspects of the picture of American maleness, but again only in part, especially if they were Jewish immigrants. What a source of surprise and pride it was to me that Barney Ross, a Jew, was a world champion fighter! Even *my* parents took pride in that. I am reminded here of the time when I was in my late fifties and found myself in Israel talking with an Israeli who was a commander of a tank corps. He was dressed like a commander, looked like one, talked like one, and, by God, he was one—and a Jew, to boot! And I met scores of other Israelis, an experience that forced me to understand in the concrete what I knew in the abstract: To be a Jew in Israel was a different cup of psychological tea from what being Jewish in America was for me as a child. I am not explicable in terms of a psychology that leaves out the America my family coped with. In my case, the clear and loud messages I was getting about masculinity were always on a collision course with family values and context. My Jewish family and America are in my psychological bloodstream. Yes, different Jewish families "produced" different kinds of males in America. And America was not the Eastern European *shtetl,* or what was then a Palestine kibbutz. If this is a glimpse of the obvious, it is one that American psychology (indeed, Western psychology, including that of Freud) has not confronted squarely. It took me a long time to understand it in a truly personal way.

At the beginning of this chapter, I said that I saw myself (and still see myself) as ambitious but not competitive. If that is valid as "seeing," it may be invalid by the criteria others used to describe me. To me, competitiveness has always meant that you vie with others for some reward (symbolic or material) and that, therefore, there are winners and losers. You strive to win, and if you lose it is a defeat. And at no time is a defeat more poignant, less easy to rationalize away, less easy to compensate for than in the preadult years. When Vince Lombardi said about pro football that winning is what it is all about, he could also have said that about what the American boy was expected to feel. And no one in all of American sports, past or present, has been revered (or quoted) as much as Vince Lombardi. The name of the game *is* winning! And writing this autobiography has told me that it is most unlikely that I escaped the consequences of the virulent American virus of competitiveness and winning. I offer a few examples. Each year in Hebrew school, two religious plays were staged for parents. You tried out for a part, and usually there were a handful of boys vying for the "big" part. I competed, and very successfully. Indeed, I always won. A more compelling example is from my senior year in high school, when I still had my right arm in an airplane splint. It was announced that a teacher was organizing a radio production of Dickens's *Great Expectations,* and that it was going to be broadcast on WNBC in Radio City in New York. You can well imagine the flock of students who wanted to be in the cast. It was like the scene in the movie *42nd Street* when, before the opening curtain, the director says to the chorus girl who will fill in for the inebriated star something like: "You are going out there a nobody, but when the show is over tonight you will be a star and your name will be in lights." Airplane splint and all, I competed against the others, and I got the lead part. I achieved local stardom, helped no end by a photograph of the show's cast around the microphone of a studio in Radio City.

These and other instances force me to the conclusion that I was literally an actor—that is, I could act as if I were competitive even though I saw myself as otherwise. If anything is clear about the me of those years, it is that I had a fear of failing and losing, never really being clear about what would happen if I failed. Indeed, winning presented

a problem, because I knew how a loser would feel, and that decreased the strength of
the satisfaction derived from winning. I felt as sorry for the loser as I would for myself
in his position. So, when I came up for tenure at Yale, I perceived the department as having to choose between me and a colleague. I had absolutely no doubt that he would be
chosen, and that would be understandable to me: He was very "intelligent" and productive and, to me, he looked as a Yale professor should look. When I was informed of
the decision, my immediate reaction was less one of surprise than of pity for my colleague. I sought him out to tell him how bad I felt! This speaks volumes about my "psy-
chodynamics," but here, too, I do not think it is the whole story. If engaging in competition, tournament style, is encouraged and rewarded, it is also true in America that we
are taught that it is unseemly to parade one's competitiveness, and we cloak it in a variety of garments that hide from us and others how much we want to be better than
everyone else, how deeply we want to stand on the mountain of success. We are supposed to appear modest, as if what we have achieved is simply a recognition of objective performance relatively independent of the strength and content of our private fantasies. It is my impression that in no other country are people as sensitive to the concept
of "public image" as we are in America. And that concept bespeaks a cleavage between
public and private image, the former possessing none of the unseemliness of the latter.

I have in this and previous chapters described aspects of my world of childhood and
adolescence. I did not do this because I thought it was intrinsically interesting, let alone
distinctive. Put in another way, I am not a "great man" who wants to explain to the
world how greatness was achieved, requiring that its origins in early life be plumbed and
the threads of continuity carefully traced, making it all seem near inevitable. However
interesting the autobiographical accounts of such people have been, I have long been dissatisfied with the ways they locate and weight the influence of the culture of their countries on their development. For example, in the past decade a spate of books has been
written by those who were part of what has been called the New York Intellectuals of
the 1930s. Their impact nationally was far out of proportion to their numbers. Unlike
me, they are household names in academia and beyond. Without exception, they try to
portray, and usually do it well, how their childhood and adolescence bore the imprint
of the fact that they had lived in the Bronx, or Brooklyn, or Manhattan. They were New
Yorkers from head to toe.

But as they bring their stories to their later years, a new theme emerges: how *American* they were (and are) but did not recognize or want to recognize, and it was more the
latter than the former. That recognition did not arise *sui generis* but as a result of events
in the world posed by Hitler Germany, Stalinist Russia, and World War II. If that recognition came to the fore in midlife, it is not a recognition the substance of which is made
clear to a reader like me. And if I felt that way, it was because in the middle of my career in psychology I found myself engrossed with the relationships between America and
American psychology, and, therefore, when I would be reading an autobiography, I
found myself judging it in terms of how directly the writer confronted the fact that he
or she was born into, reared in, and socialized in a particular country in a particular period of its history.

Geographically, intellectually, and politically, I was on a distant periphery of a circle in the center of which were the New York Intellectuals of the thirties and subsequent decades. I met some of them, I read what they wrote, and I felt kinship with them. But there was always a part of me—what some of my friends said was the "bourgeois" part of me—that could not accept the readiness with which this influential group disparaged American culture and society. . . . I wish to emphasize that my developing interest in this problem increasingly had little or nothing to do with political ideology, let alone patriotism, which so often is "the refuge of scoundrels." It was at the same time both far more simple and far more complex than that. How does one become an American? That is a simple question. The answer is fantastically complex, no less so than the answer to the question of what is an atom. For example, it takes a good part of one's life to begin to appreciate how America is composed of regions geographically distinct, each of which has a distinctive ambience that becomes reflected in a distinctive world view. And yet, despite these differences, there is a common core that leaves no doubt in the minds of foreigners that we are American. The issue has a pressing urgency, because we are well into a unique phase of human history in which all nations and their cultures are struggling with the consequences of the fact that they do and must interact with each other. The vicissitudes of that struggle in the past are warning enough that we have to better understand radically different outlooks, a significant part of which remain, at best, unarticulated and, at worst, beyond the fringes of awareness.

What I have recounted about my childhood and adolescence may strike some as coming from another world or an era no longer with us. The world has changed in terms of appearance, problems, knowledge, expectations, and feats of human creativity and stupidity. We like to believe that we learn from the past, that we have overcome it, and that the future is ours to shape. Those beliefs do not reckon with the strength with which our socialization into our society implants in us unarticulated attitudes and outlooks that ensure that the past will be part of our present and, therefore, influential for our futures. Of course the world has changed, but it is a non sequitur to conclude that those changes are completely or largely independent of continuities (the cultural DNAs) that derive from our social-psychological heritage. As we shall see, American psychology was and continues to be *American* in very distinctive ways, an obvious fact to foreign psychologists. When Freud, rightly or wrongly, feared what would happen to psychoanalysis in America, he was reflecting a perception of America quite different from that of American psychology and medicine. Freud, the European pessimist, did not look kindly on American optimism. For somewhat different reasons, Piaget feared what would happen to his work when American psychology "discovered" what he learned by talking to children.

CHAPTER 15

Columbine High School and Contexts of Productive Learning

Focusing on one of the most horrific tragedies in modern school history, Sarason asks us to consider: "What is the purpose of schooling?" and calls back "the Man from Mars" to help us reflect on how poorly the practices of our schools mirror our most-often stated goals of personal growth and cognitive skills development for children. He wonders why so few psychological experts and observers commented on the large student population of Columbine High School, the anonymity experienced within such an environment, and the inevitable "we-they" nature of student/teacher interactions, as at least partial explanation for the perceived lack of a sense of community there.

Sarason reflects upon the nature of human learning from early childhood onward as part of a review of the major features required for "contexts of productive learning" within school and society. He views the emergence of charter schools as expressing our need for smallness in educational settings, and he challenges psychologists to engage their understanding of human development in helping to make schools more human-friendly places. Sarason worries that if the field of psychology continues to ignore schools, future Columbines may not be prevented. He says, "if American psychology continues to train psychologists, the large bulk of whom have no experience in schools and there is no desire or incentive to gain such experience, American psychology is manifesting . . . social irresponsibility."

Question for Seymour Sarason:

Are you firmly in the "small school" camp, believing that smallness is a criterion that must be included in any significant reform?

Reprinted with the permission of Teachers College Press from "Columbine High School and Contexts of Productive Learning" in *American Psychology and Schools* by Seymour Sarason (New York: Teachers College Press, 2001).

Sarason's Response

Smaller schools—which normally offer a more personalized setting for teachers and students to get to know one another—*are* a necessary attribute of any significant school reform strategy. But too many people attempt to short-circuit that issue by proposing, instead of smaller schools, smaller classes within traditionally large schools. I am on record as saying that whereas, *overall,* smaller class size may have a small positive effect, it is by itself an insufficient factor in the larger picture.

I would not put a lot of money on the "smaller-class-size" horse, because when such classes are taught by teachers who are only average or below average in their ability to help students want to learn, the results will still be average or below by *conventional* criteria of educational outcomes. Without radical transformation in the selection and preparation of educators, nothing of much consequence will occur.

More about issues involving the well-being of children and human dynamics in educational settings may be found in:

Educational Reform: A Self-Scrutinizing Memoir (2002)
Crossing Boundaries: Collaboration, Coordination, and the Redefinition of Resources [with Elizabeth Lorentz] (1998)
Barometers of Change: Individual, Educational, and Social Transformation (1996)
Revisiting "The Culture of the School and the Problem of Change" (1996)
Parental Involvement and the Political Principle (1995)
School Change: The Personal Development of a Point of View (1995)
You Are Thinking of Teaching? Opportunities, Problems, Realities (1993)
The Case for Change: Rethinking the Preparation of Educators (1992)
The Predictable Failure of Educational Reform (1990)
The Challenge of Art to Psychology (1990)
Schooling in America: Scapegoat and Salvation (1983)
Educational Handicap, Public Policy, and Social History: A Broadened Perspective on Mental Retardation (1979)
The Culture of the School and the Problem of Change (1971, 1982 [included in *Revisiting "The Culture of the School and the Problem of Change"*])
The Psycho-Educational Clinic: Papers and Research Studies (1969)
Anxiety in Elementary School Children: A Report of Research (1960)

It is impossible for me to discuss Columbine or any other school without asking and at least trying to answer the question: What is the purpose of schooling? I say purpose rather than purposes because I assume that the reader, like me, knows that there are many purposes to schooling and they are not of equal importance (to me or the reader). Even if unanimous agreement could be reached on a short list of major purposes, it is most unlikely that each of us would consider each purpose on the list of equal importance. It is a basic axiom in economics that resources are inevitably limited and we have to make choices in allocating resources: This purpose is important, that purpose is important, and there are other important purposes, but precisely because resources are finite, however we wish it otherwise, we have to decide by some criterion (or criteria) where each purpose should be on our priority list. . . . Is it possible that our short list of purposes is faulty, wrong, incomplete, self-defeating? . . . Should we examine and challenge our short list of purposes? Can it be that our short list of purposes and even the ways we prioritize it is on target, but we have not taken its practical implications seriously? That there is a difference between rhetoric and decisions consistent with it?

The two most frequently stated top purposes of schooling are:

1. To aid each child's actualization of his or her potential; the assets of each child should be identified and developed.
2. To insure the learning of subject matter and those cognitive skills which together prepare the student for a productive adulthood.

In practice, of course, the two purposes are seamlessly intertwined; they can be considered two sides of the same coin. The first purpose emphasizes the importance of respect for *individuality;* the second reflects or implies or assumes a *societal* consensus about what a student should learn over the school years about human knowledge, experience, and accomplishments. The store of human knowledge is vast and (again) choices have to be made in selecting from that store what is deemed essential. So, for example, music and art are considered important but not essential and, therefore, are allocated fewer resources, if any, compared to "basic" ones: literature, science, history, math, social studies, and a foreign language (not always). In times of financial crises no one suggests that any of the basics be eliminated, but that is what is done in the case of those subjects and activities which are judged as less important, or as a luxury, or as a frill. Prioritization comes with two obligations: to create the conditions which are consistent with priorities and then to test for the outcomes.

How does a high school containing somewhat more than 2,000 people achieve the two purposes to which practically everybody pledges allegiance? So let us go back to our Martian, who now is fluent in English, and ask him to direct his x-ray–like technology to provide us with "data" relevant to several questions:

1. How many times in the course of a month do students talk *alone* with a teacher or any other adult in the school? How many of those times are during the school day or after school?
2. How many times and with what durations do teachers or other adults talk with each other during or after the school day?
3. For any one teacher, with how many of the other teachers does he or she *never* interact?
4. During whatever is the classroom period, how much of the time does the teacher talk? The student? How many students never talk to or with the teacher or do so one, two, or *x* times?
5. How often do two or more teachers meet, and for how long, to talk about individual students?
6. Because the number of school personnel is not small, how often are there general faculty meetings? Where are they held? How many times does a teacher raise a ques-

tion or issue? What is the total time teachers talk? The principal and/or some other administrator?

7. After the school day how many students stay to engage in a teacher led or supervised school-related activity? How many teachers perform in such a role? (Athletics requiring being outside the school building are not included.)

8. How many times does a teacher phone or write a parent asking for a meeting? How many times, invited or not, does a parent come to school?

9. At the end of the school year several hundred students are graduated; they never return. They are replaced two months later by several hundred younger students. Are the data we request from the Martian in any way different for these replacements compared to the older cohorts who are still in the school?

There are no existing data relevant to the overt behavioral regularities for which we seek the help of our Martian friend. But does anyone doubt that regularities the Martian would provide us are relevant to the two most frequently stated purposes of schooling? I did not dream up the nine questions out of whole cloth. They do not derive solely from my personal observations, although they are far from small in number. They derive from talking to scores of parents, teachers, and students. I never asked any one of them in a direct, explicit way these questions: How well do you think your child is known to and understood by his or her teachers? How well do you know and think you understand the 100 to 125 (or more) students you teach each day, divided as they are into four or five non-overlapping classes or sections? How well do you feel your teachers know you? Would you say you have a personal relationship with most, if not all, of your teachers? With some exceptions, I did not "confront" those with whom I talked. On several occasions when I was meeting with a small group of teachers whom I had gotten to know well—who did not see me as an intrusive professor foraying into matters about which he knew little—I asked: "Given the number of students you teach, how long does it take you to associate names with faces?" That always drew a laugh. By far the most frequent answer went like this: "By the end of the first month I could associate correctly the names and faces of the 20% or so of the dumbest, brightest, and misbehaving students. Even at the end of the semester I would still have to consult my seating chart like the law professor in the TV series *The Paper Chase*."

The second exception was when I was asked to evaluate three high schools participating in a school reform project. The schools were in different parts of the country. In each school I met with several small groups of students. The purpose of the meetings was to determine if the juniors or seniors in the school had noted any changes in their school. Without exception the answer was no, even when I pressed in regard to several changes which had been initiated. At the end of each meeting I asked, "How do you like school?" The only way I can describe their reactions was their facial reactions. It was as if I had asked a stupid question in that it assumed that one should like school. One or two in each group finally said, "It's O.K.," the socially desirable response to a stranger whom the principal had obviously invited to the school. No students ever said they found school interesting, quite the contrary. They were never vehement and certainly not expansively critical; they simply did not see the point of my questions. School was not a place you were supposed to enjoy. After one of the groups left, I remained in the room to jot down some notes. There was a knock on the door, and two students entered to tell me that they had not wanted to convey to me the impression that they disliked the school as if there was nothing good that could be said about it. It was, they said, "an O.K. school but it could be better." Beyond that they had nothing more to add.

There are high schools with significantly more students than Columbine. They are bureaucratic in that, like the university, those in one department know very little about those in other departments, and there are no incentives to change this. In addition, the layers of administration are not small and their contacts with and relationships to teachers are indirect, relatively infrequent, and more often than not take the form of written (or Xeroxed) messages concerning procedures, information, record keeping, and the like. It is understandable if many teachers regard themselves as workers at the bottom of a mountain on top of which is Kafka's castle from which emanate policies and directives; there is not a safe and effective way for messages from below to reach the top or if there is a way, it has no consequences.

You do not have to be a sage to conclude that "helping each student to realize his or her potential" is empty rhetoric of the emptiest kind. To achieve that purpose implies that students are known and feel known, that relationships with teachers and other personnel are not fleeting and superficial, not as strangers passing in the night, not as people assigned narrow roles with rigid boundaries not to be crossed. . . .

. . . An organizational purpose explicitly or implicitly says, so to speak, that to achieve the goals of that purpose you must judge how much time to allocate to that purpose. Time is a finite, precious commodity to be judicially allocated in accord with the priorities of stated purposes. Time is not democratically allocated as if all purposes are of equal importance. For example, the federal Senate has one fifth the number of members compared to the House of Representatives. (This disparity is not happenstance. It is in accord with the stated purposes of the Founding Fathers, but that is another story, a most fascinating and instructive one.) With its 500 plus members, and its changing composition every 2 years, the House is a place where a small number of people make the most important decisions, not every member knows everybody else in a meaningful way, "freshman" members experience an unwanted anonymity, and the time a member has to address the house is severely limited. With its 50 members the Senate has been described as a "club" in which its members know each other, each is elected for 6 years, a freshman senator does not remain anonymous for very long, and each senator has more than ample time to address his or her colleagues—in the case of filibusters "time" can be many hours, even days. Practically all members of the House—not including its small number of party power brokers—would rather be in the Senate. What is most relevant for my present purposes has to do with time. Although both have the same stated, overarching purpose to legislate for the public welfare—to debate, pass, or reject—each allocates time to the purpose in very different ways. To achieve their identical purpose, the Senate allocates time to its members which the House realistically does not and cannot do. It is understandable if the general public has a higher opinion of the Senate than of the House, a judgment with which the Senate, of course, concurs.

The above was prologue to how the time perspective enters the educational picture. I have over the decades had discussions with individual teachers, or small groups of them, about their reactions to what I have said as an invited speaker at their professional meetings and conventions. Since I am a Johnny-One-Note about understanding the learner as an individual, it is rare that I do not sermonize about it. I cannot do better than to paraphrase what teachers have said regardless of whether they were elementary, middle, or high school teachers, although the intensity of feeling in the latter two is always dramatically higher than in the first one. "You talk as if teachers are not interested in students as individuals. If that is what you are implying, you are being both unfair and wrong. For example, students are in school for about 6 hours a day, but when you deduct settling down time in the morning, lunch time, gymnasium, only about 4 and a half hours are left for basic subject matter and instruction. It is not really different in middle and high schools, maybe it is worse. There is limited time and don't ever forget that. Given limited time is one thing, but you have to see that in terms of a curriculum we must cover because we are under a gun: At the end of the school year we as teachers will be evaluated by standardized tests to see how well we covered and taught the curriculum. The pressures from administrators and parents are real and enormous. Keep on track with the curriculum, everything else is secondary. Of course, each student is a unique person and learner. Do we ever know that! But there is precious little time to fathom and adapt to individuality. If teachers suffer from anything, it is guilt that we know there are kids who need more help than we have the time to give them. We have to teach by the clock and the calendar because there are deadlines and consequences. Of course, we are in favor of individuality, however you define it, but for all practical purposes we have very little time to take it into account. And please don't forget that if you have one or two troubled disruptive kids in your class, you cannot ignore them, and the extra time you are forced to give them takes time away from teaching the curriculum and from the very small amount of time, if that, we can give in a one-on-one to the other students."

My response had several parts. The first was that they were largely correct; I agreed with them but had to say that there are teachers, a small minority, who deal with the issue of individuality better than others. The second was that in agreeing with them we were both conceding that "helping each child realize his or her full potential" was empty rhetoric. The third part was in the form of a question: Why are you telling me this in the confines of a professional interchange, while as individuals and the formal organizations of which you are a part you monotonously repeat the rhetoric to the public? Does this not border on hypocrisy?

In response to Columbine High School, I zealously read what psychologists were saying on TV, what they were quoted as saying in newspapers and national magazines, and letters to editors and op-ed columns. In all that I read, saw, and heard, there was only one time that someone mentioned size of school. That exception was in a three-sentence letter to the editor of the *New York Times* where the writer, Dr. Sidney Trubowitz, a professor of education, plaintively wondered why no one was discussing the implications of size of school. The psychologists were not hypocrites, they simply do not know any

better because neither their training nor accustomed professional role gives them an understanding of the school culture or brings them into meaningful contact with school
personnel. . . . That, I should hasten to add, does not mean that school personnel are
the experts. As I learned and pointed out decades ago, it is the rare educator whose socialization into the school culture has not dramatically narrowed the direction and range
of his or her comprehension of the school culture.

I say this sympathetically because as a psychologist, an academic one to boot, I had
to struggle to unlearn what I thought I knew about the school culture. Psychology prides
itself, as it should, on the emphasis given in training to the difference between opinion
and conventional wisdom, on the one hand, and demonstrated and tested truths, on the
other hand. It is because of psychology's emphasis on the individual, its neglect of organizational tradition, structure, and dynamics, that the response of psychology to
Columbine was so conventional, superficial, and an unwitting reinforcement of over-
simplifications, if not irrelevancies. Psychology rightly reveres the role of the experimental method which, to state it succinctly, derives from the axiom: If you want to test
your understanding of an existing state of affairs, do nothing with one group and try to
change it in a comparable group. The experimental method requires action and some
understanding of that state of affairs before you go into action. You do not fly into action. You act on the basis of personal experience and available or existing knowledge.

I am in no way suggesting or advocating that the experimental method is the best answer to understanding and improving schools at the present time. I brought up the experimental method as a way of underlining the importance—*importance* is too weak a
word—of gaining a secure familiarity with the state of affairs you seek to understand,
evaluate, and change. The experimental method is not inherently virtuous; it has its time
and place, and in regard to the major problems of schools, its present virtues are few
and obstacles to applying it are many and gargantuan. What I do consider inherently
virtuous, especially at this time, is the effort to describe, clarify, and conceptualize what
we think is the state of affairs in what Goodlad called and described as *A Place Called
School* (1984). But if American psychology continues to train psychologists, the large
bulk of whom have had no experience in schools and there is no desire or incentive to
gain such experience, American psychology is manifesting, in my opinion, social irresponsibility. . . .

[Sarason turns to the idea of "contexts of productive leaning" as a way of highlight-
ing a vital element missing from a large high school such as Columbine. He asks and
briefly answers the question:]

What are the major features of a context of productive learning?

1. From our earliest days we are curious, question-asking organisms. Differing as we
   do in temperament (and more), our curiosity may attach to very different things. In
   order for curiosity to be manifest it must be reflected in some form of overt action.
2. Curiosity is not necessarily motivating. Whether curiosity becomes motivating depends on the response it elicits in adults (in some cases from a cat or dog or other
   pet).

3. Curiosity and question asking occur before a child can talk. The facial expressions we associate with the two—attentiveness, puzzlement—which parents and other adults may or may not perceive and respond to are early manifestations of curiosity and non-verbal question asking. Around 9 months of age many children display what is called stranger anxiety: a reaction of staring, puzzlement, frowning, and then a turning away and/or a clinging to the parent. Again the consequences of this reaction depend on how the parent understands and responds to the child.

4. From the time the child begins to talk, the rate of question asking steadily mounts to the point where some parents become annoyed and give an answer which to the child is unrevealing and unsatisfactory. The answer of the parent or other adult plays an important role in determining how curiosity and question asking play a role in the child's exploration of self, others, and the world. Parents differ widely in how they regard or value or support the role of curiosity and question asking in cognitive and personal development.

5. When children come to school for the first time, they come with loads of questions about what their experience will be. If asked, they will say they will learn to read, write, and so forth. But they hope and expect more which they do not or cannot verbalize. Will *I* like or be liked by the other children? Will *I* like or be liked by *my* teacher? What will she ask *me?* What will *I* be able to ask her? What if *I* do not understand what she says? Will *I*, should *I*, tell her *I* do not understand? Will she think *I* am dumb? The questions are legion. The pronoun *I* is italicized as a way of suggesting the obvious: The child is self-absorbed, the self is the center of the child's world. That, so to speak, is where the child is coming from.

6. How well and how much of the substance of that self is recognized and exploited for intellectual and personal development depends on the teacher's conception of individuality: what obligations this requires of her, how and to what extent she can adapt to a child's individuality, how to allocate precious time so that her response is not interpreted by the child as insensitive or a brush off. Time, no less than the conception of individuality, is always part of the context if only because the context includes other children. (In our schools time is the major enemy of innovation, individuality, and creativity for students and teachers.)

7. Students know the difference between needing or being required to learn and wanting to learn. They may not object to the former, but they want to feel that what they are required to learn has some personal significance for the questions they have about the world they see and experience, for the roles and places they have or may have in that world. Subject matter matters, but so does the relationship between subject matter and the world they experience matter. They want to experience the sense of cognitive and personal growth, the sense that one is changing, horizons are enlarging, that the more one learns the more one wants to learn.[1] . . .

In the millions of words written about the Columbine tragedy, the focus has been solely on the causes of violence in young people: absence of more stringent gun-control legislation, TV Hollywood movies, and a society historically noted for the frequency of displays of violence. In invoking these as precipitating causes, no one was suggesting that schools could do much about them. As more than one person said, "Schools are for the purposes of learning, not for the purpose of lobbying to change this or that in the society." But there were things schools could and should do better. And one of those things derived from the fact that other students in the school were aware of something of which school personnel apparently were not: The two boys were part of a small group who dressed in a strikingly flamboyant, attention-getting manner, who often were heard in and out of the classroom to express hostile thoughts and intentions, and were loners. If no student thought they were dangerous, they saw them as relatively asocial and different. But what was apparent to some students was not known to school personnel who, even if they knew, took no action of any kind; we can say that no teacher or administrator was quoted as saying that they had concerns about the boys.

What could and should schools do? To that question countless commentators, including psychologists, offered the same bromide they gave to parents: to be more knowledgeable about, sensitive to, and vigilant about what children are thinking, feeling, and doing. I label it a bromide because it will do no good (or harm) because it bypasses the question: What is there about a school as densely populated as Columbine that fosters and sustains a psychological cleavage between students and teachers? You do not have to do more studies to confirm again that students and teachers inhabit different worlds and that each of their worlds—in this case the school world—is comprised of many groups which vary in numerous ways: transiency, fluidity, boundaries, composition, degree of gender mix, and hierarchy. Those factors are more pronounced for student than for teacher groupings, if only because the number of students is so large and one of the purposes of their groupings is to give and receive personal and social support, a kind of safe haven that dilutes the sense of unwanted privacy and allows for some degree of intimacy. It is the rare student who begins high school who is not from day one scanning the surround to determine with whom he or she will feel comfortable and safe. That scanning frequently has the quality of desperation; the need to belong can be as pressuring as the need to eat. The strength of their need to belong, to be accepted, to be understood, cannot be overestimated.

In their groups the students talk about many things and that includes teachers and administrators: their personalities, their quirks, whether they are likeable or not, whether they are good or bad teachers, fair markers, and what the gossip in the rumor mill tells them about the lives, families, the outside-of-school activities of this or that teacher, as well as relationships among school personnel which are in one or another way "juicy." These groupings reinforce and sustain a "we-they" dichotomy in the world of the school, and it is frequently a dichotomy which has an adversarial flavor.

In a general way school personnel know, feel, experience that cleavage. They regard it as going, so to speak, with the territory called generational gap. There are individual teachers, albeit few in number, who try to bridge that gap with this or that student, especially if this student seeks out the teacher. Students are well aware of who these unusual teachers are even though most students do not feel personally secure or safe enough to approach them. Most teachers regard the cleavage as one that students "cause" and is desired by them. In the dynamics of the self-fulfilling prophecy, teachers react in ways that sustain the cleavage.

We say—we certainly are told ad nauseam—that teachers are role models for students. But the concept of teacher as role model clearly implies that teachers create and foster a social-interpersonal context in which the learner regards the social and intellectual life of school as stimulating, interesting, mind expanding; that one is changing as a thinker, that the more you know the more you need to know, that what you are learning has a personally meaningful direction you willingly take. For students in middle and high school the school is frequently *socially* interesting, and even enjoyable, because that is where they have friends who they feel understand, accept, and support them. *That interest does not extend to the classroom,* a point that is confirmed in studies and readily acknowledged by teachers. As one teacher said to me, "Trying to get students interested in what I teach them is like pulling teeth. Their minds are elsewhere. They dutifully show up and go through the motions." Scores of teachers have said versions of that to me literally scores of times. There are, I hasten to add, exceptions but they are just that, exceptions, which is to say exceptional teachers.

Why is it that in the hundreds of interviews reported on TV, radio, and other mass media of Columbine students, school personnel, parents, and assorted others, nothing was ever said about the classroom context of learning? There is more than one reason, but there is one I have to mention, and that is because in an affluent Denver suburb test scores of the students were at, and probably above, national norms. So what is there to say about the context of the classroom that has bearing on cleavages, reduced interest, values and goals, the sense of apartness or alienation or adversariness? No one, including so-called expert psychologists, counselors, educators, seemed to know what has long been reported, studied, known: As students go from elementary to middle to high school their interest in and their motivation for learning, for intellectual inquiry, steadily decreases. Why is it that no one mentioned that even in our most respected colleges and universities faculty bemoan the fact that entering students too frequently cannot write clear sentences, paragraphs, and essays, and that they do not know "how to think." This, I should emphasize, is never said with the intention of tarnishing all entering students but rather to indicate that a number of them have educational deficits that were unexpected given their test scores. And in some, perhaps all, of these esteemed institutions, they offer remedial programs. In other colleges and universities whose standards for admission are discernibly less stringent, faculty complaints are louder and more poignant, and remedial programs are elective standard fare, sometimes required fare.

For students, especially those in middle and high school, the classroom is an uninteresting, unstimulating, boring place where you do what you are told or expected to do, you answer questions, you do not ask questions, and only when you leave the classroom can you do, think, and talk about what "really" interests you with other students who you understand and who understand you. Such relationships with and feelings toward teachers are the exception, not the rule.

The classroom is not (again the usual exceptions aside) a context of productive learning. It has few, if any, of its features. That students learn subject matter and pass tests is not to be sneezed at, but neither should it be judged as proof that what has been learned has been absorbed in ways that are personally and intellectually meaningful, a goad to want to learn more and give direction and shape to emerging interests and goals, to visions of a career. As I have said elsewhere (Sarason, 1996a, 1998a, 1998b), there is one overarching criterion by which schools should be judged: If when a student is graduated from high school, that student wants to continue to learn more about self, others, and the past and present world, that school has done a good job. At the present time that criterion is very infrequently met.

If your doctor tells you that you have normal body temperature, he or she will not say that you are well and healthy because he knows that in fact the symptoms you report may indicate you are not all "well." Body temperature is by no means a totally valid indicator of health: The physician goes beyond that single indicator. Similarly, passing tests does not mean that the student is intellectually "healthy," that the student has assimilated knowledge, attitudes, and a style of thinking that have sustaining, productive consequences.

It is totally understandable that the nation riveted on the Columbine tragedy and in unusually muted, non-polemical way agreed, among other things, that school personnel should be more sensitive to and vigilant about what students are doing, talking, and thinking. In focusing only on violence, the nation ignored a critical question: Is there something about the size of high schools, the way they are organized, the way time is perceived and allocated, and the selection and preparation of educators that should caution us to look beyond extreme violence, that may suggest a preventive approach rather than an exclusive dependence on repair, the track record of which is by no means significantly effective?

One of the distinctive contributions of American psychology has been devising and applying statistical techniques to determine the degree to which psychological characteristics and performances cluster within individuals and within and among groups of individuals. Which characteristics to study as well as which tests to be used to measure them are determined by theoretical considerations, the previous findings of others, and what may be called hunches. It is an approach that takes the obvious very seriously: No single psychological characteristic is comprehensible apart from its degree of relationship to other characteristics of an individual.

What would it mean if we were to take seriously what is obvious in that approach for the purpose not of understanding one school (like Columbine) alone but rather to pursue this question: In order to evaluate what we think we know about Columbine, as well as the appropriateness of our suggestions about changing and improving it, should we not determine whether there are trends or developments *in schools generally* which may confirm or disconfirm what we think we know and recommend for Columbine? Columbine is not an individual human being but rather an organized collection of individuals who vary in many ways. The question we are now asking is not about discrete individuals but about discrete schools. Let me put it more concretely and personally: Is my analysis of Columbine illuminated by developments in other schools where violence has not been an issue? When the unit of analysis is not an individual person but individual organizations, American psychology is of no help even though potentially it has much to offer. The interest is simply not there.

What is a charter school? Why have a large majority of states enacted legislation creating charter schools? Why did President Clinton ask for and receive congressional funding to create 3,000 new charter schools? A charter school is one that is created and administered by a small group—teachers, parents, and other community individuals—based on what has been considered to be an innovative plan that gives promise to increase and/or enlarge what students experience and learn. Crucially, the charter school is exempt from the usual rules and regulations of the existing school system; the charter is permitted to go its own unfettered way to achieve its stated goals. They are "free" of the existing system.

Although it is rarely stated explicitly, the justification for charter schools derives from a conclusion: If you want to innovate in order to demonstrate a more productive context of learning, you have to be free of the stifling rules and regulations of the existing school system whose capacity to change, let alone innovate, is not far above zero. That conclusion can be put more succinctly: For all practical purposes the existing system is unrescuable if the goal is to change and improve it.

I have read scores of applications submitted for approval of a charter school. I have talked to many individuals starting or planning to start a charter school. For my present purposes here, there are characteristics the creators of charter schools state without exception.

1. The school will be small. It will start with a truly small cohort of students, that number will increase in subsequent years but not to the point where size defeats the innovative purposes of the school.
2. Students will be known, treated, and respected as distinctive individuals, not as part of a homogeneous group in which individual differences are ignored, or glossed over, or not capitalized on.
3. The collegial relationship among teachers will be close, even intense, in order to insure that their knowledge of and experience with students are shared, discussed, and utilized in ways appropriate to the needs and characteristics of individual students.
4. The relationship between teachers and parents will not be a superficial or transient one. Parents should and will have a responsible voice and role not only in regard to their child but to the overall, innovative purposes of the school. The usual gulf between parents and school, community and school, will be bridged.

Even if these purposes were recognized at Columbine and similar high schools (and middle schools), they could not be realized. Their size and the balkanization of subject matter in unconnected departments make it impossible. It is understandable if those who commented on the Columbine tragedy said that teachers should be more vigilant about and sensitive to what students are thinking and doing. If it is understandable, it also exposes an appalling degree of ignorance—more charitably, a total unfamiliarity—of the size and organizational features of these schools. What should be the frequency and quality of the relationship between Columbine parents and teachers? What roles and responsibilities should parents assume? Neither question got raised or discussed in all that was said about that school. Is it that parents are uninterested? They feel strange and unwelcomed in the school? No one has ever said that they have a crucial role to play? Or is it that in subtle and non-subtle ways the message has been conveyed that parents should do only what the educators ask them to do, that all other matters are the exclusive preserve of the educators? The charter school movement, in addition to the growing support of parents for vouchers, plus the dramatic rise of the number of parents who opt for home schooling are symptoms of both parental interest and dissatisfaction with schools as they are. . . .

Note

1. These seven points, I must emphasize, are less than the bare bones of the features of a context of productive learning. But, I hope, [the list] gives the reader some basis for distinguishing between contexts of productive and unproductive learning. If I have emphasized the universal human features of curiosity and question asking, it is because their manifestations in classrooms are truly rare, less than frequent (much less).

CHAPTER 16

An Overarching Goal for Students

Sarason turns his attention to the basic question of what a school should be about and laments the lack of attention to the obvious answer: to foster in children "the desire to continue to learn about self, others, and the world." He asks us to recognize that children "come to school already possessed of the major psychological attributes crucial to productive learning."

Arguing that the "educational reform movement, today and in the past, has not come to grips with this overarching aim," Sarason warns us not to look at children in terms of their deficits but rather as young persons who are asset rich in regard to their potential as learners. When we do so, he avers, we will recognize that the regularities that create and sustain the present school culture must be changed.

Question for Seymour Sarason

When educators argue for an asset-rich (as opposed to a deficit-laden) approach to children from poor or minority neighborhoods, they sometimes get accused of ignoring or downplaying the very real differences in the levels of preparedness of such children entering school as compared to kids from highly educated, middle class families. Or they are accused of "celebrating multiculturalism" at the expense of "essential skills." Are these fair criticisms, or does your "overarching goal" demand that we place nurturing a child's "desire to learn" above all else?

Sarason's Response

I think it is a false dichotomy. You do not teach assets or deficits, you teach children. You start where the student is, and that means you know enough about him or her to begin by nurturing the child's desire to learn. The artistry and creativity of the teacher inhere in when and how such nurturing accesses the child's multicultural knowledge and vice versa.

I have to say that the more I read (and have observed) about multiculturalism and the classroom, the more I fear that "multiculturalism" may become a refuge for unimaginative teachers. I have seen, in my life, too many classrooms in which students ask few if any questions and dutifully conform to and regurgitate what the teacher has said. It was no different in classrooms with a multiculturalist focus.

More about issues involving goals and roles for productive learning for students and schools may be found in:

Educational Reform: A Self-Scrutinizing Memoir (2002)
American Psychology and Schools (2001)
Teaching as a Performing Art (1999)
Political Leadership and Educational Failure (1998)
Revisiting "The Culture of the School and the Problem of Change" (1996)
Parental Involvement and the Political Principle (1995)
School Change: The Personal Development of a Point of View (1995)
You Are Thinking of Teaching? Opportunities, Problems, Realities (1993)
Schooling in America: Scapegoat and Salvation (1983)
Educational Handicap, Public Policy, and Social History: A Broadened Perspective on Mental Retardation (1979)

There is, in my opinion, an overarching goal we should have for students. Although I am not downplaying the importance of other major goals, I consider the overarching goal to be one that, if not achieved and sustained, impoverishes educational experience not only during the school years but also in the years thereafter. Let me use as a text for this final sermon the "mission statement" issued by the New Rochelle (New York) public schools in June 1987.

> The mission of the New Rochelle School System, acknowledging its richly complex history, is to produce responsible, self-sufficient citizens who possess the self-esteem, initiative, skills, and wisdom to continue individual growth, pursue knowledge, develop aesthetic sensibilities, and value cultural diversity by providing intellectually challenging educational programs that celebrate change but affirm tradition and promote excellence through an active partnership with the community, a comprehensive and responsive curriculum, and a dedicated and knowledgeable staff.

That is an exemplary mission statement in three respects. First, it identifies the major stakeholders in the educational enterprise, suggesting that the mission is incapable of realization if any of them is absent or relegated to a secondary role. The phrases "an active partnership with the community" and "celebrate change but affirm tradition" have the virtue of suggesting that the boundaries between the community, on the one hand, and the encapsulated school and its encapsulated classrooms, on the other hand, will become far more porous than heretofore. In the context of the mission statement, these phrases are not intended, I assume, to imply that the role of the community is only to support educators to do what they want to do. Comprised as it is of individuals and groups, containing as it does resources and sites relevant to educational goals, the community can be used to change and enhance the experience of students. Mission statements are not prescriptions for action and, therefore, we cannot say what "active partnership with the community" means in this instance. It is fashionable today to be in favor of such an active partnership, although far more often than not such assent on the part of educators means: "How can we get them to support what we are already doing?" At least in the case of the New Rochelle statement, the partnership is for the purpose of change. So, if one were to study New Rochelle schools before the mission statement was publicized and for subsequent years, one should be able to discern changes in relationships among the stakeholders—that is, the quality, substance, and frequency of relationships and the ways in which the different resources of the stakeholders are exploited. Exploited for what purpose? That brings us to the second and more fundamental respect in which the mission statement is refreshing, if not novel. Indeed, of the hundreds of such statements I have read (fortunately, most mission statements are brief), I cannot recall one that says so clearly that the overarching goal is to engender and sustain in students a desire "to continue individual growth, pursue knowledge, develop aesthetic sensibilities . . . by providing intellectually challenging programs." It is noteworthy that such goals are hardly captured or measured by our usual tests.

However atypically refreshing the New Rochelle mission statement is, I have to fault it on two grounds. The first is that . . . the statement reinforces the axiom that schools exist primarily (really exclusively) for students. . . . The second is that it begs the question: Why have schools not "produced" the citizens envisioned in the statement? I do not expect a mission statement to answer that question, and one should be satisfied that the statement suggests that change is in order—that is, what is should no longer be, and what the statement envisions will not be realized under existing structures and practices. But I have to raise that question in order to point out that many of the characteristics of students that the mission statement seeks to engender are already possessed by the students when they start school. Why do they get extinguished or go underground or get manifested outside of school?

If there is anything we can say about the biologically intact, preschool child, it is that he or she is a question-asking, question-answering, questing, knowledge-pursuing organism, pursuing knowledge about self, others, and its world. That is truly a glimpse of the obvious but, remarkably, it is not taken seriously. Our schools (beginning in kindergarten), in a myriad of ways and with the best of intentions, require the student to make a sharp distinction between "what I am interested in and what I am supposed to be interested in, what I am curious about and what I am supposed to be curious about, what I know and what I am supposed to know, what kinds of questions I would like to ask and what questions I am told I should or it is permissible to ask." Put more succinctly, schools do a remarkably effective job, albeit unwittingly, of getting children to conclude that there are two worlds—the one inside of school and the one outside—and they have no doubt whatsoever about which of the two is intrinsically more interesting and stimulating. It is probably the case that students have always drawn that conclusion, and it is not relevant here to try to decide to what extent the conclusion about two worlds is inevitable. But it is also the case that in this century, especially since World War II, the perceived gulf between the two worlds has widened and their contradictory or conflicting purposes (as perceived by students) have become more stark.

Let me now state what should be our overarching goal for students. I say "our" goal, but it is also one that students hold and which, they will tell you, is so poorly and infrequently approximated as to make classrooms very uninteresting places, intellectually and interpersonally. The overarching goal rests on the recognition that children start school with the expectation that their curiosity about a myriad of things—about people, places, growing up—will receive some answers. If you ask children why they are in school, they will not regurgitate a mission statement. They are likely to say that they are in school "to learn," for example, reading, writing, and arithmetic. Some come with feelings of awe, wonder, and excitement, others with an anxious enthusiasm, and some with a fearful reluctance. For all of them, however, school is a source of curiosity and expectations. We can legitimately describe starting school as a rite of passage, the crossing of a dividing line separating a known from an unknown world, moving from a familiar role of existence to an unfamiliar but desirable role with new tasks and responsibilities. Albeit inchoately, children know that life will now be different for them in terms of their responsibilities and the expectations of others. If they know, as they do, that they will be learning, they expect that it will be challenging, interesting, and meaningful. And to the young child, learning means what it means for any learner regardless of age: It will in diverse ways make personal sense in relation to one's interests, questions, skills, and growth. And to "make sense" means concrete sense, that sense of possession and of illumination that carries one willingly forward. It is, apparently, easy to overlook the fact that children have two truly burning interests: themselves and the social world around them. And in regard to each, their questions are both concrete and countless.

All of the above is, once again, obvious, but if one were to observe classrooms from kindergarten onward, one would be hard put to find instances where the obvious is being taken seriously. . . . Two . . . examples will suffice here.

President Kennedy was assassinated on a Friday. In New Haven, schools remained closed until the following Wednesday. That was the day of the week I met with a group of new teachers . . . after the school day. When I entered the clinic conference room, the teachers were talking to each other, rather excitedly, about what they had experienced that day in their classrooms. And what were they talking about? They were voicing their reactions to the assassination and saying that, from the standpoint of learning, it had been a fruitless day because children seemed unable to attend to their tasks. No teacher denied that the assassination took center stage in the minds of the children. No teacher really expected that when the children came to school that day they would be other than overflowing with questions about the assassination. And yet, the teachers proceeded "to try to teach" as if it were a normal day. There was a curriculum, there was a lesson plan, and they took precedence, as if what was gripping the students was irrelevant to educational purposes.

Fortunately, assassinations are infrequent events. If the example is an extreme one, it is nevertheless not atypical of how what is interesting to children so infrequently gets reflected and exploited in learning. How many times in this century has it been said that "you teach children, not subject matter"? When that is said, it is intended to emphasize that learning is arid, unproductive, and stifling to the degree that it does not take into account the interests, curiosity, and questions of the learner. To the degree that classroom learning requires of children that they conform to what others say is important, learn it in ways that others say is the way to learn, and separate this learning from all other contexts of experience and learning children bring to school, the school then is remarkably and predictably effective in getting children to regard the classroom as an uninteresting place. That does not mean that children do not learn what others say they should learn, although it is obvious that a fair number do not. It means that what they learn (what tests measure) is not viewed by students with a sense of growth or achievement but as the overcoming of hurdles in a compulsory obstacle course, which when traversed presumably frees one to pursue one's real interests. In the words of the New Rochelle mission statement, it does not produce citizens who desire "to continue individual growth," certainly not in the educational arena.

A second example is more personal. On the second or third day of my geometry class in high school, the teacher drew two connecting lines on the blackboard and said: "That is an obtuse angle." Why is it called *obtuse?* Why that word and not some other word? Why a word that I had never heard before? Why should I care about obtuse angles or, for that matter, geometry? What does geometry *mean?* Who invented the curse of geometry and what relation did it have to anything in my world? That geometry course stimulated more unanswered questions in me than any other course before or since. In that sense, it was a stimulating course! But it was also a course in which I was in an ever-enveloping fog, and I almost flunked it. One secure conclusion resulted: Only under the threat of death would I take another math class.

And I did not, until my last year of college when I needed a four-point course and the only one that I could fit into my schedule was Richard Henry's math course. I had come to know Professor Henry, a most delightful, funny, challenging, and creative individual. When will you take a course with me, he would ask? I told him about geometry but promised that when hell froze over, I would take his course. If I wanted to graduate, I needed his four-point course. It was quite an experience. For one thing, he was amazingly sensitive to what today we call "math anxiety." Second, any question was on limits, not off, however foolish you might think it was. Third, if you were having difficulty, it was your obligation to say it out loud and his responsibility to help you. Fourth, I never got the feeling that his pace was determined by a curriculum, only by where you and others were. His job, and he said so explicitly and his actions were consistent with what he said, was not only to help you learn math but also to understand and enjoy it. Fifth, and in some ways the most psychologically significant point, he never began with abstractions or formulas that we had to memorize but rather with concrete examples (or tasks) with which we could easily identify from personal experience. He had the most masterful grasp of the need for and the processes required for going from the concrete to the abstract, and he knew how to stimulate students to use their concrete experience.

I know that there are few Richard Henrys among math teachers, but that is not the point of the example. The point is that he taught students, not subject matter, and that is a feature lacking almost totally in teachers generally, including those in higher education. I have observed mathematics and science courses in many public schools, and my dominant reaction is that these courses are reflections of curricula aimed at the achievement of an efficient rote memory at the expense of interest and meaning. Countless other observers would agree. I am not scapegoating teachers or any other group. Teachers teach the way they have been taught, and those who teach them teach the way they have been taught, and so on. Children who begin school are nascent scientists and artists. They are already formed and forming explorers of themselves and their world. That is far more overtly clear in relation to artistic than to scientific activity, but those are surface differences. The preschool years are the awe and wonder years: Why do clouds move? Why is the sky blue? What keeps an airplane in the sky? How do they make pictures on a TV screen? How can you talk to someone who is far away? How are babies made? How are they born? Why do boys have a penis and girls do not? What is a germ? How to you "catch" a cold? Why do people fight? Where is God? If you say there is no God, then who made the world? What is a dream? Why are they sometimes so scary?

. . . That young children are question-asking, answer-seeking characters is among the most obvious features of human development. And that is true regardless of family, race, ethnicity, economic background, or where on this earth children are found. When children start school, a message is conveyed to them that is as influential as it is subtle and unverbalized: "Forget or set aside your world of questions and interests. Your job, our responsibility, is to get you to learn rules, facts, and skills, without which you are nothing. School is not for play or for dreaming. It is work, serious work. And if you pay attention, work hard, some day when you are big, you will understand." There is a distinction between work and labor. To labor, as on an assembly line, is to engage in an activity the products of which in no way reflect characteristics of the laborer; the relation between laborer and product is completely impersonal. To work is to engage in an activity that, in some way to some degree, bears the imprimatur of the worker. To most children, not all, school is where you labor, where much of your world of interests and curiosity becomes alien or unrelated to what you are required to do. School does not extinguish in children the interests and probings of that "other world." That is impossible. What school does is erect a barrier between two worlds, a kind of Berlin Wall that seems in no danger of being torn down.

The overarching aim of schooling should be to recognize, capitalize on, and exploit the obvious fact that children come to school already possessed of the major psychological attributes crucial to productive learning. They are thinkers and doers before they come to school. They are eager to remain thinkers and doers, to integrate new worlds into their old ones—an integration not a separation. They already know that there is much they do not know and are eager to learn. Motivation is not a problem. They want to conform, but to them conformity does not mean giving up or setting aside the world most familiar and intriguing to them. There is a difference between willing conformity and an unwilling and puzzled submission. That children generally experience school as boring and uninteresting should occasion no surprise. What would require explanation is if they felt otherwise.

What is at stake here is what happens to children not only during the school years in regard to this overarching aim but in their adult years as well. The aim of education is not simply to keep students in school and to graduate them, just as the aim of imprisonment of criminals is not to make sure that they serve their sentences. On the level of rhetoric, we are told that the aim of imprisonment is to reduce the likelihood that the criminal will engage in illegal activities once the sentence is served. The realities, unfortunately, contradict the rhetoric. Analogously, we want students to do more and learn more than is symbolized by a diploma or test scores. Surely no one would disagree with this excerpt from the New Rochelle mission statement: "to produce responsible, self-sufficient citizens who possess the self-esteem, initiative, skills, and *wisdom to continue individual growth [and] pursue knowledge.*" Should not our aim be to judge whatever we do for children in our schools by the criterion of how we are fostering the desire to continue to learn about self, others, and the world, to live in the world of ideas and possibilities, to see the life span as an endless intellectual and personal quest for knowledge and meaning? Should we not be upset that so many students come to view the life of the mind, the world of ideas, the history of man, as derogated arenas of experience?

The educational reform movement, today and in the past, has not come to grips with this overarching aim. One can alter curricula, change power relationships, raise standards, and do a lot more, but if these efforts are not powered by altered conceptions of what children are and what makes them tick and keeps them intellectually alive, willingly pursuing knowledge and growth, their results will be inconsequential. As I said earlier, the problem is a long-standing one, but precisely because the worlds in and out of school have become increasingly separated, and the school world suffers by comparison in terms of interest, stimulation, and motivation, the consequences of that separation are more dangerous for our society. Until the sixties it was valid to say that education reform was cyclical—that is, about every decade or so the fire for reform (which never went out) would become a four-alarm blaze that the society sought to extinguish. Since the sixties, however, the reform movement has never been far from societal center stage. What has happened is that every segment of our society has come to see, although for diverse reasons, that the inadequacies of our schools are having and will continue to have untoward consequences for the health of the social fabric and the changing relationship of the society to the rest of the world. The concern is warranted, but when I read the plethora of reports that essentially recommend what has been recommended and done before (variations on a few themes notwithstanding), I see no indication that the overarching aim I stated, and which has been stated by many others in the past, is acknowledged and taken seriously. And by this I mean two things. First, you must understand and digest the fact that children, all children, come to school motivated to enlarge their worlds. You start with *their* worlds.[1] You do not look at them, certainly not initially, as organisms to be molded and regulated. You look at them to determine how what they are, seek to know, and have experienced can be used as the fuel to fire the process for enlargement of interests, knowledge, and skills. You do not look at them from the perspective of a curriculum, classroom, or school structure. You enter their world to comprehend and reinforce the psychological assets they already possess. You do not look at them in terms of deficits: what they do not know but need to know. Far from having deficits, they are asset rich. You enter their world in order to aid them and you to build bridges between two worlds, not walls.

Second, if you take the first point seriously, you are required not to start with an unreflective acceptance of schools as we know them but rather with the question: What should schools be in order to accomplish what pursuit of the first point suggests? As long as you start the reform effort with that unreflective acceptance of the culture, traditions, and organization of classrooms and schools as we know them, the implications of the first point will not surface. If you take that first point seriously, you will find yourself asking: If we were to start from scratch, what would schools look like? But, it can be argued, we are not starting from scratch. We have schools. How do we begin to change schools to make them more consistent with that first point? That question sounds more practical, not an exercise in wishful thinking.

In my experience, those who ask that presumably more practical question—usually saying that to disagree with my overarching aim is to be for sin and against virtue—have no comprehension of the radical changes that would be required in all of those variables that are part of the educational enterprise. When I point out what some of those changes might be and the time perspective one must adopt in regard to them—the obstacles that will be encountered, the resistances, the experience we need to gain to learn from failure, the knowledge that where we want to go in no clear way tells us how to get there—they react to me as if all of my genes converged to produce a wet blanket. What they seek are answers, and by answers they mean elevations in test scores. Although they regard the overarching aim as obviously virtuous, they are both unable and unwilling to confront two questions: What is there about classrooms and schools that is inimical to that aim? Why should we expect that the reforms now being proposed will positively support that aim? Today the fashionable buzzword is "restructuring." Granted that restructuring (whatever that may mean) is necessary, and granted that it can have desirable consequences for parents and educators, on what basis, other than hope and prayer, will it bring about classrooms consistent with the overarching aim? . . .

. . . In my experience, too many people have concluded that too many teachers are not as concerned as they should be about the performance of students. That is an unjustified and demeaning caricature. If many teachers burn out, it is a consequence of frustration and disappointment with the fruits of their efforts. . . . The logic or structure of subject matter should, whenever possible, be related to something in the experience of students. There are classroom teachers who understand and act appropriately in regard to that insight. They are few in number, and for two major reasons. The first is the pressure teachers feel they are under to cover a curriculum, causing them to focus on subject matter and not students. That, of course, does not explain why some teachers are able to overcome or not succumb completely to such pressure. The second reason is that the formal preparation of teachers is grossly inadequate in helping them to understand and implement the insight. It is easy to state and agree with the overarching aim; it is not easy to comprehend it in that visceral way that gives stimulus and direction to action. Teachers are taught the way they have been taught in their preprofessional years and before.

No one who seeks to become a teacher is incapable of gaining the insight. That teachers, like any other professional group, will vary in the ease with which they gain the insight and in the quality of their efforts at implementation is not the issue. The issue is that the overarching aim and the insight it requires are far from central in their professional training. Earlier in this book I briefly discussed the intractability of medical schools to efforts at making issues surrounding caring and compassion more central to medical training. As a result, physicians who are caring and compassionate are that way despite their training, not because of it, which is why there are relatively few of them. I should point out that medical students are selected by criteria that absolutely have no relationship to the attributes of caring and compassion. We are far better off in regard to those who seek a career in education. In my experience, they seek such a career because they see the role of the teacher as quintessentially expressive of the desire to be caring and compassionate. But these are not superficial characteristics. What they require is the effort to comprehend someone else's world and to use that comprehension to help that individual. In the case of the teacher, that should mean comprehending and utilizing that which in a student's experience is relevant to the task at hand. I am obviously not suggesting that teachers become psychotherapists or philosophers, but that they be helped to understand that their primary task (not their exclusive one) is to figure out how the experiences of students can be brought to bear on subject matter—that is, how to make the wall between two worlds more porous and permeable. That is no easy intellectual and personal task. Given the way our classrooms and schools are organized, the effect that has on teachers and students, and the values and goals that are dominant, the task is an impossible one.

On the very day (January 10, 1990) I write these words, the mass media are reporting the results of the most recent national assessment of student performance. The Secretary of Education deemed them "appalling." Scores had not declined, and he and others made valiant efforts to take heart that the test scores of this racial group or that age cohort had increased somewhat. (This is akin to the difference between being run down by a car going forty or one going forty-four miles an hour.) So what is to be done? The secretary proclaims that schools have to be restructured, that more groups have to be related to matters educational, and that we must do better than we are doing. His heart, not his head, is in the right place.

What if the results of the national assessment had been dramatically better? What would the secretary (and many others) have said? Does anyone doubt that he would have joyously said that we are on the road to recovery and that our major educational aims are being realized? It is important here that I emphasize that such a dramatic improvement would be cause for satisfaction. Having said that, I must go on to say that such improvement in no way can be interpreted to mean that students are now more motivated to continue their intellectual growth, that they are more interested in the world of ideas and history, that they regard schooling more positively and enthusiastically, that they understand themselves and their worlds more deeply, that they are better "thinking" organisms, and that they have acquired those attributes that will make them better citizens and those attitudes and interests that will permit them productively to exploit themselves in a troublesome world. In brief, what do these improvements in test scores signify for the overarching aim I have stressed? The answer has to be in two parts. The first and most justified answer is that we do not know, and not knowing that (because we do not seek to know) speaks volumes about how seriously we take the overarching aim.

The second answer is that we have learned enough to know that changes in test scores can be due to factors, at least in part, that are not all that praiseworthy—for example, teaching for the test and emphasizing facts. So, for example, on the front page of the New Haven Register for January 6, 1990, there is the headline "Slight Gain Posted by Pupils on State Tests." In Connecticut these "mastery" tests for reading, writing, math, and language arts are administered to fourth, sixth, and eighth graders. The Commissioner of Education is quoted as saying: "I think we are upbeat and moving in the right direction. But we can't declare victory. We still have a long way to go." The article goes on to report that the commissioner "believes teachers have learned 'to teach for the test'—a practice educators usually criticize . . . because students may learn only what is necessary to pass, not a broad range of knowledge. But because the mastery tests evaluate dozens of specific skills, teaching for the tests means pupils are learning what they should know, the commissioner said." Knowledge and skills—attaining them is the aim of education! All else is a dispensable luxury, and that includes the overarching aim I have been discussing. Pour in the facts, hone their skills, measure them objectively, tote that bale, and old man river keeps on rolling along. With friends like that, education need never worry about enemies. And let us not scapegoat tests and testmakers whose business it is, after all, to give the policymakers what they want. It is not their business to change the priorities of their customers.

I have presented what I believe should be our overarching aim for students. It is not the sole aim of education, but it should require us to ensure that it informs and directs any other aim. Take, for example, the teaching of a foreign language, which some states (for example, New York) have mandated. I have sat in classrooms in which a foreign language was being taught. Predictably, the teaching rationale was no different from that for the more traditional subject matter in terms of how the classroom is organized, the length of a period, and the intervals between classes. Also predictably, because my observations were made in classes that were elective not compulsory, the students began with a good deal of interest and enthusiasm. (I could tell this story with my own experience in Spanish and German classes when I was in high school, but I will refrain except to say that it led me decades later to observe these kinds of classrooms.) Interest and enthusiasm did not last long, which is not to say that they were extinguished. But in the main these became joyless affairs as the students became mired in matters of grammar and conjugation, as the gulf between what they were learning and what they wanted to learn widened. Learning a foreign language—its structural logic, idioms, inflections, and those inevitable exceptions to the usual rules—is no easy matter. There is no way you can learn without struggle. In any event, neither the teachers nor the students I observed were satisfied with what was going on. The students were dutiful and respectful, but not very motivated. To say that they had been "engaged" would truly be an overstatement. The teachers were painfully aware of this, but a curriculum is a curriculum and they rarely diverged from it.

With one of these teachers I felt I could be intrusively direct, and so I said to her: "Neither you nor your students seem all that happy about the class. Is there not another way to think about it? Forget you are in a school. What if it were summer and the parents of these children asked you to teach them Spanish and you had them all day for a month or so and you could teach them in any way you wanted. Would it look like an intensive version of this classroom?" To which she replied (paraphrased): "You are right. I am not happy with the class. But then again, I never am satisfied. These are a good bunch of kids. The problem is that I have them for forty-minute periods three times a week. Except for these periods, they live in a world of English. What would I do if I had them all day, every day, in the summer? The short answer is that we would, for a good part of that time, *live* Spanish. No grammar or anything like that. That's the way I learned Spanish, and quickly, when in my junior year in college I lived for a year with a family in Mexico. I knew next to nothing about Spanish, and their English was no better. It was quite an experience that for the first week or so was both frustrating and exciting. After the first week, I was sorry I came. After a month, I was amazed that I had become semi-fluent. I had my Spanish books and dictionary, which during that first month were not all that helpful. So what would I do in the summer with kids like these? We would live Spanish and we would have a ball. They would eat it up. I can just see the looks on their faces as they hear themselves conversing in real Spanish."

I then asked her, with as deadpan an expression as I could muster, "Why can't that be done during the school year?" In staring disbelief, she answered: "Are you kidding? How could that be possible the way school days are organized? They have to take other courses. How could they be freed for a month to learn only Spanish? It simply is not possible." She was right, of course. Once one accepts the traditional way in which high schools are organized—which means accepting a number of dubious assumptions about factors that make for productive learning—then my question is nonsensical. But if it is nonsensical, her answer explicitly concedes that by virtue of the way the school is organized, she and her students are shortchanged. Both have to conform to that organization. The organization cannot conform to what this teacher considers a more productive way of learning Spanish, a quicker way, not a way of convincing students that learning a foreign language is not for them. So the question becomes: Are there ways of thinking about the organization of schools that would make it more possible to try and evaluate contexts for learning that hold promise of being more consistent with the overarching aim? If you start by accepting the present structure, if you insist that those who seek to change it must guarantee ahead of time that it will work, you guarantee one thing: Nothing will change. If you unreflectively assume that the psychological rationale undergirding the present structure is valid in whole or in part, you possess all of the attributes necessary to reinforce the status quo. . . .

I am not aware of any report by a commission appointed to recommend educational reform that characterizes its recommendations as radical or revolutionary. Those adjectives smack too much of political movements on the extreme left of the political continuum. If the aim of some of these reports is to bring about radical change, that aim is cloaked in language that obscures the intent. To say that, however, attributes aims to these reports that the report writers did not intend—that is, they seek no radical change, the system stays pretty much as it is, and what exists must be improved, not discarded. If *radical* implies getting at the root of a problem, these reports are the polar opposite of radical. I am by no means alone in this view. If anything characterizes the attitude toward these reports of people in diverse groups—those with an interest or stake in what happens in and to our schools—it is not renewed hope but a puzzled pessimism, puzzled because they want to be hopeful or optimistic and yet cannot understand why recommended changes should have the desired consequences. As one person said to me: "I view these reports the way I do an alcoholic's promise to go on the wagon. How many times can you be disappointed?" Actuarially speaking, this person was making a prediction that the future will confirm. . . .

Note

1. It is more complicated than that because unless the teacher begins with an understanding of her or his particular way of learning, *a* way among several "learning styles," each of which is characteristic of some but not all people, each of which is legitimate in that it is productive for some learners, the teacher will be unable to grasp the different starting points of students, that is, flex to their individual styles. No one more than David Hunt of the Ontario Institute for Studies in Education has stated this problem so clearly, researched it so thoroughly, and applied it so productively to real teachers and real classrooms. His book (1987) has the very apt title, *Beginning with Ourselves: In Practice, Theory, and Human Affairs.* As best as I can determine, his work and book have had no influence in teacher-training programs.

CHAPTER 17

Students as Teachers

Departing from his habit of refraining from giving advice, Sarason argues that "students in middle and high schools . . . be encouraged to learn what is involved in teaching." He looks at several school settings in which this already takes place and proposes an eight-year study of the impact of training secondary students to serve as voluntary adjunct teachers of younger children.

Using kids' mastery of new technology as an example, Sarason argues that we seriously underestimate what young people are "capable of learning and doing" and asks that this experiment be subjected to a rigorous analysis, something that he finds missing in most educational reform endeavors.

Question for Seymour Sarason

One can accuse schools of a tendency to infantilize everyone (especially students and teachers), such that people in school act in a less mature, less responsible way than they do in other social contexts. If this is so, does it not militate against your proposal to involve students in teaching?

Sarason's Response

1. In the legendary one-room schoolhouse older students regularly taught younger ones.
2. Parents with two or more children frequently have the older ones instruct younger ones.
3. There is a vast literature on group learning in which students teach other students, although the students and the teacher do not label the activity as teaching.
4. There are scads of early teenagers who spend their summers as informal "teachers"—called "camp counselors."

None of the above is infantilizing. What is infantilizing is when a teacher assumes that students are empty vessels that have to be filled. Necessity is not only the mother of invention, it also stimulates a redefinition of what a resource is. And children are one of

Reprinted with the permission of Teachers College Press from "Students as Teachers" in *Teaching as a Performing Art* by Seymour Sarason (New York: Teachers College Press, 1999).

our most tragically underutilized teaching resources. I encourage readers interested in the redefinition of resources to read *Crossing Boundaries,* a book I co-wrote with Elizabeth Lorentz.

More about issues involving goals and roles for productive learning for students and schools may be found in:

Educational Reform: A Self-Scrutinizing Memoir (2002)
American Psychology and Schools (2001)
Crossing Boundaries: Collaboration, Coordination, and the Redefinition of Resources
    [with Elizabeth Lorentz] (1998)
Political Leadership and Educational Failure (1998)
Revisiting "The Culture of the School and the Problem of Change" (1996)
Parental Involvement and the Political Principle (1995)
School Change: The Personal Development of a Point of View (1995)
You Are Thinking of Teaching? Opportunities, Problems, Realities (1993)
The Predictable Failure of Educational Reform (1990)
Schooling in America: Scapegoat and Salvation (1983)
Educational Handicap, Public Policy, and Social History: A Broadened Perspective
    on Mental Retardation (1979)

. . . [Here is a] proposal I shall make about students learning to teach: Students in middle and high schools will be encouraged to learn what is involved in teaching.[1] The idea of students as tutors and mentors of younger students has been taken seriously in some schools, but the purpose of this practice has not been to use it as an initial step in learning how to teach. That is to say, the purpose has been solely to help students at risk and not to further or broaden the intellectual and career education of the student tutors whose "rewards" are largely, if not exclusively, of a personal nature. Why has the use of students as tutors not spread? The reasons are many but one of them is how middle and high school students are viewed as resources. Let me illustrate what I mean by several examples.

The first is a long-standing program in the Shoreham-Wading River Middle School on Long Island in New York. A book about the program was written by a teacher, Mr. Vlahakis, *and* his students (Vlahakis et al., 1978).[2] In any one week approximately 300 of that middle school's 600 students spend several hours . . . in a helping relationship in a community setting (such as nursing homes). Initially, the directors of these settings were very skeptical, to say the least, about students, on average 11–12 years of age, in an active relationship with old or handicapped individuals; these students could be a burden or a nuisance, perhaps even a danger, given their immaturity. But the arrangements were made in part because the teacher would act as supervisor as well as conduct sessions with the students, going over their responsibilities and duties as well as determining how the students were making personal and intellectual sense of their experiences. It did not take long before the directors said they would gladly take more students because they were providing a very valuable service. As the book indicates, there were memorable personal and educational experiences for the students who had never seen themselves as resources of use to others, just as others had viewed them as young, immature *children* whose place was in a classroom and school. Of course they were young, of course they were immature by adult standards, of course they would require close supervision, and of course there was no guarantee they would not make mistakes. But equally, of course, they were students with a burning curiosity about themselves in relation to an "outside" world which represented a challenge they wished to accept.

The second example (Butterworth & Weinstein, 1997) is a K–6 private, far-from-affluent school created by parents who ensured that there would be a significant number of minority students, many of whom would require tuition scholarships. In addition to the regular academic program (which differs perhaps by virtue of specialist teaching in the elementary grades and by the requirement of a second language), there existed a variety of additional programs which enhanced the daily classroom activities. These included student government, a school economy, publishing, theater performances, an outdoor education program, community experiences, an after-school program, and holiday celebrations.

The school had a system of student government in which a mayor, vice-mayor, secretary, treasurer, and social coordinator were elected by the whole school twice a year. Each individual running for office appointed a campaign manager who, along with the candidate, prepared a speech as well. Representatives from each class completed the membership of the governing body. Two teachers helped the students plan activities and fund-raisers for the school.

The school also had an economic system in which children held regular jobs around the school and were paid a weekly salary in the local scrip, "keybucks." Jobs ranged from aiding in the classroom or office to maintenance around the school grounds: Adults in the school supervised jobs related to their interests and classroom/subject area needs. Jobs were listed, students wrote applications, and were interviewed for positions. Students could save keybucks in the bank (run by the sixth grade) or spend keybucks at the school store (run by the fifth grade) or bookstore (run by the fourth grade) and for field trips and the use of special equipment like computers.

Publishing was a third area of activity for the school. A student newspaper was published monthly, staffed by students from all the grades, and a literary magazine was published twice a year by the fourth grade. A yearbook with photographs was also published by a student staff with teacher help. The principal wrote a weekly Wednesday letter to parents and children, and classroom teachers routinely sent home newsletters about class activities.

During the year, two school-wide performances were held, a musical for the holiday season, and a dramatic or musical comedy at the end of the year. Scripts were modified so that every child in the school performed in the play. In addition, each grade put on a play for the school and for parents.

An outdoor education program involved fourth to sixth graders in a 5-day camping trip to an area of ecological importance and younger children in one-night camping trips. Class visits to community theatre, concerts, and museums were also regular parts of the program. Students brought their own performances to local homes for the aged. Community resources also visited the school, for example, two architects collaborated with fifth-grade students in designing a model community for their social studies assignment.

The year was also punctuated by celebration—Halloween parades, Thanksgiving luncheon, Martin Luther King's Birthday, Grandparent Day, and Graduation dinner, to list a few. These traditions have developed rich, elaborate rituals which brought energy to the school periodically during the year and warmly involved the family community.

The Butterworth and Weinstein description is of a setting in which what we could call "small kids" are given and accept duties and responsibilities rarely if ever given in public elementary schools. What the writers make clear is that the principal and teachers did not regard the students as *just* small kids unable to accept diverse responsibilities, too young and inexperienced to confront tasks that require initiative, planning, creativity, and cooperative endeavor. The students did not do what they did because it was required or demanded of them. Of course the teachers offered ideas, advice, and guidance, but that does not explain the enthusiasm, energy, and the accomplishments of the students. I had occasion to talk to two high school students who had attended that school, and they said that their years there were far more than what is ordinarily meant by "going to school." In fact, they said, their subsequent years in middle and high school were less challenging, required less initiative, and certainly provided less of that sense of community in which ideas and purposes could be tested in action. If I had to put it in my own words, what they seemed to be saying would go like this: "We were accorded that degree of respect that made it easy for us to engage in the variety of tasks and projects we did. We were not regarded as dependent, guidance seeking, dutiful kids from whom not much was expected. We were made to feel that we had something to contribute to each other and to the school."

The third example is about high school students. A colleague of mine, Dr. Richard Sussman, had obtained a master's degree in child development at Columbia's Teachers College. Several years later he visited a professor there whom he had found very helpful and stimulating. Dr. Sussman was interested in the current research program she and her graduate students were planning and doing. The professor described the research program, which would require studies of elementary school children. She finished her account by saying that the research was not likely to be done because it would require a number of schools and most of those she had approached did not wish to cooperate. For purposes of brevity, here is what Dr. Sussman asked:[3]

1. If I can provide you with 10 or so selected high school students, would you explain to them the goals and significances of the research?
2. Would you train them to collect your data?
3. Would you give them a mini-seminar on data analysis?

The professor was predictably, understandably, more than surprised and skeptical. How could you trust high school students to collect research data? Was it not likely they would make errors of one kind or another? After all, the one thing we know is that they have had no experience in research and the moral and scientific obligations of the researcher. After brief discussion Dr. Sussman played his trump card by saying, "If you can agree with what I have suggested, I can make available to you all the elementary schools you need." That research went so well that the students were invited to make a presentation at Teachers College and made a similar presentation to their board of education.

We pin labels on individuals and groups which implicitly define what they can do and what we can expect of them. And the implications of labels are in the form of either positive or negative self-fulfilling prophecies. In the positive form *you define and act* toward individuals (or groups) in ways that make it likely—we are dealing with probabilities—that they will be able to do what your label indicates they can do. In the negative form your definition says what this or that person *cannot* do, and you act in ways consistent with that label and definition, thus making it likely that you will "prove" the validity of the label or definition. . . .

Inevitably we categorize, pigeonhole, slot, and label people in terms of ability, aptitude, interests, motivation. That is certainly justified when we can point to credible efforts which have challenged the validity of our labels and support rather than undermine the labels we use. Unfortunately, however, we are frequently totally unaware that we apply our labels on the basis of custom, or our socialization into our culture, or conventional wisdom which is certainly conventional but not necessarily wise, or sheer prejudice. I did not present the three examples to convey the impression that labeling and defining (and their implications) are inherently pernicious or unwarranted. My purpose rather was a form of plea, specifically in regard to students in our schools, that we re-examine the ways we define them as resources because if we do so we are very likely not only to begin to redefine them, but to understand more clearly the obstacles that institutional custom and practice place in the way of taking the redefinition process seriously. So let me after this long prologue present my proposal for students as beginning teachers.

My proposal calls for an eight-year study in which, beginning in the third year of the study, 10 students are chosen by criteria indicating that they might be capable of performing a teaching function in the classroom, which in no way means that they would be teaching their peers but rather students in lower grades. Nor does it mean that by the end of the initial study they would have demonstrated other than a very circumscribed but real teaching function. And by *real* I mean that if you sat in the classroom, you would not be in doubt that they are endeavoring to teach something of educational value.

I said that selection would begin in the third year of the study for several reasons. The most obvious reason, of course, is that those who will be participants in developing a course of action will have had no previous experience to use as a guide. They will confront many knotty questions. What grade should we start with? Should we initially start the students in one-on-one relationships, and if so, how would we want to differentiate that experience from what we call tutoring? If, as we hope, they will learn to perform in a classroom, what do we have to do to help them gain an understanding of what has been learned about learning? And to gain that understanding how do we help them to use their own educational experiences? The aim is not to give them a course in the psychology of learning but rather in a step-by-step fashion over several years to make them sensitive to the fact that what a teacher does or does not do is a direct reflection of how a teacher thinks and, in addition, that for any aspect of subject matter the teacher has to know that aspect very, very well. How and when do you begin this learning about learning process? How and when do you start to help them see and accept the fact that teaching is an art, a performing one, requiring of the teacher imagination and a grasp of where the learner is coming from, a grasp the sources of which are both cognitive and intuitive? Because the student is, after all, a student who is learning other subject matter, what would be the minimal time the student should devote as a study participant, a minimum below which subverts the goals of the study? . . .

. . . That the proposal challenges conventional views of the ability of students and their role in a classroom and school is obvious, but it is not a challenge that deserves out of hand rejection as pie-in-the-sky musings. Let us not forget that one way you can write human history is as a series of battles centering around the question: What are people capable of learning and doing? So, for example, take the question of whether people—all people, not only ruling elites—should have a voice in governance. Up until the eighteenth century the answer was a clear no; you could not trust people to make wise decisions about governance; they were too inexperienced in the ways of the world, they were too gullible and too ignorant to be given responsibility. Besides, they not only needed to be ruled with a firm hand, they wanted such rule, they wanted to be told what to think and do. Even today, there are many places on this earth where that battle continues. I am not contending that all challenges to how we define individuals and groups are of equal merit. I am contending that my proposal does have that degree of merit as to be taken seriously in action. The purpose of this chapter is to provide an underlying rationale for my proposal, not to take up the methods and research design of an initial study. There is no one best way to proceed in a study for which previous experience gives us no guide as to method and evaluation and more. When I say that this has to be viewed as an exploratory study, "exploratory" does not excuse sloppiness, diffuseness, or an undue dependence on opinion or anecdote. And precisely because of the importance of such a study, it should not be undertaken unless there are sufficient time and funding to do justice to it. We have had a surfeit of initial studies in education where the pressures of time and money contributed to compromises that made it virtually impossible to come to any secure conclusion about the findings. An initial study is not a fishing expedition; it is a reasoned exploration which should determine when, if, and how further studies should be conducted.

My proposal raises some very practical issues of which the most important is: Who will have responsibility for working with and overseeing the students? Before you can think about that question there has to be agreement on three points: Teachers do not have time to be other than part-time participants; not every teacher has the motivation, knowledge, and interpersonal skills to instruct, guide, mentor these students; the goal of the study is *not* to select and train tutors but to provide these students with a degree of understanding about learning and teaching which will allow them, albeit in a *circumscribed* way and time, to teach a class of younger students. I italicized circumscribed to emphasize the obvious point that we would not be training teachers but young people for the purpose of providing them the opportunity to begin to experience and comprehend what teaching requires.

Over the decades I have gone to see student productions of plays and musicals. In each instance the students were selected by a teacher-director who, I assume, was not compensated (or was very minimally compensated) for this extracurricular activity. That teacher-director was essentially self-selected; it was something he or she wanted to do. Although the audience was never in doubt that they were witnessing an amateur performance, several things were noteworthy. First, the students were giving their all; to say they were luxuriating in the opportunity to perform is no exaggeration.[4] Second, some of those productions were surprisingly good, leading me and others to say (proudly), "Some of those kids have what it takes to become real actors." Third, in a few of these atypical instances I knew the teacher-director, and therefore, I was not surprised by what they got out of their cast. They went far beyond ensuring that their students knew their lines; they would make an effort to explain the "psychology" of the role and the importance of timing, facial expression, body language, and voice projection; they encouraged students to imagine the kinds of feelings of the person they were portraying. (Some of these teacher-directors were members of a community amateur theatrical group.)

All of this is by way of saying that I have known teachers who I believe had what it takes to do justice to the students in my proposal. The degree to which that kind of teacher could participate in the study would depend on funding. In an initial study of much potential significance, the first question should be: *What do we need to know, have, and do in order to be able to determine at the end of the study that we are on the right road, that we should be allowed to learn and do, or that further expenditure of funds is not justified?* Ignoring that caveat is precisely why I wrote *Charter Schools: Another Flawed Educational Reform?* (1998)—because proponents of charter schools had (and have) a grievously unrealistic conception of the inadequacies of the resources charter school legislation imposed. I hope I am wrong in my predictions that (1) the majority of charter schools will fall far short of their mark, and (2) we will never know why one charter school was successful and another was not. In the case of charter schools, I should hasten to add, unrealistic funding was but one reason for my predictions.

Who should have responsibility for developing and implementing such an initial study? There are more than a few *individuals* in our colleges and universities who would be appropriate because they know schools and their culture, they truly understand young students; they are careful observers, investigators, and reporters; they have worked with or have participated in the preparation of teachers (or both); they are imaginative people with interpersonal, diplomatic skills; they are serious workers whose ideas and investigative programs attract others to them either as students or colleagues; they are risk takers. Some are in schools of education, some in departments of psychology, some in institutes of child development. I would have no trouble coming up with a list of *indi-*

viduals who, if they were interested, would do justice to the study. They have a proven track record, they are well known to others in their arena of interests and work. It would be a list of individuals and not of places or institutions because it would be an egregious indulgence of parochialism to think that because it is a study of students and schools the responsibility for it should be given to a school of education. Only a few of the individuals on my list are in such schools. I could come up with a short list of school teachers I have known who could play a very important role in such a study but who lack the knowledge and experience to be given the responsibility of an action research program. The list is short for the obvious reason that although I have had occasion to observe and know many scores of teachers, they are a very minute sample of the approximately 2 million people who teach in our schools.

I have talked about a single study but only to simplify this discussion. There should be several such studies and for two reasons. First, precisely because we cannot count on previous experience and an extant literature, and because each of the several sites predictably will proceed in different small and large ways—there is no one best way to proceed—we will learn more than if there is only one site. Second, it should be made possible for each site to be in meaningful contact with the others: to be able to observe and learn from each other; not only on the level of ideas and method but also on the level of personnel exchange. Differences in approach are virtues to be protected, but that does not rule out cooperation. You learn a lot when you design an appliance, a car, or a program, and one of the things you learn, and it is the most important thing, is how to capitalize on what you have learned for the purpose of *redesign*. That is why Kenneth Wilson titled his seminal book *Redesigning Education* (1994).

Some readers may have asked themselves why my proposal is about students in middle and high schools where it is not unusual for students to serve as tutors and even perform a community service. Although I would have no objection to starting in high school, I prefer starting in middle school because it is in those years that so many students begin to lose interest in and motivation for school learning because (among other things) so much of what they learn has no particular personal relevance; it is for so many of them arid book knowledge which tells them little about themselves or others or what to them is the unexplored world. They are told they are no longer "children" in elementary school but not big or mature like high school students, a message that implies they cannot be given meaningful responsibility for almost anything except to learn what they are told to learn. It is, in my opinion, an example of a negative self-fulfilling prophecy. I am again reminded here of the enthusiasm, seriousness, and energy middle school students manifest when they engage in dramatic productions, especially in those instances where the students had a voice in choosing the play or musical to be performed, or in instances similar to those I described earlier. If my proposal should turn out to achieve even modest, positive results, it should dispel any doubts that similar efforts with high school students will be even more productive. I prefer to start with students with whom "conventional wisdom" says the outcomes will be uniformly negative, which is by way of saying that I like to operate on the basis of the dynamics of the positive self-fulfilling prophecy. But I must say again that I have no principled objections to starting with high school students. The important point and task is to start.

Imagine for the moment (if you can!) that the studies, at whatever levels from which students are chosen, produce credible, positive results. That is to say, the students gain an increased understanding of themselves in relation to the nature and complexity of learning and teaching; they know they are not teachers and they also know that far more is involved in teaching than knowing subject matter, that between teacher and pupil is a demanding process requiring the teacher to be a performer ever sensitive and adaptable to what his or her audience is thinking and feeling. If they have manifested increased understanding and a very modest level of competence, they have also acquired both humility and respect for the nature of learning and teaching.

So what? Assuming that these studies begin to have a *general* impact—that these studies do not, as most studies usually do, remain a local affair—then teachers of "younger" pupils have a pool of "older" pupils who can be helpful to them. Teachers have fallen into three groups when I presented my proposal to them. One group almost instantly and unequivocally agreed that using the older students would be a pain in the neck, their contributions not compensated by the time and responsibility the teacher would have to assume. Not a few of these teachers regarded the proposal as outlandish. The second group consisted of teachers who were intrigued but balked at the idea that these students should ever be permitted to teach a class, however circumscribed in time and scope it may be. They had no trouble with using them as one-on-one tutors—indeed they would welcome them as tutors—but not ever as "teachers." As almost all of them said, "I have pupils who are at risk to whom I cannot give the attention they need, so if I had tutors with some training, it would be a boon. But to help and supervise students teach a class is asking too much of the teacher and student." The third group, smaller than either of the first two, in one or another way said, "That would be an interesting challenge that would introduce novelty into my days, especially if a few other teachers in my school went along and we formed a working group. But I would not participate unless I knew my principal, other higher-ups, and parents were solidly supportive." This third group consisted of no more than 20% of the teachers, a fact that I found both surprising and encouraging. I should add that one teacher in this group said that she had given up on preparatory programs for teachers and that school systems should select and train their own teachers "so why not start with students in the system?"

My proposal challenges our accustomed way of defining the interests, aptitudes, and abilities of students. I am reminded here of many middle and high school teachers—and a few elementary teachers—who are astounded and chagrined that they have students who can use computers better and more creatively than they can; indeed in some instances the student has taught the teacher. The reaction of teachers stems in part from *their* view of how complicated learning to use the computer can be, and in part from the way they regard the capacities of their young students. Teachers are not alone in this respect. Most teachers are women and are familiar with the past history of how women were narrowly defined in terms of work and career. But they, like most of us, may know a lesson from history but do not generalize it to other groups. More to the point of this chapter are those studies which have demonstrated that carefully selected individuals can effectively conduct brief psychotherapy (with circumscribed goals) even though they have had no formal training. More important than the labels appended to the kind of work in which they were normally engaged were the kinds of people they were: sensitive, supportive, nonconfrontational, capable of listening and engendering trust.

My proposal, if the results are positive and accepted and implemented generally, can increase the number of people who seek a career in education for the best of reasons: They have had experiences that indicated a match between their interests and aptitudes and teaching young people. . . . In the conventional performing arts the individual's interests in a career in this or that performing art begin early in life. That is infrequently the case among those who choose teaching as a career, which in part (and only in part) explains why many teachers come to wish they had chosen another career path. . . .

Notes

1. As I will make clear later, my proposal is a complicated one because it not only requires programmatic and other changes in schools but in preparatory programs for teachers as well. The idea of students as teachers was suggested to me by Kenneth Wilson who, with Bennett Daviss, wrote the very seminal book *Redesigning Education* (1994).

2. The book was generally not available and is out of print, which is why, with the permission of Mr. Vlahakis, I excerpted a large part of it for my book *You Are Thinking of Teaching?* (1993c).

3. The rationale undergirding his questions would take us too far afield, but the interested reader will find that rationale in *Crossing Boundaries* (Sarason & Lorentz, 1998), a book to which Dr. Sussman contributed.

4. In Chapter 4 I noted that it is by no means unusual for professional actors to say that their choice of career had its seeds in their middle and high school experiences in student production. This, as I shall discuss later, is one of the consequences I would hope would be true for some of the students in regard to choice of teaching as a career.

CHAPTER 18

Parental Involvement and Power Struggles: Applying the Political Principle to Relationships Within the School and Beyond

In this selection, drawn from three chapters in his book *Parental Involvement and the Political Principle,* Sarason extends his definition of *the political principle* ("when decisions are made affecting you . . . , you should have a role, a voice, in the process of decision making") to include parents specifically and the community generally. He reminds us that "parents and educators [are] unequal in the possession and exercise of power" regarding schoolchildren, and he points to the 1954 Supreme Court decision on segregation as a reflection on how quickly the parents' role as instigators of change was bypassed by governmental and bureaucratic actions.

Sarason cautions parent and community advocates to recognize that while power is unequally distributed both without and *within* the school system, the struggle becomes "unproductive" when "the relationships between the two sides center around power and turf." He urges teachers to reflect on how vulnerable they are likely to feel, as parents, when they approach school personnel on behalf of their own children. He also reminds them how much they share with parents in their feelings of powerlessness when faced with seemingly arbitrary decisions that come down "from above."

Sarason chides educators to reflect how their profession, "no less and no more than any other profession, has been awfully slow to become sensitive to the issues of rights . . . and even slower to begin sincerely, courageously, and seriously to alter its professional traditions."

Question for Seymour Sarason

In the years since you wrote this and other books about "the political principle," have you seen more of an indication that educators and parents are realizing that they just can't solve real problems without working together and, inevitably, sharing power? Or have our schools and school leaders remained intransigent here too, in defiance of common sense and our political history?

Sarason's Response

In some respects there has been real progress. You just don't find, for example, urban school leaders who deny the absolute importance of parental involvement. And whenever budgets are tight (and even, sometimes, when they're not), school leaders everywhere give voice to the need for dialogue with and support from parents and community members. However, it is frequently the case that school personnel engage in rhetoric as a cloak for inaction.

Politicians, on the right more often than on the left, have jumped in with demands for vouchers and for high-stakes testing that will, supposedly, put more "power" in parents' hands to deal with schools that are seen as failing to serve children. We must denounce such demagoguery whenever we suspect that its real purpose is to punish children and defame public education.

The trouble is that too many professional educators are allowing the political principle to be used *against* them (by irresponsible as well as responsible agitators) instead of reaching out to parents and citizens as allies in the struggle to make schools more interesting—and, thus, more successful—places to learn.

More about issues involving parent involvement and power-sharing in school governance may be found in:

How Schools Might Be Governed and Why (1997)
Revisiting "The Culture of the School and the Problem of Change" (1996)
The Case for Change: Rethinking the Preparation of Educators (1992)
The Predictable Failure of Educational Reform (1990)
Anxiety in Elementary School Children: A Report of Research (1960)

The political principle justifying parental involvement is that when decisions are made affecting you or your possessions, you should have a role, a voice in the process of decision making. You may call it a principle, a value, a right. It is not a *formal* rule, law, or a contract mutually agreed upon. It is a principle undergirding and embodied in our legal and political systems. How or when it should be reflected in relationships or practice depends on circumstances. It is not a principle without justifiable exceptions. So, for example, if a group of your friends or relatives decide to honor you with a surprise party—an occasion that is intended to affect you and stay in your memory—they will not include you in the decision. You do not, of course, resent having no voice in the decision.

But take the situation where a friend invites you to a dinner party in his or her home and when you get there you find that your host also had invited someone whom your friend knew you cordially disliked or, worse yet, with whom you had severed relationships. You would direct your anger at your host for not giving you the opportunity to decide whether to come or not. You will justly say your host was insensitive, by which you mean that your host made a unilateral decision that would negatively affect you. What if your host did not know that you disliked the other invitee? You would expect that person to say that if he or she had known, a unilateral decision would not have been made.

These are, clearly, nonmomentous examples, which is why they were chosen to make the point that in the relationships we label friendship, well-intended, unilateral decisions may not be in our best interest. But, one could ask, why are these trivial instances illustrations of the *political* principle that is concerned with uses and allocations of *power*, more specifically, relationships in which participants possess different types and degrees of power (e.g., parent and child, teacher and child, supervisor and staff, Congress and the president, a state and the federal government)? The point is that power is not absent between friends but rather that friends have implied equal power; that is, power is not on the interpersonal agenda. The termination of and alterations in friendship frequently occur because of the perception that one of the friends has violated equality in the balance of power.

The call for and the predictable consequences of parental involvement in school matters are not comprehensible apart from the fact that *in regard to the child in the school, parents and educators are unequal in the possession and exercise of power.* Yes, educators had always recognized that parents have a legitimate vested interest in what happens to their children in school, but that did not mean to educators that that interest should be formally accompanied by the power to influence how schools and classrooms are structured and run, the choice of curriculum, selection of teachers and other personnel, and so forth. Those matters were off-limits; they were the concern and responsibility of the professional educators. And for a long time that was that; no serious challenge to the status quo was mounted.

The opening challenge was the 1954 Supreme Court desegregation decision, the significance of which was initially less in the fact that the plaintiff was a parent than in the more obvious fact that there would be an external force influencing *and* monitoring educational decision making. It was a force more powerful than the powers of educational decision makers (i.e., the latter *had* to comply with the decision, no ifs, ands, or buts). It was predictable that this instance of a legally sanctioned, unilateral decision would meet resistance from certain groups and regions. That is what almost always happens when a "superior power" acts unilaterally toward a less powerful person or agency (i.e., the latter resents having had no voice in a decision altering the style of its existence).

Generally speaking, the educational community was very slow to sense the less obvious implications of that decision: There were many individuals (black and white, parents and others) who would be watching schools to see and judge how seriously, speedily, and effectively school people would change policies and practices to be in accord with the judicial decision that by its very nature was a *national* decision. And, as we know, "seeing and judging" became rather quickly an insistence on the part of parents and others in the community that they be part of the decision-making, policy formulation process. It is an understatement to say that educators were unprepared for the challenge to their power and its exercise. It is not an understatement to say that the preparation of educators was (and still is) woefully deficient in regard to the theories and history of power, its uses and allocation, moral dilemmas, and, perhaps most fateful, the predictable psychological consequences in those who are in relationships of unequal power. It was unpreparedness guaranteeing conflict and led to "parental involvement" becoming a rallying cry giving expression to resentment, anger, and militancy.

The 1954 decision started a train of events in the center of which was the issue of power—who had it and abused it, who should have it but did not. It was a train whose first stop was the station called the sizzling sixties. The long and short of it is that the 1954 decision and its immediate aftermath became a part of a widespread challenge to every major societal institution: churches; the government and the political establishment; business (especially big business); the military and the police; primary, secondary schools, and colleges and universities; and what is suggested by the advice that "You can't trust anyone over thirty." If anything was clear in those days—and few things were clear—it was that these institutions were being accused of aggrandizing power, unilateral, authoritarian decision making, and a gross insensitivity to the needs and rights of society in general and their different constituencies in particular. The timing and force of the call for parental involvement has to be seen in the context of an era in which challenges to power were directed to and far beyond schools, especially in urban areas. And it is important to note that the term "parental involvement" was (is) misleadingly narrow because in regard to schools the call was for "community control" and "community participation." The word *control* was used advisedly, because its proponents meant what they said: drastically to change the balance of power between community and educators.

It is beyond my purposes to say more about the origins of the call for parental involvement. I trust that what I have sketched helps the reader understand how several strands of events combined to make parent-community involvement an issue, a force, and a response to the perceived inadequacies of our schools. It is not an issue that will go away; it is safe to assume that its force will increase. As I said earlier, several states have formally mandated some form of parental involvement, and many school districts have also supported some form of involvement. I shall have more to say about these measures later in this book. Let us in the rest of this chapter pursue the role of motivation of educators in accepting or rejecting the political principle.

A story is appropriate here. It was in the late sixties that I was asked by a suburban school system to meet once a week for ten weeks with elementary school teachers as a forum to discuss matters of practical importance in the classroom. My role was less as a workshop leader and more as a moderator. The first five sessions went well in that a lot of strong feelings and conflicting and conflictful stances got expressed and discussed.

One of the themes that came up with heat and regularity is contained in the question I asked early in the sixth session:

I have been reviewing past meetings as a result of which I want to ask a question. Imagine that the board of education asks you to choose between two proposals. The first is that your salary is increased by a thousand dollars next year. The second is that you never again have to meet with a parent. Am I wrong to expect that you would have trouble making your choice?

The nervous, anxious laughter that greeted my question was indicative of the obvious ambivalence the teachers had previously expressed to parents in this affluent community. I should hasten to say that, as a group, these were bright, decent, likable, committed individuals. But in dealing with parents they found them intrusive and difficult, too quick to offer advice and criticism about matters about which the teachers thought them to be uninformed. As one teacher put it, "Some parents approach me with a chip on their shoulders, unrespectful of what I know, what I do, or why. And before I know it, we are talking past each other." Another teacher said, "If some of my parents talked to their child's pediatrician the way they talk to me, he probably would tell them to go elsewhere." Still another teacher said, "When I tell some parents what they can and should do to help their children, it is as if they think I am trying to cut back on what I do."

It would be unfair to say that these teachers were, so to speak, anti parents (i.e., wishing that they would go away and stay away). What was nettlesome to them was when parents, directly or indirectly, challenged their professional knowledge and practices, and sometimes the scope of their authority. *That response is not peculiar to educators; it is a response quite characteristic of those in all of the professions.* It is both incorrect and unjust to single out educators in this respect. However you define a professional, that person's training makes clear that there are *boundaries* of responsibility beyond which "outsiders" should not be permitted to intrude. Those boundaries are intended to define and protect the power, authority, and decision making derived from formal training and experience. Conflicts on this score are by no means only between the professional and nonprofessional; if anything, the conflicts between different kinds of professionals have been more frequent and no less heated. Someone once remarked that animals are not professionals, but both share the characteristic of brooking no invasion of their turfs.

It is unrealistic to expect that a profession will, without external pressure, be motivated to take the initiative to include outsiders in its customary decision-making ways. It is no less unrealistic to expect that when the external pressure is strong and insistent, conflict is avoidable. That is small balm to participants in the conflict, who tend to see it as a zero-sum game: What *they* win, *we* lose. Nor is it reassuring to the participants to know, as it is quite knowable today, that their particular conflict is no different from that of other professions whose powers are being challenged by outsiders on the basis of the political principle. Nowhere is this more clear than in physician-patient relationships. It used to be that physicians unilaterally decided what course of action was best and when for the patient. In the best circumstances that course of action was arrived at after the physician had considered the universe of possible actions and the safety and dangers of each, an internal, cognitive process not shared with the patient. "Second opinions" were rarely recommended. Doctor knew best! It was the rare patient (parent) who felt secure enough to interrogate or challenge the wisdom or logic of a physician's (educator's) thinking, let alone to insist on a second opinion. That type of relationship began to be challenged on the basis of the political principle at about the same time that educators began to be challenged on the same principle by parent-community forces. And it was at the same time that the political principle became part of environmental protection legislation. Those who would be affected by a proposed highway, or dump waste, or building complex, and more, had to have a voice in the final decision; that is, the professional planners could not plan in a social vacuum.

The point here is not that because the political principle is, so to speak, in the air, that the educator should succumb to it. That, as I indicated, has not and is not happening. Controversy and struggle are unavoidable. The point is rather that the educator, *any* professional, has to come to grips with where he or she stands about the *legitimacy* of the principle, *independent* of possible actions that may flow from the principle. In other words, that person is faced with two struggles: the internal struggle about legitimacy of the principle, and then the one about how to handle the consequences of accepting or rejecting it. Accepting the principle "solves" one problem and brings in its wake a host of problems around actions consistent with that principle. Rejecting the principle also is a form of solution, but it, too, leaves one with thorny problems about how to deal with those who are pressuring for parent-community involvement. Each is an instance of problem creation through problem solution. It goes with the territory. In any event, in some ultimate sense the most important question confronting the educator is where he or she stands in regard to the political principle.

A story is relevant here. I came to know well a school principal whose youngest child had a mystifying illness requiring an array of diagnostic procedures and several hospitalizations. He and his wife were upset and angry about many things: the paucity of information given them, puzzlement about who was "on top of the case," the unwillingness or inability of medical and auxiliary personnel to listen to (let alone to follow) the advice of the parents about how to handle *this* child, and resentment, to put it mildly, about being treated as anxious, intrusive ignoramuses. To someone like me who has spent a fair amount of time in and around medical-hospital settings, what the principal related was not an unfamiliar story. But this was a principal who in his own bailiwick saw parents through the lens of professionalism; that is, parents were to be shown respect and given an opportunity to express their opinions, but that in no way meant that what parents thought and felt should determine what he or his teachers decided was the best way to proceed, educationally speaking. He had no trouble identifying parents who were demanding and intrusive (by his lights), parents whom he sought to placate without violating the boundaries of his "professionalism," which meant that he had more than a few parents who viewed him as he and his wife viewed most of those dealing with his sick child.

All of us, like the principal, are not noted for clarity about principles, examining their applicability across situations and problems, and acting consistently in regard to the principles. But if we indubitably have our imperfections—and no one has ever doubted that assertion—are we not obligated to be more humble, or at least more self-critical, about the rigidity of the boundaries we erect around our profession? If stone walls do not good neighbors make, neither do rigid professional boundaries. I said earlier that the first task of the educator is to determine where he or she stands in regard to the political principle independent of its implications for concrete action. I would like to add to that task a subtask: to determine, on the basis of personal experience, how you viewed the political principle when you were the "outsider" trying to get an "insider professional" to take your ideas, feelings, and recommended actions seriously. It is one thing to accept or reject the political principle in the abstract; it is quite another thing to do so on the basis of experience in diverse professional-nonprofessional relationships.

Generally speaking, educators are aware of the political principle but it is not a self-scrutinizing awareness, nor is it one about which they feel sufficiently secure to express openly. It is as if they know that they are under attack, that they are not respected or even liked as much as they feel they should be, and if they were to say out loud what they say to and among themselves, the attack would gain force. They avoid public discussion of the principle except to say (sometimes) in the most general, inoffensive, and unrevealing ways that *of course* parents are vital to the education process, without implying that that affirmation of principle requires some alteration in existing power relationships. So, for example, the Connecticut section of the *New York Times* carried an interview with the president of the Connecticut Education Association to which 28,000 of the state's 36,300 teachers belong ("Evaluating [and Defending] Teachers," 1994). In the course of the interview is the following:

Q. Is there a widening gulf between teachers and parents?

A. If I talk to prospective teachers I tell them there are certain conditions that go with this job. One is that there are people who believe you are not earning your keep, you can never do enough. For many children you will be successful but there will be people who say you did not meet the needs of their child. There are people who when you have their children in your school will advocate for the school. They want small classes and the best for their children and when they leave they no longer have a vested interest. These are the conditions of employment.

I think as teachers we do the best that we can. If there are those who are not doing the best that they can then we ought not to have them there. Someone should take care of that. Someone who is paid that administrative fee.

It is noteworthy that this official does not answer the question, although in his reply there and elsewhere in the interview he conveys the impression that teachers feel embattled and misunderstood. In no way does he ever suggest that *some* of what critics say *may* have validity, or that if parents and others had a role in educational policy and decisions, they would better understand why educators think and practice as they do. At one point he says that in Connecticut "[w]e ought not to be bemoaning the fact that teacher salaries are the highest in the country. We ought to be saying you pay for what you get." That is a strange statement in two respects. First, if Connecticut teachers are the highest paid in the country, why are so many citizens dissatisfied with what they feel they are getting? Second, there is no evidence whatsoever that increasing salaries increases educational outcomes, a fact that bewilders both citizens and educators. Indeed, I have no doubt that his statement increased the gulf between educators and "outsiders."

In brief, this educator had the opportunity to state and discuss the political principle but did not do so, leaving the reader with the impression that the political principle does not deserve discussion. I drew the conclusion that he knew full well the significance of the principle but that if he stated his position—leave things as they are—it would not, to indulge understatement, be greeted warmly; the gulf would widen. The point here is *not* if and how the political principle should be implemented but rather that it demands discussion, that it should be on and not under the table, that it is an issue that will not go away, that if undiscussed will ultimately be "solved" by legislative fiat, a process not noted for its efficacy.

I said earlier that when the political principle comes to the fore, conflict is unavoidable. But there is conflict and there is conflict. What we should seek to avoid, for as long as possible, is conflict solely or largely around power, its allocations and uses, conflict in which if one side "wins," the other "loses," the type of conflict the consequences of which are too often self-defeating for all participants. We like to think of ourselves as pragmatic; that is, we judge our intentions and goals by how well our actions achieve our purposes. In regard to parent-community involvement in schools, we are currently in the situation either where the political principle is in the picture but undiscussed, or dealt with superficially, gingerly, and insincerely, or where power (sometimes naked power) obscures everything else.

In my experience, where power struggle became a central feature, it was not the original purpose of the participants to make power so central but rather in some way to improve the substance and quality of the educational experience. The reasons for the power struggle were many, but the most obvious and common one was the failure or inability or reluctance to begin the discussion with where the participants stood in regard to the political principle. After all, the political principle is not new; it is rooted in our national history and political system; it is one everyone has experienced in his or her life; it is a clear, simple principle (at the same time it is "messy" in implementation). What happened in these instances was that none of the participants ever discussed the *political principle qua principle* but rather became embroiled, almost immediately, in the specifics of power redistribution and the mechanisms of implementation.

I am in no way suggesting that if the discussion of the principle had taken place, what followed would have been sweetness and light. What I am suggesting, and I do not think I am being overly or unrealistically optimistic, is that such a discussion would have gotten more agreement about the principle than the open warfare indicated. If such agreement could have been reached, it could have served as a preventive, in part at least, for a hostile "we win, you lose" atmosphere. Instead, what happened is that the professionals started with the Custer-like stance of being surrounded by deadly enemies, and the parent-community groups started with the stance that the professionals had erected impenetrable, high walls to keep "outsiders" outside. Both sides proceeded as if no agreement on anything was possible, and superior power would be the ultimate arbiter. Of course, matters were not helped any by the fact that little or nothing was contained in the education of educators in regard to the history, dilemmas, and opportunities of the political principle. Nor were matters helped any by the fact that the outsiders were far from clear (I am being charitable) about *why and in what ways* their possession of power would improve the quality of education.

That is, it does not follow as night follows day that because power would be differently allocated and used, education would be improved. The political principle is just that: a political principle about who should participate in some way in decisions vital to his or her welfare. It speaks to governance, not to the core problems governance seeks to ameliorate. The virtue of clarity about the political principle is that it requires you to ask, How do we concretely act on the basis of the principle to alter and improve an undesirable situation that is extraordinarily complex? But when a conflict, potential or actual, degenerates into power plays, the limits of the political principle and the complexity of the educational issues are given short shrift. The political principle is a starting point. Reaching agreement on it is, in some respects, easier than deciding how to proceed to diagnose and treat the deficiencies in the educational process. In the instances I have observed or read about (and I have a good counterintelligence network) the substance and contexts of the educational experience remained where they initially were: on an unlit back burner.

. . . I have discussed the obstacles professionals in general and educators in particular have in enunciating, confronting, and accepting the political principle. If only because parents know and have more contact with teachers than with other personnel, it is not surprising that when parents are critical of schools, they have teachers in mind. Someone once said that the cold war (before the Soviet Union dissolved) really started with the cold war between teachers and parents, a war that, far from remaining cold, shows signs of heating up. Teachers, of course, did not greet that remark warmly. But there is one group of teachers among whom there are more than a few who, albeit reluctantly, saw truth in that quip. I refer to teachers whose sons or daughters (or both) were in a public school and therefore, as parents, met with the teachers of their children. It was not infrequent in my experience over the decades to hear these parents criticize teachers for treating them "as if I was just a parent whose opinions were to be politely heard but not taken seriously." I cannot, of course, say that these parent-teachers responded more or less sensitively to the parents of the children in their classroom. But I bring this up to emphasize how one's own experiences as an "outsider" can and should be used to understand how the boundaries of professionalism work against recognition of the political principle. But that lack of recognition is by no means unusual *within* the profession (i.e., between those within the same profession but differing in status, function, or responsibility). . . . However insensitive teachers may be to the political principle in regard to parents, they are acutely aware of the principle in their relationships with those administratively above them, and in turn each layer of the educational hierarchy is no less aware of the principle in their interaction with the layers above them. Awareness of the principle—more specifically, violations of the principle—depends apparently on whose ox is gored.

If, as I have said, it is understandable that parent-community advocates for taking the political principle seriously primarily have teachers in mind, that focus betrays an ignorance of how power is allocated, experienced, and protected *within* the educational hierarchy of a school and school system. We are used to thinking that as one goes up the layers of the hierarchy (in any complex organization) there is an increasing correlation between status and responsibility, on the one hand, and the exercise of power, on the other hand. That correlation is far smaller than people realize. So, for example, we unreflectively assume that a school principal has and exercises more power than a classroom teacher. And when we make that assumption we mean that the principal, more than the classroom teacher, determines the educational policy of that school, or can alter an existing one. And by educational policy I do *not* refer to making up bus schedules, arranging for supervision of the cafeteria, getting substitute teachers, arranging field trips, or insuring that report cards are handed in on time and in some way conveyed to parents, and so forth.

By educational policy I mean such things as how new teachers are to be selected; establishing criteria for and observing teacher effectiveness and classroom climate; how disciplinary problems are to be handled; the obtaining and allocating of existing or new educational materials; providing intellectual-educational stimulation to teachers; serving as spokesperson for the school in discussions of budget; conducting "foreign relations" with higher administrative personnel, parents, and the surrounding community; and more. In matters like these the principal, as the title indicates, is seen as having more power than teachers. The domain of the teacher is the encapsulated classroom, a domain directly or indirectly subject to policies of the principal. A teacher is "just" that: low person on the totem pole of power. As one would expect, it has long been the case that, as a group, teachers have resented being subject to educational policies in the formulation of which they have had no role. Indeed, the rise of militant teacher unions is understandable only if one comprehends the substance of that resentment (which was directed only in part to principals); that is, in their self-interest teachers began to take seriously the political principle. If they were to be affected by policies, they wanted a role in their formulation. It is not happenstance that they began to take the political principle seriously at about the same time that the call for parent-community involvement in educational policy began to be articulated, *although neither of these groups perceived their kinship in regard to the political principle, then or now.* Phenomenologically, teachers are themselves in relation to their administrative superiors precisely the way parent-community groups see themselves in relation to school personnel: outsiders looking and wanting "in." One can only hope that some day these two "outsiders" will better understand their kinship in principle: What is sauce for the goose *is* sauce for the gander.

I am, I suppose, indulging the hope that that understanding will lead to an acceptance of the political principle, an acceptance that could prevent the worst excesses of the resort to displays of naked power.

But what about the principal? How does he or she view the power of the position? I have discussed this question with scores of principals, and their answers can be put into three categories, overlapping and cumulative as sources of frustration, as restrictions on the exercise of power. The first category contains the perception that teachers look kindly on a principal who leaves them alone to do what they have always done and/or accedes to requests for this or that; they do not take kindly to suggestions that require the teacher to change what and how he or she teaches, how a class should be organized, how a particular child or type of child should be managed, or to explain why children are performing below standard and to come up with an approach that will improve performance, or to explain why previous suggestions have not been followed.

The second category has to do with the "union contract," *a document about which the principal had no role whatsoever* but that contains sentences, phrases, and clauses that either constrict the scope of his or her power or inhibit its exercise because it may result in a grievance procedure, which may make a bad situation worse. As one woman said to me shortly after she became principal of a troubled and troublesome school, "If I did what I know I should do, and what on the level of rhetoric I am expected to do, I would have time for little else other than engaging in grievance procedures, and I would have to defend that to those above me who, despite what they say and expect, would not like it."

The third category is the most poignant: the realization by principals that they must follow and implement educational policies legislated by those higher up in the hierarchy, policies in the formulation of which they played little or no role, and usually no role. I say poignant because those who seek to become principals usually have a vision of what an ideal school should be. They do not seek to be principals to implement the vision of others. So, when they become a principal and begin to experience the culture of the school from that position, it is almost always sobering and frequently disillusioning. As teachers they understood, they experienced, what violations of the political principle meant. As principals they did not expect that again they would be outsiders looking in. It is that kind of experience or reaction that makes it difficult for principals sincerely and seriously to act on the basis of the political principle in their relations with teachers or parent-community groups, actions they perceive as a further dilution of their power.

We are used to hearing that the presidency of the United States is the most powerful position in the world. Few, if any, presidents would agree with that statement on the basis of their experience with the House of Representatives, the Senate, the Supreme Court, their political party and that of the opposition, let alone countless special interest groups. Formally and informally, the presidency is subject to all kinds of restrictions on the explicit powers of the office. Our most effective presidents have had several characteristics. They quickly learned the difference between having power and being influential. To the extent that they were influential it was because they took the political principle seriously; that is, they sought to work with and influence those who had some kind of stake in regard to a proposed policy. They made the boundaries between themselves and diverse stakeholders permeable; they respected (even expected) that those who would be affected by a policy would want some kind of input in the final shape of that policy. And, needless to say, "those" includes the "outsiders," the nonprofessionals, the people who vote and whom the political system is intended to serve.

What I have said about some presidents can (and should) be said about some schools. Although they are admittedly few, I have known schools (*not* school systems) where the political principle informs relationships among school personnel and between them and parent-community individuals. But in every case respect for the principle was not a matter of formal policy of the school *system* but rather of an unusual and refreshing array of people for whom the principle was, so to speak, second nature. They did not formally proclaim the principle or even put it into words. I cannot put it any other way than to say that they were the kinds of people whose lives seemed to be based on the principle. I put it that way because in some instances the appointment of a new principal and the hiring of one or two new teachers created severe problems because the rhetoric of these new arrivals turned out to be just that: rhetoric devoid of consistency with action. I am certain that there are readers of this book who will have experienced what can happen when new arrivals, especially when they are principals, have little respect for the political principle. The fan can blow other than air!

I have discussed the political principle in the case of teachers and principals. But there are other layers of administrative power above them. Indeed, in our urban school systems, the hierarchy can be quite complex to the point where it is next to impossible to determine who has the power to do what. The lines of power may seem clear on an administrative chart, but the chart has little to do with the realities. Whatever I have said about the sources of disillusionment of principals is true for those "above" them even though most of them had been principals and could have known that the grass is not predictably greener elsewhere. Hope does spring eternal.

In brief, it is an egregious instance of missing the trees for the forest to see the call for parent-community involvement in decision making as a new or challenging expression of the political principle, or to see the resistance of educators to that expression as sheer perversity, or narrow-mindedness, or solely as rampant professional imperialism. *Leaving parent-community advocates aside, resistance to the political principle characterizes relationships among the different layers of administrative power in the school system.* The parent-community advocates are latecomers to the scene. . . .

. . . Let us now turn to the deficits of parent-community individuals and groups in regard to participation. As we shall see deficits are not of a piece, nor are they irremediable.

1. Parents have little basis for understanding the culture of a school and school system: the axioms and assumptions undergirding behavioral and programmatic regularities; the nature and rationale for decision making in regard to scores of problems and responsibilities; how organizational-educational goals and practices are experienced

and interpreted by *adults* in that culture, varying as they do with status, power, and experience; and how within that culture, and between it and the "outside," are attitudes or stances the origins and substance of which are rooted in a present and past. A school or school system is a complicated affair that did not have a virginal birth and is not easily described or comprehended. Nor is it a static affair devoid of tensions, conflicts, and doubts about goals, practices, and outcomes. If most people know (or think they know) more about how and why the federal government operates with varying degrees of effectiveness, than they do about a school or school system, it is because there are media whose job it is to inform the public about this or that aspect of government policy, action, and effectiveness.

2. Parents' knowledge of and attitudes toward schooling in general and school personnel in particular derive primarily from their experience as students. That is both an asset and a deficit, an experiential asset not to be ignored but at the same time a deficit because that type of experience gives rise to attitudes about classrooms, teachers, and subject matter that are narrow in perspective, that cannot be understood in terms of the perspectives from which school personnel perceive students, classroom practices, subject matter, educational goals, and more. Just as children and their parents comprehend "family life" very differently, schoolchildren and school personnel comprehend schooling very differently. *That does not mean that the comprehension by parents and school personnel is necessarily adequate or valid but that their "pictures" are different; that is, they are differences that make a difference in the real world of action and relationships.*

3. When parents and others call for involvement of some degree or kind in the decision-making process, their emphasis is on issues of power—they want "in"—and not on substantive educational issues (e.g., what life in a classroom should be, the classroom contexts for productive learning, the pros and cons for the use of tests and test scores, how one becomes aware of alternative conceptions of curriculum, how resources outside of the school can be made available to buttress and expand the substance and effectiveness of classroom learning). To seek power is to raise and begin to answer the question: To seek power to change *what?* Changing the forces of power in no way guarantees that anything else will change. To seek power in order to become more knowledgeable, which does not mean becoming an expert, requires confronting your assets and deficits. To seek power without asking the "what" question is not only to beg the question but to avoid it and, therefore, to collude in cosmetic changes.

There are those who will conclude that these deficits are reasons enough to resist involvement by parents and others. That conclusion is justified if you make several assumptions. The first is that the political principle is inappropriate in this instance, or that it is appropriate only in very narrow confines (i.e., educational issues are off-limits). The second assumption is that the assets of parents are not assets. That is to say, they are not assets relevant to educational issues. The third is that the deficits are not remediable, in part at least; parents cannot become more knowledgeable to the point where they have something to contribute to changing and improving the quality of schooling, perhaps to bring new life, new blood to an educational arena about which few within and without it are satisfied. The fourth assumption is "this too shall pass"; that is, the issue, like a lot of fads and fashions, will run its course. I have heard that said by more than a few educators at the same time they bemoan the fecklessness of many schools, and some, in fact, see the situation getting worse.

If I do not agree with any of these assumptions, it is not because I consider parent involvement a proven means for improving schools but because my adherence to the political principle requires it, and there is every reason to believe that the issue will not go away. When the political principle will be taken seriously and sincerely (hope springs eternal, I know), it will take educators off the hook of being *solely* responsible and accountable for the plight of our schools. At the present time, educators feel like General Custer surrounded by enemies, with no supportive constituencies, and dependent only on hope for a secular miracle. But there can be a supportive constituency, a participating one possessed of assets and remediable deficits, a constituency that at the very least will seek to prevent efforts (mindless for the most part) to bypass, or weaken, or even dismantle the public schools. Those efforts will gain force to the extent that the public's criteria for judging schools continue not to be met. That, in fact, is what I have predicted (orally and in print) over the last thirty-five years, and candor requires that I say I now believe the situation will get worse. . . .

Whatever I have listed and said about the assets and deficits of parents is in principle precisely what educational administrators have said about the role of teachers in educational decision making. When I articulated this kinship to groups of teachers, there were several reactions. The first was a mixture of silence, reflection, and then consternation. The second was (paraphrase), "The analogy does not wash. Community people do not know schools; they have little basis, if any, for understanding why a teacher does what she does, or even a quarter of the things that go on in a school. As teachers we know schools. No one can deny that, not even administrators." To which I would reply, "I do deny it. I think it is a fact that over the decades I have known and talked with more administrators, usually principals, than anyone in this room. Given my age, it may well be that the number I have talked with exceeds the combined number of all administrators under whom all in this group have worked. If there is anything about which they agreed it is that the individual teacher does not know all that goes on in a school. Indeed, they would say, each teacher sees the school in terms of *her* thinking, practices, problems, and biases and, therefore, does not comprehend why things cannot be otherwise. Teachers are *individualists* in terms of their space and psychology; they do not know, and often they are not interested in, how a *whole* school works and why. We thank God when a teacher does her job in the classroom well but that does not mean that because she does her job well she understands the larger picture and can contribute to it."

I would sometimes bring up a personal example relevant to the above. It was when I was director of a psychoeducational clinic at Yale. I was sitting in my office trying to understand why I was having difficulty with my department in regard to obtaining additional resources. "Suddenly" the clouds parted and the sun shed its light. You have, I said to myself, to ask two questions. Who tries to "make it" in the university? Whom does the university select? The two questions had one answer: *rugged individualism*. Put briefly, by virtue of factors of selection and self-selection the university guarantees that it will be comprised of bright, ambitious, prima donna types who do not seek or know how to work with each other and frequently do not know how to talk with each other. And each sees the university in idiosyncratic, self-serving ways (of which I was a fairly good example). I began to understand why university administrators see faculty as lovable, demanding, pouting children who have confused *their* world with the world of the university. And that is what educational administrators were conveying to me about teachers. The irony is that university and school administrators are victims of the self-fulfilling prophecy: They pin their labels on the faculty and then act in ways that prove to them that the labels are appropriate (i.e., the "deficits" of the faculty are irremediable). If that is not nonsense, it comes close to it. I am *not* suggesting that the problem has a "solution" in the sense that four divided by two has a solution. In the realm of human-organizational relationships we rarely, if ever, deal with problems that have once-and-for-all solutions. But if those kinds of problems have no final solutions, it does not mean they cannot be ameliorated.

In regard to parental involvement the major obstacle at present is that the relationships between the two sides center around power and turf, a situation conducive to nonproductive struggle. Some would argue that altering power relationships never occurs without struggle. More specifically, that the ideology of professionalism is so strong, so concerned with boundaries of authority and responsibility, as to make alterations in power anathema to professionals, and educators are by no means unusual in that respect. But we are discussing educators and cannot ignore the fact that a good fraction of the general public perceives educators as unable and unwilling to agree to changing power relationships, and, as I have emphasized, that is also true for relationships between teachers and their professional "higher ups." . . .

. . . Over the decades I have learned a lot from teachers who were parents. Here, briefly, is how a fair number described how they felt after meeting with their child's teacher, or principal, or the school psychologist. Unlike ordinary parents, of course, they did not regard themselves as amateurs; they were peers. In all instances (if memory serves me right) it was the parent who initiated the meeting.

1. The parent approached the meeting with unease and dysphoric anticipation, as if she (all shes) knew the teacher would "feel on the spot."
2. The parent felt she was regarded as a "know-it-all."
3. Without saying it in so many words, the teacher implied that the parent's view of the particular issue was a prejudiced one (i.e., the parent had a one-sided view, while the teacher saw things whole).
4. The suggestions of the parent were reacted to by what may be termed a "you stay on your turf and I'll stay on mine" stance. The parent was made to feel she was being intrusive, directive.

5. In instances where there was no meeting of minds, the teacher's facial and body language seemed to say, "You are being contentious."
6. Throughout the meeting the parent was poignantly aware of the danger of putting her child in between two warring camps (i.e., if the parent said what she really thought, her child might be adversely affected).

It should be said that none of the parents generalized their reactions to all teachers or other personnel. But it also has to be said that these parents were in no doubt that many personnel were not at ease with parents, did not trust them to the point where they could be spontaneous, revealing, and admit error or imperfection.

It is not an unjust extrapolation to say that these instances tell us a good deal about why parent-school relationships are as unproductive as they frequently are; why parents approach school personnel with a mixture of respect, deference, fear, and anger; why trust is such a rare commodity in these relationships; why school personnel believe that keeping parents at a distance is less troublesome than sincerely involving them. On this last point educators could not be more realistic in the sense that once you take parent-community involvement seriously life becomes more complicated, messy, and even more unpredictable than it was before. That life can *become* more interesting, exciting, less isolating, protective of the existence of the public schools, and potentially an aid to their improvement is a goal and possibility educators have difficulty envisioning. And that is what is called for: a vision that pulls us to a future, not one riveted on a present satisfactory to few. . . .

The . . . profession of education, no less and no more than any other profession, has been awfully slow to become sensitive to the issues of rights, in particular the political principle, and even slower to begin sincerely, courageously, and seriously to alter its professional traditions. It is the lack of meaningful response, the lack of articulate leadership, that is my basis for assigning blame. To understand all is not to forgive all.

. . . Clearly, if educators take the political principle (and its derivative issues) seriously, time, the most precious of commodities, will become far more of a problem than it is. . . . Schools can be justly criticized for lack of clarity about priorities and the lack of courage to resist taking on programs that further obscure the issue of priorities. Communities have required schools to initiate programs, to help "solve" racial problems, *at the same time they are dissatisfied with what schools accomplish in other matters educational.* You could argue that to be consistent with the political principle and parent-community involvement, I am not entitled to criticize schools when they initiate programs parents and others want and educators may or may not want. I agree. But my criticism is not that schools took on these programs but that they did so without an effort to engage the community in the issues of priorities *and* existing educational inadequacies; that is, the community was provided no basis for judging between and among educational priorities and problems. It was too often the case of knowing the price of everything and the value of nothing. It was hard to figure out what educators stood for.

And, I must remind the reader of what I have said earlier about the political principle: taking it seriously in no way means that the outcomes of the process will always be salutary. But it does mean that the important issues stand a chance of getting on the table. Concretely, and from my standpoint, the most important issue is in the form of this question: When a child is graduated from high school, what are the one or two characteristics you want that child to possess, characteristics previous schooling has reinforced? All else is commentary. . . .

However sincerely I advocate for parent-community involvement, it will ultimately have to be judged by how educators and parents respond to the question I have just asked. You cannot answer a question you have not raised. But the question has been raised many times before. Neither educators nor the public have taken it seriously. And, here again, I place major responsibility on the education profession because they know that the question is the central one that practice has to reflect. Ironically, in the many times I have raised the question with parent groups, I have gotten two reactions, without exception: The first is puzzled (and long) silence about how to answer the question, and second, after I have broken the silence with *my* answer, they whole-heartedly agreed with me. That may come as a surprise to many educators; they have far more kinship to parental goals than the gulf between them indicates. . . .

CHAPTER 19

The Governors:
Teachers and Parents

Sarason assumes that parents and teachers, in settings beginning with elementary school, have much to learn from each other regarding their mutual stake in promoting productive learning for students. He reiterates his proposal for individual parent-teacher meetings before the school year begins, indicating that such a collaborative relationship will help to avoid the "estrangement and the censorship of thought and feeling" that characterize too many parent-teacher interactions.

Sarason broadens his agenda for parents and teachers to include mutual accountability. "No longer will teachers be *solely* responsible for the educational-intellectual development of students. Parents and teacher will be jointly responsible, by which I mean that parents, no less than teachers, have obligations to understand and take seriously what they can and should do at home to support the concept of productive learning."

Question for Seymour Sarason

The issue of parent-teacher "ownership" of a school has perhaps been most effectively realized in independent schools and also in charter schools—schools that depend for their very existence on such a partnership. Can such shared ownership ever realistically be extended to conventional public schools whose principals and teachers strongly advocate, in principle, such a shared partnership?

Sarason's Response

Yes, but probably not in my lifetime. We will have to wait until school systems acknowledge the impossibility of achieving any significant improvements *without* the full participation of parents and students working with empowered and receptive teachers. And I have to add that achieving this goal of shared ownership requires that teacher prepara-

Reprinted with the permission of Teachers College Press from "The Governors: Teachers and Parents" in *How Schools Might Be Governed and Why* by Seymour Sarason (New York: Teachers College Press, 1997).

tory programs face up to their obligations to make future teachers welcome and anticipate such partnerships.

We must accept the fact that, in such collaboration, there will always be ups and downs,
tensions. There is no way the existing gulf can be bridged, all problems solved, and the
glorious future realized without encountering all the problems of a democratic society.

More about issues involving parent involvement and power-sharing in school governance may be found in:

Revisiting "'The Culture of the School and the Problem of Change" (1996)
Parental Involvement and the Political Principle (1995)
The Case for Change: Rethinking the Preparation of Educators (1992)
The Predictable Failure of Educational Reform (1990)
Anxiety in Elementary School Children: A Report of Research (1960)

I start with the elementary school years because they pose all of the important issues
about the relationships between governance and productive learning in the later school
years. Those relationships are not determined by the age of the student. They are required on the basis of an agreement about an overarching purpose, an understanding,
and a value judgment. The purpose is to sustain, reinforce, and support students' wanting to do and learn more. The understanding is that the purpose cannot be achieved unless students perceive that learning is in some important ways meaningful and necessary
for what they are and want to become. The value judgment is that it is a "good," a
moral, obligation, so to expand students' knowledge of self, others, and the world that
they increasingly feel more competent to make choices that living does and will present
to them; they are choices that should always take into account the knowledge, opinions,
values, and experience of others. Choices are not exercises in narcissism or reflections
of mindless permissiveness. If adults "owe" something to children, we also want children to feel they owe something to adults as well as to other students.

What do we want a teacher to know about a child? How might a teacher go about
acquiring that knowledge? Consistent with what we know about productive learning we
take for granted that a teacher will want to know "where the child is" and "where he
or she is coming from." And we take it for granted that parents will want to provide
whatever relevant knowledge they have, if appropriately and sensitively asked. Such
knowledge is obviously important in the case of children starting school for the first
time. Because that knowledge is sought in order to be maximally helpful to student,
teacher, and parents—especially to the teacher who wants seriously to take account of
a child's individuality—this question arises: When should that knowledge be sought?
The answer is *not* after the child has started school but *before* he or she has started
school. And the answer explicitly assumes that that initial meeting establishes a relationship between teacher and parent that makes it easy for both to arrange subsequent
meetings whenever each of them thinks a meeting would be helpful. Parents are resources to teachers and vice versa. For a teacher to regard meeting with a parent as a
form of noblesse oblige guarantees estrangement and the censorship of thought and feel-

ing. As soon as a parent feels that he or she is being "talked down to," that parent will regard the teacher as the child is likely to regard the teacher who sees that child as an unformed vessel who has no sense of identity or individuality. The parent is part of the context of productive learning.

I am sure that many readers are asking themselves several questions. "Does he realize how much time it would take it for a teacher to see each parent before a child starts school? And how much time it would take to meet with each parent, say, several times or more during the year? How many teachers would be willing to spend a good part of the month of August meeting with parents? Who would pay the teachers for that extra time, which will not be minuscule? And when do we see working parents? At night? On weekends?"

These are legitimate questions, but they miss the point I made earlier. If you agree with and take seriously what I have said about contexts of productive learning, then what I have said about parent-teacher meetings (in the case of children beginning schooling) is not only important but a necessity. It is not a frill, an empty ritual, or play acting. Of course teachers should be paid for their time. And, again of course, teachers should, within reasonable limits, be flexible in regard to working parents. Teachers should not be expected to be philanthropists but neither should they regard themselves as exempt from the professional obligation to try to accommodate to the life conditions of others. If you are a professional, you have something to profess, a something that is substantive, ethical, and moral.

What does this have to do with governance? It means that the community and the legislative and executive branches of government—who collect and spend taxes—would be obliged to regard the funding not as a gift or bribe but as a necessary way of supporting productive learning. We hear much from these sectors about the bedrock importance of parent involvement, and what I have advocated is *one* way of demonstrating how seriously that involvement should be taken. When a governor calls a special session of the legislature, those legislators are paid for their time. That is taken for granted. Similarly, if you require teachers to give more and special time to discharging an agreed-upon responsibility, the system should make that possible. But that will only be possible if the policy makers and funders are crystal clear about the overarching purpose of schooling. It would also be the obligation of the funding sources to pass legislation that would allow working parents to be released from work for a half day x number of times during the school year to attend meetings with teachers regardless of whether it is the parent or teacher who seeks the meeting. Nothing would be deducted from the parents' pay. Just as teachers and others have paid days of personal leave, so should working parents be able to meet with teachers without penalties when necessary. I said "x number of times" because I do not want to be bogged down in trying to decide on whether it should be 3, 5, or 7 days. In this case the devil is not in the details but in the principle. Once the principle is accepted numbers will not be a thorny obstacle.

But there is another aspect to what I have proposed that is not concerned with time and money but is no less important, and I would argue that in some ultimate sense will be more important. The purpose of the parent-teacher meetings is not only to share information or as a vehicle for getting to know each other but to define accountability. No longer will teachers be *solely* responsible for the educational-intellectual development of students. Parents and teachers will be jointly responsible, by which I mean that parents, no less than teachers, have obligations to understand and take seriously what they can and should do at home to support the concept of productive learning.

The context of family can be congruent with or in opposition to productive learning. Allowing a child to watch TV for hours on end is doing the child no favor. And that is true if no one reads to the child, or tells him or her no stories, or does not elicit or respond to a child's questions, or does not provide the child with toys that sustain his or her interest, or shows no interest in what the child is doing and experiencing in school, or never or rarely takes him or her to community sites or happenings that would stimulate the child's interests and curiosities. Just as parents will hold teachers accountable for what goes on in the classroom, teachers will hold parents accountable for the quality and context of learning in the home. Aside from meeting and discussing these matters with parents, the school will be required to provide parents with a brochure containing, among other things I will take up shortly, the responsibilities of parents and teachers for the education of their children.

What about parents who are poor, uneducated, and may not even be able to read? Are those features to which educators are expected to be sensitive but to which they are not expected to take some concrete actions? On what moral and pedagogical grounds can one justify inaction in regard to features that negatively affect learning, directly or indirectly or both? At the very least, each school should have a fund that is used to purchase age-appropriate books and toys that are then given to and owned by child and family. It would also be the responsibility of the school to be of whatever help is realistically possible in regard to why and how those materials might be employed.

Here, again, the objection will be made that another time-consuming task is being given to the school. And some would object to what appears be an intrusion by the school into family life. The first objection implicitly concedes the point that what I recommend is desirable and should be put into practice, but it is impractical and self-defeating. The objection is valid only if one is judging on the basis of how schools are *now* organized, funded, and function. As they now are, schools cannot regard my proposal as other than utopian musings that have the virtue of allowing one to escape from reality. It is one thing to escape from reality—to leave it alone, so to speak—it is quite another thing to take it seriously enough to seek to change it. I must also remind the reader that one of the conclusions derived from the long history of the literature on utopias is that over time many aspects of those publications became standard in what later became quotidian reality. The constitution of 1787 was regarded by many, here and abroad, as a utopian document.

The second objection is on the grounds of the protection of privacy and parental authority against the "big brother," freedom-constraining stance. I said earlier that parents will be given a brochure spelling out the rights and responsibilities of teachers and parents, i.e., the constitution of the school. I then went on to say that teachers will provide some parents with books and toys that they will be helped to use in productive ways with their children. And so we come to the heart of the matter: the political principle, which is that if you are going to be affected by a policy, decision, or practice you should stand in some relationship to the formulation and implementation of any or all of them. Concretely, whatever I have said (or will say) assumes that parents and teachers, in equal numbers, will decide the substance, purpose, and means of implementation of educational policy. *The political principle is not only about rights but about accountability.* Parents, no less than teachers, are accountable for the development of children. Whether and to what degree a school achieves its intended, agreed-on purposes, no longer should praise or blame be directed to one source, i.e., educators. Just as war should not be left to the generals, education is too encompassing and important a task to be left to educators; it is not a task educators have ever or could ever or should have been allowed have as their sole responsibility. If it takes a village to raise a child, it takes more than teachers to educate a child. . . .

. . . To the extent that the governing board of the school willingly assumes the responsibility to act consistent with the overarching purposing of schooling because it is *their* task and obligation, not a task and obligation imposed on them, the goals of productive learning stand a chance of being realized. And when I say "stand a chance," I mean just that. Good intentions are necessary but not sufficient conditions for achieving purposes. Not in the crucible of human affairs.

There are several objections (to put it mildly?) to what I have proposed, but two require reply at this point because they are interrelated. The first would take the following form: "What do parents know about schools, teachers, teaching, curricula, budgeting, assessment, and more? You are being irresponsible when you advocate giving parents an equal status with educators in matters for which parents are not even amateurs. You say that a professional is one who has something to profess based on preparation, personal experience, and the experience of other professionals. On what basis do parents have something to profess? Are we to give what they profess the same status as that which we profess? You are always quoting Mencken's caveat that for every social problem there is a simple answer that is wrong. Your proposal confirms Mencken's wise remark. It is as if you want to appear as the super democrat for whom obvious distinctions among people do not exist, or can be easily overcome or erased. Come off it, Professor Sarason, you have been in the halls of ivy too long. If you once thought you knew schools, you certainly do not know them now."

Let me begin my defense by saying that since I retired in 1989 I probably have been in more classrooms in more schools, I have talked to and with more teachers, I have read more articles and books about or by teachers than almost all of my objectors. Having said that, I can assure my objectors that I know that in and of itself experience does not automatically confer validity on whatever conclusions I have drawn or proposals I have advocated. *That, I must emphasize, holds no less for my objectors than it does for me. That is not an argumentum ad hominem.* Between experience and conclusions is a minefield of traps with such labels as wish fulfillment, illogic, imprisoning habit, blinding partisanship, and selective perception and attention. I take it for granted that the human mind is a fascinating amalgam of assets and deficits. Therefore, I cannot cavalierly dismiss objections to what I have said. . . . By the same token I ask that what I say be given a hearing, however strange, disturbing, and unfamiliar it may be. I must remind the reader that the purpose of this book is to start a discussion about the inadequacies of our schools. If you hold the belief that, generally speaking, our schools are achieving their purposes as those purposes are currently proclaimed by both educators and the public, I see no point in your continuing to read this book. And if you hold the belief that, again generally speaking, our schools, especially our urban schools, are improving or can be improved without radically changing the system, this is not a book for you. This is a book for those, by no means small in number, who are wrestling with the question: Why in the post–World War II era, after spending scores of billions of dollars, can few people generate any optimism that the public schools can be improved, and find themselves looking with favor (or with far less skepticism) on diverse efforts—ranging from vouchers to charter schools to privatization—that directly attack the system qua system?

Let me now give parts of my answer.[1]

1. The substance of the objections is in every respect identical to that which was raised by many people (in the convention of 1787 and during the ratification process) against the constitution. Were people up to the responsibilities and power that were going to be accorded them? Could you trust the masses to be wise and to resist fads, fashions, and the blandishments of self-serving, power-seeking scoundrels? Could you entrust the fate of a nation to the ordinary citizen, whose passions and unsophistication would overwhelm what was in the best interests of the larger collectivity? Did we want mob rule? If the constitution had the substance it did and obtained the ratification sought, it was with prayer and hope as well as the realization that the blatant inadequacies of the Articles of Confederation required a new direction, albeit one that had its risks. I do not point this out as a way of saying, "Look, they did it, they placed their faith in people, so why object to what I have proposed?" I point this out to my objectors only to remind them that *their argument is not self-evidently valid*, historically, morally, and conceptually. Are there risks? Of course. Is what we have now demonstrably inadequate? Of course.

2. The objections, again, are identical to those voiced by many educational administrators, legislators, and boards of education against giving *teachers* the authority and responsibility to determine educational purposes, priorities, and use of resources. Teachers, they say, are unsophisticated in matters of administration, law, finance, and budgets. They are unprepared for this new authority and responsibility, and on what basis should one expect they can become competent in these matters? What you are proposing is that we go from the frying pan into the fire. No thank you. And to compound this felony in misguided thinking, you want teachers to share this authority and responsibility with parents who are even more ignorant and unsophisticated than teachers! Someone said that it is hard to be completely wrong and that is true here.

Suffice it to say here, the question is not what teachers now can do but what they can learn to do, and how quickly. The self-fulfilling prophecy can work in one of two ways.

One way assumes than an individual or a group cannot learn something and/or be trusted with this or that responsibility, you act toward them in accord with that assumption, and you end up proving that assumption, unaware that your initial, untested assumption already contained the "final" proof. The other way is that you assume that the individual or group can learn, you act in ways consistent with that assumption, and you are not surprised if, more often than not, your initial expectations are realized. In my experience, at least, the first way produces far fewer surprises than the second way. For example, the modal American classroom is not comprehensible apart from the unverbalized assumption that students cannot be trusted to govern themselves, to learn with and from other students in small, semi-autonomous groups, or to play a meaningful role in determining the constitution of the classroom, i.e., the rules, regulations, and values governing social relationships and learning. It is as if students require taming and socialization, otherwise they would run amok. There can only be one source of control, power, and direction. The teacher, and only the teacher, knows best. The "good" student is one who conforms, one who is unformed and needs to be formed, in much the same way that Professor Higgins shaped Liza Doolittle in *Pygmalion* and in its musical play and movie version, *My Fair Lady.* I said the "modal classroom" because there are classrooms, albeit clearly in the minority, governed by dramatically opposite assumptions and where anarchy, turbulence, volatility, or passive conformity are not in evidence. Assumptions are just that: assumptions about what people are and how they should and need to be managed. Assumptions are not empirical facts, however much we lull ourselves into believing they are factual.

3. My proposal was not dreamed up in an armchair. It was stimulated by countless stories, anecdotes, frustrations, resigned musings, and the articulated personal perspectives of a large number of teachers and administrators. If these were sources of stimulation to my thinking, congruent with what I personally observed, the fact is that no one came up with alternatives to the way things are. If they agreed on anything, it was that there was nothing basically wrong with the system that an infusion of better and wiser people would not remedy. The possibility that it was far more the system than the personal attributes of those in it that made the current situation what it is was never considered. And, I should add, no one asked of themselves: How did it happen that the enthusiasm and idealism with which I entered the profession so quickly got diluted, if not extinguished? Why do so many of my colleagues feel the same way? . . .

. . . If the beginning teacher has been sensitized to anything, it has been the bedrock necessity of leaving students in no doubt about who is in control of learning and who is the source of discipline. I have never met a teacher who denied that when he or she started to teach their first class their major concern was: Will I be able to control the students? Will I be an adequate and fair disciplinarian? Will they go along with me? What will I do if a student challenges my authority in some way? These questions reflect a stance resting on a psychology that views children as teacher-adult devouring animals, who will demand a mile if you give them an inch, who have no intrinsic desire to be understood, to be competent, to seek answers to questions about themselves, others, and the world around them. Their deficits are far greater than their assets; they are unformed, they need to be shaped; they can get shaped only by external others; they have to be instructed, informed, directed; they have no internal compass or sense of direction. The modal American classroom is incomprehensible apart from that kind of psychology and the pedagogy derived from it. . . .

The objectors to my proposal could raise another issue: "Not only do you propose that teachers be given an unusual, if not unheard of, degree of responsibility and authority, but you also expect them to work hand-in-hand with parents who have the most superficial understanding of learning. It's not a case of the blind leading the blind but it comes awfully close to being just that." This criticism could be made by the objectors, but it has not and will not be raised because to raise it is to expose how egregiously deficient preparatory programs for teachers and administrators are in regard to what parents know or would like to know; how they perceive schools and how they see how schools perceive them; the political principle justifying and requiring their deep involvement and commitment; and why parents no less than educators should be held accountable for what schools are and how well goals are being met. Teachers view parents no differently than they view children, just as administrators view teachers, which is to say that administrators regard teachers as people whose place is in the classroom and only the classroom because beyond its borders are roles and problems about which they know little and are incapable of comprehending and confronting.

To deal and work with parents is not only a matter of technique. Technique is the overt manifestation and implementation of a rationale containing philosophical, moral, psychological, and political facets. If I had to put it in a most succinct form, it would be as follows: Technique is revealing of what you think people know and can know, what they are and can become, what your obligations are to help another person become more than what he or she is, all of this revealing of the degree to which you are aware of the difference between the positive and negative consequences of the self-fulfilling prophecy. In the realm of human affairs we have no choice about whether or not to adopt a self-fulfilling stance. We do have a choice, at the same time that we have the obligation to justify that choice, never to forget that how and why we choose affects the lives of others.

Have I not, the reader may ask, rather thoroughly given my objectors justification for their position? Have I not said that teachers are not prepared for the responsibilities I propose to give them? Are the objectors right in saying that it will be a case of the blind leading the blind?

My answer is in several parts. The first is that I wanted to emphasize that preparatory programs are part of the system and that unless they change in appropriate ways the likelihood that school change will be even relatively successful (and sustained) will be somewhat above zero. Granted that current major reform efforts call for new roles and responsibilities for parents and teachers—albeit to an obviously lesser extent than in my proposal—why have the inadequacies of preparatory programs been exempt from criticism, especially since the results of these reform efforts are very far from robust? How do you justify an effort at "systemic change" and ignore preparatory programs that are indisputably part of the system? Why is so much criticism directed to schools and their personnel and practically none to the programs that select, prepare, and credential those personnel? The second part of my answer is that in the existing system accountability is so diffuse, if not chaotic, as to guarantee that no part will learn anything from any other part of the system. What we have now is the antithesis of a self-correcting system. Even worse, it is a system with no agreement on an overarching purpose, e.g., the creation and sustaining of contexts of productive learning. My proposal assumes that there should be an overarching purpose and that the commitment to it, and the implementation of it, are the responsibility of the two groups with the greatest stake in the enterprise, the two groups most immediately and personally involved, and, therefore, the groups that will be accountable, explicitly so.

The final part of my answer is that I do not regard parents and teachers as so ignorant and unknowledgeable, so lacking in the capacity to learn, so devoid of whatever is meant by wisdom and reason, so unable or unwilling to comprehend the differences between productive and unproductive learning, and so unwilling or unable to move in new directions as to be proof positive that they will make the present situation more dangerous and feckless than it now is. That does not mean that I regard teachers and parents as having more wisdom and insight than other groups, because they do not. What I am saying is that they do not have less wisdom and insight than others, and their capacity to learn is not less either. Put in another way: If parents and teachers are given and assume the roles and responsibilities explicitly and implicitly contained in my proposal, and if they are not constrained by existing rules and regulations of a failed tradition, and if they are truly free to take innovative actions that to others seem strange and risky, they stand a chance of demonstrating the crucial significances and consequences of productive learning. A reform effort not powered at all points by a conception of productive learning will have no demonstrable, percolating effects.

In my book *The Creation of Settings and the Future Societies* (1972), I emphasized and illustrated a point that is relevant here. If you ask members of a university faculty, "How do you justify the existence of a university?" the answer, with few exceptions, will be that a university is a place that creates the conditions in which its faculty can learn, change, and grow. You can have a university without students. The assumption is that by discharging its obligation to the faculty that faculty will be able to create those same conditions for students. Now, how would teachers in an elementary school justify the existence of the school? The answer is that it exists for the education of children. That is a very different answer from that given by university faculty. I would argue that an elementary school should exist for the productive learning of both teachers and students. If contexts for productive learning do not exist for teachers, those teachers cannot create and sustain those contexts for students. Those contexts do not or hardly exist for teachers. On the contrary, in the modal school teachers are in a context of discouragement.

My proposal does not assume a "Here are the keys to the kingdom" approach. What it does assume is that: (1) parents and teachers are willing to embark on the venture; (2) they have been provided and discussed materials (written, films) illustrative of contexts of productive learning; (3) they are enabled as a group to observe such contexts; and (4) they have access to individuals who potentially can be helpful as consultants, sounding boards, and support. *In short, they are not catapulted into a sink-or-swim situation but rather made aware that they, no less than students, are in a context of learning the pur-*

pose of which is clear but the course of which cannot be described in a predictable, step-by-step fashion. That is not to say the course is unpredictable but rather that productive learning cannot be driven by calendar time. Further, they have been sensitized to their obligation to develop forums and procedures that alert them to when and how the venture can be changed and improved, i.e., you can plan, plan, plan, and discuss, discuss, and discuss, but you have to be prepared for the reality that the process of creation and implementation brings to the fore issues, problems, and ambiguities ignored or glossed over. The change process is not for the fainthearted, let alone for those who paint themselves into a corner in which the admission of imperfection is a signal of defeat or failure. That is a glimpse of the obvious but the history of educational reform is a history of not taking the obvious seriously. The governance of our educational system is not one that has the overarching purpose of supporting productive learning for students and teachers, and it should occasion no surprise whatsoever that parents are not even in the picture. My proposal puts them in the picture because they are one of the two stakeholders most immediately and personally involved with and concerned for the quality and the outcomes of the enterprise, and that determines why they should be given the authority and responsibility to govern that enterprise.

Will there be some mistakes and conflicts? Of course. Will there be schools where parents and teachers are unwilling to give the time that governance will require? Of course. My proposal does not require that form of governance; it makes the opportunity possible. Legislation should require that parents who wish to be available for their role but cannot because they are working will be released from work up to x days a year without loss of pay. I expect, and they should expect, that they will be giving more than the equivalent of x days but they should also expect they should not be "paid" for time they will have to give in evenings and weekends. They are not going to be running a business but a nonprofit enterprise involving the present and future of children. Yes, I do assume that many parents will be willing to give the time, will not view it as an oppressive burden, but rather as an opportunity to enlarge their knowledge and experience, an opportunity not ordinarily available or possible in the lives of many people.

My proposal dramatically enlarges the authority and responsibility of teachers. It was not many decades ago that teachers overcame their resistance to joining a union in order to have more power in matters of salary and working conditions. On the surface it appeared they were interested only in increasing what then was a scandalously low salary. Without in any way denying the justice of their grievances, what the teachers sought was *respect* for what they were and did. They did not want to be treated as peons who did what they were told by those above them. They were "told" they had to conform and submit, they saw others as seeing them as children who could not understand or participate in important matters of educational policy and procedure. If in subsequent decades their salaries have increased, it has not been accompanied by the feeling that they are truly recognized and respected by those above them in the system.

When we say we respect someone, we mean we understand and accept what they are and think as well as what they want to become. In the present system teachers have good reason to believe that others do not respect the capacity of teachers to be other than what they are: someone whose work is in an encapsulated classroom and who should not and cannot be expected to take responsibility for anything beyond that classroom. Socialized as they are in that kind of institutional culture it should occasion no surprise that a fair number of teachers come to esteem themselves as others esteem them. It also will not surprise me if teachers regard my proposal as another downgrading of their status.

Do you mean, some will say, that teachers will share authority and responsibility with parents who are not professionals? As I have pointed out in detail elsewhere (Sarason, 1995b), the spirit of that question is precisely that which informs the stance of educational administrators in opposing giving teachers any role in matters of policy and decisions. If I expect that there will be teachers who will not embrace my proposal, I do expect there will be far more than a few who will, provided that two conditions are met. The first is that their compensation will be appropriate to their new roles and its time demands. Second, that the rules of the game will be clear that parents and teachers will have the freedom to go their own way, and not to be watched, supervised, and ruled by others who, however well intentioned, are not totally involved in *that* school, and who are more concerned with uniformity among schools than with individuality.

It was not my purpose in this chapter, as it will not be in subsequent ones, to deal with all of the criticisms, questions, and reservations my proposal will elicit. But there are two issues I can safely assume will have occurred to the reader. The first has to do with giving the school control over the allocation of funds, i.e., removing control from the central office. In a document *Reinventing Central Office: A Primer for Successful Schools,* Chicago's Cross City Campaign for Urban School Reform (1995) deals forthrightly with that issue. The document is clear about what it needs to change:

Abolish:
- the centralized control of funds
- the central office's monopoly on services
- the present allocation formulas
- the unnecessary categorical and restricted federal and state funding rules
- the requirement to return unspent funds to central office
- the obscure and overly technical budget documents

The document then sketches the steps that can be taken and that obligate the council of the school periodically to make public how the funds were used. I found their suggestions reasonably clear, responsible, and realistic. The document is the fruit of the collaborative efforts of eight individuals whose credentials establish, at the very least, that they are people who know the current system and are not engaged in witch-hunts. What is so refreshing about the publication is its unequivocal recommendation that the governance of the existing system is a self-defeating one in which accountability is diffused or masked or both. What is disappointing is the absence of a commitment to what I consider to be the overarching purpose of schooling. That is to say, the document does not address the question: Is there an overarching purpose that, if not realized, makes the realization of all other purposes unlikely, if not impossible?

Can one come up with a plan that *guarantees* that a parent-teacher governing group will expend funds in consistent, efficient, honorable ways? The answer is no, and that answer would be the same if the organization was a private company, a church, or a so-cial club, and it is certainly the answer one has to give in regard to existing school sys-tems. To ask for a guarantee, at this time, is an effective way of distracting attention away from the task of recognizing the inadequacies and failures of the current system in creating and sustaining productive learning for students *and* teachers, and from de-vising a new governance system that is clear about the differences between productive and unproductive contexts of learning. If there is no clarity about that, we will continue to reinvent past wheels that turned out to be flat tires. The Chicago document is one of many indications that people in diverse sectors of the society find themselves driven to the conclusion that the existing system of governance is hopelessly unrescuable.

The second issue that will have occurred to readers can be put in the form of ques-tions: "Let's say you have the kind of school your proposal calls for. What assurance is there that the school is being consistent with the overarching purpose, and how will the larger community be able to judge that consistency and the achievement of educational goals? To whom and in what ways will it be accountable? What basis will be provided so as to allow some external agency to say 'Stop, no more,' or 'Right on,' or 'Some changes are necessary'? What self-correcting procedures will there be? Good intentions are one thing, getting to or near your goals is another thing. Will the teachers and par-ents be accountable only to themselves?" Those, of course, are legitimate questions. . . . I know that devising a new governance system should not be done in isolation but rather in a context and through a process maximizing awareness of the universe of alternatives that should be considered. As I said earlier, what is required is something akin to the constitutional convention of 1787, where its participants engaged in a competition of ideas and possibilities, where different interests were represented, where common ground could be found for seemingly opposing views, where it could become apparent that the problems being confronted and discussed did not have one, and only one, so-lution, where it could be acknowledged that any resolution or compromise brought risk and uncertainty in its wake. In the realm of human affairs we are never dealing with problems that have a solution the way 4 divided by 2 [has] a solution.

Those are the reasons I resisted writing this book. It is not about a set of problems and proposals one individual should be expected to "solve." It is not only because the problems are so complex but also because they are problems taking us over uncharted seas. I am in the same position as the kind of school I am trying to describe and justify, with the crucial difference that, unlike me, that school will have external sources of ideas, support, counsel, and evaluation. Productive learning requires, among other things, feedback. The kind of school I am proposing will not operate in a vacuum.

Note

1. My answer in regard to parents is given in much greater detail in my book *Parental In-volvement and the Political Principle: Why the Existing Governance Structure of Schools Should Be Abolished* (1995b).

Part IV

The Political and Policy Agenda

CHAPTER 20

The Non-Learning,
Non–Self-Correcting System

Sarason's deep frustration with the education system is captured by the title of this selection. He acknowledges most people's tepid acceptance of the current system of public education and their general pessimism that "something is wrong somewhere." He fears that the system is, in fact, beyond repair—it must be replaced. And he buttresses his critique with five assumptions about learning and school governance. These assumptions, which are generally accepted in principle by thoughtful educators, are ones the education system consistently undermines.

Sarason describes the key assumption among the five as follows: "There is one goal that, if not achieved, makes the achievement of all other goals very unlikely. That goal is to create those conditions that make students *want* to learn; *not* have to learn but *want* to learn more about self, others, and the world."

He concludes that "every major reform effort accepts the system as it is, which is why I have predicted, and continue to predict, they will have little or no general impact or staying power," but he holds out a possible exception in the charter schools movement. But even with charter schools, he worries that the lack of well-funded and well-designed research efforts to examine the schools will mean that we will learn much less from their successes and shortcomings than we might.

Question for Seymour Sarason

You say that "teachers cannot create and sustain contexts for productive learning unless those contexts exist for them." Yet many of us have had at least one or two teachers who worked under the same deeply flawed school systems as everyone else but managed to create productive contexts for some or most of their students. How do you explain this?

Reprinted with the permission of Teachers College Press from "The Non-Learning, Non–Self-Correcting System" in *How Schools Might Be Governed and Why* by Seymour Sarason (New York: Teachers College Press, 1997).

Sarason's Response

I have observed such teachers, although they are few in number as your question implies. The only thing I can report is that those teachers were independent, inner-directed people. They were that way before they became teachers. In my experience I have observed the same among physicians, who, generally speaking, are not noted for their caring, compassionate behavior. The few who are caring and act appropriately were that way before they entered medical school.

Years ago Leonard Eron conducted studies comparing medical and law students from the time they entered training to when they finished. Idealism was one of the characteristics studied. The two groups were not different to begin with, but by the end of training, medical students had become dramatically less idealistic than law students. A student of mine, Prill Ellis, did her doctoral dissertation in this area and found the same disparity.

The point is that one cannot depend upon finding a whole school full of such teachers nor, for that matter, can we be sure that such teachers will want to remain in the profession for long once they realize that teachers such as they are few and far between. By "creating the context for sustained and productive learning for teachers as well as for students," all I am saying is that if we want better than that, we have to create within schools the contexts for such.

More about the obstacles to educational change at the system and national level may be found in:

Educational Reform: A Self-Scrutinizing Memoir (2002)
Charter Schools: Another Flawed Educational Reform? (1998)
Political Leadership and Educational Failure (1998)
Revisiting "The Culture of the School and the Problem of Change" (1996)
School Change: The Personal Development of a Point of View (1995)
Letters to a Serious Education President (1993)
The Case for Change: Rethinking the Preparation of Educators (1992)
The Predictable Failure of Educational Reform (1990)
The Challenge of Art to Psychology (1990)
Schooling in America: Scapegoat and Salvation (1983)

In recent years I have been asking people this question: Are you satisfied with the present governance system of public education? The answers were a qualified yes. The qualifications had to do with financing, inadequate educational outcomes, community-parent participation, regionalism, and the bureaucratic mentality. No one questioned the system *qua* system, i.e., the need for, the powers of, and interrelationships among a state department of education, a local board of education, a superintendent of schools, a principal, teachers, colleges and universities, and parents. As one person put it, "Politically and philosophically it is in principle a democratic system that can accommodate to a variety of needed changes. If it doesn't work as well as we like, it says less about the system and more about the people in it and the strong conflicting social pressures impacting on it." There were a few individuals who were so deeply critical of the system and its outcomes that they were disposed "to give up on it," although all but one of them could offer no alternative. The one exception was a person who semi-facetiously said, "Let's privatize the whole shebang." It will come as no surprise to the reader that no one with whom I talked expressed any optimism whatsoever that, generally speaking, schools would discernibly improve. That was true whether or not the respondent was an educator, another type of professional, or an ordinary citizen. It was difficult for most of them to explain or justify their pessimism. It was the feeling that "something was wrong somewhere," but they could be no more specific than that. Some indicated that much was amiss in our society, and schools were no exception.

These answers were predictable. Leaving the educational arena aside, the literature on organizational change is replete with instances where the approach has been to change personnel or to change the perspective of existing personnel, or to improve speed and quality of communication between and among levels of authority, or to provide incentives for increased motivation and commitment, or to adopt a more equitable reward system, or to alter who should participate in what ways and to what degree in decision making, or all of these. Frequently these may require changes in the organizational chart by changing or eliminating boxes in that chart or by changing the directions of arrows indicating how the boxes should be in relation to each other. Although these changes are intended as "systemic" ones, far more often than not they hardly alter the hierarchy of power despite the rhetoric of power flowing down-up as well as top-down. That, I hasten to add, does not mean that no changes take place but rather that little or no changes take place in the basic features of the system.

There is a difference between a new system and changes within an existing system. I should also add that I am in no way implying that a new system is inherently virtuous. When the Bolsheviks gained power in the Russian revolution, they changed the system of governance and for 70 years ruled the country in a tyrannical, murderous fashion. They sought escape from a Czarist tyranny and in short order instituted their own brand. Whether in the political, business, or educational arenas, to be in favor of system change does not automatically confer brownie points on you; the verdicts of history are about consequences, not motivations. Henry Ford introduced the assembly line system in industrial production, and he paid his workers what was then a high daily wage, five dollars a day. He was considered an organizational genius pointing the way to a rosy, prosperous, technological future. Today we think otherwise because we see the assembly line as a cruel, insensitive, debilitating enslavement of workers to an ever-moving production line. Henry Ford's ideas impacted on and were emulated by educators and others in the then political-social-educational establishment. More about that later. Suffice it to say here, his overarching criterion justifying his system of production—and he did have such a criterion—was increasing production at ever lowering costs. His overarching criterion said little or nothing about the lives of workers.

Let us turn to an instructive, more heartening example quite relevant to this book. I refer (as I always do) to the constitutional convention of 1787. That convention initially was intended to repair the dangerous inadequacies of the Articles of Confederation. (Indeed, when Thomas Jefferson learned that his friend James Madison was supporting the

move to scrap the Articles of Confederation and come up with a new system of governance, he was surprised and somewhat opposed to such a departure.) What the convention came up with was a new system of governance, unlike anything in history. What
is most relevant to my present purposes is that the new system of governance had one
overarching goal: how to harmonize political power with individual freedom. Put in another way: Given all that history contains about power, its uses and misuses, its necessity and yet the necessity to constrain it, what system of governance stands a chance of
securing individual liberties by allocating, distributing, and constraining the exercise of
power?

That was the central problem and one that was morally, politically, and realistically
complex, which explains why that convention occupied several months, during which
scores of proposals were discarded, examined and reexamined, compromises arrived at,
compromises undone. If they did not need to be taught about how political power could
be abused, they also did not have to be taught that the citizenry, as individuals and in
groups, did not always make wise and reasoned decisions. They were not devotees of
the concept of rational man (women were not in the picture). They were not armchair
theorists. They were practical men confronting a historically vexing problem. And when
they were through, they were far from certain that the new system of governance would
achieve its central purpose. They included an amending process in the final document.
And in order to secure approval, it was later necessary to include a Bill of Rights that
made individual rights more explicit.

. . . What is so instructive about the constitutional convention of 1787, and explains
its length, is the interplay, the clash, the creativity of ideas and personalities. What kept
them together was the acknowledged brute fact that the Articles of Confederation were
dangerously inadequate. When they were through, no one was completely satisfied but
all could live with the compromise. We are still in their debt.

What follows in this book is informed by several considerations, assumptions, judgments.

1. Education has multiple goals, but not all goals are equally important. How should
   we scale these goals, and having scaled them how should governance of education
   take seriously and support the ordering of the priorities?
2. There is one goal that, if not achieved, makes the achievement of all other goals very
   unlikely. That goal is to create those conditions that make students *want* to learn; *not*
   have to learn but *want* to learn more about self, others, and the world. The overarching purpose of schooling and its governance is to support that goal, i.e., to create
   and sustain contexts of productive learning supportive of the natural curiosity and
   wonder with which children start schooling.
3. Contexts for productive learning are no arcane mystery. They require that adults start
   with where the child is: his or her curiosities, questions, puzzlements. The artistry of
   teaching inheres in how to capitalize on that starting point so as to enlarge and support what the child *wants* to learn. That is to say, you seek to help the child forge
   connections between what he or she wants to know and what the child needs to

learn. I say artistry because those connections cannot be forged by a fiat that requires the child to conform to a predetermined or calendar driven program. You can teach by the calendar, you cannot learn productively by the calendar. This is not permissiveness or a mindless indulgence of a child's whims and fancies. It is a way of "hooking" the child, enlarging the child's view in line with the maxim that the more you know the more you need to know.

4. Teachers cannot create and sustain contexts for productive learning unless those contexts exist for them. Teaching is not a once-and-for-all learned craft. It is (should be) a developmental process that today is hindered by teachers being in an encapsulated classroom with no time, opportunity, or forums where the issues and problems of teaching are discussed, not in the abstract but in terms of concrete children and teachers. To be helped and stimulated by others, or to stimulate and help others, requires forums where that is expected and possible. If teaching is a developmental process, it must also be a self-correcting one. Contexts for productive learning are as necessary for teachers as they are for students. Where they exist for neither—which is generally the case today—you get learning but not productive learning: the sense that one's understanding is being enlarged and propelling one willingly to the future.

5. Bedrock to a system of governance should be the political principle: If any one or any group is going to be affected by a policy, they should have some role in the formulation and decisions about that policy.

This book will not sit well with those who believe that the existing governance system of education is rescuable. It is not rescuable if by that is meant that it can be restored to an earlier state of grace and efficacy. It never was an efficacious system. It arose largely as a way to tame and socialize the children of scores of millions of immigrant children. The concept of individuality and productive learning was never in the picture. What was in the picture was rote learning, memorization, drill according to a predetermined calendar-driven curriculum to which the student had to conform. It was basically a shape up or ship out approach in which being shipped out could mean not being allowed in school, or being segregated in special classes, programs, or tracks from which one could never emerge. They were "rejects" from an assembly line of education, rejects in no way interpreted as casting any negative light on the system. There were always a few educators who saw the system for what it was: an educational factory in which a student's interests, curiosities, questions were of no account. Schools were contrived oases from real life and that included the life of the mind; the life of the mind and the social life outside of the oases were off limits, i.e., interferences to what a child *had* to learn. In the reigning pedagogy individuality and productive learning were foreign concepts.

As time went by the rhetoric of individuality and productive learning gained currency, less because of the power of ideas and more because the children of immigrants were not content to have their children receive an education that consigned them, as it had their parents, to lives of drudgery. Following World War II, *and precisely because of that war* (Sarason, 1966), the inadequacies and failures of the public schools could not be kept off the societal agenda. The era of educational reform had begun. Whereas earlier movements for educational reform came in cycles—every ten years or so cries for reform were sounded and curricula changed—educational reform now took on an urgency and degree of continuity as never before. As one looks back over the post–World War II era, one cannot avoid the conclusion that it was an era of increasing disappointment with and criticism of the efficacy of the public schools, and that is putting it mildly. Although the rhetoric of individuality and productive learning was increasingly heard and taken seriously in a classroom here and a classroom there, a school here and a school there, it was neither taken seriously, let alone implemented, in schools generally. And in the case of the minuscule number of exceptions, they occurred despite, not because of, the system. My own experience, as well as a review of the literature on educational reform, substantiates the conclusion that these exceptions traversed a minefield of obstacles in order to survive, and many did not survive.

I am in no way suggesting a conspiracy against the concepts of individuality and productive learning. Indeed, I have never met an educator, a public official, or a citizen who argued against the primacy of these concepts. Rather, I am making two points. First, there is a reluctance or inability to pursue the *practical* implications of these concepts. Second, when they are seriously pursued, it becomes obvious that the existing governance structure would require such a radical overhaul as to be regarded as an indulgence of utopian thinking. If by utopian thinking is meant the exercise of imagination to depict situations that do not and cannot now exist, what I have said (and will say throughout this book) is not utopian. There are instances, albeit few, in some public and private schools where the concepts are taken seriously and appropriately implemented. They do not exist in a never-never land; they exist today, e.g., the school created and recently described by Weinstein and Butterworth (1996). And the knowledgeable reader knows that it is these concepts that are powering the movement for charter schools, which is an effort to get these schools "out from under" the present governance system. And, I must reiterate, there is no reformer who leaves us in any doubt that the success of his or her efforts requires a governance change.

Unfortunately, none of these reformers confront the governance system as a system that includes the school, the school system or district, the board of education, the state department of education, the university, parents, the legislature, and the executive branch of government. These are stakeholders in a very complicated educational system. They are not passive stakeholders; they have similar but by no means identical interests and agendas; more often than not they are in conflict with and mistrust each other. *It is a system so balkanized as to prevent meaningful discussion of, let alone agreement about, educational goals and priorities. It is not a system that can initiate and sustain meaningful reform.* On the contrary, its features are such as to make reform extraordinarily difficult and even impossible. Under severe and unusual pressure it may permit tinkering, even the appearance of reform, but as time goes on and the pressures decrease, the leadership changes, the tinkering and the reform lose force and purpose, confirming the adage that the more things change the more they remain the same. *It is not a self-correcting system; there are no means, procedures, forums through which the system "learns."* It is a system with a seemingly infinite capacity to remain the same in the face of obvious inadequacies, unmet goals, and public dissatisfaction. *It is a system in which accountability is so diffused that no one is accountable. It is a system that has outlived all of its reformers, and will outlive the present generation of reformers.* I made that prediction 30 years ago, and I have no reason to think otherwise today.

We are not used to thinking in system terms. We hear much about the need for "systemic" reform, and what is almost always meant is either some kind of change in a single school or in a single school district. Sometimes, but not always, the called-for change involves altering power relationships or giving greater autonomy in policy making or resource allocation to the individual school, or both. I heartily endorse such goals but only on the basis of the political principle: Those who are going to be affected by an educational policy should have some role in the formulation and implementation of the policy (Sarason, 1995b). But why should such changes be expected favorably to affect educational outcomes? That question hardly receives an answer. What is implied is that by changing power relationships, teachers and others will be more creative, more willing to be bold in thinking and action, and, therefore, the quality and level of student learning will be enhanced. To the extent that existing power relationships destroy, as they do, the morale of teachers by reducing them to the level of alienated ciphers, changing those relationships may have positive effects on teachers.

But, again, why will those changes have positive effects on students? And the answer is that unless those changes specifically and concretely focus on individuality and productive learning, there will not be such positive effects on students. To seek to change power relationships ("systemic" reform) without those changes being in the service of clear conceptions of individuality and productive learning is a missed opportunity. Put in another way, changing power relationships is a necessary but *not* sufficient basis for improving the quality and context of learning. For example, in an increasing number of states parents, by legislative fiat, have been given parity with educators in educational decision making. From personal observation as well as reports I received from observers, there has been no change whatsoever in regard to taking seriously individuality and productive learning. Needless to say, teachers viewed such legislation as another instance either of taking potshots at teachers or blaming the victim or both. But, again in my experience, the story is only slightly better when teachers have asked for and been given a greater voice in decision making in their school. In most instances, what passes for site-based management is a charade. In a few instances it is not a charade, but they are instances where the teachers learned rather quickly that taking individuality and productive learning seriously was impossible given the nature of the larger system. They lowered their sights.

I do not relish being perceived as a wet blanket or as someone who, if he cannot have the whole loaf, would rather eat nothing. Basic to my stance are two brute facts. First, the educational reform movement in the post–World War II era has been, generally speaking, a failure. That is not to deny that we have learned a lot but rather that the system has not "learned" the lessons to be drawn from that history. And the second fact is that the reform movement has not dealt with the stakeholders who are part of the system and who play crucial roles, directly or indirectly, in setting goals and priorities. More correctly, these stakeholders and their relationship to the system insure that the important issues will be obscured. To put it bluntly, the system is incapable of confronting the sources of its inadequacies. Far from being a self-correcting system, it is a problem-producing one.

There was a time when the defects of the system were seen as deriving from a lack of financial resources. Today, few hold that position. Beginning with the 1954 desegregation decision, the moral dimensions of the system's inadequacies could no longer be ignored. It was then that we began to hear that the overarching goal of the system was "to help *each* child realize his or her potential." That, it turned out, was (and is) empty rhetoric because no one saw fit to raise the question: Is the system capable of taking the concepts of individuality and productive learning seriously?

There was a period, by no means over, when the chief culprits were seen to be teachers who had an inadequate grasp of the subject matter they taught. . . . How does a teacher's increased grasp of subject matter get communicated to and absorbed by students so that it is psychologically "owned" by them and motivates them to *want* to learn more? On what basis can one claim that teachers' increased grasp of subject matter is *alone* adequate to deal with the fact that as students go from elementary to middle to high school their desire for learning steadily decreases? Does what we have learned about child development tell us nothing about contexts of productive learning?

With one exception, every major reform effort accepts the system as it is, which is why I have predicted, and continue to predict, they will have little or no general impact or staying power. The one exception is the charter school, which is by legislative fiat *relatively* independent of the system. They are minuscule in number. They are too new to justify passing judgment on them. From what I have read or have been told their rationale takes seriously the concepts of individuality and productive learning. My concern is threefold. First, will they implement their rationale appropriately and consistently? Second, because they are *relatively* free of the existing condition, will they be able to resist efforts "to bring them into line"? Third, will they be able to discharge their obligation candidly and inform the general public about what they are doing, experiencing, learning, and accomplishing? The third point is the most important one because if it is inadequately dealt with, we end up with an "experiment" from which we learn nothing, an old story in the history of educational reform.

One would (should) expect that in a major departure from traditional practice—a departure of great *potential* value—resources would be provided adequately and impartially to discharge the reporting function. As best as I can judge, those resources are not in the picture. What would be surprising would be if they were in the picture. The legislature and executive branches of state government—who, let us not forget, are stakeholders in the educational system—have never understood, or have been helped to understand, that the reforms they initiate or approve will not serve the public interest unless they and we have a secure basis for passing judgment, i.e., how, when, and why predictable and unpredictable problems arose and how they were dealt with, what self-correcting actions or procedures were employed, etc. I have no doubt that legislators and executives in state and federal government approve of the Federal Drug Administration's practice of not making a drug available for public use until there is a good, impartial basis for concluding that the drug achieves its intended, positive effects. But that understanding and approval by elected officials does not transfer to the educational arena, which is what I meant when I said that the existing governance structure of education is not capable of self-correction or learning. On a purely actuarial basis, I am skeptical that over time charter schools will remain an exception to what I said earlier.

In the chapters that follow I attempt to describe features of a new governance system for education. I do so for several reasons. First, I have long been a critic of the existing system. Second, it took me years to confront the fact that the system was not rescuable. Third, the inadequacies of the system are having percolating, negative consequences throughout our society, especially in our cities where issues of race and poverty force me to regard cities as time bombs. Fourth, despite the fact that people knowledgeable about education, to say the least, have grave doubts about the system, I have been singularly unsuccessful in getting funding sources and/or the powers that be to take actions that would give currency to the need for a different system. Fifth, despite my unsuccessful efforts I feel obliged to, so to speak, go it alone. I do not do so with a firm sense of security that what I have come up will be clear or compelling or as comprehensive as it should be. If it stimulates discussion and debate, or if it leads others to come up with better alternatives, my effort will not have been in vain. Time is not on our side. Public dissatisfaction with the existing system is real and deep. In the quiet of their nights most people know there is something very wrong with the existing system.

I entreat the reader to assume the obligation to try to take distance from the system as it now is. That is a lot to ask of readers who, like me, have been socialized to regard the system as if it had been given to us on an educational Mount Sinai. It was not easy for me, and it will not be easy for the reader. But the time to use whatever conceptual creativity we possess is now.

CHAPTER 21

Are Schools
Unique Organizations?

Reflecting on the twenty-five years since publication of *The Culture of the School and the Problem of Change* (1971), Sarason places himself, imaginatively, first inside the head of a corporate leader who reflects on how the private sector has had to transform itself in light of the "total quality" revolution based on Deming's principles of management. A preoccupation with "quality" at every step of the process, and shared ownership of key goals at all levels of the organization, are what stand out. Next, Sarason imagines how a typical, well-meaning but besieged public school educator might respond to a corporate leader's arguments today—that "schools have a lot to learn from us in regard to how we had to change, the turmoil of change, and why in the long run it is worth it."

What Sarason is doing here is comparing some imaginary conversations between private sector leaders and school leaders that he first wrote in the 1971 edition of *The Culture of the School and the Problem of Change* with another imaginary interchange between the two some 25 years later, when he rewrote the book under the title *Revisiting "The Culture of School and the Problem of Change."* In the 1971 edition, Sarason also characterizes the model laboratory school developed in Chicago by John Dewey as an example of a school where the "culture" was seriously and deliberately attended to. At that time, Sarason lamented that the failure of most educators to take Dewey's ideas seriously—or to even read them! He begins the present selection by explaining that his perspective on the culture of schools derives, in part, from looking at education through the lens of his primary discipline, psychology.

Sarason finds the contrast between the private sector and schools particularly striking. In response to an acknowledged crisis, the typical educational leader will emphasize his or her lack of control over critical elements rather than the need to move ahead boldly. Sarason also faults schools, as organizations, for refusing to accept valid criticisms or to

Reprinted with the permission of Teachers College Press from "Are Schools Unique Organizations?" in *Revisiting "The Culture of the School and the Problem of Change"* by Seymour Sarason (New York: Teachers College Press, 1996).

create a climate of self-study and reflection. He states, "Schools do not contain the forums in which serious discussion of educational issues . . . can and are expected to take place."

Question for Seymour Sarason

Has the focus of leaders on "quality" in education (à la Deming), so prominent in the early nineties, been completely overshadowed by a crass political insistence on the "accountability" to be found in "high-stakes testing" and "teaching to the test"? Is there anything of value that the private sector has to contribute to educational reform today?

Sarason's Response

I do not blame the private sector for the current absence of discussion on quality in education. That is an incomplete and even inappropriate attribution. On the level of action and implementation, concern with quality has never been a *notable* feature of school learning contexts. The impetus for the ways schools have been structured, organized, and their governing rationale for learning was the taming and socialization of the children of immigrants, beginning in the late nineteenth century when compulsory education took hold.

It is more complicated than that and it should not be overlooked that what Henry Ford did for the assembly line mode of factory production had a major impact on how schools were organized—albeit in the last three decades many business leaders have recognized the quality variable at the same time that they were puzzled by the intractability of school reform efforts. There were, for all practical purposes, few people in the educational community who could get them to understand that variable in relation to learning and schools, the way Deming did for the Japanese. If I am not about to take the private sector off the hook, I also do not want to take the educators off the hook.

One more time: Unless and until there is a consensus about the differences between contexts of productive and unproductive learning "quality" in education will be visible in a paltry number of classrooms. That is why I was so delighted and encouraged by your two books. You gave concrete examples of real teachers and students in real classrooms. I have tried to do the same thing. Dewey tried. Who listens? Who *acts* in accord with it? The private sector is not the culprit. There is no culprit, not in the sense that any one or any group willed the current situation. I continue to be amazed that the issue of clarifying the productive/unproductive dichotomy was hardly ever discussed before our political leaders began to proclaim "accountability and standards"—a "shape-up or ship-out" stance—as the educational wonder drug.

More about the obstacles to educational change at the system and national level may be found in:

Educational Reform: A Self-Scrutinizing Memoir (2002)
Charter Schools: Another Flawed Educational Reform? (1998)
Political Leadership and Educational Failure (1998)
How Schools Might Be Governed and Why (1997)
School Change: The Personal Development of a Point of View (1995)
Letters to a Serious Education President (1993)
The Case for Change: Rethinking the Preparation of Educators (1992)

The Predictable Failure of Educational Reform (1990)
The Challenge of Art to Psychology (1990)
Schooling in America; Scapegoat and Salvation (1983)

. . . In my adult years I came to public schools as an outsider, primarily as a researcher and then as a helper to teachers in their classrooms. Nothing in my professional education as a psychologist in any way prepared me to understand schools. I saw myself as an outsider and I was made quite aware that I was seen by school personnel as an outsider, i.e., I lived in one world, they lived in another. You have to be unusually dense and uncurious not to ask yourself why you are seen not only as an outsider but as a somewhat unwelcome one. I saw myself as a sympathetic, harmless character; they tended to see me as kin to the visitor from Mars. How to explain that? . . .

I was in the role of a helper and, being a somewhat friendly person, over time I established friendly relationships with school personnel. We did not have to be on guard with each other. As a result—and it took time—I became aware that I was being told things that made it obvious that life in a school was very complex, far more complex than those with whom I talked realized, and dramatically more complex than I had imagined. It was an example of a maxim that we know to be true but we do not take seriously: "Part the curtain, go behind a person's words, style, and appearances and you find another world you did not suspect." And what I found required me to begin to conceptualize the culture of the school.

One of the most fruitful ways of gaining insight into the culture of schools (or any other organization) is to determine how its members respond to alternative ways of thinking about and organizing a school because their responses tell you, directly or indirectly, what they regard as right, natural, and proper: the underlying rationale and the practices and structure they require and justify. I included the chapter on the Dewey school [in *The Culture of the School and the Problem of Change,* 1971] not only to indicate that there had been such a school, but also to tell the reader how the culture of today's schools is a mammoth obstacle to anything resembling a dispassionate and serious effort to assess the possible virtues of the alternatives, i.e., it is "impractical" or "utopian," or the stuff of fantasy. Those are the kinds of responses that define that which *is* right, natural, and proper—what is the "right" rationale, structure, and practice—and what is "off limits."

. . . I must relate one of my "discoveries" about the school culture [circa 1970] because of what it says about changes that have occurred since then in the school culture and about which I will say more later.

I came [to the study of education] from the field of clinical psychology. It is a feature of the clinical professions that in their training and practice individuals spend a lot of time in case conferences. As a friend and colleague, Dr. Murray Levine, once quipped, "Every clinic needs two staffs: one to go to case meetings and another to do the work." I was not long in schools before I realized that the tradition of frequent and regular meetings to discuss individual cases—for that matter, to discuss any meaningful issue— did not exist. That floored me. Each teacher dealt alone with his or her problems; there was no give-and-take forum where one could learn anything from anyone else. That is what Murray Levine meant by "teaching is a lonely profession."

How to explain this? Why did teachers say nothing about the absence of such a tradition? Teachers, no less than those in the clinical professions, always have to deal with difficult or hard-to-understand individuals. Why is it expected that a teacher will *always* deal *alone* with those kinds of problems? How was the absence of the collegial case conference reflective of the school culture? What would have to happen for that absence to be recognized and its self-defeating consequences confronted? The questions multiplied. I was not dealing with a personality problem. I was faced with the problem of the culture of the school. Again, one of the reasons I initially included the Dewey chapter was to contrast collegiality in Dewey's school and the public schools of 1970. In that respect, as in many others, the contrast is stark. On theoretical, practical, social-philosophical grounds, Dewey's school *required* a high degree of collegiality.

But the major reason the answers we would have gotten from [our imaginary interviews with] educators and corporate people [to the question of whether schools are similar to corporate institutions] in 1970 were historically, inexcusably wrong is far more serious than ignoring Dewey and his school. Briefly put, it goes this way:

1. With the advent of universal, compulsory education, in large part a consequence of waves of immigration, the main purpose of schooling was to tame and socialize the children of immigrants, to make them respectful of American values, beliefs, work ethic, and political institutions. "Tame and socialize" may seem harsh, but only if you read the present into the past. Given the times, schooling was seen as the major means of divorcing children from the "foreign" speech, thoughts, and ways of their parents. Education was indoctrination. The concept of individuality of students was never in the picture.

2. Especially in the growing metropolitan areas, schools became very large; classes of 50, 60, or more students were not unusual. The administrative structure of schools became more differentiated, complex, bureaucratic. The main purpose of schooling did not change.

3. Schools resembled factories. That was not fortuitous. Educators were very much taken with the concept of the efficiency of the assembly line, of a rigid organizational structure, of everyone having his place in the scheme of things. Henry Ford was a revered icon because of his organizational genius, i.e., things went according to a clear, predetermined plan that left no room for individual initiative. Educators sought to emulate Ford who, it should be remembered, said that a customer could have any color car he desired as long as it was black. *Not only were educators influenced by the industrial model but industrial leaders made clear that schools should take that model seriously if they were to "produce" the kinds of workers industry needed.* (That influence, please note, was precisely what Dewey explicitly criticized.)

In short, in our imaginary 1970 interviews with educators and corporate types, there would have been no recognition of the historical fact that schools as organizations were incomprehensible apart from the ways they had been influenced by the private sector. Therefore, they could not see that even 1970 schools, organizationally speaking, were obvious lineal descendants of schools as they were a century ago. And . . . for all practical purposes the overarching aim of schooling had changed little. The situation is somewhat different today.

What if we asked today, 25 years later, the same question of educators and private-sector people [about whether schools are similar to corporate institutions]? I shall give the "average" response of each group even though it masks somewhat the range of answers. And that average response is based on what educational and corporate leaders have said orally or in print. I did not dream up the answers.

▶ *The Private-Sector Response*

There has been a noticeable change in emphasis on how we in the private sector look upon the nature of productive organizations. And that emphasis did not come about by sitting in a chair and thinking. It came about because we were hit over the head by foreign competitors who were making better-quality products and getting a larger share of markets we once dominated. We were in trouble and we knew it. We tried to understand what was so different about these foreign organizations. We did several things. One was that we began to listen to organizational theorists and consultants whom we never had taken seriously. And we began to read about these foreign organizations. The best way to put it is that we began to unimprison ourselves from a self-defeating parochialism. We had our comeuppance.

We learned many things, but two stand out. The first is that you can never take your eyes off the *quality* of what you are producing. At every step of the process you judge quality and that is the only way you can make the necessary changes quickly. You don't wait for the end of the process to judge quality. You are always judging it from step one. That is the preventive orientation in contrast to the old days when we knew what was wrong only at the end of the process when there was little we could do except to repair this or fix that, and that was very expensive and not all that helpful for our ability to compete. We had to change the way we were organized. Those who have changed found it a wrenching experience; so did our stockholders, but they not only survived, they prospered. They satisfied their customers; they listened to them; they even sought their help—quite a contrast to the Henry Ford mentality. Indeed, Ford today is an outstanding example of organizational change in the service of quality and it is not fortuitous that the Ford company began to take seriously the ideas of the person (Edward Deming) who after World War II put Japanese industry on the right road, as a result of which he became one of their secular saints.

The other thing we learned, and this represents a real change (if not a revolutionary one), is that you cannot achieve your goals unless all members at all levels of the organization meaningfully participate in some important way in the organization's affairs. The top-down type of organizational structure made that impossible. Unless everyone has reason to feel respected, listened to, involved, and committed, you may be able to change structure but not the ineffective use of the human resources that make up the organization.

Are schools like private-sector organizations, at least the growing number who are really changing? The answer, unfortunately, is no. Organizationally speaking, they remain what they always were, despite the fact that the world has changed and the educational outcomes of school are near totally lousy. The leadership of our schools is unimaginative or worse in the sense that they seem incapable of self-scrutiny, bold actions, and a willingness to admit that they are part of the problem and not of the solution. Unlike some of us, they have not gotten their comeuppance. They roll with the punch, hoping that their critics will go away. They will not go away. If schools remain what they are, the puzzlement of the general public, especially its tax-paying segment, will turn to anger and you will begin to see the demise of our school systems. And why not? If you are not accomplishing your goals—if your "customers" are dissatisfied—why should you be supported? That is what happened to a lot of companies and it is and will be happening to others. Schools, like some of us, will have to change, and the change cannot be cosmetic. Schools have a lot to learn from us in regard to how we had to change, the turmoil of change, and why in the long run it is worth it.

The Educator's Response

What have we got to learn from private organizations? They have their problems and we have ours and the differences are enormous. What can they tell us about how children learn? They have "customers" and so do we. Our customers are children, parents, and the rest of the community and we have absolutely no control over who our customers are or will be. We have to take all comers regardless of ability, of parental support and interest, disability, and a host of other factors with which the private sector does not have to deal. That variation is dumped on us and we are supposed to perform miracles at the same time as our budgets are static or decreasing. We are not only a teaching institution but a social service one, and sometimes we are an arm of the police. We keep many of our older students in school even though they are not interested, motivated, or even appropriately behaved. As soon as society becomes aware of a social problem, they ask us to do something about it, e.g., drugs, guns, teenage pregnancy, AIDS, delinquency, smoking, racial conflicts, and more. Does a private company have to deal with those problems at the same time it produces what it does? Does the productivity of a company worker suffer because he or she watches TV at night? What our students are supposed to learn and do does suffer from the hours in front of the TV set. We can suggest, implore, and plead with parents to cut back on TV watching, to be more attentive to whether a child is doing assigned homework, but, at best, we only get to first base.

   That does not mean that we have done as well as we should have. We are not saying that we have not made mistakes. But when critics from the private sector take potshots at us, it is for several reasons. They don't understand the nature of the learning process, they don't understand schools, and they ignore the things we have tried and are trying, the changes that are taking hold, and they don't understand why schools are organized the way they are, and why, unlike a private company, we cannot snap our fingers saying, "There shall be change," and the change begins. We know our private-sector critics are well intentioned but that does not mean we should refrain from saying that they are basically ignorant of what we are up against. For example, take the case of a large company that has a board of directors. Ninety-nine times out of a hundred, if the CEO of the company makes a recommendation for a change, it will be approved and supported. When the CEO of a school system, the superintendent of schools, makes a recommendation for change, she is far from certain that the board of education will approve. Remember that board members are chosen via the political system and each member has his or her own loyalties and constituencies. We will never know how many times a superintendent refrains from making a recommendation for change because he or she knows that it will be turned down or create a community controversy. The number of those times is very large. And also remember that school systems are creations of the state and that the local system is legally responsible to the state board of education. Can you imagine a private company having so many "owners"? Could they change quickly under such a system?

Private-sector critics are fond of saying that schools are monopolies, they have no competition, no incentive to change, the private-sector marketplace is thoroughly competitive and only those companies survive that have changed in order to compete. So introduce competition into the educational marketplace! So they and other critics are gung ho for vouchers, charter schools, "break-the-mold schools." We have been accused of two things. First, we are too smugly conservative. Second, we uncritically take on new fads and fashions. One says we are stick-in-the-muds; the other says we are always trying this or that. The fact is that we are and should be conservative in the sense that we should hold on to what is best in our traditions and what is best is our unique concern with the learning process in children. But because we are conservative and resist anything that diverts us from the learning process does not mean that we have not made changes that will influence that process in positive ways. We are constantly requiring our teachers to take advanced courses, attend workshops that will inform them about what researchers are reporting, about new techniques of stimulating the minds of children, about new curricula, and, very important, about how to deepen their grasp of subject matter. We have been in the forefront of the fight to reduce class size. We support the utilization of cooperative learning approaches because they supplant the traditional model of one teacher pouring information into the minds of children, which does not permit children learning with and from each other. We have encouraged parents as never before to participate in the formulation of educational policy and practice. And we are supportive of the movement to give teachers a greater role in policy matters, and the number of schools that are dedicated to site-based management by teachers and parents—giving them more opportunity to be responsible and accountable—is certainly increasing. We are moving forward in new directions, but it takes time. There are no quick fixes when it comes to improving the learning process for all children in a classroom, if only because of the variations among them on the factors significant for learning. ◀

There are similarities and differences between the responses of each group in 1970 and 1995. In 1970, the private-sector position was that schools were unique organizations but inadequate ones. Being unique was no excuse for doing a poor job. In 1995, their position is the same, but with the difference in saying or implying that if schools go on as they have, they deserve extinction. Whatever the reasons, they say, schools are failing and educators are unwilling or unable to confront the need for radical change the way some companies in the private sector found themselves forced to do. However, although the private-sector critic seems not to deny that schools are unique organizations, he or she is very clear that as organizations they have a lot in common with the private sector in regard to change. Both require bold, visionary leadership capable not only of critical self-scrutiny but of instilling such a stance in everyone in the organization. Also, and again in regard to change, everyone in the organization has to understand what is at stake, they have to be provided with forums where they can be heard, and in their working roles they must participate meaningfully in decision making. Put in another way, the effective leader is one capable of reexamining past ways of regarding and using the human resources in the organization. So, if an organization considered unique is failing of its purposes, it says a lot about leadership and a faulty rationale for its organization. In that respect, schools are in no way different than failing companies.

Neither in 1970 nor in 1995 do the educational spokespersons come to grips with these criticisms. They do not indict inadequate leadership and they avoid saying anything about redefining and utilizing existing resources in more productive ways. What they do say is that by involving more people (teachers, parents) in school affairs, improvements will follow, although they say nothing about why increasing the number of participants should or could affect organizational structure and functioning that for so long regarded that involvement as inimical to its purposes. The private sector was quite clear that desired change required not only a new ethos but a thoroughly transformed organizational rationale adapted to new values, attitudes, and responsibilities. Yes, the private-sector spokespersons are likely in favor of charter schools, break-the-mold schools, and vouchers, but that is primarily because they hold out the promise of increasing competition, and by holding out the promise of demonstrating that these bold ventures will be successful, schools will be forced to consider the kinds of transforming changes of which they have been incapable. Educational spokespersons look with disfavor on these developments and they do not expect them to be successful and they expect that these developments will only make more severe the problems of schools. The spokespersons may or may not be right, but they seem to miss the point that these ventures are getting increasing support not because the private sector is intent on dismantling the public schools (there are critics who have such intent, but I have heard no one in the private sector say that) but because they will consider anything that seems truly bold, i.e., an obvious departure from an obviously unacceptable state of affairs. In 1970, the educational spokespersons were resentful of criticism. In 1995, they not only are resentful, they seem embattled.

The strength and scope of the criticisms have increased over 25 years and there is no reason to believe that these criticisms will not gain added force. Why is that a likely scenario? The answer to this question derives in part from a feature of the school culture that I discussed in 1970 and that has become more obvious and glaring as the years have passed. In a literal sense it is not a "feature" you can observe, record, and chart. It would be more correct to say that it is a feature one should *expect* to observe but does not, i.e., it is nonobservable, an absence, a silence.

Imagine that for a period of months you are able to sit in on *all* meetings, formal and informal, that take place in a sample of randomly selected schools. You are an observer, not a participant. Your sole task is to note those occasions when discussion centers around the criticisms leveled against schools by external critics. What is the frequency of such occasions, their average duration, the seriousness with which those criticisms are discussed, the willingness to entertain the possibility that at least some of the criticisms have merit, and what courses of action, if any, should be considered and pursued? When you have completed your observations, you should have a good deal to say about how knowledgeable school people are about the substance of the criticisms and about the conceptual-philosophical basis for their positions.

What I am asking the reader to do is in principle analogous to the study I describe in the school culture book about how the "constitution" of the classroom was forged, by whom, and why. For the first month of school, observers sat in classrooms recording those occasions relevant to the "laws" governing behaviors between students and between students and teacher. All classrooms have a constitution; their structure and ambiance are not random affairs—they are reflections of conceptions, almost always unverbalized, about what is right, natural, and proper. Challenges to those conceptions are literally regarded by the teacher as countercultural and, therefore, to be resisted, and that resistance is spontaneous and automatic, not reflective, not a spur to self-scrutiny.

Our study of the classroom turned out to be an uncomplicated one in that the constitution was *always* "written" by the teacher and written means that there was never *discussion* about what was right, natural, and proper. The rules were articulated by the teacher without any attempt to engage students in a discussion about the whys and wherefores.

Now to our imaginary study of meetings. For all practical purposes, we would not have observed any meetings or series of meetings in which (a) the criticisms of schools were clearly articulated in a semi-objective way; (b) that articulation was based on participants having read and digested those criticisms; and (c) the participants had or developed a reasoned, thought-through response, i.e., they offered more than unreflective, knee-jerk opinion that had no conceptual, philosophical, historical foundation. In short, the discussions could not be dignified by such adjectives as serious, sustained, probing, reflective, and self-scrutinizing. Keep in mind that the issues surrounding school reform are not simple. We should never ignore Mencken's caveat that for every complex problem there is a simple answer that is wrong, nor should we forget another caveat: It is hard to be completely wrong, and that is as true for you as it is for your critics.

Schools do not contain the forums in which serious discussions of educational issues —serious discussions that are going on outside of schools—can and are expected to take place. Schools are not places for surfacing and debating the issues that have and will continue to impact on schools. The culture of the school is one which makes it unsafe to bring up controversial issues that implicitly or explicitly are critical of existing practice and call for change. The point here is not why this is so but that it is so. That accounts for the perception on the part of external critics that schools are unresponsive to the call and need for change, that they are so inwardly oriented that they are unaware of how they remain the same in a world that has dramatically changed, and that one should no longer expect that schools as they are can be changed from within the school or school system.

Over the past 25 years I have visited several scores of schools. For no more than a handful of schools could I say that they tried to have regular discussions, the main purpose of which was to become sophisticated or knowledgeable about controversial issues the educational community can no longer ignore. I have *never* known of a *school system* that as a matter of policy encouraged and supported systemwide forums for discussion. I have known of instances where a school sought to change itself by setting up such forums and met subtle and not-so-subtle criticisms and obstacles from the larger system.

My experience in schools, since the school culture book was published, forced on me a conclusion that I should or could have reached earlier but did not. With the usual few exceptions, school personnel hardly read books, journals, and similar periodicals that could make them knowledgeable about the most important criticisms and controversies surrounding school reform. For example, I would ask a school person (teacher, principal, superintendent, board of education member) what were the rationales for the different voucher proposals being discussed by political figures and others external to schools. I was not asking if they agreed or disagreed with any voucher proposal. What I was after was how well they understood what these proposals contained and why they were seriously being proposed. Again leaving the usual exceptions aside, the word *voucher* was pounced upon as if it represented evil incarnate, and that those proposing vouchers were intent on dismantling the public school system. No one was able to give a sustained, coherent analysis of the different voucher proposals, although such analyses were plentiful in the educational literature. From their standpoint there was nothing to discuss!

Occasionally I would point out that some proponents of vouchers wanted to maintain the public school system and argued that vouchers might be one way to introduce competition and incentives to change. That possibility was inconceivable to these school personnel. And, sometimes, I would ask if vouchers ought not to be put to the test of implementation. How else can we determine whether they will have their intended positive effects? That suggestion received short shrift. The point here is that these school personnel seemed unaware of two things. First, that within the past several years a relatively large number of state legislatures had begun seriously to consider vouchers; in some states some form of voucher system had become law; and there was good reason to believe that the "voucher movement" would gain, not lose, force. Indeed, a fair number of those with whom I spoke were totally ignorant of the seriousness with which legislatures were considering a voucher system, a degree of ignorance I still find mystifying in light of all that has been written about vouchers.

The second point is that the bulk of my interviewees were unaware that the passion with which they denounced vouchers, and their inability to come to grips with the problems of school inadequacies that so troubled some voucher proponents, would be interpreted as an argument for the status quo, i.e., educators were "stonewalling," they were opposed to any basic changes, they were incapable of self-scrutiny.

Another example. In recent years we have heard much about site-based management, which its proponents endorse as a way of bringing about fundamental changes in our schools. A good deal has been written about site-based management, much of which is more intended as promotion and not as description or as conceptual rationale. However, in the past several years there has been a growing literature on site-based management and, as one could have predicted, it is no simple affair: It involves a departure from tradition, a reallocation of power, the assumption of responsibilities for which teachers have not been prepared, and the brute fact is that it requires a degree of time for meetings that simply does not exist in the usually structured school day. That should not be surprising or disheartening because any meaningful alteration of the school culture should be expected to be beset with problems. What is dismaying is that when I ask teachers what they mean by site-based management, they truly cannot give an informed reply. To say that "site-based management means that teachers will run the school" is not an informed response; it is an oversimplification bordering on the tragic. And it is further dismaying because most teachers have not felt compelled to find out, by reading and other means, what site-based management entails: the predictable problems, the minimal conditions below which one should not attempt such a change. In addition, many teachers are not interested in being part of such a venture. It is as if they are only interested in what they do and are confronted with in their encapsulated classrooms in their encapsulated schools—an outlook that reinforces the view of external critics that schools are not capable of change from within.

I said earlier that there is reason to predict that the gulf between schools and the general public will widen. I have endeavored in this chapter to indicate two reasons for that dysphoric prediction. The first is that there is validity to the criticism by private-sector individuals and theorists that schools, unlike segments of the private sector, seem incapable of organizational change because they are mired in tradition, or they lack the bold and visionary leadership that could gain the energy and commitment of their people to changes that will allow them to better achieve the unique purpose of schools: to create and sustain productive contexts of learning for students that will prevent disinterest, lack of motivation, dropouts, etc. The private-sector critic is on target when he or she says that when an organization—any organization—is not achieving its purposes, one *has* to assume that the structure and culture of that organization is part of the problem and not the solution. The second reason, not unrelated to the first, is that schools almost totally lack forums both for self-examination and for becoming and remaining sensitive to how and why other organizations (e.g., religious, private sector) found themselves forced to change in truly significant ways.

CHAPTER 22

Our Expectations of
Political Leaders

Sarason asks, "What are the likely consequences of an educational system that cannot narrow the gap between the haves and have-nots, and, in addition and in general, decreases rather than increases interest in and motivation for learning?" He takes a look at the impact of the GI Bill of Rights that, following World War II, allowed so many returning war veterans to access a college education. He views the GI Bill of Rights as a successful example of the government actually changing how Americans learn—placing most of the "power" in the hands of individuals while fully funding the costs.

He decries the lack of a sense of immediacy regarding the achievement gap between privileged and disadvantaged students, especially those in decaying urban school systems. And he faults our policy leaders for (quoting Richard Darman, then advisor to President Reagan) "a continuing surrender to ignorance." Sarason complains that our "recent presidents have never . . . become knowledgeable about the problem" or viewed it as a sophisticated, systemic failing.

He demands that the American public begin to hold its political leaders accountable—if not for bringing about needed reforms, at least for demonstrating "a willingness to learn" about the complexity of our educational system. The selection includes one of Sarason's most plaintively eloquent statements about the educational system, beginning with the words, "There are no villains. There is a system. You can see and touch villains, you cannot see a system."

Question for Seymour Sarason

Do you have any indication that our political leaders are doing anything but continuing to "surrender to ignorance"? Is there any hope in the expressed determination to "leave

Reprinted from "Our Expectations of Political Leaders" in *Political Leadership and Educational Failure* by Seymour Sarason. Copyright © 1998 by Seymour Sarason. This material is used by permission of Jossey-Bass, Inc., a subsidiary of John Wiley & Sons, Inc.

no child behind" that at least promises continued governmental attention to glaring disparities in educational achievement?

Sarason's Response

Why blame political leaders? From their standpoint, educational officials and their nostrums have failed: They were given billions upon billions of dollars to improve education and they have had next to nothing to show for it. So the political leaders—ignorantly, but presumably with worthy intentions—came up with charter schools, vouchers, higher standards, cereal-and-tests for breakfast, memory drills, etcetera.

And let us not gloss over the fact that governors and presidents now have educational advisors who cannot or will not tell them that, as far as obstacles to change are concerned, we have met the enemy and it is *us*.

Thomas Jefferson is the only serious education president we have had. Where are you, Tom, when we need you? For Jefferson knew that we could not sustain a new and free society unless its youth were educated to be free, independent thinkers and persons who came to understand the opportunities and obligations of liberty—not people who lived lives of dutiful and mindless conformity.

More about the obstacles to educational change at the system and national level may be found in:

> *Educational Reform: A Self-Scrutinizing Memoir* (2002)
> *Charter Schools: Another Flawed Educational Reform?* (1998)
> *How Schools Might Be Governed and Why* (1997)
> *Revisiting "The Culture of the School and the Problem of Change"* (1996)
> *School Change: The Personal Development of a Point of View* (1995)
> *Letters to a Serious Education President* (1993)
> *The Case for Change: Rethinking the Preparation of Educators* (1992)
> *The Predictable Failure of Educational Reform* (1990)
> *The Challenge of Art to Psychology* (1990)
> *Schooling in America: Scapegoat and Salvation* (1983)

We are used to depending on the forecasts of meteorologists to tell us what weather conditions we might expect over the next three or four days. We know, because they have told us, that forecasts beyond a few days get increasingly unreliable. Yet meteorologists are encouraged and supported to seek more accurate forecasts for longer periods of time, not for the hell of it, so to speak, but because increased accuracy will prevent loss of life and property. Most weather disasters are of a kind that come with ferocity and confront us with an immediacy we pray we will be able to endure until our world takes on aspects of accustomed normality. But there is another kind of disaster that never "comes," we do not know it is "here," we do not label it until its implacable destructiveness becomes visually apparent. Drought is the clearest example; civilizations have disappeared or been damaged forever by droughts. Today we are witness to a raging scientific controversy about a possible "greenhouse effect": Has the ozone layer become dangerously thin, has our atmosphere heated up and, if it continues, will the levels of our oceans and the contours of our continents change? And what about the climatic consequences of the elimination of rain forests because of human thoughtlessness and ignorance? In these kinds of instances the fear of some people is that an irreversible change has occurred and we are not taking steps to contain it, or we are acting too late.

Social change, of which school change is but one aspect, is in the second category—that is, we become aware of a change only after that change has begun to be recognized and labeled. Social change is not an intended phenomenon; it is largely (not exclusively) an unintended, unpredicted phenomenon even though the initial cause of the social change is no great mystery. So, for example, the social change so much a feature of the past five decades is inexplicable apart from an understanding of how World War II started, was conducted, and ended (Sarason, 1996a). Indeed, that wars transform societies is an old truth; predicting the substance and form of those transformations is quite another matter. It is one thing to say that World War II guaranteed a mammoth postwar social change, regardless of which side won; it is another thing to claim that the social change was immediately apparent and not preceded by an interval in which the desire to return to normalcy made early recognition of the social change virtually impossible. What is fascinating about social change is that it becomes understandable retrospectively but that understanding (right or wrong) brings to the fore the prospective question: How will that discerned social change get played out?

In regard to school change the prospective question is very high on the list of social anxieties: What are the likely consequences of an educational system that cannot narrow the gap between the haves and the have-nots, and, in addition and in general, decreases rather than increases interest in and motivation for learning? *Unlike any other time in our national history, that prospective question has not been off the social agenda for the past half century.* A lot of other aspects of the social change have been on the social agenda during these decades but none has had the insistence and persistence of schooling and race. . . .

Some readers will be surprised to learn that there was a truly massive educational program, legislated near the end of World War II, that forever changed this society in ways that no one has ever seen fit to criticize. I refer to the GI Bill of Rights, of which millions of veterans took advantage. Let me sketch the background and purposes of that bill because of its possible significance for schooling below the college level.

The catastrophe called the Great Depression was still fresh in the minds of all adults, veterans or not. And there were a great many veterans; of a population of 150 million people, approximately 15 million served in the armed forces. The number of veterans incurring a physical or mental impairment was very high. Between the veterans and their friends and families, it is not an exaggeration to say that the lives of very few people escaped the negative impact of the war.

It was a long war. Plans and ambitions had to be put on hold. Careers were interrupted. Personal lives and outlooks changed in response to ever-present dangers, sexual deprivation, military life, and exposure to new cultures. An anxiety-arousing social question arose as the end of the war neared: Could the economy accommodate several million eager-to-be-released veterans, especially in the face of the fact that a substantial part of the war-oriented economy would no longer remain in production?

The long and short of it is that political leaders saw the immediate postwar years as perilous ones, containing the poisonous seeds of social upheaval and another economic depression. Side by side with these forebodings was the felt moral obligation of a grateful society to do whatever could and needed to be done to give veterans the opportunity to reshape their lives in whatever ways they saw fit. The crucial word in the title of the bill is "rights." Veterans had rights that a nation was obligated to respect; they were not a homogenized mass for whom officialdom would set a direction and make decisions. Here are some of the features of the bill:

- A veteran could enroll in any program in any accredited college, university, or vocational school, here or abroad.
- Tuition and fees were paid by the government.
- There was an allowance for books.
- There was a monthly subsistence allowance for the veteran, wife, child.
- Centers for personal and vocational counseling were available to veterans.

It is unfortunate and deplorable that the social sciences never saw fit to study the GI Bill in terms of how many lives were redirected, of careers changed, of alterations in the stability of the nuclear family, of changes in the culture and complexity of colleges and universities, and the like. Keep in mind that we are not talking about a few thousand or a few hundred thousand veterans but of somewhere between five and ten (or more) million veterans who sought to take advantage of the unprecedented opportunity to refashion their lives through education.

For my present purposes, the significances of the GI Bill are several. First, the political leadership knew that it was confronted with a prospective scenario that could dilute, if not negate, the fruits of victory in war. Second, that scenario was to a significant degree informed by the still vivid memories of the Great Depression—it was also informed by experience with World War I veterans, who responded to the Great Depression by demonstrating against what they regarded as a niggardly, ungrateful government. Third, and quite unusual, decision-making power as to how and where the veteran would exploit the legislation was the domain of the veteran, a power largely respected and supported by colleges and universities willing to be flexible and sensitive to returning veterans for whom the campus was the polar opposite of military installations. Fourth, having decided on a course of action that was basically preventive in orientation, the political leadership did not shrink from the financial costs of that course of action.

I am not trying to convey the impression that the GI Bill was an outgrowth of a linear, rational process in which uncertainty and fear were in the background, the outcomes clear and desirable, and the law of unintended consequences had been repealed. What I wish to emphasize is that there was a knowledge of and respect for a troubled economic past that had taken a war to submerge; the fear that that past would reappear; the specter of millions of veterans returning to a civilian life unprepared and unable to meet their needs and expectations; the dread of civil strife. It was a mix of attitudes, memories, fears that required bold action before the social scene would become marked by civil unrest. Political leaders acted more because they felt they had to act and less because they were convinced that the legislation would serve its intended purpose, let alone that it would alter lives and institutions in the most pervasive ways.

In regard to school change the situation is both similar and different. It is different in that there is little or no perceived sense of immediacy. The problem is seen as serious, but it has been around a long time, its threat to the social fabric real but not yet immediate; in the future as in the past the problem can be contained. Furthermore, we really do not know why our past efforts have been so without success.

It is similar in that we know that the inadequacies of our urban schools—related as they are to issues of race, ethnicity, and class—are year by year increasingly consigning students to jobs that do not exist or for which students are unprepared; they are catapulted into an electronic-computer-telecommunication world that has no place for them. In a very abstract way some political leaders know that when there is no place in the arena of work for a significant part of the population—the young part not noted for its passivity and lack of hopes and dreams—the odds that there will be trouble ahead markedly increase. It is a part of the population that has no voice, that does not convey its individual and group dynamics to the rest of society except as its attitudes and actions are read or heard as worrisome signals by the others.

What these political leaders know in the abstract they cannot use as a basis for school change because the evidence is clear that their proposals have been tried in the past, with no discernible effect. In regard to the veterans of World War II political leaders did not have to ask questions about prewar policies and practices because the evidence was overwhelming, truly overwhelming, that the VA medical programs were qualitatively and quantitatively deficient, and there had been no educational program for veterans. In regard to school change, political leaders know that the history of school reform is a thick and discouraging one in which it appears that what could be tried was tried—except that no one suggested that perhaps the traditional undergirding assumptions of our school systems should be radically altered. As I have indicated, the concept of the charter school is the first indication that political leaders, perhaps unbeknownst to themselves, are challenging the legitimacy of the system qua system. It is also (perhaps) an indication that the need for school change is taking on a degree of immediacy and compellingness it did not have before.

In his book *Maximum Feasible Misunderstanding*, Moynihan (1969) tells the story of how in light of the Job Corps program in the War on Poverty he thought it would be instructive to read about the Civilian Conservation Corps (CCC) in the New Deal of the 1930s. He found that the government contained no record, no description, no evaluation of the CCC program; the government had no basis for learning from past successes or failures. In that same book, Moynihan concentrates on the Community Action Program of Johnson's War on Poverty and concludes that the government did not know what it was doing; and what it was doing was legislating a transfer of power from the political system to indigenous community groups. As one who observed that transfer firsthand I can only criticize Moynihan for understatement. That does not mean that in principle I was opposed to that transfer but rather that there was no evidence whatsoever that such a transfer of power *in the way it was being proposed* stood a chance of achieving its stated purposes. Nor does it mean that you do nothing unless you have evidence to justify doing something.

Richard Darman (1996) has put it well: "The problem is not the visions. Americans across the political spectrum want to improve education, reduce violence, eliminate substance abuse, strengthen families, restore traditional values and increase opportunity for achieving the Dream. The problem is that we know little more now than we did in the 1960s about how, on a large scale, to achieve these shared objectives. And the reason is a continuing surrender to ignorance. Major public-policy initiatives are routinely advanced, but rarely do we organize to evaluate what works. We thus allow politicians to mislead us. Then we act like helpless victims." Darman is no left-winger or liberal, nor (to use his own words) a "pointy headed" academic. But neither is he a conservative ideologue who would take pleasure from a government that disconnected its telephone service and went away for a long sabbatical.

Whatever he is, he has put his finger on the theme of this book: We have a right to expect that politicians in high office will feel obliged to become so knowledgeable about the important problems besetting the society that they will refrain from taking a blunderbuss stance where the target has not been identified and there is no way one can learn from failure. In addition, in a relatively small number of instances, they will support—fiscally and time-wise—the implementation of a reform in real-life conditions and with built-in means to pinpoint errors of omission and commission that will be corrected and tested in a subsequent, more sophisticated demonstration. As with other parts of government (for example, the Food and Drug Administration, Department of Agriculture, National Institutes of Health) no new solution will be encouraged or supported without prior credible evidence that most of its intended purposes can be achieved.

Good intentions are not enough. Personal anecdote and opinion are not to be sneezed at, but certainly they should not be confused with evidence. Fashionable terms or labels like "high standards," "charter schools," "vouchers," "privatization," "site-based management"—or anything that suggests technology as a universal solvent of educational problems—may sound innovative and attractive but, in Darman's words, you do not bet the system on a hunch or feeling. Hunch and feeling do play a role in new learning but one should never assume ahead of time that these inner promptings should be treated other than with respectful skepticism.

In regard to educational reform I agree with Darman's assertion that politicians have misled the general public (and misspent its money). I would go so far as to say that these politicians had little interest in, and therefore gave little attention to, the substance and history of the post–World War II educational reform movement. I say that because our more recent presidents have never given the slightest indication that they made it their business to become knowledgeable about the problem—they deserve the description "deep down, he is shallow." It is a problem they say is crucial for societal traditions and welfare, a problem they say has defeated us in the past, a problem they say is deserving of our moral and fiscal support—having said this and more, the fact remains that their articulated concerns mask a pervasive ignorance. They do not mislead us in direction—

that is excusable—but in conveying the impression that they know what they are talking about. In regard to educational reform they do not know what they are talking about, and on those rare occasions when they say something that suggests they are getting near the heart of the problem (for example, the significance of charter schools), it soon becomes obvious that they feel no obligation to test their proposals in the real world in a limited number of places. They are not able to distinguish between an assumption and a demonstrated fact.

Earlier in this book I asked this question: "When your child is graduated from high school, what is the one characteristic you hope your child has?" In regard to political leadership and educational reform I would put the question this way: "When a president leaves office, what is the one characteristic you would want that president to have demonstrated?" My answer is that the president (or others in high office) should have demonstrated a willingness to learn, a modesty that acknowledges that the more you learn, the more you have and want to learn, and the courage to share personal experience of change and complexity with a public for whom the words *courage* and *leadership*, when juxtaposed, form an oxymoron. When it comes to school change, we should cease regarding our political leaders as exempt from criticism, as if there are more important things for them to think about. There are no more important things. What happens to our schools (especially urban ones) over the next two decades will be fateful for this country. To proceed as if that prediction is an indulgence in hyperbole, that somehow or other we will muddle through, is to take stances that produced the educational problem in the first place.

Nothing I have said in previous pages was meant to suggest that those elected to high political office should seek to gain more power to implement programs of school change. The further the seats of power from the sites that are the objects of change, the more likely the spirit and letter of change will be violated. That assertion may not deserve the status of a law but it does rest on a lot of experience with a lot of people in different times and places.

The power to educate, stimulate, and legislate is not synonymous with the power to influence, if by influence you mean that people are disposed to seriously consider what such leaders think and propose. To be influential does not require the exercise of formal power; it is the difference between making people feel that they must do something and that they want to do something, between their going along with you because they fear the consequences of not going along and because they choose to do so. In terms of consequences neither power nor influence is inherently superior to the other; when one resorts to one or the other (or some combination of both) depends on time, place, and experience. History is replete with leaders who had a great deal of formal power that they exercised in ways that limited their influence, just as there have been people whose influence was great but did not depend on formal power.

What I have done in previous pages is to criticize leaders more for errors of omission than for those of commission, because the demonstrable inadequacies of what they sought to require others to do were in large measure the consequence of a failure to become knowledgeable about the failures of past leaders; to formulate that knowledge in clear ways; and to impart that new vision to people generally—that is, to give currency to ideas that need to be pondered, digested, and examined for utility.

If leaders are elected because a majority of the people agree with what those leaders say they will do, it is also the case that we expect them to bring to people's attention ideas, issues, problems that will at some point have untoward societal consequences if not put into currency. After all, we do not call people leaders because they are riveted on the present, ignorant of the past, and aware of the future only as extending to next month or perhaps to next year. We do not elect leaders only for them to act because they want to be perceived as responsive activists. We want a vision, some kind of map to the future, a proposal for a journey that most of us cannot conjure up if only because we are not paid to think about such things. But that is precisely what we pay those in high office to do: to use all resources of their office to track a present that has a past and a future. That is what they tend to do in regard to many problems, with a few notable exceptions of which education is in an ultimate sense the most fateful. In regard to education it has been all sound, no fury, no bangs, all whimpers, an audiocassette that endlessly repeats itself.

My criticism of political leaders is not a form of *argumentum ad hominem*. I do not impugn their motives, their personalities, or their intelligence. What I criticize is their failure to gain some understanding about why the consequences of the reform movement have been so discouraging and, no less important, their inability to entertain the possibility that the educational system as we know it is unrescuable in the sense that if we continue to do what we have done, the society will undergo transformations far more destabilizing than in the present or past. *When over a period of time a condition has been intractable to efforts to improve it, it is a sure-fire sign that something is radically wrong with the assumptions on which our actions are based.*

My conclusion about the unrescuability of the system was one I initially had difficulty accepting. But as years went by my resistance crumbled in the face of all my experience in schools. What finally convinced me was the recognition that no one—not teachers, not administrators, not researchers, not politicians or policymakers, and certainly not students—willed the present state of affairs. They were all caught up in a system that had no self-correcting features, a system utterly unable to create and sustain contexts of productive learning, indeed, a system in which the differences between these contexts of learning were hardly (if at all) discussed. The icing on this cake of vexation was provided by my meetings with policymakers and politicians in Washington and elsewhere. I realized that, however sincere their intentions, they knew nothing about schools and why the school culture, honed over many decades, would resist and defeat reforms attempting to alter the status quo. *There are no villains. There is a system. You can see and touch villains, you cannot see a system.*

You have to conceptualize a system, and you do that on two very different occasions: when you are essentially creating a system and when an existing system is faulty and you want to understand why. On both occasions the purposes of the system are the governing consideration. The fact is that most people—and in the case of political leaders it is all of them—think of education not as a system but in terms of its parts—teachers, administrators, local boards of education, colleges and universities, parents, state boards of education, and the legislative and executive branches of local, state, and national government. Clearly, there are many parts, each of which is and sees itself as a stakeholder in the system. Equally clearly, precisely because no one is satisfied with educational outcomes, one would expect that reform efforts would be based on answers to two questions. In actual practice how do these parts relate to each other? Among those parts how much agreement is there about the purposes of the educational system? These questions have hardly been formulated, addressed, or studied.

As a result the reform movement has been about parts, not about the system, not about how the purposes of parts are at cross-purposes to each other, not about how the concept of purpose loses both meaning and force in a system that is amazingly uncoordinated and that has more adversarial than cooperative features. It is no wonder that people within the system as well as an increasing fraction of the general public privately conclude that nothing will change. It is obvious why no one has ever said to me that if they were to start from scratch to create an educational system, they would come up with what we now have. They could not say what they could come up with because they had never thought of schools as being embedded in a very complicated system. And, I should add, when I pressed them to identify the parts of the existing system, it was surprising how many parts they left out.

What I have said here, as well as in earlier chapters, can be concretized by reference to *The Politics of Education* by John Brademas (1987). For two decades in the House of Representatives, Brademas played a major, often the crucial, role in the passage of education-related legislation. Perhaps more than any member of Congress, Brademas understood that improving the quality of schooling was no less than protecting the future of the country. His book deserves serious reading if only for its description of the obstacles the legislation encountered, the compromises negotiated, and how political leaders were defining problems. Several things are crystal clear in this book.

• *No one thought in terms of an educational system but rather in terms of discrete problems or discrete parts of the existing system.* It is not unfair to say that the cascade of legislation was a cascade of Band-Aids. There are times when Band-Aids are useful and effective—but only if the condition is not a systemic one. When the condition is systemic (and you do not know it), Band-Aids are at best useless and at worst harmful if they prevent you from examining the system.

• *Basic to the thinking of legislators was the assumption that what schools lacked were the resources to deal with the problems confronting them.* That is to say, there was nothing basically wrong or self-defeating about schools that an influx of money, materials, and personnel would not remedy. Put in another way, all the problems and inadequacies of schools *as they were* were in no way a reflection of how schools were organized and administered, of a narrow, stultifying conception of classroom learning, of a school culture in which collegiality and self-examination were absent. It is worth repeating: The legislation rested on the belief that money was the universal solvent that

would permit schools to do more good for more students. One could say, to be charitable, that it was hoped that not only would schools do more for more students but they
would do better for all students than they had been previously—that is, schools would
transform themselves. It was a hope that ignored the realities.[1]

• *Rhetoric aside, presidents spend little time with matters educational, a reflection of
the degree of their interest, curiosity, and sense of responsibility.* That was not true for
President Lyndon Johnson who, like Brademas, was passionate about education but
who had no understanding of what the problems were and whose tendency to act
quickly short-circuited thinking.

At one point in his book Brademas says:

> Support from the national government has been crucial in enhancing our understanding of
> ourselves and our universe through, among other entities, the National Science Foundation,
> the National Institutes of Health, and the National Institute of Education. I felt a special
> commitment to the last initiative. When I introduced the bill to create the National Institute
> of Education, substantial percentages of the annual federal budgets for defense, agriculture,
> and health were earmarked for research and development. Yet when it came to education,
> which has such an enormous impact on our society, *the nation was not spending the small
> amount needed to generate thoughtful, objective, analytical evidence concerning how peo-
> ple teach and learn.* (p. 13; italics added)

The italicized sentence is especially revealing of the view that teaching and learning—
what takes place between teachers and students in classrooms—can be understood apart
from the features of the system near and far—that is, apart from the culture of the
school, from the local school system, and from other parts of the larger system. Teaching is inevitably an interpersonal affair but it also inevitably has the imprimatur of that
larger system. I certainly am not opposed to research on how teachers teach and students learn—but from my personal experience and reading the research literature, we
know a good deal about these issues already. What we know should compel us to ask
why teachers teach as they do, why classrooms are contexts for unproductive learning.
The why question takes us beyond the encapsulated school and requires that we seek to
understand how the system sustains and reinforces unproductive contexts for both
teachers and students. As I have said countless times in my writings, teachers cannot create and sustain contexts of productive learning for students if those contexts do not exist for teachers. Those contexts do not exist for teachers now, and that is in large measure a consequence of the nature of the system. If Brademas makes anything crystal clear,
it is that he came to have a very sophisticated understanding of how Congress works
and why the actions, successful or not, of any individual congressman are totally inexplicable apart from the system of governance in which the individual operates. In his role
as congressman he thought in system terms, which is why he came to be as respected as
he was, as successful as he usually was in the passage of legislation. But when he thought
about educational problems, he could not think in system terms, he accepted the system
as it was, he dealt with parts. He could not transfer what he learned in the political system to the educational system.

Again, am I being unfair to political leaders? Am I expecting them to be more knowl-edgeable than they can or should be? I believe I am not. I expect them, no less than I do any other person, to face up to the fact that when efforts to improve a serious condition have generally failed one has to seek answers in the nature of the system in which the conditions arise. Yes, I expect political leaders to have that kind of wisdom, a kind of street smarts that at least some political leaders do acquire and apply in their political bailiwick.

Note

1. The one exception to those criticisms concerns Public Law 94-142, the 1975 Education for All Handicapped Children Act, which in the most explicit way said that the schools could no longer treat handicapped children and their parents as they historically had. That act required that schools take the *individuality* of these students seriously, a respect for individuality not then or now accorded nonhandicapped students. Brademas fought successfully for that legislation, al-though he fails to see the relevance of that requirement for all students.

CHAPTER 23

America's Only Serious Education President

After noting that "the word *education* does not appear in the Constitution," Sarason examines Thomas Jefferson's holistic vision of public education, which Jefferson first proposed to the Virginia legislature in 1779. He notes how Jefferson's appreciation of the qualitative advantage of smallness contrasts with how America organized its public schools during the twentieth century.

In comparing Jefferson's view of his new nation with the elitist, undemocratic regimes of Europe, Sarason poses anew the question of that day, namely, "Why educate people who could not assimilate or benefit from education?" and comments, "To Jefferson and everyone else in the new nation, that question was politically and morally sinful."

Sarason wonders, with dismay, how Jefferson would judge the typical school of today, once he became aware that "as students traversed the grades, the strength of wanting to learn, to be motivated and interested, decreased; that students were passive, non-questioning learners." The point Sarason makes is not just that Jefferson was the *first* "serious education president" but that he was, unfortunately, "our first and last serious education president."

Question for Seymour Sarason

You speak of the Jeffersonian era as "a time and place where there was an unexcelled awareness that freedom should suffuse all areas of individual and institutional existence." In your vision of the good school in the good society, what will it take to bring such freedom and exuberance to American public schools?

Sarason's Response

It will take both a national crisis and luck to have an education president like Jefferson, who was a probing, visionary leader. What happened in New York, Washington, D.C., and rural Pennsylvania on September 11, 2001, was a crisis that forced us to recognize that our assumptions about this country in this world were dangerously wrong. Whether our political leadership will take the right courses of action we cannot as yet say.

More about Sarason's views on political leadership and the political principle in education may be found in:

How Schools Might Be Governed and Why (1997)
Revisiting "The Culture of the School and the Problem of Change" (1996)
Parental Involvement and the Political Principle (1995)
School Change: The Personal Development of a Point of View (1995)
Letters to a Serious Education President (1993)
The Predictable Failure of Educational Reform (1990)
Schooling in America: Scapegoat and Salvation (1983)

The word *education* does not appear in the Constitution. Indeed, from all that was written at the time about the shaping of a new nation, one might conclude that there was no interest in why, where, how, and by whom youth should be educated. There were two major reasons for the omission. The first was that it was a matter of *obvious* principle—political, moral, and pedagogical—that education was a responsibility of family and community. It was not a responsibility of a central government far removed from the sites of education. The framers of the Constitution had no need to articulate the strong belief that only those who obviously were the most direct stakeholders in formal education should decide what that education should be. It was literally inconceivable that it should be otherwise. Besides, it was axiomatic that centralized government and authority were evils, albeit necessary ones, which had to be constrained and prevented from increasing in power, and—as history documented—any increase in government's assigned powers was a threat to individual freedom. I think it is fair to say that if the leaders of the time were to observe today's educational scene they would be aghast at the degree to which the substance and process of formal learning are determined by individuals and groups (near and far) who have no direct, concrete knowledge of and no personal, intimate relationship to the context of learning. We, today, could try to explain to them how this change came about, but our explanation would be unconvincing because to them the history would be about a step-by-step departure from the principle that in matters educational only those with the most direct, personal responsibility for children should determine what goes on, why, and for which purposes. And to them that meant parents and the small, local community.

The second reason, related to the first, was no less obvious: The purpose of education was to give youth the tools to become free individuals who would live in and protect a free society. That was not empty rhetoric. The framers of the Constitution saw themselves and their fledgling nation in a world containing enemies, internal and external, and to withstand those threats required a citizenry educated to understand the nature and history of tyranny. The Bill of Rights was to be taken seriously: Individuals were encouraged and expected to speak their minds, however controversial and idiosyncratic their spoken or written words. In his first inaugural address, Jefferson said, "If there be any among us who would wish to destroy this union or to change its republican form, let them stand undisturbed as monuments of the safety with which error of opinion can be tolerated where reason is left free to combat it." And it was Jefferson who near the end of his life articulated what Commager (1975, p. 5) called "the animating principle of Jefferson's age": "We believed that man was a rational animal. . . . We believed that men, habituated to thinking for themselves, and to follow reason as guide, would be more easily and safely governed than with minds nourished in error and debased by ignorance." The earlier Pilgrims and Puritans saw learning to read as absolutely essential for comprehending and defending biblical teachings. Satan was the enemy of God's ways. That conception of the overarching purpose of education had changed markedly by the time the colonies became the United States of America, as Commager beautifully summarizes:

> [There was] no need to campaign for the secularization of education. It was, by Old World standards, already secularized. One of the purposes of creating public schools in the Bay Colony was to outwit "ye ould deluder Satan," but that maneuver was directed by the secular branch of the community, not the ecclesiastical, or—if it was difficult to make this distinction in the 1640s—that was certainly true during the era of the Enlightenment. No religious tests sifted applicants to colleges and universities (not until 1871 could dissenters attend the universities of Oxford or Cambridge), nor were there religious tests for professors. In the seventeenth century a Baptist sat in the president's chair at Harvard College, and in the opening days of the nineteenth century a Unitarian was elected to the Hollis Chair of Divinity (As late as 1862, Cambridge University turned down a professorship of American history on the ground that the incumbent might be a Unitarian!). The charter of the College of Rhode Island, established especially for the proper training of Baptists, provided that "all members shall forever enjoy free, absolute, and uninterrupted liberty of conscience" and that the board of trustees should include Anglicans, Congregationalists, and Quakers. So, too, trustees of the new College of Philadelphia included Presbyterians and Anglicans, as well as Quakers, and Franklin, who was a deist, served as the first president of the board. Jefferson's new University of Virginia was based on "the illimitable freedom of the human mind." "Here," he wrote, "we are not afraid to follow truth wherever it may lead, nor to tolerate any error as long as reason is left free to combat it." (1975, p. 15)

The thrust of these introductory comments is that in Jefferson's era leaders understood the difference between education and indoctrination, between encouraging curiosity and stifling it, between the freedom to express and the fear to express, between a marketplace of ideas and one with nothing or little to sell or buy. They were not, I should hasten to add, educational theorists who developed a pedagogy consistent with their conceptions of the needs, minds, capabilities, and ambitions of *American* citizens, and I italicize American for the simple reason that no one was in doubt (including foreign observers) that the new country's people were and should be a breed apart. In brief, it would be quite misleading to attribute to these early political leaders a sophistication about the relation between educational theory and practice they did not have. But it is not wrong to say that they had an extraordinarily clear conception of the overarching purpose of education: to nurture and sustain independence of thinking, expression, and action. To be sure, there were other purposes—but none as important as independence of view and expression, without which European class-political-economic inequities and tyrannies would transfer to these shores. When these political leaders spoke of freedom, it was because of the reality and immediacy of threats to that freedom.

There was another point that these early leaders, and people generally, considered so obvious that it did not have to be made explicit. Education took place in more than formal sites of learning. From an early age children were expected to assume household responsibilities, a kind of division of labor, ranging from cooking, sewing, repairing to the care of siblings. In what was primarily an agrarian society those responsibilities were many, varied, and crucial. Children were not only expected to perform these tasks, they wanted to. The legendary one-room school was prototypical in this respect in that each school contained children varying in age and ability (and probably interest) and older children had to be given some responsibility for teaching or supervising or caring for younger children. One teacher in one such classroom had to devise some degree of division of labor.

The important point is that the worlds in and out of school were not as psychologically and intellectually separated or divorced from each other as they later became. That, of course, was not a matter of any educational theory or pedagogical practice. It was a matter of necessity and a conception of what children could and should learn and do; and these two matters were taken seriously. If the political leaders did not have an understanding of or articulate the relations between a theory of productive learning and pedagogical practice, they were very familiar with Rousseau's theory of learning and its political and developmental implications. If Rousseau was clear about anything, it was the importance of exquisite sensitivity to a child's interests and curiosities, which were the starting points of a process for awakening, broadening, and deepening the child's capabilities, skills, and knowledge. Rousseau's writings played a significant role in the events and thinking that culminated in the French Revolution of 1789, a fact of which American leaders were quite and approvingly aware. If we cannot truly say that American leaders consciously and deliberately sought to apply Rousseau's theory to formal schooling, we can say that they viewed children as precious, multifaceted resources whom it was the duty of a free society to nurture and support in ways that would produce free individuals, not individuals who would be required to conform blindly to unexamined doctrine. When you read the observations and conclusions of foreign observers who came to these shores in those early days, they express surprise at how individuals of differing ages, status, and economic level gave voice to opinion, thought, and criticism. Obeisance to long-standing tradition and practice was notable by its absence. It was the duty of one generation of free people to reproduce the next generation of free people. The concept of freedom cannot be defined in brief, simple terms. But in the late eighteenth and early nineteenth centuries one of the most obvious features of the concept exemplified in quotidian living was the obligation to give expression to what one thought and felt, and it was the obligation of everyone to respect expression of the thought, opinion, and feelings of others.

I am not trying to convey a picture of an early utopia where everything was sweetness and light and harmony reigned. It was not a Garden of Eden, although the early settlers so described the new continent. But it was a time and place where there was an unexcelled awareness that freedom should suffuse all areas of individual and institutional existence. That awareness was matched by boldness and a degree of consistency unmatched in history. I cannot refrain quoting from Commager's lecture on an occasion celebrating the upcoming 1976 Bicentennial:

> What happened to that deep sense of obligation to the past that animated most of the Founding Fathers, the obligation to preserve the heritage of civilization from Judea and Greece and Rome and, in the political and constitutional arena, from the Mother Country—a commitment which linked the new nation, even as she was embarking upon the boldest of experiments, irrevocably to the Old World, so that the most innovative of revolutions was also the most conservative? What happened to the deep and passionate sense of fiduciary obligation to posterity which animated all the Founding Fathers and admonished them to pass on their heritage intact to their descendants, even "to the thousandth and thousandth generation"? What happened to that devotion to the commonwealth which animated a Franklin, an Adams, a Jefferson, a Washington, a Mason, a Madison, a Wilson to wear out their lives, and their fortunes, too, in the public service, and which gave us, in a single generation, a galaxy of public leaders we have never been able remotely to duplicate since then? What happened to that ingenuity, that resourcefulness, that creativity which fashioned, again in a single generation, all those great political institutions on whose capital we have been living ever since? What happened to that confidence in Reason, and in the ability of men to solve their most formidable problems by the application of Reason; to that confidence in the ultimate common sense and even wisdom of the people—a confidence which was at the basis of the passion for freedom of the human mind in every area, religion, politics, science, and morals?
>
> When we have answered these questions we may perhaps set about restoring the intellectual and moral world which the Enlightenment created, and which we have lost or betrayed. That is the most important item on the agenda of the Bicentennial years. (1975, p. xix)

As Commager frequently notes, slavery was a glaring, mocking exception to the "passion for freedom." Ironically, there was one aspect of slavery that emphasized how people understood (too weak a word) the indissoluble connection between education and freedom: The Southern states made it illegal to educate blacks. If slaves were taught to read and write, if they were exposed to the history of the struggle for freedom, they would get the "wrong ideas," the very ideas that powered the American "white" revolution. These Southern states were paying tribute to the overarching purpose of education at the same time they denied that education to blacks. They correctly knew that education that was not deliberate indoctrination was dangerous precisely because it opened up vistas on what the human mind could be, create, and accomplish. They knew that indoctrination was not education as they understood it. As Commager says, the passion for freedom had to put its stamp "in every area, religion, politics, science, and morals." As we shall now see, and as Commager's essays make plain, "in every area" included education. That, in those earlier times, was a glimpse of the obvious. Today it is not. The modal American classroom, public or private, secular or religious, has more of the features of indoctrination than of a passion for freedom. More of this later.

Let me now list Jefferson's accomplishments and leadership in the educational arena. He castigated the European tradition of two types of education: that for "gentlemen of the elite" and that for "the rabble." Even a fervent libertarian like Voltaire looked upon education for the lower classes as, at best, semi-wasteful. Jefferson, like many of his cohorts, pronounced anathema on such a view and practice even though he was part of an American elite. For Jefferson, the democratization of education required that it go beyond the elementary school into higher education.

In 1779, he proposed to the Virginia legislature a three-part plan: a system of elementary schools feeding into grammar schools, and then into the university. He also proposed that the very low quality of the College of William and Mary be radically reformed, including new chairs of law, medicine, and modern languages. He considered it essential to establish a state library. In 1816, he proposed a more ambitious plan that included what Commager (1975, p. 69) described as "the astonishing provision of a literacy test for citizenship."

The creation of the University of Virginia was Jefferson's doing. He was chairman of the Board of Trustees. He was the first rector of the university, and indeed he designed every building, every column, every window, every door, and every mantelpiece. He planted every tree, shrub, and flower, laid out every path, and built every wall. He provided the library, chose the professors and students. He drew up the curriculum and dedicated the university "to the illimitable freedom of the human mind."

As Commager delightfully comments, "Not bad that for a man in his eighties." The university was at its birth not only the most eminent in the United States, as Jefferson said, but the most enlightened and the most liberal, the most nearly like some of the great universities in the Old World. And it was also Jefferson who was chairman of the committee that drafted the Land Ordinance of 1785 containing provisions establishing the policy of setting aside public lands for the support of schools and universities, a policy that was later extended to all newly acquired territories.

Bear in mind that throughout his life Jefferson was formally or informally a major figure on the American scene. If the descriptive label workaholic had been in currency at that time, it could have been legitimately applied to him. I say that only semi-facetiously to make the point that one of the tests of great political leadership is the courage, strength, and persistence with which a leader pursues an issue he or she regards as essential for the public welfare, even though that issue may arouse resistance and controversy. Not all of Jefferson's proposals met ready acceptance. Not everyone considered education as important as he did, although they considered it important. No other leader at the time immersed himself as he did in the details of the organization of an educational *system*. No one articulated more or as well as he that the overarching purpose of education was to free, not indoctrinate, minds, to produce questioners and not narrow or mindless conformists, to inculcate the morality undergirding freedom, not a morality that closed minds to new or alternative ideas. And Jefferson was never in doubt that what he wanted for people was what people wanted for themselves and what alone would prevent the new nation from regressing to the class distinctions of the Old World.

Jefferson had standards of quality. He was interested in far more than building schools, universities, and libraries. He wanted teachers capable of stimulating minds. He was most clear on that in regard to universities. So, for example, he did not succeed in reforming the College of William and Mary, one means for which was his proposal to bring over the faculty of the University of Geneva, one of the most respected European universities! He sought quality wherever or in whomever it was. Education was too important for the individual and nation to be entrusted to pedestrian minds. . . .

I do not think it is unwarranted speculation to suggest that he assumed   one of those "of course" assumptions that did not require articulation—that the people of the new, small nation wanted and hungered for education for their children, and that that hunger would be transmitted to them. He could count on that. Today it is hard for us to grasp how concerned those people were about the fragility of the new nation in its efforts to survive, confronted as it was with enemies and a paucity of those human resources required for nation building. National pride required an educated citizenry. That message required no hard sell to the adult citizens and neither did parents have to sell it to their children. What I am suggesting is that Jefferson did not have to articulate that wanting was crucial for productive learning. That articulation was necessary by educational theorists in a class-based Europe whose ruling, nondemocratic elites viewed education of *all* of its masses as dangerous and wasteful; maintaining the status quo was their aim. Why educate people who could not assimilate or benefit from education? To Jefferson and everyone else in the new nation, that question was politically and morally sinful.

There was another "of course" in Jefferson's outlook on education and that was that the schoolhouse would be a small place with, by our standard today, a very small number of children. The one-room school was the norm. Jefferson never looked favorably on the possibility that America would be other than a predominantly agricultural nation. He looked upon Europe's large, crowded, and conflict-ridden dominating cities as something the new nation would and should not foster. This was a comparatively large country. It became much larger as a result of actions Jefferson took during his presidency. Nevertheless, he wanted a country whose institutions and communities were small and literally connected to the land, not divorced from it. So when he envisioned a school, it was the polar opposite of what schools ultimately became. However imaginative a mind Jefferson had, he could not imagine the size of our schools today. If he never articulated a theory of learning and pedagogy, everything we know about him permits the conclusion that he would have regarded the size of today's classrooms and schools as patently inimical to productive learning. He would have readily agreed that a context of productive learning requires a degree and quality of teacher-child relationships possible only in a small group. Jefferson increased the size of the country—but not for the purpose of increasing the size of communities and the institutions they needed and for which they were responsible. Jefferson would have applauded the saying "small is beautiful."

Now for the second and more speculative reason. Jefferson was, among many other things, a writer. Practically all that he wrote was deeply personal, concerned as those writings were with hopes, fears, issues, all very strongly felt. He wrote about the world as it had been, was, and should be in the future. Nowhere was this more true than when he wrote about education. My speculation—which I really do not regard as such—has two facets. The first is that Jefferson knew and appreciated that *he* had had opportunities, stimulation, and resources (for example, books and teachers) that vastly enlarged and enriched his understanding of himself, others, and his world. It is to indulge understatement to say that he was an introspective and reflective person. When he wrote, he drew upon personal experience. All writers do that, however marked, indirect, or unacknowledged the expression of that experience may be. When Jefferson wrote about education, his statements were informed by personal imagery from myriads of sources. The second aspect is that Jefferson wanted his and future generations of young people to have the educational opportunities he had and that meant a quality and context of learning that would be the opposite of indoctrination, of knowledge divorced from personal significance or practical and social applications, of instruction that would not sustain the distinctive human attribute to want to know and explore.

Jefferson did not write about a pedagogy for the classroom. Pedagogy is more than how to teach, or techniques or approaches geared to obtaining stated objectives. Pedagogy is the overt expression of the relationships among a theory of the learning process, conceptions of the needs and abilities of learners, and strategies that reflect the theory and conceptions. Pedagogy is a form of the self-fulfilling prophecy. That is to say, if you start with theory X, conception Y, and strategy Z, you expect to achieve the desired objective; that is the way you set it up. You may know there are other X's, Y's, and Z's, but you eschew them because you regard them as inappropriate, inadequate or harmful in some way, unnecessary, or downright wrong. How should one decide between different pedagogies? That question is in principle identical to asking how we should decide between different forms of government—for example, democratic or authoritarian. If you believe that people are both interested in and capable of participating in the political process, that they want to be heard and their opinions respected, that forums should exist where opposing ideas are articulated—if your thinking goes in that direction you will opt for one form of government. If you believe that people need to be directed and instructed, that they do not know what is good for them, that they need to be firmly led and controlled, that if you give them an inch they will demand a mile because they cannot tell the difference between freedom and license—if you think in these ways authoritarian government will appeal to you. The two forms of government lead to very different pedagogies.

It is no different in the case of classroom pedagogy. How would Jefferson have judged today's modal classroom and school as he learned that as students traversed the grades, the strength of wanting to learn, to be motivated and interested, decreased; that students were passive, nonquestioning learners; that the gulf between life in school and life outside of it was enormous to the point of unbridgeability; and that despite these facts the existing pedagogy continued to be employed and justified? To a Thomas Jefferson whose devotion to and clarity about freeing the mind from any source of restriction and con-striction, the modal classroom would be a disaster.

Thomas Jefferson was not an educational theorist and he did not leave us an explicit pedagogy. He was a political and educational statesman who throughout his long life in public office and service saw the connections between a freeing education and a free society. That is why, despite his countless obligations and responsibilities, he considered his achievements in the educational arena as among the most important. He not only wrote about education, he acted in very concrete ways. If he had done aught but leave us with inspiring generalizations about a free people in a free society, history would have regarded him favorably. If he said that the pressures of time and office limited his con-tributions to education to generalizations, we today would say we understand. But that is my point: He understood very well that generalizations were not enough, that actions at *all* levels of education were required. He did not create the University of Virginia as an exercise in the aesthetics of architecture but as a place in which faculty and students would interact and intellectually struggle with the most important problems of history and the day.

In Jefferson's day the problem was creating sites and gaining fiscal support for edu-cation for *all* young people at *all* levels of education. Improving education was far less a problem than making education possible. Today our task is to improve education. There is complete agreement that that is our responsibility. About how to discharge that responsibility there is nothing resembling agreement either within the educational com-munity or among public officials. In the first presidential debate in the 1996 campaign both Senator Dole and President Clinton emphasized their total commitment to improv-ing schools. In an hour-and-a-half debate, between fifteen and twenty minutes were de-voted to a give-and-take under two headings: the Department of Education and school choice. (In addition to that give-and-take each candidate referred to education many times.) Senator Dole advocated the elimination of the Department of Education and ad-vocated for school choice. President Clinton was for school choice; he was not opposed to vouchers that would use private funds to send students to private schools, and he fa-vored the creation of several thousand schools "created by teachers and parents, some-times by businesspeople, called charter schools, that have no rules."

Jefferson was our first and last serious education president, by which I mean that he was clear, knowledgeable, and *inquiring* about the means and purposes of learning, and what some European educational theorists had written. And when one reads about the many roles he played in creating the University of Virginia, to say that he was an active educator is an understatement. By contrast, Senator Dole and President Clinton come off as rank, uninformed, well-intentioned amateurs who for all practical purposes are not interested in becoming knowledgeable. Their working knowledge of schools and school systems appears to be virtually nil.

Let me explain that statement by analogy. During the Cold War a president had to develop, or change, or take action in regard to the then Soviet Union. Being personally unfamiliar with the Soviet Union he had to depend on what he had read on his own and what different parts of the executive branch provided him, most notably the State Department, the Joint Chiefs of Staff, the CIA, and the National Security Council. He not only had to read a great deal, he frequently met with representatives from these agencies. What he read and discussed concerned many things but they all focused on such questions as: What are we dealing with? What changes, if any, have occurred in power relationships among the ruling elite? What is the health of the Soviet economy? Have any changes occurred in Soviet foreign policy? There were many more questions for each of which there were data varying from hard to soft, from clear to ambiguous in significance, from relevant to tangential to this or that particular issue, from sheer speculation to educated guesses. And all of this in varying degrees had to be placed in the context of Soviet history and our relationship to it. Precisely because the Soviet Union was a totalitarian society, Kremlinology became a specialized field of study, one aspect of which was intuiting the Soviet mind-set. The point is that the president did not have to be convinced that he had to be knowledgeable about all facets of our relationships with the Soviet Union. No convincing was necessary; he knew the problems were too important to allow him to be simply a passive recipient of data and opinion. I have no doubt that the president spent a significant fraction of his time reading, talking, and thinking about the Soviet Union.

I also have no doubt that by comparison the president spends an insignificant fraction of his time on public education; that he feels far less compelled (if compelled at all) to become knowledgeable about the history and complexity of educational problems. Looking back to the Cold War, it seems clear that to the president of the time, the Soviet Union was far more "sexy" a problem than American education. After all, one could ask, was not the Soviet Union a clear, immediate threat to our leadership of the free world and to our national security? Of course it was. It needs to be noted, however, that there was one assumption on which our policies and actions in regard to the Soviet Union was based: The Soviet Union would remain the familiar Soviet Union we had known. No one in government was prepared for the speed with which the Soviet Union crumbled and disintegrated, which is another way of saying that available data, their interpretation, and opinion about the Soviet Union had been grievously misleading or wrong. What we have been learning since the demise of the Soviet Union is that there were people there who years before its demise had already concluded that it could not continue as it had. And, as we now know, their beginning efforts to change the society unleashed forces that could not be controlled. The system was unrescuable.

It is ironic that in that first 1996 campaign debate it went unnoticed that despite sharp surface differences between the candidates they were in implicit agreement about one point radical in its implications for what each was proposing, a point that if not taken seriously could negatively transform the society. More correctly, it could continue to transform the society; the transformation has been going on for decades but, as in the case of the Soviet Union, its dynamic nature has not been recognized. The point of unrecognized agreement was that the current educational system is grossly flawed and we must seek ways to bypass it—for example, through vouchers, schools "without rules" and not part of a school system, and lessening and disempowering educational bureaucracies. Those and other similar proposals—by the candidates and many other people—can only be offered on the assumption that the system as it is is incapable of achieving desired outcomes. But neither candidate could draw that conclusion, let alone contemplate or discuss it. Just as presidents assumed that with all its weaknesses and inefficiencies the Soviet Union would be with us in the foreseeable future and beyond, the candidates assumed that our educational system is basically rescuable if we apply the right kinds of Band-Aids or if by demonstrations of a few thousand new, unencumbered schools, the thousands of encumbered schools will change their ways.

Although I believe the system is not rescuable, I do not expect others to agree with me. After all, it took me decades to come to that belief and I had to overcome a lot of internal resistance even to verbalize it. But I am not asking for agreement. I am asking that it be discussed because it speaks to the vague feelings of many, many people that the future is gloomy. In regard to our urban schools those feelings are not inchoate. Those school systems are written off as hopeless, even though people who hold that view agree that what happens in urban schools will adversely affect our society. And yet neither candidate said anything about urban schools except in the most indirect and allusive ways.

What do I mean when I say that I expect a president to be knowledgeable about education? The simple way of answering the question is to say that I expect him or her, like Thomas Jefferson, to be as interested in the many facets of classrooms, schools, and school systems as in foreign policy, agriculture, commerce, the environment, and the like. The president should be knowledgeable enough to realize that there are some questions that require confrontation and that must be answered:

- Why is it that despite the scores of billions of dollars spent on education in the post–World War II era, there is little to show for it?
- Why is it that as students go from elementary to middle to high school, their interest in and motivation for learning decreases?
- Why is it that when there is credible evidence that a particular school context in a particular school system achieves desirable outcomes—in some cases where those outcomes exceed previous expectations—that demonstration does not spread elsewhere in the school system or beyond?
- Why is it that when people are asked that if they were given the opportunity to start from scratch and create a school system, they do not say they would create the system we now have?

I am not asking a lot of a president whose most minimal knowledge about education must indicate that the situation is too serious, too fraught with adverse consequences for the society, to justify inaction or proposing programs that are retreads from the past. I am not asking the president to be able, initially at least, to answer these questions in any depth. The president has many ways of getting answers to these questions. The questions will generate a variety of answers; that is clear ahead of time. But unlike past presidents he or she will be posing some very concrete questions, in contrast to asking open-ended questions of such generality or vagueness as to get answers that wander all over the lot and more often than not are hortatory, empty rhetoric. There is a vast difference between a president who passively asks others how and what he or she should think about, and a president who asks: "Here are some troubling, puzzling questions to which I would like some very detailed answers so that I have a basis for deciding what I must do, how I should lead."

Before he became president, John Kennedy was a member of the Congress that established the Joint Commission on Mental Illness and Health. He, like many others, knew three things: Mental health was a serious national problem; the state hospital system was glaringly, immorally inadequate; and the disjunction between the number of people who required help and the number of relevant professionals was very great. Crucially, his interest in mental health issues was personal in that one of his siblings required sustained hospitalization. The commission issued its report in 1961, although its substance was known before publication. In 1963, in his address to Congress, President Kennedy presented proposals that went beyond the commission's report and had the effect of radically transforming the mental health system—for example, giving it a community-based orientation in addition to emphasizing the promotion of health, of wellness, and prevention as coequal in importance with the repair orientation. That was an instance of a president who for personal, societal, and political reasons had become knowledgeable about a major problem that compelled him to exercise bold leadership.

My comments about education and presidential leadership were not for the purpose of saying that the president should act. Indeed, I would argue that at the present time any action is likely to be as fruitless as past actions. What is required is presidential action that will give us a far more secure basis for answering the four questions I posed earlier. Those answers will be provisional; there will be no unanimity; they will vary in imaginativeness and boldness; they will (or should) stimulate debate and controversy about relatively concrete questions, not questions that have the characteristics of inkblots. And that debate and controversy cannot take place absent political, presidential leadership.

I am of the opinion that one of the four questions is the most crucial. I refer to the fact that there have been many isolated examples—the "heres and the theres," many of which never get published—of classrooms and schools that changed from unproductive to productive contexts of learning. As luck sometimes has it, I began to write these words on the day (October 20, 1996) that an article appeared in the Connecticut section of the New York Times. The article is by a reporter, Fred Musante, who—among other things—sought and attained his teaching credentials. The article is about New Haven's High School in the Community (HSC), an alternative high school created in 1970, a time when social unrest in the city was on the front pages of major newspapers around the country. The Black Panther–Bobby Seale trial was in progress, the National Guard was called out, most people had a siege mentality, racial conflict in the schools was a daily occurrence. A handful of teachers sought permission to create their own small high school. Trickett's 1991 book describes in detail how the school was created, its unusual governance and structure, and its accomplishments. It is important to note that permission was not enthusiastically granted. The powers that be were desperate;

anything that would or could be a place for troubling and troubled minority students (and some vocal, militant teachers) should be tried if only to prevent escalation of criticism of the city's school. Musante summarizes aspects of the story well:

In 1967, Hillhouse High School erupted in racial violence, explained Matt Bornstein, High School in the Community's math teacher, computer coordinator and unofficial historian. Some of Hillhouse's teachers were upset at their school administration's solution to the riots, which was to cut short the school day to keep opposing white and black students separated. "That is still a problem in our society," he observed.

He, Ms. Wolf and some other teachers felt another approach would be better, and in 1970 they opened their "high school without walls" with 150 students in a former auto parts store. The following year, a second unit started in space in a girdle factory. They were later combined in a community hall of a public housing project.

When its Federal grants ran out, High School in the Community settled into an abandoned elementary school built in 1888, where it stayed for 20 years. The building was decrepit, but with poverty came the freedom to experiment. . . .

Most of all, the hallmark of its educational philosophy was a democratic organization. As close as possible students are admitted to maintain a balance of one third each white, black and Hispanic, half male and half female, but otherwise by lottery with no advantage for higher levels of ability. As a result, the school is not a collection of angels or geniuses like some other magnet schools that "skim the cream."

HSC has no principal!

Several years after the school opened I met semi-weekly over a year with the teachers of the school, far less for whatever help I could be than because I wanted to check out what friends and Yale colleagues (Edison Trickett, Edward Pauly, Willis Hawley) connected with the school had been telling me. They were for me inspiring meetings. They were especially instructive (and discouraging) in regard to the countless obstacles encountered in dealing with the system.

What lessons did the system draw from HSC? How did that system seek to spread the significance of HSC to other parts of the system? It is true that one of the creators of HSC years later started a somewhat comparable high school. But it is also true that, these two schools aside, New Haven's schools have been influenced not at all. I consider that failure to spread to speak volumes about why the educational reform movement has had no generalizing effects.

But there is another reason why the lack of spread of an HSC and other "heres and theres" is so important to confront: We have learned a lot about the differences between contexts of productive and unproductive learning. We are not babes in the woods in these matters. That is not to say we know all we need to know. But we know enough to conclude that unless we seriously confront and comprehend the system's failure to spread what we do know, what has been demonstrated, the inadequacies of our schools will continue—or, more likely, get worse.

The lack of spread aside, diverse answers to the other questions have been put forth. Some of them have their kernels of truth—but the proposals derived from those kernels have been far from encouraging, let alone widespread. The significance of the spread question is that it forces one to come to grips with the system qua system, not only with classrooms, or individual schools, or school districts but with all the different stakeholders in our educational system, including state departments of education, parents, legislatures, executive branches, colleges and universities, and unions. *The lack of spread is quintessentially, blatantly, a symptom of system malfunction.* Up until now reform efforts have dealt with this or that part—really parts of parts—as if the system in which those parts are embedded does not present mammoth obstacles or does not support attitudes, practices, and purposes inimical to reform.

An analogy may be helpful here. One of Freud's contributions was his emphasis on the complex, subtle, and unintended ways individual symptomatology arises and is supported by family dynamics—that is, the family drama. Despite that emphasis he developed an individual psychoanalytic therapy that mightily influenced almost all other approaches to helping individuals. The results were and are far from robust. It took decades after Freud for some therapists to ask: If neurotic symptoms of an individual arise and are maintained in the context of the family, should we not deal with the family as a family, as a system of interacting individuals, rather than dealing only or primarily with the individual? That question led to the development of family therapy, which in the case of children is more economical and effective than prolonged therapy with the individual child. In brief, once the fact that the family is a social system was taken seriously, the technical problem was one of how to deal with and alter that system in appropriate ways.

We have not taken the concept of system seriously in regard to education. A recent, notable, and stimulating exception is Kenneth Wilson's *Redesigning Education* (1996), in which he clearly emphasizes the significance of the lack of spread of deserving innovations. And his emphasis is powered by many examples outside the field of education that illuminate how far we are from thinking about education in system terms. I do not consider it happenstance that Wilson came to education from a field in which the concept of system is second nature to its members. Wilson is a physicist, a world-class one. There are other hard scientists who got interested in education but who did not at all take seriously or apply the concepts of system so fundamental in their previous work; their contributions to education have been minor or nil—or have added to the confusion. Wilson is an exception.

The immediate task is not how to answer the question but how to give it currency. And by currency I mean alerting the general public to the importance of the question and to the real possibility that when answers are forthcoming, they may require changes that will be unfamiliar, controversial, and critical of current stakeholders, who understandably will not respond enthusiastically. To expect an unprepared public to respond with serious interest to such answers is to make the most frequent mistake of reformers: to spring a proposal or program before those who will be affected by it have had time to think about it, to digest it.

To give currency to the questions I posed can come about in different ways but none is as influential as presidential-political leadership, with its power to investigate heretofore intractable problems. I can [write], as I have, . . . about these questions. Wilson has and will continue to do the same.[1] Our audiences are minuscule. The point is not whether Wilson or I have come up with answers but rather that the questions have not been brought to the attention of the general public. What is at stake here is no piddling matter. What is at stake is the future of the society. In such matters the presidential role is primarily moral and educational—that is, to become knowledgeable, to seek answers in diverse ways, and to present the issues concretely, clearly, and frequently. We know all too well that presidents are politicians used to compromise and very able to speak out of both sides of the mouth. But, as I have emphasized, I am not asking the president for answers but rather for action to launch a commission charged with the task of providing relatively concrete answers to relatively concrete questions. Although its members will not be asked to cover the waterfront, they will be unable to avoid coming to grips with the system as a system and seeing its familiar parts in an unfamiliar way.

Jefferson knew well that posterity is the cruelest of critics, that it would judge him, other political leaders, and the new nation not for their idealistic philosophy of freedom and democracy but for the courage, wisdom, and persistence of actions to implement and protect those ideals. He had an eye on posterity in regard to all that he proposed and did. Today and in the recent past it is unfortunately fair to say that in regard to matters educational our presidents and political leaders generally have been content to do what they think *can be done* and remain oblivious to what *needs to be done*, even though, as posterity will undoubtedly note, what they did plainly was of no avail. If I believe that, it has been and will be no reason for me to stop saying what I say (repetitively?) in this and previous books. The stakes are too high.

Note

1. John Goodlad's books of recent years are very much on the mark and I urge the reader to give them serious study. Unlike Wilson or me, Goodlad has throughout his long career held important roles in educational settings; for example, he was long dean of the School of Education at UCLA. His most recent book, *In Praise of Education* (1997), is a good place to start and it contains references to his previous writings.

CHAPTER 24

What Should We Do?

I end this collection with a rather dated entry from one of Sarason's almost-forgotten and out-of-print books. Sarason begins by acknowledging that "to entertain alternatives to traditional practice is never easy. The process usually begins with the recognition that what you are doing simply is not having its intended consequences."

Sarason disdains the conventional excuses for the repeated school failure of large groups of nontraditional students, and he asks us to do more than condemn the system's tendency to "blame the victim" for such failure. To this end, he poses a deceptively intriguing question, wondering, *If it were illegal to teach math, science, or any other subject matter in a classroom or school, how and where would we teach it?* He asks us to consider the wide range of community sites where such learning might, indeed, take place.

His purpose, here, is not to abandon school buildings but to suggest that a radical restructuring of education—from pre-K through graduate school—must be seriously considered and that the broader community not be excluded from becoming part of the reconstruction of American education. The alternative, he comments, is that we find ourselves continuously reinventing a "poorly functioning wheel." His task, Sarason reminds us, is not to recommend a policy or a course of action but to goad us to begin with and move on from the realization that "our schools have been, are, and will continue to be uninteresting places."

Question for Seymour Sarason

Ultimately, if your skeptical vision is to bear fruit, schools must become inherently interesting places for young people (and their teachers) to learn in. What are some simple, doable actions that can provide your readers with renewed hope that they, in small but significant ways, can "do the right thing" in making schools more interesting? And, while we are at it, how is it that you seem to be able to address these complex issues so effortlessly as a writer?

Sarason's Response

It has by no means been my purpose to give teachers "hope." I would rather give them some ideas that may provide them with a basis for examining—in new ways—themselves, their students, their colleagues, and their students' parents. And by "examine" I mean to flush out and challenge assumptions about these players. It is all too easy, unfortunately, for teachers to fall into a rut of conformity and routine, with the result that they can no longer change and learn but can only wait and hope.

Many people say they envy me because I can write so much so easily. My answer goes like this: "You are grievously wrong. What you do not know are the tortures I experience in thinking before I write; how much self-examination I go through; how frequently I see that I have no choice but to change my mind; the exhilaration I feel when I see myself, and my ideas, in a new light—and yet how overwhelmed I get by the complexities of educational reform; how dangerous and yet easy it is to be smug and arrogant, to think that one knows the truth, and you don't have to change it or think about it anymore."

Yes, writing is easy for me because it is preceded by a soul searching that is the opposite of pleasurable. I am my best friend and my worst enemy. That internal battle never ceases, with the result that I am always changing.

No, it is not my purpose or obligation to give hope. When I have worked one-on-one with teachers, I have sought (if the teacher seemed willing) to reinforce, support, help that teacher to engage in self-examination, to see which assumptions should be reexamined, what alternatives should be explored, and which initial steps must be taken by the teacher on the level of action. I did not determine the action, the teacher did. I should add that I had no difficulty whatsoever sharing with teachers the concrete personal experiences that led me to this or that idea and that required me to give up a previous way of thinking and acting. End of sermon.

More about Sarason's views on political leadership and the political principle in education may be found in:

Political Leadership and Educational Failure (1998)
How Schools Might Be Governed and Why (1997)
Revisiting "The Culture of the School and the Problem of Change" (1996)
Parental Involvement and the Political Principle (1995)
School Change: The Personal Development of a Point of View (1995)
Letters to a Serious Education President (1993)
The Predictable Failure of Educational Reform (1990)

. . . To entertain alternatives to traditional practice is never easy. The process usually begins with the recognition that what you are doing simply is not having its intended consequences. But that recognition, more often than not, leads to a resolve to try to improve what you are doing, making changes here and there that allow you to continue doing what you have been doing but with the hope of better results. If these efforts are ineffective, a variety of explanations can be offered that direct blame away from what you are doing.

As we have seen, that has been happening in the case of schooling, especially in the post–World War II era, in regard to diverse groups that for one assigned reason or another do not succeed in school and are considered unable to do so. Indeed, such students at the middle and high school level have been channeled into programs that either do not require them to be in school very much or expose them on only the most superficial level to traditional subject matters. These instances of "blaming the victim" (although more than that is involved) are justified on the basis of the fiction that the intended consequences of schooling are being obtained by the bulk of students. In short, if you get rid of those youngsters unable or unwilling to do well, the school will be able to provide what society has always expected it to do.

As I have noted, this so-called solution fails to recognize that for most students "making it" in school, schooling is a bore; that getting a passing grade (overlooking grade inflation in the process) says little or nothing about interest or fruitful assimilation of subject matter; and that functional illiteracy, scientific or other, seems to be on the increase. One comes to expect descriptions about a ray of hope here and a ray of hope there; and a slight increase in test scores, or the arrest in decline of certain test scores, is greeted as an indication that the worst is over and the corner turned. There is a desperate effort to justify continuing to do what has always been done. There was and is no disposition to examine the basic assumption that schools are places where subject matter can be productively experienced and assimilated.

. . . *If it were illegal to teach math, science, or any other subject matter in a classroom or school, how and where would we teach it?* That is far less of a radical question than it would appear. The evidence is overwhelming that middle and high school students can be engaged in structured and supervised experiences outside school that maintain their interest and have obviously beneficial intellectual and educational consequences. But, with some notable exceptions, the core subject matters have not been touched in these contexts and, therefore, the student spends most of his or her school day inside the classroom. We are so used to thinking of subject matter in terms of a particular physical site that is organized in a particular way—and for which there is a particular curriculum—that our minds go blank when we are asked seriously to come up with alternatives. As I have emphasized, that inability or unwillingness to come up with alternatives is testimony to how well we have been socialized to accept and to think within a particular world view.

Let me give an example that has the additional virtue of emphasizing the insidious consequences of the ahistorical stance. As recently as thirty years ago, a college student, for example, a sophomore or junior, who requested a year off to gain experience through travel or some kind of work appropriate to his or her interests was looked upon as deviant and therefore suspect. You were expected to go to college for four uninterrupted years, take a curriculum for the most part required, and then enter the larger society or go right on to graduate or professional school. You could absent yourself from the sequence for medical reasons or you might fail. Few students would have dared to state directly that they wanted to further their education in ways not possible in the college program. From the standpoint of the college, such a student would have been viewed as arrogant or unmotivated or irresponsible or dilettantish or all of these. Likewise, graduate and professional schools would have viewed as suspect any student who did not seek admission immediately after college. The situation is different today. In fact, many colleges now encourage, organize and supervise a year of experience away from the college, justifying this option on intellectual or educational grounds. These programs, of course, are not of a piece, varying from being aimless, content-free, and poorly supervised to tightly integrating subject matter and out-of-school experience. The important point is that one no longer needs to defend the principle that there are places and ways of learning outside the classroom that foster intellectual or educational growth. But at the college level, as on preceding levels, that principle is not invoked in the case of the so-called core curriculum. The principle is admitted for certain subject matters; that it may be no less applicable for most, if not all, other subject matters cannot even be entertained as a possibility. . . .

. . . As soon as one admits that many community sites could serve the purposes of education, intimidating questions arise—intimidating precisely because of the changes that such an admission brings in its wake. What would we do with school personnel educated and trained to work with traditional curricula in traditional classrooms in traditional school buildings? Would it not be necessary drastically to alter teacher training programs? What would be the role of educational personnel in selecting and working with community sites? How, when, and where would these personnel meet with students? Would it be necessary to abandon school buildings? Given the number of students, is it not wildly unrealistic to expect to find enough sites with educational potential? These and other questions really speak to two points that are not logically related but are presented as if they were so related. The first point is that institutional change, not only in schools but in colleges and universities as well, is necessary. To conclude that efforts to improve schools have been spectacularly unsuccessful, that prospects for future improvement are gloomy, that schools as they now exist are incapable of achieving their goals, that alternatives have to be seriously considered—to come to these conclusions *and* to expect that any serious alternative will not (should not) require substantial institutional changes is remarkably unrealistic. Here we come to the second point: Many people suggest that it is better to stay with familiar and manageable setups than to grapple with the problems of institutional change, which inevitably will create turmoil. These points derive from an even more fundamental misconception, which I will leave for the moment. I wish to turn next to an objection that is intended to deliver the coup de grace to my argument.

The objection can be put in the form of a question: Granted that the situation is as intractable as you say as long as we stay within the confines of our usual ways of thinking about schooling, and granted even that the changes you suggest have merit in principle and in another kind of world ought to be acted on, is it not wishful thinking to assume that community organizations (public and private, formal and informal, profit and nonprofit) will agree to become schooling sites? Will organizations that justify their existence on noneducational grounds, whose survival depends on performing functions (e.g., making a profit) unrelated to public schooling, cooperate in such a venture? These questions betray ignorance of two related facts. First, cooperative arrangements between schools and noneducational organizations have dramatically increased in number in the post–World War II period. In saying this I am not passing judgment on the direction and efficacy of these arrangements but only emphasizing their prevalence. Every school system with which I have had direct contact over the past twenty years, and the number is not minuscule, not only has had these relationships but also has sought to expand them.

Second, noneducational organizations in the community have, more often than not, been receptive, rather than resistant, to overtures from schools. In an earlier chapter I noted that whatever merits programs of experiential education may have, they too frequently lack an intellectual-educational direction that would make subject matter meaningful, useful, and heuristic. One could argue that it is one thing for noneducational organizations to provide students with experiences that fit organizational purposes and quite another to expect them to become truly educational sites. That objection misses the point that the two purposes are not antithetical: The domains of theory and practice are separate only in an artificial way. But, the argument could continue, what would be the relationship between teachers and those in the organization with whom the students would apprentice? And, assuming that the preceding question could be answered satisfactorily, would not the effort cave in under the weight of the number of students involved? Moreover, would not the problems that my suggestion would entail create an administrative nightmare, a cure worse than the disease?

In light of all of these objections, let me elaborate further on my reluctance to answer the question of what we should do. The reader will recall that this question presupposes, at a minimum, that one has concluded that alternatives to present thinking and practice have to be seriously considered. However, whether one is dealing with an individual or an organization, the pressure to change, to consider unfamiliar alternatives, is on a collision course with the quest for certainty: the desire, quite understandable, to judge any alternative by the criterion of certainty or predictability, i.e., the degree to which it provides a blueprint or a road map that clearly tells one how things will look and how one will be able to go from here to there. When one has come to the understanding that customary imagery, ideas, and practices have to be given up—and the adjective "customary" hardly conveys the hold that our imagery of schools has on our thinking and, therefore, on our attempts to free ourselves from its hold—it requires no special insight to realize that we will want to feel certain that the new direction is *the* answer. Convinced of the inadequacies of the present, pressured to move in new directions, bewildered by alternatives that are both unfamiliar and upsetting in their implications, it should occasion no surprise if we resort to the quest for certainty as a way of avoiding the implications of the initial conclusion that we must move in new ways. We can never overestimate two processes (in the case of either individuals or organizations): the effectiveness with which we have been socialized to view the world in particular ways and, not surprisingly, the extraordinary difficulty of taking distance from (let alone gaining control over) the consequences of our socialization.

The sources of the objections are not understandable in terms of our extant psychologies of the individual organism—psychologies that focus on the individual inde-

pendent of time, place, and social history (Sarason, 1981). The objections to Coperni-
can theory, Darwinian theory, and psychoanalytic theory are not understandable in
terms of the workings of individual minds isolated from all of the factors that shape and
give direction to a world view. And it was (and still is) no different in principle in the
case of objections to alternative views of women, racial and ethnic minorities, the handicapped, etc. Whenever some aspect of a world view is challenged—like the proper lo-
cus of schooling—objections to the challenge, precisely because they are voiced by so
many people, say far less about these people as individuals than they do about the formation of their shared world view. To expect, therefore, that a proposal that clearly
challenges centuries-old conceptions about how and where schooling can occur will be
responded to dispassionately is to ignore how much a product of a long history we are.
This, of course, does not automatically confer merit on a proposal or invalidate any or
all objections to it. But it should alert us to the ease with which our treasured world view
can defeat the goal of recognizing, confronting, and acting in accord with alternatives
to what is perceived as an intractable state of affairs. . . .

. . . We are at the beginning of a new era in which the back-to-basics movement in-
sures that subject matter will again be center stage and in which, given our ahistorical
stance, every past mistake stands a good chance of being repeated. To reinvent the wheel
is a tremendous intellectual feat, however redundant it may be. To reinvent a poorly
functioning wheel is no basis for commendation. Today, that malfunctioning wheel is
being reinvented around the country. No place is the reinvention proceeding as quickly
and self-defeatingly as in Washington, where empty administration speeches express pi-
ous commitments to excellence and fear about the nation's military and industrial leadership but cannot hide the fact that not one new idea has surfaced and that a serious effort to explain past failures emanating from Washington apparently has been ruled off
limits. Let me be clear that what is emanating from Washington is not peculiar to the
Reagan administration; it was no different under Carter, Nixon, Johnson, or Kennedy.
If Reagan were to spend the money for education his critics are recommending, there
literally would be no difference between what he would do and what his predecessors
did. Each president presents a new wrinkle, e.g., Nixon's experimental schools program, which could not have been more of a failure than it was despite its enormous cost
(Sarason, 1982). They are wrinkles in the same fabric.

I believe that the mastery of subject matter is essential on a number of grounds. Indeed, my firm belief that such mastery is crucial for adaptation over one's lifetime drove
me to the conclusion that far from facilitating mastery over subject matter, the classroom
extinguishes interest. The school is not the solution. The problem inheres in the school's
existence, more correctly, in the narrow limits that our conventional imagery of schools
imposes on our imagination.

Although . . . I have focused on subject matter, . . . my critique rests on two assumptions. The first is less an assumption than a well-validated fact: An educational activity
that does not derive from or spark a person's curiosity and interest *and* take place in a
context that is personally meaningful, permitting actions that affect and in turn are affected by that context, stands little chance of being productively integrated into that per-

son's knowledge and orientation. The second is the assumption that the world view of people born in the post–World War II era, profoundly altered by changes that have occurred in this society and the world, makes it extremely unlikely that our schools will be able to contain these students, or hold their interest, or help them to understand their world for the purposes of adaptation and mastery. When one starts with these assumptions, the crucial significance of subject matter, far from being devalued, becomes critical at the same time that the fate of subject matter in the lives of students is unfortunately gloomy.

I assume that no reader of this book is satisfied with our schools. I also assume that readers do not need to be convinced that what our schools do or do not accomplish has had and will continue to have serious consequences for our society. I am also safe in assuming that most readers are puzzled and troubled by the failure of past efforts to improve schooling. What I cannot assume is that the reader has been able to avoid assigning blame to this group or that. However understandable the assignment of blame may be, when one is faced with a serious problem with which one must deal, this stance will prove counterproductive. A final assumption I make is that most readers have responded to my arguments with their own questions. If you are saying that we should not be teaching what we teach in classrooms in our schools, what should we *do?* Granted that your argument has merit, does it not lead to wildly impractical conclusions? Are not your recommendations another example of the road to hell being paved with good intentions? Have we not had a surfeit of utopian schemes and panaceas of which your argument is a version? . . .

The question about what we should do has another source that should make one wary about a direct answer. Associated with that question are imagery and conceptions about how social change comes about, more specifically, that ideas should be formulated into a policy statement, which will lead to actions aimed at solving the problem at hand. And when we say "solving" we are unaware that we are using the word in its natural science sense, i.e., in the sense that four divided by two gives the solution "two." We dearly want to believe that the problems of schools have solutions in that sense; consequently, we dismiss alternatives that do not appear to be solutions—a variant of the quest for certainty. The fact is that the problems with which we are dealing do not have clear-cut, sure-fire solutions. But there is more to this difficulty than that because in practice—and nowhere is this more demonstrable than in the educational arena—new ideas embedded in new policies are produced by a few top-level staff members, who frequently are insensitive to the needs of those who will be affected by the new policy, those who will have to implement it, to understand, to work through, and to act fully in accord with the new policy.

The belief that good ideas will survive and win out, Darwinian style, in the realm of implementation has contributed more than its share to the current malaise. Regardless of the new policy's merits, its fate turns on the extent to which the people most closely involved in its implementation agree about its substance, appropriateness, and consequences for action. If anything is clear in the history of educational innovations and improvements, it has been the failure of policymakers to put ideas into currency before putting them into action. Telling people what they should do before they have had the op-portunity to examine and work through the significance of a new approach is inherently unproductive, especially if in doing so one is reinforcing the tendency to be satisfied with answers which do not prepare you for what is ahead, answers given as "solutions" that are not digested and to which something akin to an allergic reaction develops.

It should be clear that my proposal about schooling is not intended either as a policy or a course of action. If I had the power to put the proposal into action, I would not do so. The proposal is not, initially at least, a problem in social engineering, conjuring up, as that phrase does, how-to-do-it, blueprint imagery. The proposal is intended to achieve several purposes. The first is to ask consideration of the possibility that our schools have been, are, and will continue to be uninteresting places that are inimical to the assimila-tion and utilization of areas of knowledge that help one understand the social and phys-ical world and that give direction to one's life. The second is to gain recognition of the fact that schools are what they are in part because they reflect a world view that says that schooling should take place, best takes place, in a school building. The third pur-pose is to suggest that there are alternatives against which we struggle precisely because they require us to alter our world view. Finally, if these three purposes are achieved, if we can seriously "play with" alternatives, we are starting a process in which our imag-inativeness and creativity will render the unfamiliar less troublesome and more realistic.

I put quotation marks around "play with" to indicate a feature of numerous conver-sations I have had with people about how subject matter can be learned in sites other than classrooms. A few people are literally unable to think of subject matter as other than *something* you learn in a classroom. However, most people with whom I have talked (and these were not brief encounters several minutes in length) began to enjoy "playing around" with the idea and had little or no difficulty in describing ways that subject matter could be learned outside of a classroom. Here I must add the fact that with few exceptions the two dozen or so people with whom I talked were from the hard sciences: physicists, chemists, mathematicians, biologists, and earth-environmental sci-entists. This was not happenstance. For one thing, I chose these people because of the current (and recurrent) concern about the role of schools in producing scientific illiter-ates. More personally, my own public school education came perilously close to extin-guishing any interest I might have had in the sciences, a result that was hardly remedied in my university education but somewhat more remedied in subsequent decades. I felt comfortable playing around with my proposal in relation to history, social studies, and literature, but not with the sciences. If I had to summarize the most frequent reactions of these people to the conversations, it would go like this: "*Of course* you can learn some of the basic concepts in my field outside of the classroom in a context where these concepts are being applied; it was in the field, not a classroom, where *I* learned the most; your proposal in theory makes sense, but is it *practical?*"

A fascinating issue about schools surfaced in the post–World War II period to chal-lenge our world view and, up to a point, to alter that view. However, this issue—who owns the schools?—takes on a different cast when viewed in relation to my proposal. In a legal sense this question is easy to answer, but its import is broad: Who has or should have responsibility for our schools? Put in that way, the issue is political; people who directly or indirectly are affected by educational policies (i.e., parents, teachers, and others with a vested interest in what happens in school) have sought to have some voice in their formulation. In terms of the political principle this view of responsibility and participation requires no defense (Sarason, 1982). However, the emergence of this principle as a source of controversy and pressure for change reflected the assumption that to the extent that the principle was accepted, schools would improve: Education would be more relevant to societal realities, and the academic performance of pupils would improve. It has not worked out that way and there was no good reason why it should have, because "community participation" advocates of every description implicitly believed that schools are the primary site at which education should take place. Indeed, in many instances, those who sought a voice in educational decision making were critical of schools because they were not achieving their academic goals in traditional ways. Whatever clarity was attained about the political principle and whatever alterations were achieved in the allocation of power and responsibility, no one reexamined the basic assumption that schools are the best place for instruction to proceed.

Just as war is too important to be left to the generals, education is too important to be left to the professionals—that is another way to describe the position of those who adhered to the political principle of community control. There is an irony here bordering on the unfair. Although there is no doubt that in practice the professional educators "owned" the schools, arrogating to themselves the dominant role in formulating and implementing school policies, the community nevertheless complied with what was happening. We have always both revered and mistrusted experts, and the history of America contains many periods in which that ambivalence became manifest. In the main, however, we have been content to let professionals like educators, physicians, lawyers, and city planners exercise leadership and power until changes in the larger society have evoked and helped coalesce opposition to their practices. Anyone familiar with the education of professionals is never surprised at their resistance to the idea of shared responsibility. Just as Winston Churchill said (in relation to the movement for the independence of India) that he had not been chosen prime minister to preside over the dissolution of the British empire, so the professional does not see himself or herself as properly sharing decision making with lay people. Accordingly, when the issue of community participation in educational decision making appeared on the national agenda in the 1960s, especially in our urban areas, there was a serious power struggle. In reality, it was a struggle between parents and educators, with the rest of the community on the sidelines. And that is the point: The way in which educational issues were posed (when they were posed at all) restricted the issue of responsibility to these two groups. How and why other groups in the community should assume responsibility for schooling were questions that could not arise. As long as education was a process that took place in a school building, only parents and teachers had a vested interest in assigning responsibility for schools.

It is obvious that my proposal requires groups other than educators and parents to assume responsibility for education. After all, if education is to take place (can take place) in a variety of community sites, if these sites are to make accommodations to the educational needs of students, it will only be because they have been given and accepted a responsible role in the formulation and implementation of educational policy. In some vague, abstract, civic sense, community groups other than parents and teachers feel responsibility for the performance of schools. But isolated as that feeling is from any relationship to schools, it is no wonder that their opinions are, at best, superficial and, at worst, ill founded and prejudiced. I have argued, as have many others, that separating education *in* schools from education *outside* schools defeats the purpose of education by maintaining a gulf between the two worlds of learning. Here I am similarly arguing that to the extent that most community members are kept apart from the educational process, have no role in that process, their learning and understanding about the two worlds will be next to nil. I must emphasize that my proposal derives not from any political principle but rather from a conception about the characteristics of settings that make learning interesting, adaptive, and sustaining, i.e., that maximize the chance that students will see a close relationship between subject matter and the world in which *they* live. If to do this requires changing our views about where and how education should take place, if it requires looking at our communities in terms of the sites that can accommodate to educational goals, then we are confronted with the implications of the principle that those who are affected by educational policies should have a role in determining those policies. I use the word "confront" advisedly because the implications of the political principle are for most of us unfamiliar and upsetting.

Several people have responded to my argument by calling it "an idea whose time has come." That response troubles me for several reasons. For one thing, it suggests that ideas have a power and persuasiveness before which tradition crumbles, a version of the belief that truth and justice ultimately win in the marketplace of living. No less troubling is the failure to recognize that any idea worth its salt is an expression of time and place: It is a challenge to, or a criticism of, conventional wisdom embedded in the features of society, features that do not change easily. That optimistic view is not the case even in the relatively narrow confines of science, about which most people mistakenly believe that good ideas are irresistible even if they require scientists to change their thinking and *doings*.[1] It is far less the case in the social arena when the idea requires the construction of novel relationships among individuals and institutions. In the field of education, the graveyard of ideas is strewn with good ideas that died because their makers were enamored more with the idea's truth than with its institutional consequences. Separating an idea from the institutional arrangements to which that idea is a reaction, as well as from the predictable social dynamics the idea sets in motion, is unrivaled as a formula for failure, another example of the separation of theory and practice, of treating ideas as asocial products of the human mind.

Let us return to a question that has undoubtedly troubled the reader: Why should community sites accommodate to the educational needs of students? This question has to be seen in light of the answer to another question: how does one explain why in the post–World War II period there has been an apparently very significant increase in the frequency and variety of relationships between schools and other organizations (both public and private) in the community? I touched on this subject earlier; here I want to add that these organizations have come to see that it is in their self-interest to provide life and work experiences to students. And by self-interest I refer to several things: the perception that, like it or not, they should cooperate with schools in regard to programs directed at youth who need career guidance or who might otherwise get into trouble; and concern that many people entering the labor force from school are ill equipped to handle available jobs, thus contributing to inefficiency and rising costs. I could summarize these and related points by paraphrasing what a company executive once said to me:

> ▶ We are caught in a bind. On the one hand, we are here to make a profit, not to be distracted by having to "make work" or be teachers. On the other, we are in this community and it has a lot of problems and sometimes we feel we are sitting on a powder keg. We have to appear as if we were concerned and wanted to be helpful, and the fact is that we *are* concerned not only for our particular company but for what is happening throughout our society. Sure, the bottom line is green, but that does not mean that we do not have a conscience. Some of these kids are a delight; others are not. Some of our employees really get a kick from helping and teaching these kids; others do not. I feel sorry for a lot of these kids, and there are days I feel sorry for myself. But the day is past when we can blithely say no to a school request and not have to worry about consequences. We can no longer go it alone and, I suppose, neither can the schools. ◀

This passage suggests a change in attitude about the responsibility of community organizations for education. I do not want to overestimate the depth and scope of this change but neither do I want to underestimate the profound puzzlement of these organizations about how and what they can do to improve education. They feel they are in a bind but that fact alone represents a change from earlier times.

In my talks with people in public and private organizations providing some kind of experience to students, I come up against two familiar beliefs, the contradictions between which go unnoticed. The first belief is that learning is productive, meaningful, and quick when it occurs in a context in which it is directly relevant. As one company supervisor said, "You can lecture to kids about work habits, skills, punctuality, and a lot of other desirable things, but it is not until they are on the job observing and working with others that they stand a chance of learning what it is all about and with what consequences." The second belief is in the form of a criticism: The schools are not adequately educating students, especially in regard to the basics. The two beliefs rest on very different and even contradictory conceptions of learners, learning, and the contexts they require.

If the present relationships between schools and community organizations are fragile, problematic, and narrow in scope, it is asking too much to expect that my proposal will be viewed as credible. For it to be credible, let alone to be acted on, requires that more general recognition be accorded the possibility that the real problem is our age-old belief that education best takes place in school buildings. It is only when we are able seriously to entertain alternatives that our imaginations are liberated and what heretofore appeared impractical and utopian begins to look otherwise. As I asked earlier, how and where would one teach subject matter if it were illegal to do so in a school building? The answer is that there are diverse ways in diverse sites in which one could proceed. Not one way in one site. The possibilities, however, cannot be glimpsed until you take seriously alternatives to present thinking and practices. It may come as a surprise that when I have pressed the point with subject matter specialists, they have had far less difficulty coming up with possibilities than other people. And the specialists who had the least difficulty came from the sciences.

Liberating our imaginations (changing our world view) is no warrant for sounding the tocsin and manning the barricades to carry out a revolution. There are three kinds of revolution. The first is sociopolitical (e.g., the French, American, and Russian revolutions). In a relatively short period of violent conflict, clear expression is given to long-standing ideas and social forces. One might say that what we call "the revolution" is an outcropping and, in a sense, a legitimation of long-standing ideas and forces, accepted by some and rejected by others. The second type is exemplified by what we ordinarily call the "scientific-technological revolution": the discovery, also after a long period of latency, of new knowledge and techniques, the application of which will considerably change patterns of living. Unlike the sociopolitical type of revolution, which is resisted by significant segments of the society (and sometimes by a majority), the scientific-technological revolution is enthusiastically envisioned and its presumed future delights constitute a source of pleasurable fantasy. In large part this is because over the centuries opposition to science was overcome and we are heirs to a world view in which science and technology are deemed to serve the public welfare. The third type of revolution—in terms of time it is a variant of the second—is most relevant here because it concerns a social problem that has proven intractable, is seen as having adverse consequences for society, seems to cry out for radically new ideas and approaches, but reflects unverbalized assumptions whose hold on our minds is so strong that they cause us to oppose ideas the implications of which are both clear and upsetting. It is a problem that calls for revolutionary thinking but the revolution has hardly begun.

It would be surprising if the situation were otherwise in the case of education: The past century and a half established the idea that *everyone* should be educated *inside* schools. These battles—however justified on political and moral grounds, and without implying that no educational benefits were achieved—were conceptually flawed and with the passage of time the results of these battles have been increasingly counterproductive. It would be unrealistic for me to hope for other than a hearing as prologue to a debate.

The present is not pregnant with *a* future but with many different futures and my argument is not based on a concept of inevitability. If you are a betting person, you would be wise to act as if the traditional concept of education and schools is not endangered. As I pointed out earlier, it appears today that education is being put back on the national agenda because its inadequacies are seen as contributing adversely to national security and economic stability. How long it will stay on the agenda is impossible to predict, but there is no doubt that the issues are being posed in the most traditional terms with almost complete amnesia insofar as previous formulations and debates are concerned. I do not expect our elected policymakers to be knowledgeable about the substance and history of the issues. They depend on advisors to come up with recommendations presumably based on considerations of practicality derived from a searching examination of alternatives and history. What we are witness to today is neither practical nor based on principles that explain past failures.

The current discussion differs from past ones (in degree at least) in several respects. First, more people than ever before—professional educators, the scientific community, and informed citizens—find themselves concluding in some vague way that the problem is not one for which money is the answer. This is disconcerting to the political liberal, predisposed to believe that education is a form of salvation that society should provide to its young regardless of their ethnic, racial, or class backgrounds. It is disconcerting not because they are calling their goals of education into question but because they have become far less sure that increased budgets will have the desired effect. Paradoxically, this conclusion is no less disconcerting to the political conservative, who sees the specter of youth educationally and vocationally unprepared to play an independent and productive role in society. If money is not the answer for the political conservative, what does he or she recommend? (However bothered, the liberal holds on to the belief that increasing or decreasing expenditures for education makes a difference.) I find it a source of irony that it is among conservatives that one tends to get acceptance of radical proposals that challenge the structure and perhaps even the existence of schools as we have known them.[2] In a rather explicit way, these proposals (e.g., vouchers or tax credits) are based on an indictment of public schools and educators, another example of blaming the victim although the stone throwers cannot see that they, too, are victims of unverbalized assumptions.

What those who are participating in the current discussion (it is far from a debate) have in common, and this reflects something of a difference from earlier discussions, is the sense that we may have reached (and, perhaps, gone beyond) the point at which the gulf between what our youth learn in schools and what they need to know in a society increasingly altered by the dynamics of scientific-technological developments may be unbridgeable. In the late 1950s and in the 1960s, the debates about education contained this perception but it was far overshadowed by matters racial, economic, and moral. Those matters, of course, are still with us and they continue to contribute to that ever growing underclass that no society can long ignore without penalty. However, my experience suggests that more people now see the gulf as affecting more than that underclass.

While I do not expect our elected policymakers to be knowledgeable about the substance and history of efforts to improve education, I do expect somewhat more from those in the scientific community upset by the dimensions and implications of scientific illiteracy. That they are concerned with the problem; that they are beginning to see its implications for individuals, institutions, and the larger society; that they see the problem as getting worse rather than better are all cause for both satisfaction and despair—

satisfaction because they may succeed in keeping education on the national agenda and despair because their concern is ahistorical, unimaginative, and astoundingly parochial, bordering on unforgivable arrogance. One expects the sophisticated scientist to know, at least in the abstract, that when a problem appears to be intractable one should flush out and examine the assumptions that have been taken for granted. It may be too much to expect that the scientist who understands this point in relation to his or her field will be able to apply the principle to the arena of society. A good case could be made for the thesis that there is another form of illiteracy, far older than the scientific, that has had enormously adverse consequences for most people of widely differing background and status. I refer to economic illiteracy. Two years ago I asked a group of high school students this question: In terms of selling, what are similarities and differences between a bank and a shoe store? Not one student noted the fact that a bank rents money. That these students spend a fair part of their day thinking about, practicing, and are affected by economic questions and issues is a conclusion that we can accept without waiting for the outcome of research studies. And yet we do next to nothing in capitalizing on this student interest for the purpose of furthering their understanding of the economic dynamics and organization of our society and the international order.

At its root, science is a moral enterprise based on and protecting certain rules for behavior: that asking and testing questions about self and the world are both desirable and necessary; that the pursuit of knowledge should be carried out in as dispassionate a way as possible; that one is obliged to make public what one does in an honest fashion; and that a "good" society is one that protects the morality of science from corrupting "outside influences," i.e., just as the institution of science is based on moral rules to police itself, so should the combination of morality and self-interest of the larger society police and serve itself by protecting science. What so many scientists fail to understand is that at its root education is a moral enterprise and that by glossing over that fact we sustain fruitless controversy and continued failure. The scientist has a vision, a world view, of science, a crucial feature of which is its self-correcting nature deriving from the morality on which science is based. What is there in the moral basis of schooling that makes self-correction one of its most elusive features?

Notes

1. For fascinating and instructive examples one should read Mitroff's *Subjective Side of Science: An Inquiry into the Psychology of the Apollo Moon Scientists* (1974).

2. Over the decades there has been a surfeit of proposals based on the assumption that by changing the structure of schools one in some way affects or alters the substance of schooling. As in the case of the arts, here the separation of form and content also leads to nonsense.

Part V

Tables of Contents from Sarason's Books on Education

In the following tables of contents, the symbol ✦ indicates a chapter partially or entirely included in this volume.

2. *Questions You Should Ask About Charter Schools and Vouchers* (2002)
Portsmouth, N.H.: Heinemann

3. *American Psychology and Schools* (2001)
New York: Teachers College Press

4. *Teaching as a Performing Art* (1999)
New York: Teachers College Press

20. *Schooling in America: Scapegoat and Salvation* (1983)
New York: The Free Press

21. *Educational Handicap, Public Policy, and Social History: A Broadened Perspective on Mental Retardation* (1979)
New York: The Free Press

23. *The Creation of Settings and the Future Societies* (1972)
San Francisco: Jossey-Bass

Plus: Preface, Bibliography, Index

24. *The Culture of the School and the Problem of Change* (1971, 1982)
Boston: Allyn and Bacon

[This book is included in *Revisiting "The Culture of the School and the Problem of Change."* See the list of contents under Item 10.]

25. *The Psycho-Educational Clinic: Papers and Research Studies* (1969)
Boston: Massachusetts Department of Mental Health